In *Werner Herzog / Rogue Filmmaker*, David LaRocca draws from a fan's resolute passion for his subject to face head-on vexing Herzogian notions such as ecstatic truth, the sublime, and the beguiling spirit that animates the fittingly titled Rogue Film School, which the author attended. In our distracted, dissipating times, Herzog is an icon of penetrating acuity, vigorous resolve, poetic straight-talk, and provocative medial experiments—someone with the mettle to mount visionary adventures: shouldered, provisional, failed, recuperated. In these pages, LaRocca follows the more than half-century-long footpath by which Herzog became his own genre: with fabricated films of daring, life-lived-at-the-limits intensity; artful literary innovations; and a persistently roving persona. Marshaling the awe suited to philosophical investigations, LaRocca tracks the study of Herzog from first forays to the fraught present moment, including critical dispatches on autobiography, parody, and artificial intelligence. As with any Herzogian enterprise, this one isn't for the faint of heart.

David LaRocca is the author or contributing editor of eighteen books, including *The Philosophy of Charlie Kaufman*, *The Thought of Stanley Cavell and Cinema*, *The Geschlecht Complex*, and *Metacinema*.

Praise for *Werner Herzog / Rogue Filmmaker*

"IN WERNER HERZOG / ROGUE FILMMAKER, the notorious paradoxes and resistances of Werner Herzog and his films encounter the rigor and nuances of David LaRocca's remarkable philosophical mind at work. The result is a terrifically compelling and insightful study of one of the most important filmmakers working today."

> —TIMOTHY CORRIGAN, Professor Emeritus of English, Cinema and Media Studies, and History of Art, University of Pennsylvania; editor of *The Films of Werner Herzog: Between Mirage and History*

"GOADED NOT JUST BY THE FAMOUSLY WILD FILMMAKER but by 'Herzog the phenomenon' (the writer, speaker, prophet, performer—and including the foam and froth that trails in his wake as commentary), David LaRocca has himself gone rogue. Determined to go beyond himself, LaRocca listens to Herzog and is drawn to answer antiphonally—with the cultivated voice of his own prose—the inimitable Bavarian accent and patter of his peripatetic subject. The projected films are still mandatory, and cleverly dealt with, since they have forged indelible images of the unmanageable binaries (human/inhuman; immanent/transcendent; tender/violent) that constitute the 'humanistic sublime,' which is the genuine grail pursued to the limit by Herzog and LaRocca alike."

> —DUDLEY ANDREW, R. Selden Rose Professor Emeritus of Comparative Literature and of Film Studies, Yale University; author of *What Cinema Is!*, *The Major Film Theories*, and *Concepts in Film Theory*

"IN AN EMERSONIAN SPIRIT, David LaRocca acts as a rogue agent interrogating the full range of Werner Herzog's work: his fiction and documentary films, essays, novels, notebooks, film appearances, opera stagings, and self-presentations. LaRocca blends cross-genre comparisons and philosophical reflections with the affordances of a sharp eye and ear. The result is a model of breadth and depth of critical responsiveness and understanding."

—RICHARD ELDRIDGE, Charles and Harriett Cox McDowell Professor Emeritus of Philosophy, Swarthmore College; author of *Werner Herzog: Filmmaker and Philosopher*

"SCRUPULOUS AND EXUBERANT, David LaRocca's study captures the looming, ubiquitous, and elusive cult(ural) phenomenon of Werner Herzog's self-directed star persona, always riddling and impish in posture, for an engaging snapshot album of his optical and verbal imagination that gathers to a rich *catalogue raisonné*. Beyond auteurist, the result is a gripping *iconography* of cinema's reigning performance artist in vision and voice, *philosophe* and jester at once, sardonic wag and mage of the image, counter-pontificating guru of the intuitive and prophet of an anti-academic screen sublime—whose various local stylizations are the mark of a motivated originality and the badge of a responsive anti-style. LaRocca charts a newly lucid curriculum across the picaresque aesthetic of the artist's Rogue Film School and its vagabonding commonalities. Offering a matriculation all its own, this colorfully unfolding 'document' about the great 'documentarian' is keen to put every such indication of the given, always rethought, into quotes derived from the dedicated weight of the made."

—GARRETT STEWART, James O. Freedman Professor of Letters, University of Iowa; author of *Between Film and Screen*, *Framed Time*, and *Cinemachines*

"*WERNER HERZOG / ROGUE FILMMAKER* is the single best sustained piece of work on Herzog I have had the pleasure of reading. A masterful interpretation of Herzog's fascinating oeuvre and a gripping meditation on the gaps, cracks, fissures, and tensions between Herzog-the-man and Herzog-the-myth. David LaRocca's examination of Herzog is the culmination of a recent upsurge in studies devoted to the enigmatic Bavarian. Along with Richard Eldridge's *Werner Herzog: Filmmaker and Philosopher* and the collection of essays gathered together in *The Philosophy of Werner Herzog*, LaRocca's book is required reading for any philosophical engagement with the life, work, and words of a visionary filmmaker and author who has proven to be as elusive as Proteus to pin down."

—CHRISTOPHER TURNER, Associate Professor of Philosophy, California State University, Stanislaus; coeditor of *The Philosophy of Werner Herzog*

"AT ONCE FILM CRITICISM, PHILOSOPHICAL EXTRAPOLATION, AND LOVE LETTER, *Werner Herzog / Rogue Filmmaker* proves once again that despite Herzog's very vocal acts of protest against his interpreters, it is still worthwhile to think and write about him. And more importantly: to do it very well, as David LaRocca illustrates here. We worked closely with David and other Herzog acolytes when we put together *The Philosophy of Werner Herzog*, and we are happy to discover that there are plenty of fresh reflections inside this new book to reward LaRocca's readers. Rich in references to both filmmakers and philosophers, LaRocca gives us the chance to dive back into that deep Herzogian ocean and start explorations anew. Famously, Herzog told Paul Cronin that he throws all those 'Herzog books' into the trash. Here is one Herzog ought to keep; he (and you) will learn many things about the most fascinating filmmaker of the last half-century."

—M. BLAKE WILSON and CHRISTOPHER TURNER, California State University, Stanislaus; coeditors of *The Philosophy of Werner Herzog*

"*WERNER HERZOG / ROGUE FILMMAKER* is a serious examination of what Werner Herzog has called our 'crisis of imagery.' David LaRocca's book contains insights into the many dimensions of Herzog's 'mischief,' explores a range of lenses through which to see his films and writings—from literary fiction to *Documentary Now!*, European Romanticism to *The Mandalorian*. The many chapters of LaRocca's study reflect on Herzog's war films, the humanistic sublime, and the apparently limitless undertakings of a director who has filmed on all seven continents. *Werner Herzog / Rogue Filmmaker* takes up the challenge imposed by Herzog's 'jungle metaphysics,' presenting the director as a 'conquistador of the quixotic,' as a man with a rucksack 'laden with dreams to share.'"

—BRAD PRAGER, Professor of German Studies and Film Studies, University of Missouri; author of *The Cinema of Werner Herzog: Aesthetic Ecstasy and Truth* and editor of *A Companion to Werner Herzog*

WERNER HERZOG / ROGUE FILMMAKER

WERNER HERZOG / ROGUE FILMMAKER

David LaRocca

Sticking Place Books
New York

© Sticking Place Books 2024
© David LaRocca 2024

Cover image © Werner Herzog Filmproduktion

Designed by Goran Tovilovic

www.stickingplacebooks.com

All rights reserved.
No part of this book may be reproduced, stored in or introduced into a retrieval system, or transmitted, in any form or by any means (electronic, mechanical, photocopying, recording or otherwise) without the written permission of the publishers, except in the case of brief quotations embodied in critical articles or reviews.

ISBN 978-1-942782-72-8

In Memoriam

RICHARD MACHELOR
(1951-2005)

Who shared the Mountain West with me,
wore a leather satchel, and in it
always carried a book worth reading.

Be serious.
Don't trade your interest in being born on earth
for messy theory.
Persist in your birthright.
—STANLEY CAVELL

I don't have a philosophy.
I have a camera.
—SAUL LEITER

Man is an abyss, and I turn giddy
when I look down into it.
—GEORG BÜCHNER, author of *Woyzeck*

If we opened people up, we'd find landscapes.
—AGNÈS VARDA

Wherever you turn your eyes,
the world can shine like transfiguration.
You don't have to bring a thing to it
except a little willingness to see.
Only who could have the courage to see it?
MARILYNNE ROBINSON, *Gilead*

Our concern with history […] is a concern with
preformed images
already imprinted on our brains, images at which we
keep staring while the truth lies elsewhere,
away from it all, somewhere as yet undiscovered.
—W. G. SEBALD, *Austerlitz*

Do you know any deep man? Has any one furnished you
with a new image? For to see the world
representatively, implies high gifts.
—RALPH WALDO EMERSON, *Journals*

Why not dare to find forms that had never existed?
—WERNER HERZOG, *Every Man for Himself and God Against All*

Exordium: Assignments and Visions............................1

I / Advance Signals from the Semaphore 9

II / Ecstatic, Essayistic Pronouncements 19

III / A Transcendental Persona......................................45

IV / Anti-Sentimental Dispatches..............................75

V / The Humanistic Sublime..95

VI / Perúvian Metaphysics 159

VII / Rogue Agent in an Ambivalent Universe.......193

Excursus: After Truth..293

Notes..297
Provenance + Attestations 331
Biobibliography 341
Index...343

Exordium

Assignments and Visions

"A VISION SEIZED HOLD OF ME, like the demented fury of a hound that has sunk its teeth into the leg of a deer carcass."[1] So begins Werner Herzog's *Conquest of the Useless*—shocking us all awake with his visceral language, his startling imagery. And that voice—no Herzogian vision is complete without attention to the aural sensibilities of his vocal timbre and the outsized role that sound plays in comporting his ecstasies. I too have been seized by Herzog's visions—and voices; by run-ins with many of his more than seventy films; by reading and re-reading his books and the books he recommends; by listening to his expansive, wide-ranging interviews; and by lucky stroke, being among the participants in his Rogue Film School. We all know by now of Herzog's disdain for film schools, for film theory and criticism, and for "pedantic theoreticians" who might subject his work to philosophical commentary.[2] But here we are. We cannot choose which kinds of demented and furious hounds sink their teeth into us.

While analytic inspection of art is dubious, so too, on a personal level, does Herzog resist introspection. "I'd rather die than go to an analyst," he tells us in his memoir, resolutely titled *Every Man for Himself and God Against All*.[3] Herzog is on his own. The Bavarian foot soldier for cinema doesn't need psychoanalysis to help him sleep at night (even if he doesn't dream). Good luck with that, Freudians. "It is not healthy if you circle too much around your own navel. And it is not good to recall all the traumas of your childhood. It's good to forget them. It's good to bury them."[4] But if Herzog isn't disposed to self-analysis—and certainly we are neither invited nor encouraged to analyze him on his behalf—what about his abundant, culturally salient body of work stretching across more than a half-century of global cinema? Is that worth our time to analyze?—Probably not, he would say; theory is a waste of time. So, why exactly are we writing books about Herzog—wait, why is Herzog himself writing books? The frisson of sense and contradiction in his work, of playfulness and seriousness, of category-making and conceptual challenge, sparked the essays that comprise this book, filled as they are with a durable curiosity about the paradoxes that operate in Herzog's vast catalog of films and writing, interviews and off-the-cuff reflections.

While those who profess criticism take umbrage at Herzog's repellent relation to the matter, others (critically) accept how Herzog's resistance is a feature, not a bug. For one thing, and a prominent one at that, Herzog's lack of introspection depersonalizes the experience of his films and books. Despite his prevalence and prominence on screen (especially in his own films), he—in his inner workings, private grievances, and so on—is not our subject. Though Herzog seeks (and finds) his "inner landscapes," these are given in a Romantic register as treks and discoveries for us all—that is, for all humanity. Herzog is not self-less—prostrate before for cinema and its illustrious library of egos—but has assumed a harder or higher task for his preoccupations: someone for whom "the self" (as we know it) is not that interesting to him; rather, he holds it in sufficient regard as (merely) a context in which to make other discoveries—beyond the self.

Thus, it is worth noting, as we take our first steps here, the way that the name on the cover of this book—Werner Herzog—is a double avatar. There is the Werner who lives in Los Angeles and there is the Werner—the *Herzog*—of our imaginations. This doubleness is hard to disentangle; addressing it, however, proves to be a satisfying project: at once enticing and inciting. The doubleness reveals that we are not, nor should we be, speaking about an historical person in his private thoughts and experiences, even when we have abundant, so-called autobiographical or memoirist commentary. Part of why Herzog is so often the subject of parody and satire and imitation is the *attractiveness* of this avatar, or double vision, of a man. In a distinctive way, aspects of this double—call it personification or persona—comment on themselves or on one another, thus intensifying the meta-ness of the potential madness at hand. In *My Best Fiend*, for instance, we find Herzog in self-analysis mode because we discern the "portrait" subgenre, how certain essay films that take filmmakers and the production of their work as a suitable subject for critical interrogation—and sometimes radical self-revelation. We could underscore the point by noting that despite the prevalence of Herzog-on-screen, he is no exhibitionist. When he gives interviews, the hosts—from Conan O'Brien to Stephen Colbert, from David Letterman to Terry Gross—find themselves following *him*. Herzog is an oracle who can laugh at himself. "I know who I am and I know where I come from. And I know where I'm heading towards." He concludes: "No fear and no regrets. Sure, I've made massive mistakes, and I'm, in a way, a result of my own defeats. So be it. They formed me. They made me think beyond what I normally thought before."[5]

"You will never be a filmmaker unless you read," a claim that cuts to the quick—for we feel as if it is both true and demonstrably false. Within that tension is evidence of Herzog's mercurial presence in—and provocation to—our culture of proliferating images, sounds, and words. Herzog is doubtless one of our great seers—and sayers—but what do his haunting visions and his trance-inducing voice reveal to us about the confounding world we inhabit, a world he complicates and enriches, including the ways we inhabit ourselves? As it happens, our octogenarian still pursues his uncompromising missions with a rogue's flair while remaining serious about the art at hand; time and again, his enigmatic and illuminating remarks inform the present moment and evolve defiantly into the next one. Since at least *Signs of Life* (1968), we have stood in need of interpreters and mediators to guide our thinking about the creations and emissions of our Bavarian mystic. To be sure, Herzog himself is among the best— and most entertaining—inheritors of his own work, and yet his commentary can render still further puzzles and perplexities, still more deep thoughts fit for our critical attention as well as superficial, if persistently adherent, amusements. The same person who makes an ominous cameo in *The Mandalorian* also sits down for a gracious conversation with the last leader of the Soviet Union (*Meeting Gorbachev*, 2018). Jokes made on late night talk shows land, even as—in another key—Herzog's meditations on capital punishment (*On Death Row*, 2012) and the tragic effects of texting-while-driving (*From One Second to the Next*, 2013) are quietly devastating. The tonal shifts he manages are daring—and dizzying. Reliably, we take pleasure in profound encounters with his beautiful offerings while acknowledging sustained bewilderment before them.

In this volume, I am not trying to "solve" Herzogian dilemmas, still less construct a defensible "theory" of his work that accommodates his diverse experiments on film, in writing, pedagogy, and amidst the coursings of popular media. Owing to Herzog's charisma, ample and at times distracting, it is easy to mislay the fact that he creates art not arguments. We should not seek him out for notes on soteriology, eschatology, and how to practice epistemic humility, rather, reflect with good humored flexibility on his manner of unsettling cherished facets of culture—physical rudiments and mental attributes—that together constitute "worldviews." If he is insufficiently thorough in his case-making, or blithely ignores inherited, sanctioned, standardized methods of deliberation, we cannot take it personally. He has a business to run—a mostly self-made one: *being Werner* ... and saying and doing the sort of things Herzog should say or do, or might. He represents himself. As a freelancer, a gig worker *avant la lettre*, he founded in 1963 *Werner Herzog Film Production*, a fitting appellation for what he had in mind—and what he has been up to ever since. WHFP is not a corporate abstraction or totem borrowed to underwrite a capitalist scheme, but a plain-spoken description: it names him and his appointed labors. Whether he fails or fulfills his missions, as a genre unto himself, Herzog will either satisfy our expectations (based on what we know of him) or show us new ways of appreciating his singular realm (one composed of static and dynamic characteristics). When the philosopher and film theorist and literary critic come to Herzog, they must be prepared for the frisson made upon contact—and at most points beyond it. He will frustrate them—their methods—but also generously show them ways of out of their misery.

Paradox pervades his enterprise, gives it energy but also anticipates and deters detractors who would mobilize contradiction as a reason for dismissal. Rather, in what follows, I choose to dwell in the mystery, and better, to *roam* there, wherever such mists may appear. These fervent wanderings cover disparate, uneven territories—of thought and text, of film frame and prose line—in the spirit of an experimental *ekphrasis*: the Greek itself doubling its pursuit of *e*xpression, since "phrazein" means "to point out," while "ek" prefixes "out"—to point out *out*. I take the surfeit of propulsive power as an invitation to *describe* the arts as we find them, to make the inmost outmost, whether that means tracking a man named Werner Herzog walking on foot, scanning the films he funds for our contemplation, assessing the sentences he writes, or marveling at the moments when he stands before the camera, as if to stand for our judgment (in yet another doubling: as himself *and* as our representative).

Speaking of, though the title of the book includes the name of a man who lives and breathes and walks among us, there is no ambition here to offer a biography of him, comprehensive or in brief (though elements may be gathered in the service of such a scheme). Instead, the investigation takes Herzog's pronouncements seriously full stop *and* seriously until they become funny (and asks why that humor happens at some points and not others), treats what he says with deadly intensity until the power shifts into enigmatic ephemera (inquiring along the way how such variable meanings become at times illuminating and at other instances confounding). I am neither trying to catch Herzog in a contradiction (a philosopher's hobby) nor create an *apologia* for his opinions (a cleric's duty)—but instead allow for a fascination with his library of antinomies, his ceaseless, irrepressible curiosity and indefatigable industry. To adopt, for a moment, a scientific mindset—that of the natural historian— Herzog is a polytropic figure, botanizing the lands he visits, pollinating with the images he makes. His films and books, interviews and cameos are specimens for study, for comment. The labor of assessment, in turn, finds archives diagramed, taxonomies sketched, origins annotated, and filial connections noticed toward the end (always playfully provisional if also with an underlying seriousness of intent) of drawing philosophical illumination from profound entertainment.

The book title's intentional forward slash—a semantically laden slip of punctuation / that is no accident—signals a lean, a tilt, a perpetual onward momentum: the sign of a veritable machete cutting through diaphanous overgrowth, slicing lines, tracing boundaries, etching terrain, clearing dense passages that impel our further passage.[6] An action *in media res*: forward, *slash*. "Like a scythe when you are mowing, a machete has to be sharpened constantly," a steady care suited to elaborate, precarious, and taxing endeavors.[7] Herzog would take such a blade to the pretentions of theory, all too quick to hack off a limb if venom-laced blood circulated, threatening the body.[8] Such quick cuts must be deliberate, precise, and rare, so too the concentrated steps taken on treacherous paths to unknown vistas. A *machetero* can express proficiency by shaving his own whiskers with the edge, while Herzog notes how "[e]very machete has its own sound, like an instrument in an orchestra; together they create a unique music."[9] Even so, harmonies can be hard to discover; while cacophonies can briefly align to give sense, such congenial effects quickly dissemble and disperse.

Despite the sharpened machete in hand, a patient student emmeshed in Herzog Studies will soon enough discover that repetition is another feature of our adventurer's method. Though he may speak and write aphoristically—and thus with an economy and precision befitting a poet—Herzog remains untroubled, as it were, by quoting himself, and doing so deep into the timeline of his philosophically-inflected musings, which began in earnest in the 1970s. Inescapably then, repetition and recursion—and in a figure of filmic affiliation, looping—are intrinsic to this critical enterprise, attuned to and dependent upon the structure of Herzog's *Lebenswerk*. My tolerance for Herzog's retreads may be higher than others, but I have aimed to make the eternal recurrence of the same—or very similar—into a dimension of this inquiry that grips readers' imaginations more than it tries or tires the otherwise fit bands of concentration. To be sure, then, cinematic frames of reference from Herzog's vast archive of films cyclically punctuate the full duration of these pages as do many lines of memorable, durable Herzogian prose. Consequently, and consequentially, the very form of this book constitutes an allegory of Herzog's long and illustrious career.

In a coda to this project, acknowledged in its final paragraphs [see the Excursus], I discuss an encounter with Herzog's latest book (not yet in English translation), *Die Zukunft der Wahrheit* [*The Future of Truth*], as it turns out, a satisfying if thoroughly familiar digest of thoughts. Like a guru who has trained assiduously for decades, Herzog seeks to distill lessons to their finest precipitates even while adding novel illustrations and making connections to salient features of the present day. Among the takeaways from his up-to-the-minute report, repetition can become, as it has been, the condition for renewal (a means of siphoning from prior resources in moments of dire need—as we still instinctively and productively draw from the classics and the world's dispersed wisdom literature); far from being a confirmation of laziness or lack of innovation, the recirculation of hard-won thoughts, however modestly refined, requires a deep reserve of discipline and labor. As we learn something new from re-reading a book and rewatching a movie—because we are, in a sense, new each time we re-view them—so with the iterations of Herzog's haunting images and echoic prose reflections: each next rehearsal yields rewarding insights.

Herzog is no system builder. He doesn't propound "a philosophy." In this defiant posture, there are many admirable and attractive features to celebrate: his unapologetic refusal to systematize and to supply a defensible logic; his cool response to the instinctive fever for consistency; his waiving away of pretention; his rare self-containment as a man imbued with a clarity of vision who never tires of pursuing it. What are those resistant qualities, though, the ones that reveal him to be a man apart—questing on his own terms while the mass of humanity distracts itself and squanders its precious time on earth? Don't those characteristics call for articulation and interrogation? Yet how does one speak compellingly and coherently, indeed, systematically, of the unsystematic? Consistently of the inconsistent? When the subject of one's attention fears no contradiction, courts paradox, evades theory, and mocks introspection? Herzog is built to perplex the philosopher, thwart the theorist, cower the critic—embarrass them one and all. Still, and perhaps because of such fascinating contestations, we seem in need of saying—one way and another, once and again—why it is worth our time to discover how Herzog's avowals and eschewals amount to thoughts and lessons of perennial interest to humankind and how to go about such investigations. The following book of attempted responses to such queries—*essays*, etymologically encoding their trials, strivings, struggles, and seeking—is meant to serve as a stand-alone companion and a complement to any such sincere endeavors, joining forces with the likes of *A Guide for the Perplexed*, *Werner Herzog: Filmmaker and Philosopher*, *The Philosophy of Werner Herzog*, and other propitious titles devoted to a better understanding—and enjoyment—of a perpetually generative and vexing artist. Werner Herzog has created obstacles that test the head and the heart. Field notes from the vanguard, *Werner Herzog / Rogue Filmmaker* is a report of accumulated findings—after years spent perambulating.

David LaRocca
Lima, Perú
Malecón de la Marina, fewer than three hundred miles from
11°44'14.3"S, 72°56'04.4"W[10]

I

Advance Signals from the Semaphore

*A speculative introduction to
an imagined collection of archival
photographs from the sets and screens of
Werner Herzog's film productions*

THE MIND IS CLUTTERED WITH IMAGES, he thought—everything we see refers to something else. Perhaps only children see with absolute purity of vision; they see things for what they are and nothing else. The rest of us see signals from elsewhere, and always have done, ever since people began to think. First they see gods and ghosts and symbols and portents. And then they are battered with images of everywhere and every time and all that they see is invaded from elsewhere, and always have done, ever since people began to think. [...] We don't see plain anymore, he thought. I am an artist, and I don't see plain. I see what it has been suggested that I see. I look at a tree and I see it as Dürer saw trees, as Samuel Palmer did, as Cézanne did. Who has ever seen plain?[1]

WITH THESE WORDS from a protagonist and progenitor in Penelope Lively's *Consequences*, we are invited to ask among ourselves and anew "Who has ever seen plain?" A reader, a seer, coming to the proposed—*imagined*—album of photographs, or even just this spectral book's cover image, may recognize a contender in Werner Herzog. Still more, his candidacy coalesces, in part, by virtue of these images *of* Werner Herzog, for they are visible evidence that places him at the scene of the seen (and occasionally obscene). Yet, as with most behind-the-scenes coverage, the miracle is not revealed; rather the pedestrian comes rushing forth. Herzog is just a man, and yet, in his ordinariness and mortal form, he has assigned himself the formidable project of fashioning new and "adequate" cinematic symbols, tropes, and formulations. And he remains, as an indefatigable octogenarian, a tireless advocate for reconceiving our relationship to the way we see — and to seeing plain what we have already been given so multitudinously to see.

Herzog, of course, is now famous for saying that "we are surrounded by worn-out, banal, useless and exhausted images, limping and dragging themselves behind the rest of our cultural evolution."[2] First, we ourselves notice that someone had to point out that "our images" are, in fact, frayed and faded. And then we wonder when someone might show up who is gifted enough to make us some new — sharp, vibrant, vigorous — ones. Again, Herzog appears a candidate for both positions: a sentinel who is also, after his own fashion, an originator.

To be sure, looking across the more than seventy-and-counting films he has made, few would say that Herzog's mode of "seeing plain" is untutored, but rather that his radically insistent focus on content deflects familiar preoccupations with formalism and genre traits. In this respect, he is one of the few abiding filmmakers to get away with such a reliable pursuit of content irrespective of formal constraints, inherited expectations, familiar patterns, or what might be a vulgar word to him, *style*. Herzog has no style. It's a claim met by shouts of agreement and outraged objection. Far from an insult, Herzog would wear the declaration as a badge of honor. Though committed to films as a mode — aware that he has a personal stake in his creations, and a signature effect on them — predetermined film style is suspect. Even so, *stylization* is a watchword held dear. "Many of my documentaries are feature films in disguise," he tells Nick Schager. "Some of them are partly scripted and rehearsed and repeated and well-cast, and use stylization that you would normally not see in a documentary. But I want to do a different type of documentary that divorces itself from journalism. Almost everything we see today is a form of journalism, but documentaries can do much, much more than that. I'm after something different."[3] The Herzog difference registers itself in the range of his cinematic creations — in tone and textual subjects (including intertexts and subtexts). Style is limiting, stylization limitless. When watching his films, we recall that he saw his first moving image at the age of seventeen. He sees plain. (Therefore he thinks plain, too. And though he spices his syntax with Romantic-era vocabulary and appeals to Greek etymologies, the force of his directness assures us that he talks plain so as to speak straight.) He makes images. He may aim now and again for the head but mostly hits the heart and gut—then without delay or apology, he moves on, usually on foot.

Style can arrive as anti-style—trends and tropes being reliable and durable, opposition may be the best recourse. Richard Lanham, the rhetorician, wrote *Style: An Anti-Textbook*; his lessons were liberating for those who heeded his tuitions and intuitions. Write plainly. Say what you mean. But discover the art of grammar in the process. *Have* a style, but let it be unburdened by the weight of, say, convoluted and euphemistic, bureaucratic prose. Avoid the saccharine solicitations of marketing speak that would deign to commodify the world for the sake of aggregated capital; in that aggressive realm, even "anti-capitalism" can be a consumable (sold back to the highest bidder—even often at the cheapest rates, where humans are sold out before their wares are spent). Into this breach of model breaking and path making comes Herzog, who directs his camera and his attention to whatever subject or object draws them. The gesture itself encodes morals: protect instinctive energy and follow it; do not be swayed or dismayed by doubters and dissenters—forge ahead. How regularly do these photographs of Herzog on set provide iconography for such an ethics.

The cinephiles and philosophers run themselves ragged trying to give reasons for Herzog's images—what they mean, what they do. The moment seems to call for theory, *a* theory. Seeing plain, however, would upset and invert the foregoing terms. It would set out *an anti-theoretical style* or *a style of anti-theory*. Nervous philosophers scamper, gather snippets to set out in a system: "But look, *Fata Morgana* is experimental; it's avant-garde!" Maybe so, and fair enough. Yet Herzog would have us achieve *revelation without theory*. Show us the thing—do not equivocate and second-guess. Speak plainly even about mysteries and unknowns—do not add further obfuscations from the lecture hall and seminar table, from the dusty ledgers of the dead. Another text of reference serves here: Garrett Stewart's aptly titled *The Value of Style in Fiction*, in which we are treated to his close-grained analysis of literary works that reward such intense and extended attention spans. Herzog's partner volume may run beneath the same banner, such that we have eyes and ears for *what may pass as style* in his realm: style as self-same, self-justifying, where form and content are so tightly bonded that they are liberated to follow the author's whim.

Spicing facts with fiction may be a style—stylization itself as a style—yet it is anti-documentary, anti-journalism, anti-archive, anti-tradition, anti-authority. Herzog doesn't tether his projects to antecedents of cinematic form or subject matter (though tropes, topics, types, and themes recur). Point is: by not doubling down on style (*a* style), committing himself to following a tradition or contributing to a school (and there are many quick contenders: legacies of New German Cinema; or the subgenres that would be all too pleased to claim him: adventure documentary, nature documentary, reportage, docudrama, slow cinema, essay film, etc.), he can do all or none, do what he wants—from film to film—on his own terms. This risk-taker with justification supplied endogenously follows the path he needs at any given juncture. Call this a film-philosophy for Stoics and desert fathers, hermits and mystics, seekers and prophets, poets and divines. "Seeing plain" suits the asceticism that pervades the human enterprise—a robe, a rope, a camera, and a book. Anything more is profligate, distracting. "Seeing plain" means abiding by the unaffected and unpretentious. Not arthouse, not film school, but a workmanlike directness: drink beer from the bottle, watch soccer, fly coach.

Herzog sees mysteries where we do not; for him, the world is enchanted, bizarre, a place full of peculiarity calling out for our attention—and rewarding it. These disparate and bedeviling aspects—real and imagined—need an advocate and interpreter. Sometimes Herzog's direct address (and response) to the world—the world as he found it, the world he let make its way onto film and so remade it in the process—feels profound (a gift from a gifted mind); at other times, it appears incomprehensible ... or funny. Yet that range—from grave to parodic—confirms the quality of seriousness in a project always set on the edge of collapse and failure. "Breaking" keeps kinship with its comedic cousin. Herzog's style of anti-style, his beautiful risk of creative antagonism and constitutive perception, purports to reveal—to make plain. But do we yet or still have the patience for such ambitions? Fortunately for us, Herzog leaves behind his library of films by which we can debate replies.

If film criticism is the activity given to thinking about cinematic offerings, with this book of still images (from sets, screens, and behind the scenes), what is our business? How should we respond to photographs "from films." To be more precise, not film frames or stills, but something else—shots from occasions *of* filmmaking. We are not looking through

Herzog's—or Thomas Mauch's or Jörg Schmidt-Reitwein's or Peter Zeitlinger's—viewfinder, but askew, from other angles. Herzog is often in the frame of these images, emplaced within the context of his search for new images. Now, in this gorgeous edition (still hovering in the mind's eye rather than fashioned for handling), generously supplied from the backroom storehouse of Herzog's archive, and sourced from Los Angeles to Munich, including, notably, from the collections of Lena Herzog and Beat Presser, we have here a sequence to ponder: how do these photographs help us think differently about the moving images created by Herzog over the last half-century-and-more?

WE ACKNOWLEDGE A FEW BIOGRAPHICAL FACTS: that Werner Stipetić was born in Bavaria in 1942. With a youth framed partially by the effects of Germany's loss in World War II and the mystical energies of the Black Forest, little Werner took up the film camera as a means of addressing the world—perhaps to see if it would answer him back. Even in his first forays of filmmaking, he spoke of his work—both as imagemaker and agent—in anagogic ways that would befit sages three times his age; he offered interpretations of the ordinary and the exceptional that exceeded literal, allegorical, and moral lessons, precociously delineating instead formidable mystical connotations. By this point in his earthly progress, he had traded his birth surname for the stage name "Herzog" and never looked back. Indeed, the implied portent of his apparently self-assumed mission to create new images requires a persistent forward momentum, one Herzog himself claims is best achieved on foot. When he calls himself a "foot-soldier for cinema," we recognize something of this description from his novel, *The Twilight World*:

> You are to defend its territory by guerilla tactics, at all costs. You will have to make your own decisions. No one will give you orders. You must be self-reliant.[4]

To be sure, this is not a telegram from Herzog, but the orders Hiroo Onoda received from his high commanders during World War II—in effect, to hold the line. And yet, the sequence of second-person dictates would be perfectly intelligible during one of Herzog's installments of the Rogue Film School, his occasional peripatetic experiment in film education undertaken as a shot across the bow of those most lamentable businesses called film schools. In *his* school for scoundrels and rogues, Herzog preaches the gospel of doing what one must to make a film—how to be self-starting and self-sufficient. "Steal a camera if you have to. Forge permits." Even if these are transgressions meant to be understood by students in a *poetic* fashion, the point is for poetry to emerge from the other side of the "stolen" lens or the forbidden territory entered by way of "trespassing." In short, filmmaking is not for the faint of heart.

Because of Herzog's unique relationship to the art of *creating* images, the photographs that you hold in hand (make that head) possess a double status: each is at once an image of what it appears to be (say, Herzog on set with Klaus Kinski), but also an image of a seeker putting himself at the mercy of gods, wondering day by day what he can do to translate some morsel of significance from cosmic ineffability (or perhaps only render serial representations of precisely such inscrutability). An alternate title might be *Herzog at Work*. But the referents are scattered—caught here in a moment of him offering notes to an actor or a request to a technician, seen there lifting heavy equipment while waiting for gaffers to catch up. To be sure, rumors haunt the frame as reports from afar. A photograph of Herzog beside New German Cinema compatriot Wim Wenders can't make audible the slightly younger Wenders' first-hand remembrances when his colleague, then visiting instructor, Werner, arrived at Wenders' film school in Munich. Herzog's message to the gathered students was "intense and brutal" in its unflinching bluntness. All these years later, Wenders appears to have been privy to Herzog's earliest pedagogical lessons for budding filmmakers: "Nobody teaches cinema like Werner," says Wenders. "He told us to quit school immediately. [Werner] shouted: 'You are idiots if you stay here. It is not getting you anywhere. You have to leave this school tomorrow and start to make films. You will never do that if you stay in this place.'"[5] Part of seeing plain is recognizing how names and definitions can inadvertently mutate—become their opposites, transform into ironic mismatches before our very eyes. On this logic, "film school" becomes an unfavorable place to be educated in the art of film.

Much is made in the secondary literature, and for good reason, of the quixotic figures to whom Herzog has long devoted his attention—from Aguirre and Fitzcarraldo to Dieter Dengler and Timothy Treadwell. But the people are not the point; they are proxies for the *pursuit* of something else: call it an image of the noumenal world. Thus, Aguirre covets the discovery of a city of gold, Fitzcarraldo yearns for the ecstasy of opera in the jungle, Dengler dreams liberation through painted canvas, Treadwell hungers to capture on video a portrait of animals that belies their animality. The bold aims, lost causes, exotic desires, and the all-too-real failures of such figures (nearly all of them men) is not biographical, but simply graphical: what is the image we are presented with? What is its object or its reflected import? Can we too see whatever might be there (or not)—beyond the mirage, because of the sound, within the drawing, beneath (or above) the surface of the material world?

WHEN HOLDING A FOLIO OF IMAGES OF WERNER HERZOG at work making films, we start by asking what such images are *of*, but as appealing, we also ask what these images are *for*. Photographs from movie sets rarely make this impression; rather, in conventional instances, we are captivated by the star, indulging our knowledge of the subsequent film by making connections with what scene we are seeing "behind," and generally awestruck by the always peculiar relationship between actor and character. But *these pictures* of Herzog? Nothing of the sort. Here we hold images of a man in pursuit of *what we come to see*—on account of his mission: "I'm a curious person, forever searching for new images." The project and the pursuit appeal, yet the terms blur. Is a "new" (or as he sometimes says, as if using a synonym, "adequate") image a *memorable* one? Or *useful*? Perhaps heuristic in some way? How would we know? We don't—cannot—know in advance, and may not know even upon a first, second, or third encounter. Fact is, the "new" image may be old—lying in wait. The inked impression of a hand encountered in the Chauvet cave nominates itself as just such a "new image"—and yet its provenance (near Provence) predates the better span of human civilizations.

"Our inability and lack of desire to seek fresh imagery," Herzog assures us, means we are lagging behind—inundated by refuse when we could marshal our resources to better ends.[6] But who cares if our contemporary landscape is littered with cliché postcard images (iconic forms and norms distilled into atrophied myths), or suiting the present time, musty social media memes and endlessly circulating clips—make that infectious viral material? Are these really degradations of the human condition, confirmations of our anemic imaginations? "When I look at postcards in tourist shops and the images and advertisements in magazines, or turn on the television, or walk into a travel agency and see huge posters with those same tedious images of the Grand Canyon, I sense that something dangerous is emerging. Just as a person without a memory will struggle to survive in this world, so will someone who lacks images that reflect his inner state."[7]

Herzog's metaphysical charge—or challenge to us—draws the outer world into conversation with our inner landscapes. Mind, memory, and meaning all storm about seeking companionship and expression in art, literature, film, music, whatever. When those creations are predictable, when they are unduly repetitious or beholden to past exemplars, when they aim for stunt instead of substance, when they praise mediocrity and ignore the bold, we humans are lost. "I believe that the lack of adequate imagery is a danger of the same magnitude" as an extinction-level event, he says. "I'll repeat it again as long as I'm able to: we will die out like dinosaurs if we don't develop adequate images. We need to learn to adapt our visual language to new and unforeseen situations."[8] Despite an abundance of images, they are—collectively and individually—insufficient. We are neither nourished nor satisfied by them. Herzog's admonition suggests that novelty isn't enough (e.g., the aggregation and creative recombination of prior forms), but something like an innovation beyond the felt and found is required. What could that new thing be? Is there, in fact, anything new under the sun—now or ever? In a moment of reflexivity suited to our bewildering query, Herzog's very commendation to seek and make new imagery consitutes a new image . . . of itself. We are pictured—mythologized—as "those who pursue new images."

Like the global climate crisis, the crisis of imagery is slow moving—so unhurried, so undifferentiated that we struggle to perceive it at the scale of the human. And even when it is noticed—the painful repetition of images (the sequels and prequels), the self-referentiality of contemporary culture, how most everything now "goes meta"—people just shrug, caught in a state of numb confusion, insensible to the stakes of nonengagement. How could imagemaking even *have* a crisis—especially now in its kinetic, digitized super-abundance and with artificial intelligence in the hunt for a further exponential surge? How could the practice, the *art* (!) of imagemaking matter to our sanity and survival—or indeed, our evolution as a species? Since the 1960s, Herzog has been all too aware of the deleterious effects of such nonchalance, and has been shaking us awake to its perils. Because he has made scores of films, written a number of books, directed many opera productions and myriad other performance experiments, Herzog too—perhaps unavoidably—has become an image. Such a result is an inevitable function of the times.

Herzog's singularity—his soul-penetrating stare, his Bavarian cadence, his uncanny diction—have set him apart. Yet, whatever newness his presence has brought to his identity, culture is a greedy *combinatoire*, gathering all instances in order to reorder and repackage them for sustained consumption. Though Herzog is himself a new image, he is deployed iconographically to disturb conventional scenes (The Zek in *Jack Reacher*, The Client in *The Mandalorian*, a guest on *Parks and Recreation*, W. H., i.e., Walter Hotenhoffer on *The Simpsons*, parodied on *Entourage*, *Documentary Now!*, computationally conceived for an audio AI experiment with Slavoj Žižek, and so on). His brand *is* disturbance. For some, Herzog's participation in these projects may be taken as a diminishment of his "serious" work, and yet his jealously guarded self-awareness has always been one of his most distinguishing characteristics. Unlike comedians, he doesn't break. And so, as ever, the joke is on us.

Though Herzog reports ominously that "we need images in accordance with our civilization and innermost conditioning," we will not find them accidentally, but only through tremendous effort—even if required by laughably invented obstructions.[9] Let's not forget, this is a man who pulled a ship over a mountain—not a scale model (as the studio heads suggested), not using animation or visual trickery. But an actual ship. It is Fitzcarraldo's fever dream, but it is Herzog's reality. And it should be ours too: make life difficult for ourselves *deliberately* so that we may discern—and pay attention to—our spiritual needs. Experience becomes a false, compromised arena for doubt and disappointment unless we face it boldly—demanding that it live up to our highest expectations for it. This mood of urgency, even emergency, is our greatest sign of respect for existence itself.

IN ASKING WHAT IMAGES ARE FOR, we also ask a question about the purpose of *these* images, here gathered in our imagination, by reference to the archives that are safe but absent and those that are at our disposal, at the ready (Google image search: Werner Herzog film set; Werner Herzog filming, etc.). Without any explanation given, without any captions or commentary, or shame over our circumstances in letting this remain, for now, a speculative project—we can recognize this imagined book as a handy companion—a further spur to our onward thinking. These are not sentimental portraits of an artist, but reminders, calls to action. There is Herzog starving himself in league with Christian Bale, as the Welsh actor wastes away for his devotion to craft, eating live maggots to fulfill his self-imposed constraints for making such a film. What sacrifices will we make for our art? Will the results be worth the pain, all the hours forsaken in pursuit of quixotic conceits? Herzog, like his many talented collaborators—actors and crew alike—heralds the diminished border between fiction and non-fiction. Not that we don't still need actors to act (alas, the Method can go awry), but that we need to fathom the fantastical in our everyday lives as much as on the silver screen—or on the glowing surface of our phones. We need Herzog's reminders that we are, in fact, alive and identical with experience. There is no "I" that has visions and another that watches movies of people having visions; these are continuous, overlapping magisteria.

Open this imagined book (one conjured in mind, one curated by fiat), therefore, whenever such reminders are needed—and how often they are.

II

Ecstatic, Essayistic Pronouncements

Werner Herzog is rare among filmmakers: he is very well-read—and writes well too. Though he is closing in on the creation of one hundred films, he startles us by saying "I do believe my writing will have a longer life than my films"—another rare bit of unintuitive prognostication from one of the most iconic filmmakers of the last half-century.[1] Like Frank Gehry saying we will remember him best for his epistolary correspondence or Daniel Day-Lewis for his leather crafts. (To Herzog's credit—and for our further deliberation—he adds, in a customarily deflationary coda: "Though I may be wrong. I have misjudged quite often.") But then much about Herzog—what is seemingly apparent, well known, and taken for granted—remains variously misunderstood, contradictory, or undeciphered. Not for lack of trying: an industry of film critics, journalists, fellow filmmakers and academic scholars have given abundant time and effort to figuring out the Herzog enigma.

And yet, as this book embodies, setting off in the direction of a mystery affords no guarantee of its resolution. In fact, as the dozens of other books and hundreds of articles on Herzog have made clear, resolution is a moving target, a false objective that creates new puzzles and paradoxes along the way, resolves some matters only to yield new obstacles. The spirit that animates the present endeavor doesn't seek to outsmart the many smart things that have been said and written about Herzog, but to approach matters in the wake of them, to variously let them stand or draw from them, and in the midst of such unsettled conditions, to add a few observations for further propitious inquiries. Mountains have peaks, oceans have floors, but a philosophical investigation into Herzog has no limits—it just keeps going and going. Such indeterminacy and open-endedness can leave a seeker crestfallen by an impossible mission; or it can whisper hints about the distant, still unknown, vistas that yet await—at the heights and in the depths and often on the ordinary footpaths of the demotic realm. It is after these imagined specters, real or not, transcendental or proximate, that we rogue agents roam—

onward and all the while keeping close at hand the credo of Herzog's own Rogue Film School: "Not for the Faint Hearted."

ALTHOUGH HERZOG IS AN UNCOMMONLY well-read filmmaker and a highly articulate speaker, given to estimable literary-philosophical flourishes—especially when thinking aloud about his oeuvre in interviews and on audio commentaries for his own films—he, nevertheless, regularly cultivates a defiantly anti-institutional, indeed, anti-intellectual posture. If this is a defensiveness borne of his accomplished autodidacticism, so be it. If, for whatever reason, he refuses—and gleefully mocks—academic analysis and theorizing of his work, we must live with it. The same person who counsels aspiring filmmakers to "read, read, read, read, read," who established his own "film school" (which, by the way, includes a mandatory "before you arrive" reading list[2] as well as a film syllabus—the latter entailing a list of movies conscripts are encouraged to watch prior to joining the classroom) also unrelentingly emphasizes that "film schools are a waste of time."[3] And so, despite his double status—as a talented, illuminating analyst of his own work *and* a (playfully?) hostile antagonist to those who would dare seek deeper meanings in his films—a philosopher and film theorist cannot help but be intrigued. As Herzog has said in reply to the intellectually curious, "pedantic theoreticians of cinema": "Go for it, losers."[4] Taking the bait, as I have before[5], in this chapter I offer a critical account of selected remarks that may not amount to a veritable philosophy of filmmaking, but rather, gesture toward one. Such an objective is sufficiently daring. That is, instead of attempting to discern a coherent system (surely, a lost cause even before the expedition would get underway), I aim to glean while listening to the essayistic, often repetitive, and engagingly paratactic qualities of Herzog's pronouncements.

> People sense I am well orientated, that I know where I have come from and where I'm headed, so it's understandable that they search for some guiding ideology behind my work. But no such thing exists as far as I'm

> concerned. There is never some philosophical idea that guides a film through the veil of a story. All I can say is that I understand the world in my own way and am capable of articulating this understanding through stories and images that are coherent to others. I don't like to drop names, but what sort of an ideology would you push under the shirt of Conrad or Hemingway or Kafka? Goya or Caspar David Friedrich? Even after watching my films, it bothers some audiences that they are unable to put their finger on what my credo might be. Grasp this with a pair of pliers, but the credo is the films themselves and my ability to make them. This is what troubles those people who have forever viewed my work with tunnel vision, as if they were looking through a straw they picked up at McDonald's. They keep searching. No wonder they get desperate.[6]

When Herzog eschews calls for a system, for an over-arching explanation or theory by which to comprehend his work on a case-by-case basis or in its entirety, we note the untroubled catalog of contradictions he issues for our delight and consternation; ever on to the next assignment, Herzog leaves us pitched not between clarity and obscurity so much as between mystic profundity and shambolic philosophical musings. Indeed, the films of his that attract our interest here partake in the genre of "essay films" — those that *essay*, intentionally bypassing any presumptions to a definitive "statement" or unified "argument," mocking the syllogism and its professions of deduction, thereby presenting themselves, instead, as experiments, thematic explorations, trials, studies, assemblages, upon varied and irreconcilable sites of encounter.[7] Still, if we listen closely and take Herzog at his word, there are clues that can shape our reception. Not a system, then, but provocative filaments: "The credo is the films themselves and my ability to make them," he tells us, thereby giving us ground to theorize on his behalf: that his films are their own evidence, are not representative of anything but themselves.[8]

While we observe pertinent moments from various "masterclasses" Herzog has offered over the years (including the trademarked ©MasterClass), as well as interviews with the likes of Jonathan Demme, and more conspicuously in Les Blank's legendary portraits, *Werner Herzog Eats His Shoe* (1980) and *Burden of Dreams* (1982), I attend, in this segment of reflection, mostly to documentaries featuring the filmmaker, that is: biographical and autobiographical essay films that are by design and definition contributions to meta-filmmaking and metaphilosphy: Christian Weisenborn's *I Am My Films: A Portrait of Werner Herzog* (1976-78, with Erwin Keusch) and *I Am My Films, Part 2, Thirty Years Later* (2010); Peter Buchka's *To the Limit and Then Beyond It: The Ecstatic World of Filmmaker Werner Herzog* (*Bis ans Ende und dann noch weiter: Die ekstatische Welt des Filmemachers Werner Herzog, Ein Essay von Peter Buchka*, 1989); Kim Hendrickson's *Dreams and Burdens* (2005); and lastly, Herzog's own, *Werner Herzog, Filmemacher: An Autobiographical Documentary Short* (1989). In the following remarks I am motivated by a wish to cull and assess elements from these accomplished, intellectually stimulating and conceptually fecund documentaries, and related texts, so that they all might be drawn into service for the wider critical conversation about Herzog's philosophical contributions — in particular, what philosophers and film theorists can do with his work (despite his objections or disinterest or taunting dismissals). Yet the question that haunts the undertaking remains: do his pronouncements hinder the very efforts here proffered? When it comes to thinking philosophically about his films, what can and should we make of Herzog's consistently imposed obstructionism?

1. The Enigma Speaks

IF ONE DOUBTS THERE IS AN ENIGMA AT HAND, simply consult the nearest bibliography of articles, chapters, reviews, interviews, documentaries, and books on (or by) Werner Herzog. Given the number of works addressing the filmmaker, reports and remarks that have proliferated exponentially in recent years, an expanding archive that has been uncannily supplemented and thus amplified by Herzog's *own* industry as a prose stylist (publishing his own books, articles, and "manifestos" along the way, not to mention the capacious commentary he provides *in* his films and "upon" them, e.g., in DVD commentaries; in the aforementioned, abundant, and ongoing interviews; in a

MasterClass, etc.), we can be sure that a mercurial figure is among us. To be fair, and to be sure, Paul Cronin's *Herzog on Herzog* (2002)—which has since its publication been updated, enlarged, and enriched into the (aptly re-titled) tome *A Guide for the Perplexed* (2014)—with its double sense of "guide" as a go-to *consigliere* and a Maimonidean handbook for those of us who have sought orientation in, among, and toward Herzog's varied films and literary expositions. Many days, the zone of our interest can feel like the deep interior of the Perúvian jungle—home to such labyrinthine narratives as *Fitzcarraldo*, its companion documentary *Burden of Dreams* (1982, dir. Les Blank; editor, Maureen Gosling), *Aguirre, The Wrath of God* (1972), and *Wings of Hope* (2000), among other works—and our best metaphor for the thicket of ideas we find (or more often, lose) ourselves in. Among other galvanizing ventures in Herzog interpretation— by turns exegetical and midrashic—we find *The Films of Werner Herzog: Between Mirage and History* (1986), and *The Essay Film: From Montaigne, after Marker* (2011), both by Timothy Corrigan[9]; *The Cinema of Werner Herzog: Aesthetic Ecstasy and Truth* (2007) and *A Companion to Werner Herzog* (2012), both by Brad Prager; *Ferocious Reality: Documentary According to Werner Herzog* (2012) and *Werner Herzog: Interviews* (2014), both by Eric Ames; *Every Night the Trees Disappear: Werner Herzog and the Making of Heart of Glass* by Alan Greenberg (1976/2012); *Werner Herzog: Filmmaker and Philosopher* (2019) by Richard Eldridge; and *The Philosophy of Werner Herzog* (2022), edited by Christopher Turner and M. Blake Wilson (and featuring a foreword by Paul Cronin), among other authors, journalists, and editors gamely going at the project of making sense of Herzog's movies and musings. Yet, as I mentioned in a previous attempt at arranging some thoughts on the speculation of a "humanistic sublime" in Herzog, I found myself amused and thwarted by Herzog's insistence that academic, critical, or theoretical approaches to understanding film are bankrupt.[10]

The still-dawning illumination of artificial intelligence may become an even greater obstruction to such pursuits, since human authors will have to do their bit while writing at the pace of electro-chemical-based liquid cognition rather than the lightning-fast velocity of a generative AI algorithm. In the meantime, however, can we tell from the cover of *My Cinematic Odessey: Werner Herzog's Story* by J. M Bright that the con is on?[11] The cover image purports to be of Werner Herzog, but it comes across as the result of a DALL-E prompt to "create a photo-adjacent illustration of a man who resembles Werner Herzog—but, for copyright and other legal prohibitions, is definitely not him." Furthermore, not only will careful readers wonder why a first person "odessey" [sic] would be written by someone other than Herzog, they will also catch the misspelled "odyssey" in the main title and the lack of a supporting period after the "author's" second initial. Perhaps J. M [sic] is not so bright after all.

And so, in the aforementioned all-too-human undertakings, including in *The Philosophy of Werner Herzog*, etc., groups of seasoned scholars step up and step in to make something in human-generated prose of Herzog's cinematic sounds and images. What can be added? Given limitations—and we know how Herzog loves limits—we hazard a brief critical digest of the ways in which we could reasonably speak of a Herzogian philosophy of film, or of filmmaking; cinéphilosophy or cinaesthetics (depending on your preference)—all of which, admittedly, may smack of a decidedly Herzogian bête noire. By now, most major and mainstream directors have found themselves on camera, on screen, explaining themselves and their films—from the press junket to the authorized biography, from the critical reevaluation of earlier work, to festschrifts and encomiums, and to the now-disappearing but much-loved DVD commentary tracks and "special features" of the "extras" menu—and so we live at a time when asking about a given film (again, by a major talent) *also means* that we can find a documentary or interview or public talk (now often available on YouTube) that can provide evidence for theory-making (his or her own, or ours). Befitting the temperament of a classic Herzogian adventurer, Herzog himself often exceeds even the vast commentary of his celebrated peers (e.g., witness the director commentary on the several boxed sets of his films as well as his copious and capacious interviews, seminars, and perhaps most crucially, his self-styled, self-invented Rogue Film School).

While the above-mentioned resources (as well as the contents of the book in hand) supply indexed access to whole worlds of Herzogian pronouncements, purloined apothems, and provocative calls to action, I turn to a small, but substantial segment of the Bavarian director's vast corpus: those works in which he has made himself or allowed himself to become the subject, often the subject-in-reflection-on-his-films-and-filmmaking. Given Herzog's availability to (both sides of) the camera, it is not surprising, though certainly perplexing (that word again), that one of these documentaries is entitled "I am what my films are" [*Was ich bin, sind meine Filme*], though more often promoted under a variorum or pithily vernacular translation—viz., "I am my films." (As a moment of sideways film history, we recall how Herzog's fellow "Werner"—Rainer Werner Fassbinder—said "*Ich bin meine filme.*" As Herzog encourages lock-picking and the forgery of documents, let us add calculated appropriation.[12] Moreover, in proximity to phraseology and attribution, perhaps some attention can be granted to the standard—to many, accepted—translation of *Was ich bin, sind meine Filme*: Christian Weisenborn's two films are rendered as *I Am My Films*; a plausible variant being: "I am what my films are." Again, Herzog's claim for films-as-their-own-evidence lends orientation even as a sphinx-like Herzog sends us back to ask—What *are* your films? How would we articulate a scenario, or an understanding, in which Herzog is somehow ontologically coextensive with what he makes (or how what he creates constitutes him)? For example, if his films are fictions, then Herzog is one too (with autofiction on offer?); if documentary, then Herzog likewise becomes a creature of non-fiction; if his films are encounters with "ecstatic truth," then how would we discern this status in and of the director as well (facts fabricated to *exceed* evidence)? Of course, as suits his temperament and the tone of his mystical adventuring, his films can be all these things, and more—and so, as usual, we appear in need of another (first?) step in our discovery and appreciation of Herzog's cinematic creations. To this end (or this beginning), as we have in various "commentaries" on his own work, we look to Herzog himself to tutor us—to provide tuition—on the illumination of his enigma, in the indeterminate double state of his films (and of the philosophy they may contain, or that he adopts in making them), of his own capacities as a filmmaker, and qualities as a storyteller.

2. "All Around the Movie" Žižek's Closet Commentary on Herzog

THE MUCH-CELEBRATED CRITERION COLLECTION has made a habit of inviting people—usually famous filmmakers and actors, but also, god forbid, film theorists (!)—into its booth-like storeroom to browse the titles and comment on them. In one memorable close encounter in the closet, we find Slavoj Žižek extemporizing on the values and virtues of films by Ernst Lubitsch, Peter Weir, Louis Malle, Ang Lee, David Lean, Roberto Rossellini, Sergei Eisenstein, Charlie Chaplin, Alfonso Cuarón, Carl Dreyer, and Lars von Trier. And then Žižek's free-flowing analysis comes to a sudden halt. Plied with his distinctive syntax (preserved in an animated quotation below), globally-recognized accent (sound familiar? more on the sonic shape and vocal syncopation of Herzog and Žižek in chapter VII), and with a knowing hint of corporate advertising added to placate his obliging host, Žižek remembers an example of the type of film he *does not* like to watch:

> I must confess that I cheat sometimes: if the movie drags on, I do a little bit of fast forward or whatever and so on. But the reason I like Criterion is that even if it's a bad movie you can get, you usually get, a good running commentary and all the making-of stuff and so on. And sometimes, I must say, I enjoy this additional stuff more than movie itself. For example, Werner Herzog. *Fitzcarraldo*. I think it's a pretentious fake. The other one, similar movie: *Aguirre, The Wrath of God* is much better. But there is, I think, the title is *The Burden of Dreams*. A documentary on the making of *Fitzcarraldo*. I think it's much better than the movie itself. So that's why I like Criterion. Forget the movie. I'm a corrupted theorist. Screw the movie, I like to learn all around the movie.[13]

We will not, then, shortlist Žižek for a review of Herzog's films, since the lesson is overt: better to discuss his films than to watch them! A philosopher who has taken the bait and enjoys his feeding frenzy. Yet, Žižek's love of the paratexts Criterion makes possible on its robustly produced, high-end DVDs (and now, of course, on a bespoke streaming platform) is indicative of a behavior we see in Herzog himself: he, with seemingly peerless endurance and unflappable vigor, speaks about his own work (as he does in the rightly fêted Les Blank and Maureen Gosling film,

Burden of Dreams). Just at Žižek has, then, spotted one of the most illuminating supplemental texts in our (potential) thinking about Herzog's own films, he also gives us a clue to the way we may wish to "learn all around the movie"—and Herzog's movies more generally—in order to understand something more fundamental about what animates his (actual) thinking, let us call it his philosophical stance.

As we proceed, we might as well move forward with some candor, since we will not find a quick, consistent key by which to translate Herzog's pronouncements into the language and logic of *professional* philosophy, or for that matter, film studies (and its familiar trinity: theory, criticism, history). Herzog does not speak those languages, but instead summons mystical, archaic lexicons; feeds on terms familiar to the Romantic, poetic, and transcendental; and sometimes (as if to guard his own modesty and humble origins) undermines apparently pretencious statements with pointed clichés, parables, and everyday phrases. Whatever their provenance and shape, his remarks can seem to conjure little worlds unto themselves rather than offer a coherent portraiture or a balanced architectonic. He does not build a system or systems, but instead catches glimpses of what lies at the limit of comprehension—and often just beyond it. Indeed, nearly a half-century ago he was already at work setting his table when he declared a sentiment that has recurred throughout his career, in myriad forms and instances:

> I am not an intellectual. I do not belong to the ranks of intellectuals who have a philosophy or a social structure in mind and then make a film about it. Nor do I think that I succumbed to literary or philosophical influences. I can say, for the most part, that I am illiterate. I haven't read much and am therefore utterly clueless. In my case, making a film has much more to do with real life, with living things, than it has with philosophy. All my films were made without any reflective contemplation, or hardly any. Reflections always came after the film.[14]

All around the film! Herzog too appears willing to think critically after the fact. Doubtless we have already encountered, even here in these remarks from the early 1970s, what could be called in due time Herzog's (naturally occurring? unwittingly cultivated?) Socratic irony: his wish to appear untutored, which, as he must know, invokes the wisdom of saints and sages. The more he protests to grand theory, the more he courts self-deprecation, the more "we theorists" and film fans appear to run to his defense, as if to say: "No, Werner, you *are* an intellectual, indeed, you are *wise!*" Time and again, though, Herzog's outward contempt for theory, for the pursuits of intellectuals and philosophers, film theorists and their "schools," makes itself known; yet coupled with that rejection and brazen dismissal comes the (ironic) sense that he is, in fact, very much a (knowing) insider—which is to say, a (sincere) reader, theorist, and student. He said as much at his Rogue Film School, before an audience of aspiring filmmakers and Herzog enthusiasts: "If you don't read, you will never be a filmmaker."[15] In the intervening years, and with increasing frequency (perhaps especially in the age of social media), he has made a point of contrasting movie-watching with reading, noting on the one hand that he watches very few movies in a given year (and doesn't bother at all with social media), and on the other hand, that he prefers, quite simply, to stay home and read books. One of the enigmas, or concepts-set-in-tension, we should be working with (in what has been said thus far and in what follows) is the relationship between creation and reflection in his film production (e.g., does "reflection always [come] after the film," or does it not also, and very often, motivate its making—get it started and carry it through?); another is the extent to which Herzog's rhetoric (of ignorance, anti-theory, indeed, gasp—illiteracy!) is part of the philosophical edifice he has intentionally or inadvertently built (like a ruse that worked, but went too far).

Casting a look backwards to the first few decades of his filmmaking, Herzog showed a propensity to cast non-intellectuals in several cases, featuring prominently figures and characters whose linguistic and conceptual expression was hampered. Bruno S. comes immediately to mind.

> But of all the great actors and actresses I have worked with, one stands out: Bruno S. His appearance was always rough, as though he slept under bridges even though he had an apartment, but his face and his imposing

speech gave him an unconditional dignity. He was like an outcast, someone reeling toward you in confusion from a long bad night into a worse garish day. He had a depth, a tragedy, and an honesty that I have never seen anywhere else in cinema. Bruno himself didn't want his full name used for either our Kaspar Hauser film or for *Stroszek*; he didn't want to be a star but more something like the unknown soldier of cinema. [...] He died some years ago. The cinema will never look upon his like again.[16]

It is telling that in his vaunted valedictory to Bruno Schleinstein, Herzog describes him as he describes himself: a "soldier of cinema." They make for a memorable pair: the unknown soldier, Bruno, set in contrast to the soldier so well known to us, Werner, the public face of such ventures. One could compile a list of such Herzogian cinematic soldiers—known and unknown—who appear variously as outsiders and loners, visionaries and nonconformists, anti-social misfits and the socially outcast misunderstood. Time and again, they exist beyond the book; they are neither readers nor writers. Unlettered, unlisted, instead, they look to the horizon of an ice sheet or upwards to the stars or into the depths of frozen lakes and teeming jungles.

Given that Herzog has worked with Nicolas Cage and Nicole Kidman, Michael Shannon and Christian Bale, it is again telling that Herzog says of Bruno S.: "In all my films, and with all the great actors with whom I have worked, he was the best. There is no one who comes close to him. I mean in his humanity, and the depth of his performance, there is no one like him."[17] Bruno S., who spent years in and out of mental institutions, ascends to the pinnacle of Herzog's roster of acting talent—and we may add, of representational gravity. What Herzog admired in Bruno S. was, to be sure, not his theoretical insight.

3. Insight Without Instruction

IN CHRISTIAN WEISENBORN'S *I Am My Films: A Portrait of Werner Herzog* (1976-78), with a title, as previously noted, which can be variously translated as "I am my films" and "I am what my films are"—a distinction worth dwelling upon—our interviewer, Laurens Straub, asks Herzog a seemingly innocuous question, something to set the occasion in motion. Herzog doesn't disappoint. "What is your earliest memory," Weisenborn asks, to which Herzog replies: "My absolute earliest memory is of seeing God himself."[18] Follow-up questions ensue: "Were you scared of God?"—"No, I thought he was fine. [...] I think he was in overalls." An ecstatic image of his "savior" suddenly descends to the pedestrian, whereupon Herzog nonchalantly ends the story: "Later I found out it must have been someone from the little power station that was nearby." The shape of this vignette is iconic, and one that repeats in various encounters with Herzog—indeed, Herzog re-tells a version of this story in a different autobiographical film, *Werner Herzog, Filmemacher: An Autobiographical Documentary Short* (1989)[19]—a simple question followed by a fabulous reply, which turns back suddenly to familiar terms. For Herzog, going from God to overalls in a single breath is not uncommon, nor is imagining the tropes fused such that the deity would be wearing dungarees.

Instead of mocking or lamenting such patterns of thought and speech (and the repetitive, perhaps compulsive expression of such vignettes[20]), it is more productive—especially since such gestures are so prevalent across his films as well as in his off-the-cuff comments—to treat them as indicative of his ongoing debate between the "accountant's truth" and the "ecstatic truth." The distinction is by now familiar, but worth glossing briefly, since it may now be (inadvertently) confused with popular (if contested) phrases in our contemporary moment (or is it a post-truth era?) such as fake news and alternative facts. Ecstatic truth is not about fakes, hoaxes, and lies, but refers rather to *truth that is emergent from fabrications*. Thus, ecstatic truth is not aimed to leave one in a morass of contradictions, or lost in a field of misinformation, but, much more like a bit of legerdemain, to *conjure truth from fiction*. Ecstatic truth is, therefore, not the truth of the journalist, but of the mystic. In Herzog's case we needn't equate such a role with the mystifier, even if we come up short in "explaining" his apothems and commentaries. In large measure, because of Herzog's delivery—his unsmiling earnestness, his calm cadence, his baritone Bavarian inflection, his dramatic diction, his occasional laugh that anoints his latest thought—we have joined him in that moment of encounter with the prophetic. We are, if briefly, believers. That Herzog confesses the godhead is but an electrician who passed by the house is of little consequence to that glimpse of grandeur. The accountant's truth is admitted, but not before we are treated to a kind of truth that exceeds it. While recalling an experiencing of watching a Herzog film, we too could say of the encounter: "Once I bumped into God there."[21]

Having emphasized that he spent his childhood ensconced within a "gang" of children (a dozen or more in all), amidst a "chaotic" family, among various "litters" of siblings, and also enduring long stretches of solitude and illness (on one occasion a dysenteric fever had him dreaming he was being eaten by a shark, only to realize a lesser — but still astonishing — reality, that rats were biting into his skin), Herzog shares a formative excerpt from his educational experience:

> I really hated it in school. It was just torturous. I think we spent six months reading Goethe's *Iphigenia*. And six months on *Faust*. It was truly inhumane and terrible. I still haven't read *Faust*, simply because it made me physically sick. Back then I knew something was missing. We're forced to analyze it and pick it apart in a pseudo-academic way. It drives away any chance we have of loving these works. I always believed that the most important thing with a film or a work of literature or a painting or whatever was just to love it. [...] When I go to watch a film [...] there are moments when a realization suddenly strikes me. It flashes through me like lightning. And I know I am no longer alone. There are times like that in filmmaking [... and], yes, you find them in real life too.[22]

We are presented, then, with two primary models of encounter with art: a "pseudo-academic" style that favors "analysis," but that leaves Herzog "physically sick" and a contrasting intuitive and receptive mode, based in love, which allows "realization" and insight to strike, with the randomness, rarity, and radical intensity of lightning. As Herzog's ridicule of the academic matures over the years, we see how he drops the "pseudo" prefix since its inclusion is, in his view, redundant.

Herzog's quietist, intuitive approach, as well as a certain cultivated mysticism or even naïve wisdom, is apparent, for example, when Laurens Straub remarks "A lot of children keep secrets. Do you have a secret?"[23] How does Herzog answer a question that sets him up to admit childlike habits? First, by stating frankly, "Yes, of course, secrets played a big role," and then imposing a meta-reflexive obfuscation appropriate to the subject, "But I won't talk about that." A bit of childlike obstreperousness? In any case, the presence of a reality is constellated with notions of the unspeakable, the unsayable, the inexpressible, the ineffable.[24] For examples of this "to the limit" without a culminating result, we can look to Herzog's films about natural phenomena (e.g., in *La Soufrière* [1977], where a volcano stirs but then doesn't erupt—"waiting for an inevitable disaster" that, in fact, never comes to pass); or in his fictions that feature mutes or the deaf-blind (e.g., *Land of Silence and Darkness* [1971]) or people under hypnosis (*Heart of Glass* [1976]) or people with mental impairments (any film with Bruno S., and arguably, in a playfully provocative way befitting Herzog's relationship with him, Klaus Kinski). Time and again, Herzog convokes conditions in which we might be treated to an expression of profundity, and time and again that end is forestalled—sometimes tragically (e.g., *Grizzly Man* [2005]), that is, a man troubled by his thoughts, a man placed in trouble because of his perspective of the natural world and its non-human inhabitants), other times with parody and metacinematic trickery (e.g., *Lessons of Darkness* [1992]), on still other occasions with a kind of wry, witty withholding (e.g., *My Best Fiend* [1999]). "Yes, there are certain things which should remain sacrosanct," Herzog continues on the subject of keeping his secrets. "It's not good to know everything. You can't live like that."

Herzog extends the notion of "knowing" or not knowing (or keeping knowledge a secret or remaining [willfully] ignorant) by registering his disdain for the presumed knowledge of the mental sciences: "That's what I don't like about psychology. First, because they're so cocky, like it's a normal discipline with substantiated evidence. But actually it's reached the same stage as cranial surgery had during the mid-pharaonic period […]. Like centuries of bloodletting showed the helplessness of medicine. Psychology is the helplessness of our times."[25] Herzog's almost Nietzschean critique of psychology reminds us anew of the ways sanity (and its dissolution) is a leitmotif of his films—that is, whether people are of sound mind, or not, whether the sane are the impaired ones and the insane are the ones with clear vision, the ones to be trusted and followed. "There's a certain fatalism about [psychology] because it tries to shed light into every corner of what makes us human. [...] You can't live in a room with the lights blazing in every corner. It makes for uninhabitable, unhomely people, you know?"[26] Cinema, as a technology, is by definition a medium of illumination, yet it is also a form that invites us to gather in dark rooms (where the corners remain in the shadows). Herzog's fascination with the *primitive* qualities of the human—from mysticism to cave painting, from the untutored to the ignorant savant—seem to provide his preferred account of psychology: we are dreamers by nature, so we are wisest when we give credence to visions, when we are captivated by fata morganas. Film, as Herzog practices it, is not forensic, not for the accountability of history (say, in the way that Ken Burns' multi-part documentary portraits are meant to be both). Instead, the sounds and sights on screen form an alternate space of hallucination, where we can gather to play and replay our individual and collective phantasms.

4. The Virtue of Filmmaking on Foot

MOVING AHEAD A DECADE TO *Werner Herzog, Filmemacher: An Autobiographical Documentary Short* (1989), we catch a glimpse of another aspect of Herzog's imaginative primitivism. He speaks of a Bavarian childhood spent walking long distances—including the childlike hope of holding things together by means of personal effort and concentration (e.g., "I thought a person walking around [the country, i.e., in then-bifurcated Germany], always tracing the border, would somehow keep the country intact.")[27] When the child grows up, though, he retains his childlike sense of mystical powers, including those untutored, if honed, instincts tied to the pre-industrial human: "Sometimes I kind of jokingly say, 'My films are all films made while walking.' There is some truth to that. Because many pivotal experiences in my life were done on foot. For example, I walked from Munich to Paris one winter—that's 800 or 900 kilometers—because someone very important to me was dying [Lotte Eisner]. And I thought that walking there might save her. [...] [Walking long distances] is a completely unique way of life, of existence, that has almost completely disappeared from our everyday lives."[28]

This passage includes some of the hallmark rhetorical structure of a Herzogian pronouncement: an admission of unseriousness ("Sometimes I kind of jokingly say") followed by a very seriously presented bold irrationalism predicated on some kind of appeal to a link between mental and extramental realities ("And I thought that walking there might save her"—as just before in the notion of "somehow keep[ing] the country intact") and then, at the last moment, a seemingly trite anthropological observation ("almost completely disappeared from our everyday lives"), which, nevertheless, connects his personal experience to the realm of a shared crisis and a possible, if simplistic resolution ("completely unique way of life, of existence"). It is often very difficult to parse the logic of such a structure when it occurs, and especially when it is repeated many times in the course of a film or interview or even in his writing. A viewer (or reader) may glom onto the provocative pseudoscience (e.g., that walking a long distance might save an elderly woman from death, or keep a fragmented country unified) or dwell on the (obvious) observation that ancient man lived a different life than contemporary man, and these attachments—one way or another—will inform one's relationship to the film, to Herzog's pronouncements within it, and whether one takes them seriously or not.

Consider a further fillip on the brief remark made in *Werner Herzog, Filmemacher* about the way in which walking on foot is transitively related to filmmaking—as if walking and filmmaking are (necessarily) kindred undertakings, both literally and figuratively. For example, the outing on foot to reach Paris is not filmed (since, as we are told, Herzog walked alone), but, in time, it ends up on film as a story (as it does here and elsewhere, and in Herzog's book *Of Walking in Ice* [1978]).[29] Of his published diary, Herzog says it is "literature created more by my feet than my head, and remains closer to my heart than any of my films."[30] (Note again Herzog's elevated esteem for his writing—dearer to him than his many famous films.) Herzog's veneration of the work of writing—writing, as it were, "done by feet" (and thus not the head and the hand or by the camera), and thus overtly set in contrast with (his) filmmaking—is, in part, a testament to his affection for Lotte Eisner, who was such a crucial early and enduring support to him, but it is also an indication of his regard for the power of walking on foot from one place to another. Even so, the logical connections as well as the artistic claims remain muddled. Still, we march on.

Lesson #9 (of 13) in his now-iconic manifesto "Minnesota Declaration" reads like a epigrammatically rendered philosophical conditional: "Tourism is sin, and travel on foot virtue."[31] Herzog glosses the contrast this way: "When you travel on foot it isn't a matter of covering actual territory, rather a question of moving through your own inner landscapes. [...] The world reveals itself to those who travel on foot."[32] With the virtue of walking underscored, we could take a veritable tour of Herzog's films, scanning along the way for figures who walk—whether along a cliff-hugging mountainside trail at the beginning of *Aguirre, The Wrath of God* or atop artic ice-seas, as in *Encounters at the End of the World*; with Timothy Treadwell in the Grizzly Maze of Alaska, with Dieter Dengler navigating the jungle forests of Laos, discussing with Reinhold Messner a proposed film with Klaus Kinski ascending the Himalayas,[33] or admiring the dead who knew how to walk—and write well— in *Nomad: In the Footsteps of Bruce Chatwin*, walking informs Herzog's films even as it is figured by Herzog's own, personal peripateticism. "When walking," he tells us, "I have the most intense instances of imagination, of planning. I write profusely, work on projects and screenplays."[34]

Reading (and writing) is not, usually, something one can do while walking. And though Herzog has been known to insist that his students at the Rogue Film School "read, read, read, read, read, read,"[35] there is a counter-value in the movement of the body beyond the screen, beyond the page: "I get my ideas from real life, not books. When I hear the kind of language used by zealots and film theorists, Venetian blinds start rattling down."[36] Herzog clearly does not gain inspiration for filmmaking by reading film theory, and he seldom cites films made by others as a point of departure much less explanation. Rather, it is by means of a non-cinematic or non-theoretical activity, such as walking, that one's "inner landscapes" are revealed, as if daydreams were the better inspiration for art—"when walking I experience exciting voyages into my own imagination, and fall into deep reveries"[37]— or proof of one's inner concept(ion)s. As Gilles Deleuze has remarked on Herzog's pathways: "The walker is defenseless because he is he who is beginning to be."[38] Given Herzog's emphasis on his rural Bavarian upbringing, and the role walking played in his formative years, one can wonder if walking is more of a contingent inspiration, say, in the way that automobiles and the "road trip" figure in the imaginative landscape (both inner and outer) of many American minds from the 1950s onward, and as exemplified in cinematic form—from *Rebel Without a Cause* to *American Graffiti*, *National Lampoon's Vacation* to *Pee Wee's Big Adventure*, *Thelma and Louise* to *Little Miss Sunshine*, *Paris, Texas* to *The Straight Story*, *Rain Man* to *Captain Fantastic*, *Into the Wild* to *Nomadland*. (And in songs by Bruce Springsteen.[39]) Herzog has a way of naturalizing and thus universalizing the virtue of walking, whereas we might be better off considering his emphasis as an indication of private value and meaning—much in the same way as the mountains (of his homeland in southern Germany) could be said to stimulate his pursuit of other epic landscapes (from Perú to the Taiga). Though the landscapes beheld from his footpaths (found and made) fill the film frame, Herzog's peripateticism draws us back to cinematic origins—to the biped position of the man with the movie camera—by which the "view" "finder" stands (with eyes about five-and-half-feet off the ground) at the interstice between actual and inner landscapes, where the celluloid strip or digital stream becomes an objective correlative for what it portends to capture. After a sojourn in the jungle or a night on the mesas of the high desert, moving images confess their diminished scale: they are but proxies for what we aim to represent, placeholders for what we need. Yet, they are also reminders of our station and stature: records of the morphology of the human—how it sees and what it envisions.

5. "Construct Films, Don't Deconstruct Them"

IN THE CONCLUDING LINES OF VOICEOVER in his filmed self-portrait, *Werner Herzog, Filmemacher: An Autobiographical Documentary Short* (1989), the author pauses over a photograph of himself at work on set (preparing to snap a slate), and notes with a kind of heroic self-deprecation: "Looking at me here you can see the toll filming can take on me. But that's the life I lead. I wouldn't want it otherwise."[40] Twenty-one years later, as time continues to take its toll (and more than thirty-four years since his first documentary portrait of the director), we find Christian

Weisenborn picking up with Herzog in *I Am My Films, Part 2, Thirty Years Later* (2010)—this time very far from a cloistered room in 1970s Munich, or even from the open mountainsides of Bavaria, but instead in Venice, Italy, and in company with Nicholas Cage, Eva Mendes, and Michael Shannon. Soon enough, though, we are driving—yes, driving—in Los Angeles (Lost Angeles?), with Herzog at the wheel, and Weisenborn in the passenger seat. Herzog begins, speaking in German: "It's really a jungle out here. I always say it's a substitute for …"—with Herzog searching for the word, Weisenborn eagerly supplies a suggestion: "The Bavarian forest?" Herzog chuckles: "No, Tuscany."[41] One thing is clear, now a proud resident of Los Angeles—a denizen of a city as famous for making movies as for making walking difficult—Herzog has adapted to the car culture of his adopted home, if not the ostentatiousness of the houses of friends and associates he is invited to enter, which he declares are "totally uninhabitable."

The conversation turns, however, to, one wants to call it, Herzog's inhabitation in his films (especially his documentaries), a presence that is sufficiently distinctive that his work is fodder for parody by others.[42] Reflecting on finding himself in front of the camera in *The Great Ecstasy of the Woodcarver Steiner* (1974), standing in the foreground holding a microphone (like a sportscaster reporting on the Olympics) with a ski jumper descending behind him, Herzog notes half-a-lifetime later:

> I had my doubts and have them today with regards to my presence in the film. But it did lead me to think that what was basically right about the concept was to avoid making documentaries totally anonymously. Documentaries should always make a personal note felt in them. Because the films I made were not commissioned by someone, but were made because of my own deep fascination with the subject. […] I've now become my own commentator.[43]

Herzog here couples two distinctive attributes of his approach to filmmaking, especially of documentaries, namely, that the work should be driven by personal passion and that it should be (even if it is funded by others) driven by a fiercely independent ambition to create a film of one's own (i.e., a work that cannot be read generically or anonymously, as if it simply appeared on earth without being authored by an individual with a body, a mind, and with opinions). With such a spirit in mind — one that Herzog attributes to the success of his self-created Rogue Film School — we can assemble reasons for his antagonism to intellectual or film-theoretical approaches to making movies. In conversation with Paul Cronin, Herzog says: "One the table in front of us is a pile of academic articles about my films that you brought over for me to look at. The minute you leave here today, it will all be thrown into the trash. The healthiest thing anyone can do is avoid that impenetrable nonsense. My response to it all is a blank stare, just as I respond to most philosophical writings."[44] Herzog's fury and indifference (can he sustain both attitudes?) seems genuine, and yet, instead of alienating those of us who are braced to take the bait, it can feel like an invitation for further thinking. Herzog's earnest dismissiveness confounds those of us who care about philosophical scholarship full stop — and on film (in the latter case, what calls for and counts as thinking about cinema).[45] Invoking an image from his beloved Perúvian jungle (where all he hears is "strangulation and murder"), Herzog declares: "Academia stifles cinema, encircling it like a liana vine wraps round a tree, smothering and draining away all life. Construct films, don't deconstruct them. [...] Whenever I encounter film theorists, I lower my head and charge."[46]

On the Rogue Film School diploma, the embossed seal reads "Not for the faint of heart," and so it must be that to face Herzog — and his anti-intellectual ideology of film — one must meet his strength with a strength of one's own (should one be proud and foolish enough to do so). Perhaps, as a marker for this kind of counter-force, we can cite the life and work of Jean-Luc Godard and certain other French *cinéastes* (among them Chabrol, Demy, Resnais, Rivette, Rohmer, Truffaut, and Varda) who transformed their *intellectual* love of cinema into the making of innovative movies. (Other candidates could be marshalled too: Terrence Malick, Charlie Kaufman, Kelly Reichardt.[47]) To the joy of those who write about films, the critics of the French New Wave make one believe that criticism is a way of making films without a camera — that, in effect, criticism shows us what movies do, and how we might (or must!) think about them. In this way, the film critic does not even have to make the passage to filmmaker, since *writing* about film is a kind of writing *of* film—a creation by way of illuminative remarks. To which Herzog would surely reply, as he has in print: "Go for it, losers."[48]

To preclude pedantry and self-seriousness, and as a bid for knowing reflexiveness, that is, as we read these lines and the sentiments they contain in a book about Herzog, such as this one, it may do us some good to simply acknowledge the variations of Herzog's sense of humor. Depending on where you look in his films, Herzog can achieve rather profound moments of philosophical commentary (despite his supposed efforts to adamantly evade such results), but he can also seem ponderous—even, at times, a parody of himself.[49] If we are sure, for example, of the type of seriousness in his films that we Herzogophiles wish to defend, we can *also* spot those moments when he allows himself—and us—a bit of fun (and oblique self-critique). Consider the moment in *Encounters at the End of the World* when Herzog takes stock of the accommodations at McMurdo station and concludes with biting vitriol that the place includes "abominations such as an aerobics studio and yoga classes."[50] The intensity of his disdain, in this instance, is played for laughs; his persona as a wild dreamer is fused with that of an irascible curmudgeon. The human who walks on foot has no need for the fluorescent-lighted gym. (We could contrast such tongue-in-cheek culture [and self] critique with the bruising insights he declaims in Les Blank's *Burden of Dreams* or, indeed, in the self-portrait documentaries that have been enlisted for this chapter and the wider surveys attempted in these pages).

Picking up after such an interlude, then, if we (still) seek the spirit of Herzog's remarks to the *cinéaste* and would-be filmmaker, it may be closer to a mentor's worry that ideas (and the precedents set by others) will get in the way of one's work, attempted or otherwise. As Herzog has said: "Reading about cinema is of little use to aspiring filmmakers. […] I always felt that if you really love cinema, the healthiest thing to do is ignore books about it."[51] Note again, a certain Nietzschean strain in these comments about what is "healthiest"—as if filmmaking were an exercise in stamina (again, not on the elliptical or StairMaster), a test of one's endurance, a challenge to one's fortitude and inner reserves of vital energies (hence all the walking!—yet another Nietzschean trope). In *I Am My Films, Part 2*, Herzog goes into more detail about how he himself, and the films he has created over the last half-century, have provided a worthy model for emerging talent:

> Especially in the last ten to twenty years it has become ever clearer that many young film directors as well as writers see me as a point of orientation. I don't want to exaggerate, but that's the way it is. Some see me and my way of making films as a source of hope. Plus, the fact that I was able to start projects with practically nothing but my own energy and without making myself completely dependent on an industry. And after this pressure and this great fascination [by others] became so strong, and came towards me like a slow-moving avalanche, I've now sometimes had interactions with the public. And recently, with this becoming more and more intense, I've tried to channel this and founded my own film school, the Rogue Film School.[52]

We must deduce, then, that the RFS is in spirit and practice an anti-school: it will contain lessons that you will not find in typical, mainstream moviemaking pedagogy. The "school," such as it is, must cultivate an anti-learning (an unlearning), a way in which "students" can hear their own voices, follow their own instincts, and, in effect, ignore the "teacher" in so far as he is an impediment to doing one's own work.[53] Given Herzog's zeal for reading—though *not* reading film theory and criticism—we stumble into zones of paradox, where learning and anti-learning make company. While we can turn to a quintessential American remark on reading—say, from Emerson: "'Tis the good reader that makes the good book; a good head cannot read amiss"—we could also aim to match Herzog's spirit or milieu by reaching out to a Teutonic tradition for more astringent rejoinders to his apparent contempt for theory and criticism. Let such a tour commence with G. E. Lessing's "The Reviewer Need Not Be Able to Do Better Than That With Which He Finds Fault" and then continue with a compendium culled from Lessing's contemporary, G. C. Lichtenberg, who wrote: "A book is a mirror: if an ape looks into it, an apostle is unlikely to look out. We have no words for speaking about wisdom to idiots. Whoever understands the wise is wise already."[54] These tense contradictions—literally, counter-sayings—are as evident as they are vexing. The student must submit to an authority that insists on *her own* authority; such "instruction" is more like a summons, even if it comes in the form of a command. Though Herzog often speaks calmly, as he does in the voiceover commentary to many of his films, there is also a palpable intensity that may be mistaken for aggression or defiance.

> That's how films should be made. We are directors. We are storytellers. We are people who create. We are not people who have a camera that is surveilling a bank or till. Take action! Create! [...] [W]ith imagination, with collective dreams, with all sorts of things. That's what we have to strive for if we want to make something that will hold up for years to come. I'm not afraid of that at all. I've been attacked again and again. My response to that is always very clear: I'll lower my head and lock horns straight away. [...] I don't avoid contradiction, I confront it.[55]

With all this head lowering, some could take Herzog's bravado literally, for example, as part of some archaic, brutish, hypermasculinist ethic for any filmmaking-adventurer who aims to flaunt danger and possible death at every turn (from approaching exploding volcanoes [*La Soufrière*] to making a film in the Amazon in the midst of a civil war [*Fitzcarraldo*]). But there is a less brazen version that may more ably apply to all filmmakers, namely, to eschew the "culture of complaint,"[56] to create without excuse, without apology, without citing all the obstructions and obstacles familiar to making art, in short, to simply "Take action!" There is the fear, of course, that when such advice is stripped of Herzog's entrancing Bavarian accent and now-iconic timbre, indeed, the intensity of his person, the ubiquity of his persona, these credos become at once prosaic and predictable — like the ad copy for a brochure announcing a film school based on self-help principles.

6. Vigorous Essayism

WHILE MANY LITERARY-PHILOSOPHICAL ESSAYISTS may qualify as those who have "retired" — in the sense of pulling back from the fray in an effort to reflect and comment (Montaigne is a standard bearer, Emerson too, and his acolyte Nietzsche)— Herzog presents an active, engaged, model of vigorous essayism, where filmmaking is a full-bodied enterprise suited to one's health (unless, of course, it's taking its toll). Herzog's allergy to intellectualism started early, when he disparaged the way German literature was being taught to him in his adolescence, yet the subject—its lessons, its concepts, its inspiration—abides steadily throughout his creative life. More often than not, however, an academic approach is stultifying, and the only healthy option is to pick up a camera (maybe "lift it") and make a film (if conditions require: picking locks and forging permits along the way). Despite Herzog's faithful dismissiveness of analysis (in both the philosophical *and* psychological senses), we may yet conclude that his resolute dedication to making films— regardless of hindrances and hurdles—is a form of essaying (as noted, from *essais*), that is, of attempting, of trials, of undertaking the work of trying.

One virtue of Herzog's vigorous essayism (and it is something that would amount to a defensible philosophical position, if he should want to have it) is the artful way in which he makes films that resist being thesis-driven. Herzog himself, quite notoriously, blends or equivocates on the difference between feature films and documentary films, and part of those overlapping universes involves an unwillingness (as noted above) to share all the secrets, to spell everything out (even if one were able to do so). Despite Herzog's vaunted verbal loquaciousness, his quietism on this front especially well-serves the documentary mode, where creators are so often caught up with evidence-finding and argument-presentation that they lose sight of the mystery that haunts the cinematic proceedings (for example, how filming a subject transforms it—how a lens is creative; how an edit can distort, obscure, or illuminate, and so on).

Moreover, when Herzog's brand of essayism is confederated with his dedication to what he calls "ecstatic truth," we are presented with a unique challenge to documentary form's presumed status as a default registry of the "accountant's truth"— for example, as evidence for something: a theory, a thought, an incriminating or discriminating fact.[57] In short, *when essayism and ecstatic truth join forces*, as they do most compellingly in Herzog's "documentary" experiments, we are presented with an undeniable challenge to the standing categories of journalism and art, fact and fiction, information and revelation. As Deleuze has remarked, in a similar vein: "There is the sublime action, always beyond, but which itself engenders another action, a heroic action which confronts the milieu on its own account, penetrating the impenetrable, breaking the unbreachable."[58] Walking, making paths, trespassing, crossing, ascending—these are embodied movements to the limit, and thus put us ever closer to an encounter with the sublime.

In Peter Buchka's self-described "essay," *To the Limit and then Beyond It: The Ecstatic World of Filmmaker Werner Herzog* (1989), Herzog, sounding a bit like a Jungian and a follower of Joseph Campbell, says: "I believe that cinema is rooted in dreams and common desires. And that it's rooted more in collective wishes than it is in reality. I also think that cinema can use artificiality, fiction, and imagination to reveal a whole new reality that lies behind it all."[59] Herzog's dogged pursuit of filmmaking—in his own strenuous practice of shooting in unforgiving locations—is often allied with his interest in figures who have endured extremes (e.g., a prisoner of war, a prisoner on death row, an exile, an errant colonizer, a disquieted conquistador, a troubled "protector" of bears, or even a ski jumper). Herzog's efforts—his attempts, his essaying—are focused on cinema's power to "awaken images" that lie dormant in us.[60] He postulates that there is a "grammar of images" that we share and that they form an "inner history"—both of which can be stimulated or made evident by motion pictures. In turn, we are faced with "an image of humanity" conjured by a "humanistic sublime."[61]

In *The Romantic Sublime: Studies in the Structure and Psychology of Transcendence*, Thomas Weiskel writes: "The essential claim of the sublime is that man can, in feeling and in speech, transcend the human," and consequently: "The humanistic sublime is an oxymoron."[62] In another place, I have aimed to say something about how Herzog's war films, as I call them, "antagoniz[e] the oxymoronic status" of Weiskel's troubled syntagma. Indeed, my way into the defense of, or deliberation on, the validity and vitality of the humanistic sublime is none other than Herzog's own patented brand of ecstatic truth. There I note: "While the sublime in the romantic or transcendental sense is meant to suggest an experience that gets you out of your humanness, where you feel instead connected to the external, eternal, absolute, or atemporal, the humanistic sublime by contrast is informed by a return to, a remembrance of, or a reengagement with the human through an encounter with nature—that is, with limits, obstacles, the extremes of existence, fatality, mortality."[63] Part of the intrigue of the present investigation resolves itself into how and whether Herzog's essayism—as expressed and articulated in the foregoing films—contributes yet more evidence to a functioning notion of the humanistic sublime.

Audiences for this chapter—for this book—will vary, as they do for Herzog's films. Depending on one's sense of mission and professional identity, the "lessons" of Herzog's filmmaking will range in their coherence, transferability, and effect. The academic may be amused but unmoved, happily returning to her scholarly pursuits (which may include, irony duly noted, further analysis of Herzog's films, and the philosophy of film more generally); the filmmaker may be inspired—in part because she is freed by Herzog from any sense of needing to fulfill prerequisites, to defer to authorities beyond her own ambit; and the moviegoer may take a second look at Herzog's oeuvre, wondering if there is more than portraits of unflattering, troubled humanity, ponderous imagery, and portentous commentary, but instead, something to take up or undergo, as if movie watching itself were a form of vigorous essayism—an art, a practice, a trial that can yield ecstatic truths from the humanistic sublime evident on screen and in one's comportment with such affecting sounds and enigmatic visions.

III

A Transcendental Persona

How does Werner Herzog enter the *Star Wars* universe? Casting, of course. But why? As it was earlier in *Jack Reacher* (2012), "[t]he casting of Werner Herzog as the Mandalorian's haughty client looks like a stunt, so far."[1] But, then, why *would* such casting in *The Mandalorian* (2019) be perceived as a "stunt"? Because Herzog is not treated as an actor so much as a persona. In this way, his presence *precedes* his presence; in other words, drawing him into the story has more to do with nondiegetic elements of his personality rather than, say, attributes natively emergent in the realm of *Star Wars* characters. Herzog's successful admission into (acquisition by? commodification by?) the decades-in-the making, multi-platform space opera, in fact, depend on qualities—in him, in his pre-existing work as a filmmaker, in, crucially and most overtly, the characteristics that have already coalesced into our inner picture of him—which emerged long ago, in a galaxy very far away from the Disney-owned mega brand. How the persona of a Bavarian filmmaker famed for his contributions to 1970s New German Cinema—and a subsequently long, varied, and exotic career of auteurist film works—would be cast in Jon Favreau's marquee cinematic launch of the streaming service Disney+ by way of a *Star Wars* spin-off, needs some explaining. The following dispatch forms something of a reply to the question: how did we get to this point with Werner Herzog?

Stanley Cavell asked in *The World Viewed: Reflections on the Ontology of Film*: "Why, for example, didn't the medium [of film] begin and remain in the condition of home movies, one shot just physically tacked on to another, cut and edited simply according to subject?"[2] And he answers his question by invoking Erwin Panofsky: "Narrative movies emerged because someone 'saw the possibilities' of the medium." In particular, *aesthetic* possibilities. We, then, have a question of our own: is there reason to say that Werner Herzog explores the aesthetic possibilities of the film medium in so far as he experiments with certain potentialities of the home movie, especially intertextuality (identified in some measure by self-citation) and the fostering of fictions based upon realities (in literary circles known as autofiction)? I ask this multi-stage question, in part, because, as Cavell says: "Aesthetic possibilities of a medium are not givens."[3] Like the Herzogian quest for "adequate images," possibilities must be made.

As filmmakers *and* film critics, it would seem that we are all in the business of giving significance to works (or failing to achieve that significance, or observe it). How striking it is, then, to notice how selected films made by Herzog—that is, occasionally but also consistently over a wide swath of time— appear to court the rough-and-ready qualities of the home movie (its casual demeanor, its off-handed brilliance, its power to capture what feel like the otherwise unobserved miracles of ordinary happenstance) and, not to be missed, often by means of introducing himself, or some version of himself, into the proceedings. Call this facet Herzog as host. For these reasons, in Herzog's films created over the course of more than a half-century, we recognize elements of the home movie aesthetic coupled with self-citation and autofiction. From this triangulation something distinctive and durable emerges: Herzog's persona. And it is the creation and cultivation of Herzog's persona—as mystical host, as stalwart soldier, as irrepressible prankster—that catalyzes the attractions of this evolving research, in particular, how we might go about identifying his strategies for achieving these rare and transformative features.

Scanning back across the wide horizon of his films—to 1957—we find *A Lost Western*, Herzog's directorial debut, in which the novice is also an ingénu: still unreleased, the film's title proved prophetic. The one-room set—a bar room from the nineteenth-century American West—is populated by teenagers in cowboy hats carrying silver-barreled guns that glisten on the black-and-white film. "Wisky" is poured, a sign is swapped from "Liberty" to "*Besetzt*" (i.e., occupied), and when a man dies in the denouement, he is improbably given a sign of his own to hold (that reads "Dead"). It is positively Spielbergian in its aspiration and genre emulation (recalling those adolescent scenes and sets in *The Fabelmans*). Like young Spielberg's precocious *ciné*-experiments, the swagger of Herzog's first filmic foray comes mainly from its home-madeness—a one-camera, handheld aesthetic that conveys an intimate effort to channel raw creative energy into a work of art, a search to discover (or create) what film can do.[4]

Describing some of Herzog's work as home-movie-like is not a denigration, but something more like an appeal to a different *Gestalt*—that is, an invitation to see them (or some portions of them) *as* home movies—as a type of film constituted in ways that are familiar to the creation of home movies along with auto-documentaries. It is precisely in those moments when one addresses some of the films he makes, or are made about him, *as* home movies that one is poised to see his presence in those films *not* as an authentic subject of a veritable home movie (e.g., as a person caught unawares by the camera), but instead as a construction—as a knowing fiction and fabrication—that is, as a species of cinematic autofiction.

Herzog's films, of whatever vintage or subgenre, are not home movies in the conventional sense, but as it were in an unconventional one—as if he had gathered and mobilized certain characteristics of the home movie to serve other purposes. The hand-held camera, first-person address, lock-frame montages, or traveling shots can speak to the shared condition of filmmaking— and the intersections at which the blurry boundaries between amateur and professional may be sharpened. The fact that few recognize home movie traits in Herzog films is a testament to their transformation by his touch—call it the elevation of the everyday to the level of enduring art. Yet, if elements or aspects of the home movie aesthetic abide, if mostly unrecognized by audiences, they nevertheless contribute to the mood of Herzog's films, including the mode of his presence as an object before the camera or as an audible voice that surrounds it. In particular, and crucial to the distinctive nature of his now-recognizable persona ("As always, the frisbee is the mirror to the soul," he intones as Walter Hotenhoffer on *The Simpsons,* a show he deems full of "anarchy"[5]), Herzog relies on the presumed immediacy and authenticity of the home movie—even as he fakes it, mocks it, stages it, scripts it. Perhaps, as Herzog himself might do, we can ironize this aspect of his films by adding requisite postmodern quotation marks, so that when Herzog makes home movies they are always "home movies."

Discerning critics have articulated how such traits endanger their effects. Brigitte Peucker observes, in writing about

Little Dieter Needs to Fly (1997): "As so often in Herzog's documentaries, the camera shoots [Dieter] Dengler and the actors frontally, home movie style, thus lending the film the amateurish feel that simulates a lesser remove from reality."[6] In her account of *Gesualdo: Death for Five Voices* (1995), Holly Rogers draws upon Paul Arthur's productive syntagma, "tangled reciprocity," to discuss the relationship between different genres.[7] One of those genres is often the home movie, and its nearby variants. As Rogers puts it: "[W]hile the intrusion of the camera threatens to rupture both the reality and the fictional diegesis of Treadwell's world [as seen in *Grizzly Man* (2005)], [Richard] Thompson's epic nondiegetic (off-screen) guitar eulogies suture the 'fictive elements' whilst also softening the home-movie feel."[8]

For his own part, Herzog has been derisive of the notion of "independent cinema"—it is a "meaningless term," "a myth."[9] Adding: "There's no such thing as true 'independent' cinema, with the exception of home movies made for the family album or footage shot with a cellphone at a spring-break beach party in Florida."[10] Could it be, though, that Herzog has inadvertently, unintentionally, created just such "home movies made for the family album" in works such as *My Best Fiend* (1999)? Answering yes, an extended explanation is in order.

As a prolegomenon to that disquisition, recall how *Stroszek: A Ballad* (1977) does at times look and feel like a home movie—perhaps a sibling to Chantal Akerman's *News from Home* (1977) and Jim Jarmusch's *Permanent Vacation* (1980). While we are considering Herzog's consciousness of such home-movie-like attributes of, or in, his films, it may be satisfying to recall Jacques Rivette's contention "that all films are documents of the history of their making."[11] While Rivette states a broader claim than I wish to argue for here (indeed, it is totalizing), the remark is pertinent in so far as these films feature Herzog himself as a personal and immediate presence in the mise-en-scène—sometimes in his body, and to be sure, more often in the distinctive resonances of his voice (off-screen), the sonic signatures of his accent, and an approach to English diction and syntax that reliably keeps us guessing.

While we have Rivette in mind, consider his "Letter on Rossellini," in which he introduces descriptions that may find purchase in Herzog's context of creation—and especially his documentary work: "A filmmaker dares to talk about himself without restraint," a consequence, perhaps, of modernity since Montaigne's *Essays*, as Timothy Corrigan has illustrated at length in *The Essay Film: From Montaigne, after Marker*, and also in his chapter "The Pedestrian Ecstasies of Werner Herzog."[12] For Rivette, thinking specifically of *Rome, Open City* (1945), *Paisan* (1946), *Germany, Year Zero* (1948), *Europe '51* (1952), Rossellini's work is not just given to associations with the "temporal sketch" or "draft"—"for there is no doubt that these are hurried films, improvised out of very slender means and filmed in a turmoil that is often apparent"—but "it is true that Rossellini's films have more and more obviously become *amateur* films; home movies."[13]

Rivette usefully expands the affiliations of the "home"— when and where it is, as more recently Emad Burnat and Guy Davidi's *5 Broken Cameras* (2011) does for thinking of war films in terms of home front and war front.[14] In Burnat's case, a home movie in the midst of war suddenly becomes a war movie (and vice versa). In Herzog's case, whatever subject he decides to investigate is transformed by his distinctive framing—most often emblematized by a fusion of his personality traits and mystico-philosophical musings.[15] Herzog as disembodied voice may be a point of reference for thinking how his persona expresses itself, though his bodily presence is often a cultivated imposition—one that draws our attention, stirs our interest, perhaps unsettles us productively (e.g., his affectless facial expression, his hooded eyelids, his stare, an uneven response to humor—sometimes laughing out-of-phase with others, or remaining unmoved when the rest of us find something funny; holding a shot longer than subjects expect, thereby rendering awkward silences and faces that communicate disorientation, even alarm). Corrigan's gloss on Rivette's remarks on Rossellini's works prove illuminating when thinking of Herzog as well:

> Here "home movie," "amateur," [...] assume, I'd argue, those particularly positive values associated with an essayistic foregrounding and dramatization of the personal, a transitional, barely authorized, and relatively formless shape of the personal subjectivity, the replacement of a teleological organization with an activity defined by the object itself, and a productively distorting overlapping of subject and object.[16]

Again we see that Herzog is not alone in the "essayistic foregrounding and dramatization of the personal," though it may be that he is part of a smaller subset of filmmaking practitioners—among them Errol Morris, Michael Moore, Agnès Varda, and Ross McElwee—who make such "foregrounding" essential to the content of their films. While all of these filmmakers "craft" their presence or personality on screen, it could be analytic to say that among them Herzog is the principal advocate for dissimulation. Indeed, Morris' and Moore's documentary careers have been fairly well staked on truth-seeking and when found, truth-telling (from *The Thin Blue Line* [1988, dir. Morris], which helped exonerate a man on death row to *Bowling for Columbine* [2002, dir. Moore], which explored America's gun culture).[17] McElwee has made his particular brand of auto-documentary tied to his personal history—from his romantic life (*Sherman's March*, 1985) to the exploration of family history (*Bright Leaves*, 2003) and family life (*Photographic Memory*, 2011).

With Herzog, the form or practice of auto-documentary takes on a different register from these contemporaries. In his case, we may be better off inquiring after the *fiction* of autofiction, since Herzog does not confess (some truth) so much as create (an image). He devises a simulacrum of an ideal—an autobiographical sublime—that we simply give the name "Werner Herzog."[18] As Peucker begins her contribution (at the outset of Brad Prager's *A Companion to Werner Herzog*) with a meditation on Herzog's chosen surname, we take Werner Stipetić's free act of self-naming as a parable of self-creation (call it persona manufacture), one essential to Herzog's identity as an artist and as an embodied presence, whether on film or in person (a fact that can be difficult to navigate when talking with him, ahem, in person. Who in fact do I meet? The man or the myth?).

To underscore another contrast: while Varda's *The Beaches of Agnès* (2008) is akin to Herzog's *My Best Fiend*—in that both acclaimed filmmakers use their own films (fiction features as well as documentaries) to tell a new and different story, indeed, to supplement (at times, supplant) the narrative of their lives as filmmakers—Herzog, unlike Varda, courts the notion that his sincerity and authenticity may be in the service of telling good stories rather than achieving genuine self-exploration or self-exposure. The contrast, in fact, challenges us to consider the terms of art, especially, when personal history may transcend itself. Though Herzog can be faulted by some for fabrications, distortions, obfuscation, and (occasional) reticence, it may be precisely these artful interventions and temperamental adjustments that allow him to avoid making his films "about him"—even as he is "in" them.

While Herzog travels under his own (adopted) name, we appear to take pleasure in a sense of proximity to him—as a person. But this is our mistake. He does not walk among us; rather, Werner Herzog is what Nietzsche would call a "mask," the English word "persona" having an etymology that draws us back to Latin origins meaning precisely that: the theatrical mask; the Greek *prosōpon* delivers a still more Herzogian image: *the mask through which resounds the voice of the actor*.[19] Cavell would call such a phenomenon an "automatism," what most others would understand in terms of "character" and even "star."[20] Yet, the on-screen/off-screen dialectic troubles our recognition of these facts and features. Herzog is a modernist artist, in the sense Cavell uses the term, since such an artist "has to explore the fact of automatism itself, as if investigating what it is at any time that has provided a given work of art with the power of its art as such."[21] For these reasons, Herzog may be thought of as a performance artist, a Bavarian riff on Andy Kaufman. How do we know? Because we are perpetually confused by what it is we may—or should—take seriously and what we should laugh at; the wires are often crossed (and cross back and forth during the duration of a single film or encounter with the filmmaker). The frisson of such moments may be said to define a large measure of Herzog's power as a presence (again, on screen and off). He mocks our pretensions even as his own (likely mock-serious) pretentiousness may be illuminating, even gratifying.

Voice itself presents a case for being listed among the leitmotifs of Herzog's expansive catalog of creative works: from the near-ubiquitous status of his own vocal production (in voiceover and as voice talent) to his direction of operas, the preoccupations of films such as *Gesualdo*, and more. Along with studies of his celebrated films, assessments of his role(s) in popular culture, and analyses of his literary offerings, there remains a need for the broader articulation of a thoroughgoing thematics of voice. To amplify the project, invitations could be sent to affiliated factions, among them to Stanley Cavell, whose early apprenticeship in musical composition led him to find the stakes of performance in philosophical prose and cinematic conversation; to Garrett Stewart, whose *Reading*

Voices: Literature and the Phonotext (1990), embodied his own close-gauged attention to the spans of vocal utterance—including its subvocal enunciation, yet reaching also, in time, to the claims of Barbra Streisand's euphonic demonstrations on vinyl and celluloid; to Michael Oakeshott, for whom the intellectual adventure of unrehearsed utterances was a hallmark of philosophical exercise, as captured, for instance in *The Voice of Poetry in the Conversation of Mankind* (1959); and to L. L. Nunn, whose experiments in radical educational utopias, the Telluride Association and Deep Springs College, invited participants to hear "the voice of the desert."[22] On this last score, Herzog has treated the matter memorably in *Fata Morgana, Lessons of Darkness, Queen of the Desert*, and *Salt and Fire*.

The films by Herzog that I have invoked thus far and in what follows, among others unnoted, may be said to form variations on the unified theme of exploring the "aesthetic possibilities of the medium." One result of this decades-in-the-making—now half-century long—experimentation is a group of films that put us in a position to question not just what a home movie is (an epistemological project) but when it is (a phenomenological and ontological question). What we are exploring in assessing Herzog's contribution to the aesthetic possibilities of the medium, are moments, structures, patterns, and properties of his works that appear to participate in existing genres (say, the documentary, the home movie, the nature film, the adventure film, the essay film) and also to diverge from them (by violating a social contract with the audience, what Noël Carroll has described as our trust that documentary works are, in fact, films of "presumptive assertion"[23]).

Is it possible, then, that some strains or species of Herzog's films (the autobiographical portraits, the essay films, most of the documentaries) do not depart from the stylistics and ontology of the home movie? A reply may come by figuring Herzog as participating in a certain pedigree of cinematic history—say, in league with Dziga Vertov, where we find a "man with a movie camera." Note too that when Cavell describes the home movie in *Adam's Rib* (1949), he *also* thinks of Vertov's seminal film with its "similar pairing of automatisms."[24] Even so, we candidly admit that for most of Herzog's career the "man with a movie camera" has, in fact, been trusted accomplice Peter Zeitlinger—so even on this score, Herzog, it would appear, is *performing* a certain sensibility as the self-contained, all-in-one moviemaker. So much the better, then, to have a loyal and capable cinematographer at the ready, if a "filmmaker" wishes to put himself on screen, as Herzog has done from early on and continuously throughout his half-century of active movie creation. The collaborative nature of filmmaking impresses itself anew and in the context of a street reputation that trades mainly on the myth of the solitary explorer (the walker, the mystic atop the mountain, the man with a movie camera, & co.).

If there is Zeitlinger "directing" the lens Herzog's way, Herzog for his part wanders to other sets with willing participation in a series of films about him and his work, among them Les Blank's indelible portraits, *Werner Herzog Eats His Shoe* (1980) and *Burden of Dreams* (1982); Kim Hendrickson's *Dreams and Burdens* (2005) and Thomas von Steinaecker's *Werner Herzog: Radical Dreamer* (2022); Christian Weisenborn's tandem *I Am My Films: A Portrait of Werner Herzog* (1976-78, with Erwin Keusch) and *I Am My Films, Part 2, Thirty Years Later* (2010); Peter Buchka's *To the Limit and Then Beyond It: The Ecstatic World of Filmmaker Werner Herzog*, (*Bis ans Ende und dann noch weiter: Die ekstatische Welt des Filmemachers Werner Herzog, Ein Essay von Peter Buchka*, 1989); and lastly, it continues in Herzog's own exercises in the form, including *Werner Herzog: Filmemacher: An Autobiographical Documentary Short* (1989) and a decade later, *My Best Fiend* and *Nomad: In the Footsteps of Bruce Chatwin* (2019).

To hone things further in the wake of these distributions of Herzog on screen (before varied lenses, in myriad contexts), consider anew the theatricalization of Herzog. As the child mugs for the home movie camera, so Herzog draws us into a playful, experimental space in which he knows we know he is courting artifice (e.g., through variations on the theme of his own persona or personality) in the service of pursuing and revealing (ecstatic) truth. In other words, the goal is not to achieve something like an anthropological or even an autobiographical account of Herzog-as-a-person (as if he were creating a cinematic diary or confession), but rather to create a series of fabrications that play with the (false) idea that he has a fixed or true identity at all—to move beyond verifiable reality and toward the ineffable: hence, the autofictional or autobiographical sublime. The purpose of such filmmaking (along with those of his audiovisual portraitists: Blank, Weisenborn, Buchka, von Steinaecker, et al.) from earlier on and into the present day, has been (at least as far as his on-screen presence is concerned) to tease the audience with a glimpse of authenticity, indeed, the *intensity* of authenticity, only to allow — to taunt, to tempt, and perhaps to torment us with the notion — that the moment has been staged. In another investigation, highly pertinent to this one, I have called such a move a hallmark of "hoax *vérité*."[25] Deployed in the present deliberation, the paradoxical phrase is meant to underscore — and dramatize — the way we encounter in Herzog's films not a false pretender, but a true one.[26]

A brief taxonomy may be in order, namely, one that differentiates between "star" and other kinds of on-screen presences. I am tempted to equate what Cavell describes as the "natural ascendency of actor over character" to star qualities, and to his observations about "types."[27] If we see Brad Pitt before we see Cliff Booth (in *Once Upon A Time . . . In Hollywood* [2019, dir. Quentin Tarantino]), it is because Pitt's qualities as an actor *precede* (and perhaps also exceed) his presence as the character Booth. D. N. Rodowick has glossed Cavell's distinction between theatrical performers (the actor/character relationship) and those on film by assessing the changes underway in such moments of cinematic inscription: "Becoming on the screen is a species of (self) transformation, meaning that it is both automatic or subject to certain automatisms of recording, transcription, narration, and genre, and also that it projects reflexively a picture of self responding to pressures of transformation."[28] It is hard to find Herzog in this account, and also under the category "character actor," since even with the contested definition of the phrase, Herzog is, as we have said, not properly or principally an actor; without insulting his power to perform on screen, his scene-altering intensity — his veritable *alterity* full stop — reveals how he is hired to be some version of his recognizable persona, some shade of mercurial, menacing, or mad, or when comedic, then a send-up of these deviant traits. To test the claim, wait for the Nancy Meyers rom-com — *Something's Gotta Live* — in which Werner plays an affable heart doctor (with a heart of gold) opposite neurotic but newly self-actualizing interior decorator, Diane Keaton. The wait will be long.

For these reasons, we reach a third layer — not the star, not the character actor, but the aforementioned persona: Herzog, like many other personalities, could be said to "play himself," yet, as noted, this gets the alignment wrong. Even so, the *proximity* of persona to the particular qualities of the actor (when interacting with certain "possibilities of the medium") can be marshaled to cultivate the aesthetics of the home movie (a catalog of traits that themselves have become an automatism: repetitious, recognizable, and resolutely capable of conjuring specific emotions and associations—among them nostalgic evocations of the past). One of the hallmarks of home movies is the way everyday people stiffen up on camera or, as the case may be, ham it up. On any point along the spectrum or within the matrix of inter-related attributes, however, we are relatively sure that we are seeing authentic footage of a person—not, for example, mock-footage generated by a Hollywood studio or band of pranksters (after the fashion of hoax *vérité*).[29] Watching a given family's home movies, member and stranger alike may be able to suss out the persona of the "players" on screen. The father is earnest, the youngest child outgoing, etc. In such cases of bona fide home movies, we wouldn't say that the family members *cultivate* their personas: they are, we think, "playing" themselves, however awkwardly or confidently. To innovate and nurture a persona, as Herzog does, entails a specific—and different—kind of project: the creation of art and the contesting of its boundaries (including those that challenge lines of affiliation between the fabricated and the factual).

As Cavell wrote, it may go without saying but is worth saying nevertheless that "the home movie is meant for a private audience and the commercial movies for a public," yet the intention of having or anticipating a space for the exhibition of one's film does not preclude filmmakers from adopting the visual attributes of established genres, one way or another.[30] So, in these pages, we are urging to consciousness something like the double sense of many of Herzog's films—namely, that they would appear to operate as works aimed at a commercial audience while concomitantly drawing on the generic traits familiar to private films (such as home movies and auto-documentaries) and at times, other modes as well, including industrial films, commercials, public service announcements, and in some moments experimental, avant-garde, essay films, and slow cinema. Indeed, in a helpful taxonomic gloss, Cavell states that when looking to "the tradition of documentary film [...] home movies form a massive if peculiar species."[31] "Peculiar" because of the epistemological and ontological traits already noted, but "massive"? It may prove useful to think of "massive" in two ways: as both figuring a quantity *and* a quality. There are many, many films that qualify as home movies, even by a strict definition (how much of the five-hundred hours of video content uploaded to YouTube every *minute* would count?),[32] but it is precisely the peculiarity of the genre that gives credence to the qualitative sense of massive Cavell alludes to, one that we may identify as sustaining Rivette's broader claim cited above "that all films are documents of the history of their making."[33] Narrative cinema, then, was the deviation that became the standard.

While Herzog has become synonymous with some of the most conspicuous and influential cinematic documentarians of our age—indeed, of the age of cinema—it is a potentially misleading, even harmful designation. Given Herzog's commitment to the fabrication of "facts" in the service of "truth" (thereby, perhaps inadvertently, picking up a postmodern agenda that he would either not recognize or deride), and given his steady cultivation of a specific kind of authorial identity (what to call it? Mystic mountain poet? Semiotician of the spirit? Cinematic conjurer? Stylist of the cynic ideal?[34]), many of his films may be better categorized as experimental, as avant-garde, as cinematic performance art rather than as documentaries. Despite the brevity of the case, why does this claim feel at once substantial and substantiated? Because no one consults a Herzog film for information, for the discovery or recounting of facts, for a sense of the historical world we are said to inhabit. Werner Herzog, in short, is not Ken Burns.

Part of what makes Herzog's work antagonistic to the prevailing, indeed, canonical and established trends of documentary—i.e., films of "presumptive assertion," what we may wish to brand in contradistinction, and with no disrespect, "sincere cinema"—is his willingness to explore its logical inverse, a veritable insincere cinema. Given how I am framing his work in relation to the documentary tradition, it may be apparent that Herzog's *modus operandi* shares more than a passing resemblance with both the practice of self-citation and with autofiction. While these two aspects are crucial to Herzog's body of work, they are decidedly anathema to what passes for bona fide documentary cinema.

"Self-citations are a means for Herzog to extend his authorial signature [... into his more recent productions]," writes Brad Prager in his introductory remarks to *A Companion to Werner Herzog*.[35] That is, Herzog continually invests many of his current film projects with aesthetic, conceptual, and figurative references and allusions to the full range of his oeuvre, reaching back as early as his earliest work (from "my first real film" *Herakles* [1962] to *Signs of Life* [1968]).[36] Such "networking" or "webiness" lifts all of the works—since, in their interdependence, in the intensity of their metacinematic self-awareness, we come to regard them all as important contributions. Moreover, Herzog's casting exceeds the bounds of his own work, whether as in memoiristic documentary, such as *My Best Fiend* (1999), or in metacinematic hoaxes, such as *Incident at Loch Ness* (2004), but also and conspicuously in the work of others (Harmony Korine's *Mister Lonely* [2007] as Father Umbrillo; and as an irascible paterfamilias in *Julien Donkey-Boy* [1999]; Jack Reacher *Jack Reacher* as The Zec; *The Mandalorian* as The Client, etc.)—all of which trades on our familiarity with what precedes the work we have come to see. An unmitigated catalog of self-citation could be mounted; Chris Wahl, for example, points out the persistence of dwarfs in his films: from *Even Dwarves Started Small* (1970) to *Rescue Dawn* (2006); or jellyfish: *Invincible* (2001), *The Wild Blue Yonder* (2005), *Bad Lieutenant: Port of Call New Orleans* (2009).[37] In short, the more we know of or about Herzog's films, the more we are in a position to appreciate these modes of intertextuality. Ramin Bahrani's *Plastic Bag* (2010), in which Herzog's is the voice of the eponymous bag (an inorganic abstraction of a jellyfish?), allows us to recognize, in this brief portrait, layers of self-citation expressive or weaved together with parody, satire, irony, and wit—as well as coaxing proximity to potentially ponderous signification (the last of which emerges in films such as *Lessons of Darkness* [1992] and *Cave of Forgotten Dreams* [2010]).[38] In *Plastic Bag*, seriousness is part of Herzog's brand and yet in delivering his lines in this paratextual context, we feel his mischief: is he ridiculing us even as his trick *depends* on our knowledge of his prior (serious?) work?

The lessons of *Lessons of Darkness*, in matters of assessing the evolving (by now established if not fully ossified) Herzogian persona, are decidedly altered by the subsequent decades of his work—and especially including his comedic forays (e.g., as a voice talent, a supporting actor) and the parodic installments fabricated by others. What seemed justifiably portentous in the immediate wake of the Persian Gulf War now reads like a lark: a chapter on "the war" uses only CNN infrared footage of the brief battle, comically underscoring, or better, under-emphasizing the prominence of the historical-war-as-we-might-know-it in *Lessons of Darkness*. After interviewing a woman who appears to have lost the power of speech (along with her two sons) and another woman, holding her toddler son, who notes that the child suffers from a vocal incapacity (reporting that he even *said* he didn't wish to learn how to speak), the human trauma is slyly abandoned for an experimental microdocumentary insert on the Boots and Coots of Houston, Texas, i.e., the men provisioned from the Lone Star State to contend with oil fires and broken taps. Footage of these "blowout specialists" arrives with minimal allowances for diegetic sound, noting Herzog's preference to pair these haunting, under his direction, other-worldly visuals with the sonic intensities of Mahler, Prokofiev, Schubert, Verdi, and, of course, Wagner.

In chapter XII, *Leben ohne Feuer*, Herzog intones: "Two figures are approaching an oil well. One of them holds a lighted torch. What are they up to?" A firefighter throws an ember towards the vigorous, vertical spout of fast-flowing petroleum. "Are they going to rekindle the blaze?" Thereupon the spark becomes an eruption of fire—with diegetic sound rushing in to maximize the formidable effect. "Has life without fire become unbearable for them?" In 1992, we are mortified; in the 2020s—knowing more about Herzog's poetic mischief—we laugh. Without any context provided for how these specialists operate, we don't know if the rekindling is part of a legitimate process of capping a well or is, instead, an aggressive stunt that leads to further, abundant waste and catastrophic ecological pollution. At this late stage in the sequence, Herzog returns us thematically to the very beginning of the film—as if to those same alien figures on a remote planet who are trying to signal us to know something or to do something we cannot fathom. We have lost touch with our purported subject: notes on the aftermath of the Persian Gulf War have become a voiceless dispatch from a distant galaxy—with its unintelligible creatures doing unintelligible things. Upon (re-)viewing *Lessons of Darkness*, we too may end up losing the power of speech.

Self-citation is also related to metacinema in so far as the act forces a work of art to call attention to itself—to what lies before and beyond it. "Not surprisingly," remarks Peucker, "*Lessons [of Darkness]* also exhibits its constructedness by citing other films in the Herzog canon: self-citation serves as a means of constructing both self and text, further blurring the difference between the two. The footage of abandoned vehicles rusting in the sand is lifted from *Fata Morgana* [1971], for example, a film with which it has a great deal in common."[39] Peucker's observations help us recognize, on the one hand, the occasions when a filmmaker such as Herzog can refer to himself or his work as "citable" points of reference. Yet, on the other hand, such self-citation can, at least in the case of Herzog's history on film, bleed into citation-by-others. Herzog and his works are, in short, not only aggressively integrated into Herzog's ongoing projects (viz., self-citation as part of an authorial signature) but also drawn up by others *because of* Herzog's distinctiveness.

A brief catalog of relevant instances:

Herzog is a conspicuous inspiration in *Me and Earl and the Dying Girl* (2015, dir. Alfonso Gomez-Rejon) — invoked as both the creator of great art (*Fitzcarraldo*) and the maker of serious pronouncements about that creation (*Burden of Dreams* appears in mise en abîme). This tandem makes Herzog a kind of patron saint for these younger filmmakers-in-the-making (both in the characters of the diegesis *and* in the figure of the film's director). Still more, the author of the screenplay, Jesse Andrews, wrote a novel of the same name in which Earl says: "Werner Herzog can lick my ass-cheek. [. . .] We gotta make our *own* movie."[40] How very Herzogian of Earl, inviting a fitting paradox: as if tutored to embrace his mentor by rejecting him.

Herzog even made his way into the proceedings of the (first) impeachment of President Donald J. Trump, when Seth Meyers played a clip from Doug Collins and then borrowed Herzog's accent to provide a commentary on the former Georgia representative's contention that "the clock and the calendar are terrible masters." Collins' testimony, Meyers said, "sounds like an English translation of a German fairy tale designed to make children work harder. It sounds like Werner Herzog narrating one of his documentaries." And then Meyers, in a sustained rendition of his own Herzogian accent, continued:

> Nature has two primal forces: the clock and the calendar and they are terrible masters. But they understand common sense and you cannot outsmart them. If you befriend the clock, the calendar will kill you in your sleep. And the clock will laugh. *Tick tock, tick tock.*

> That is how a clock laughs. A clock is always laughing at you.[41]

Yet Herzog is not merely a figure or voice available for ready insertion or casual adoption (arguably challenged only by Arnold Schwarzenegger's proximate Austrian brand), he also shows up, as it were, to do his own stunts—a poignant pun in this context. While being interviewed by Mark Kermode atop a dusty Los Angeles lookout in 2006, Herzog can be heard saying "In Germany, I've somehow left the paved road. Nobody cares about my films," whereupon Herzog is shot with a bullet. He responded "it's not significant" and gestured to continue the interview.[42] Toggling between the gravest and the least consequential (what Herzog once styled "the conquest of the useless"), he encourages an unsteady alternation, thereby further entrenching the mystery of truth. Along these lines, recall the audio clip of Herzog recounting his rescue of Oscar-winning actor Joaquin Phoenix from a car that had crashed and was leaking gasoline.[43] As Phoenix, still trapped in the car, went to light a cigarette, "I confiscated the cigarette lighter," Herzog remembers, "and I then crushed the rear window and got him out."[44] The adrenalized act reported in a calm fashion adds another layer to the improbable visitation. Herzog didn't remain on the scene to accept thanks from the actor, much less accolades from the Hollywood gossip machine; having saved the star, Herzog slipped away to his own Hollywood hills redoubt. These scenes from Herzog's Los Angeles neighborhood not only convey their own strange cinematic reality—as if the city of dreams were as dangerous and bizarrely scripted as any marquee offering—but give one pause about Herzog's daring, undaunted everyday life in the city, full as it is with experiences that make existence there (and if there, then everywhere) precarious and evanescent. Far from suffering the stultifying effects of glitz and glamor, Herzog braves a Los Angeles that brings the adventure to him.

While these historical, autobiographical moments percolate to the surface of our cultural dialogue about Herzog, so do those moments when he appears as himself or as some version of himself—as in an episode of *Parks and Recreation*; yet there, the parody is so broad that it undermines any sense of his seriousness.[45] What might have been a great intensity now seems like camp; again hoax *vérité*. Likewise, Herzog is namechecked in Noam Baumbach's *The Meyerowitz Stories (New and Selected)* (2017), when we learn that Harold's (Dustin

Hoffman) dog is named after the Bruno S. of Herzog's *Stroszek*. Baumbach's now-characteristic blend of "near-farce and emotional brutality" is spiced by what we are to understand as an exotic, high-culture reference.[46] Herzog is played, in this case, for seriousness. Where some people name their dogs after cartoon or comic book characters, perhaps after Greek or Roman gods, our obscure sculptor chooses an actor/character from a lesser-known Herzog film from the 1970s — perhaps finding in Bruno S., after Harold Meyerowitz, a similarly neglected genius. Being niche and (at least conceptually) obscure is part of Herzog's brand, and yet, the more he is referenced (via self-citation and/or citation-by-others), the more his persona becomes an undeniable celebrity-unto-itself. Yet another paradox for our palate: the famous person (and voice) who no one quite knows. Even as he has become increasingly ubiquitous — a go-to style or idiom in which to fashion one's observations — the depth of cultural knowledge of him and his works becomes ever more shallow and opaque.

Given that Herzog's character, The Client, appears to die in the penultimate episode of *The Mandalorian* (s1:e7), we may be forced to concede his casting was, in fact, a stunt. While we acknowledge that in the *Star Wars* universe death is not necessarily the end of a character's life, we can study The Client's final minutes of screen time, when Herzog was paying the bills with what sounded like self-authored dialogue: "Look outside and all you see is death and chaos." Perhaps scriptwriter Jon Favreau is a sufficiently adept superfan that he could achieve a strikingly effective riff on the master's likely remarks. The line could be seamlessly inserted retroactively into or tactically extracted from *Burden of Dreams* and *Lessons of Darkness* without our awareness. As Herzog himself notes in *A Guide for the Perplexed*: "If you're interested in what I think about nature, take a look up into the night sky and consider that it's a complete mess, full of recalcitrant chaos."[47] (Of course, the very notion counters the allusions apparent in the English "darkness" [*finsternis*], such that "lessons" would be delivered beneath a sky without stars — not chaos, then, so much as a void; for the lack of orienting points of light, we would be lost, without direction). Even so, The Client, when left to freely pontificate on the role of humans, nature, droids, and galactic immensities, knows just where he is — on two feet and *terra firma* as a theorist of the berserk sublime. However much The Client is creature of fiction, in the end, perhaps as a matter of necessity, a function of Herzog's overpowering persona, he ventriloquizes; The Client's outlook and his sayings are very Herzogy.

Reflecting on the interactive provinces of Werner Herzog and *Star Wars*—both defined, as they are, by associations with rogue agency and its multifarious attributes—one feels obliged to acknowledge how, in *Episode V: The Empire Strikes Back* (1980, dir. Irvin Kershner), the Jedi-in-training, Luke Skywalker, took up the mantle of Rogue Leader (a "call sign attributed to the lead pilot of the Rebel Alliance's starfighter squadron, Rogue Squadron").[48] Similar to the circumstances by which Cornel West, prophetic philosopher and perennial firebrand of our own era, entered *The Matrix*, not as a Client but as a "Counsillor" on the Zion Council, we take note of how significant and serious ideas—inner freedom, equanimity, a view of things *sub species aeternitatis*, making contact with the cosmic—have a way of turning comic and ironic in the frenetic, sometimes melodramatic stylization of sci-fi storyworlds.[49] In the aftermath of *Rogue One: A Star Wars Story* (2016, dir. Gareth Edwards), Herzog's Rogue Film School sounds like an Alliance-approved clandestine training program for a ragtag crew of meddlesome anti-imperial propogandists.

Herzog's cameos (along with the shout-outs and impersonations) underscore that he is not an actor summoned for his talents (as an actor) but a commodity called upon (like an ingredient) for a special effect (e.g., sometimes for serious, agitating pronouncements as in *Me and Earl and the Dying Girl*; sometimes for ersatz remarks, as in *Parks and Recreation*; and at other times for his exoticism, mysticism, menace, or threat, as in *Jack Reacher*: "I only have my voice to spread terror"[50]). When he is on-screen, he is often cast for dramatic purposes as a villain (*The Mandalorian*, again *Jack Reacher*), yet when he is parodied or lends his voice—*Entourage* in the first case, where Stellan Skarsgård plays "Verner Vollstedt"[51]; *The Simpsons* in the second[52]—the effect is comedic. (One may wonder parenthetically what it would look like if Herzog ever played against type: a romantic lead, for example. Could his persona accommodate that shift? Above, the specter of a Nancy Meyers confection—*Something's Gotta Live*—was meant to test the notion). An interlude on *Rick and Morty*, when Herzog voices Shrimply Pibbles, may sow (further) doubt:

> I've dwelled among the humans. Their entire culture is built around their penises. It's funny to say they are small, it's funny to say they are big. I've been at parties where humans have held bottles, pencils, and thermoses in front of themselves and called out, "Hey, look at me! I'm Mr. so-and-so Dick! I've got such-and-such for a penis!"—I never saw it fail to get a laugh.[53]

In *Orion and the Dark* (2024, dir. Sean Charmatz), screenwriter Charlie Kaufman inserts a signature meta morsel: the imbrication of a projected film (with sound effects to match).[54] The character, Dark, admits his cinematic "passion project" didn't get into Sundance ("uh, such a boys club"), and the audience-of-one child, Orion, comments objectively at first, then supportively: "it's a little short, [...] but concise is good." As Kaufman stocks up on insider, industry jokes ("Don't say industry."), Herzog makes his debut as Herzog. In a voiceover that would be at home in his own films—though, in this case, a single sentence carries the full sweep of the micro-documentary—we hear a sonic message with trademark portent: "Dark has existed for over five-hundred million years, since early life on earth developed light-sensitive proteins." The End. Directed by Dark. Narrated by Werner Herzog. Titles by Saul Bass. —Those intertitles inlaid as a little something for Hitchcock fans as well as Herzog aficionados. Similar meta insertions of our man occur elsewhere, as in *Penguins of Madagascar* (2014, dir. Eric Darnell and Simon J. Smith), in which Herzog is animated (albeit coolheaded) as a generic "documentary filmmaker"—this time making it on screen. Attenborough-style, he riffs in the register of his mordant penguin musings in *Encounters at the End of the World*: "Tiny and helpless, the baby penguins are frozen with fear. They know if they fall from this cliff, they will surely die." Impatient, the documentary narrator turns to his two-person crew, flicks his wrist, and says "Gunter, give them a shove." Over the edge the little creatures go.

When Herzog "plays himself" in interviews, usually to promote his next project (or more than one of them!), we often catch sight of another valence of personality (and talent): the culture critic. We have been told so many times by Herzog that he eschews theory and analysis, so his forays into the critical fray catch us off-guard. Moreover, we are regularly shocked (as ever) by the juxtaposition of Herzog's brand of brogue and his objects of interest—the high and low, the profound and frivolous pulling up seats to sit beside one another. Take his unsentimental takedown of *Barbie* (2023, dir. Greta Gerwig) as representative: "I managed to see the first half-hour. I was curious and I wanted to watch it because I was curious. And I still don't have an answer, but I have a suspicion: could it be that the world of *Barbie* is sheer hell? For a movie ticket, as an audience, you can witness sheer hell—as close as it gets." But then of a movie that summons actual hell from the atomic realm, *Oppenheimer* (2023, dir. Christopher Nolan), he reports: "I have not seen [the film] yet, but I will do it."[55] On this front, there is no hurry to fulfill his duty. The *Barbenheimer* phenomenon is a bespoke assignment for the impaneled Herzog, ready-made for his kind of (unkind) commentary—trenchant though not malicious—since it captures the silly/sublime hybridization so endemic to his own trans-territorial roving and musing. Despite his proven sense of humor, Herzog's default mode is serious—stern, mystical, full of portent—so whenever he allows himself to be present in comic culture (whether as voice talent, guest star, or social critic), his mythical reputation will perpetually underwrite the moment. For such reasons, his new rom-com *Aguirre and the Wrath of Barbie* is sure to entertain.

Not so the music of The Killers, a rock band hailing from Las Vegas that Herzog saw fit to collaborate with some years ago. With the sponsorship of American Express, Herzog directed "The Killers Amex Unstaged," a sequence of words and letters that barely makes sense even after one has been debriefed.[56] To my ear, the most memorable moment of this collaboration came in the form of divine intervention: when a thunderstorm cut the live stream in the middle of the show. Talk about critical commentary.

Concurrent with the demise of The Killers' video feed, the city of Detroit, Michigan, was suffering its own catastrophic failure. The city filed for bankruptcy in December 2013. The common denominator between the fates of the Vegas alt rock band and Motor City prove to be corporate. American Express sponsored the production of a short film by Herzog entitled *Detroit* (2015).[57] The result of the collaboration with the advertising agency Rokkan is a meditative fifteen-minute commercial for the city in ruins. Herzog's presence is barely legible—no intertitles, no voiceover. Only the spare guitar score, which recalls Richard Thompson's iconic work for *Grizzly Man*, evokes a connection.

While concluding any such brief catalog of references, allusions, and invocations—varied moments of self-citation (and citation-by-others)—another category may *also* prove fecund for thinking about Herzog's transformation of the home movie for artistic purposes: autofiction. As the genre is parodied in Olivier Assayas' *Non-Fiction* (2018), autofiction is defined (and defended) as true life behind a "thin smokescreen." Yet Léonard Spiegel (Vincent Macaigne) didn't invent the method; it is familiar enough in James Baldwin, Saul Bellow, Philip Roth, W. G. Sebald, and David Foster Wallace among many others— including contemporary writers such as Roberto Bolaño, J. M. Coetzee, Elena Ferrante, James Frey (notoriously), Karl Ove Knausgård, Catherine Millet, and also, reaching back to Elizabeth Hardwick, Ernest Hemingway, Henry James, James Joyce, Laurence Durrell, and Henry Miller. Admittedly, I am repurposing the notion of autofiction beyond scenes of literary creation to those of filmic and televisual expression. In these respects, I mean to suggest that in many cases we continually encounter Herzog-on-film-and-television as if through a "thin smokescreen," or with a veneer or membrane between ourselves and him.

On this score, another brief set of examples should suffice:

We have, for instance, the way Herzog's childhood in Sachrang—and the Bavarian wilderness and mountains where it is located—figures in how he engages Dieter Dengler's story in *Little Dieter Needs to Fly*; his personal takes on Timothy Treadwell's mental state in *Grizzly Man*, which give us a glimpse of Herzog's own theory of the natural world: "And what haunts me, is that in all the faces of all the bears that Treadwell ever filmed, I discover no kinship, no understanding, no mercy. I see only the overwhelming indifference of nature. To me, there is no such thing as a secret world of the bears." We compile an index of Herzog's attraction to specific kinds of personalities, e.g., those who would stay behind in *La Soufrière* (1977) or set out for Antarctica in *Encounters at the End of the World* (2007).

Then there are "autobiographical exercises," such as Herzog's *Conquest of the Useless: Reflections on the Making of "Fitzcarraldo."* In this distinctly literary case, especially, Herzog appears to skirt the familiar beats of memoir and autobiography altogether and head straight for autofiction. Indeed, in his remarks on the time that culminates in the making of *Fitzcarraldo*, the much-vaunted literalness of his feat of conveying a ship over a mountain is countered—and we might agree, enriched—by the literariness with which the events of *Fitzcarraldo*'s shooting are depicted: both in *Conquest of the Useless* and also in Blank's *Burden of Dreams*. The reality of his achievement is better told as a romantic tale, the physicality of the act transfigured into a transcendental trope. In another case of literary expression, *Of Walking in Ice, Munich-Paris 11/23 to 12/14, 1974*, we read of Herzog's conviction that if he should walk to Paris he will "save" Lotte Eisner's life; we are, indeed, very far from making films, but, again, closer to something like performance art (and even legerdemain or occult ritual). The pedestrian—from the Latin, "going on foot"—must be transfigured into a kind of walking on air, a subliming of the ordinary.

The literariness of Herzog's *Fitzcarraldo* inspires others too, including Jacques Testard, who, when casting about for a name to underwrite his nascent book-publishing venture, apprehended at-a-glance the mythic potency of the eponymous figure's fated endeavors, a name that Rebecca Mead calls "a byword for an exorbitant, doomed adventure."[58] Testard admitted to Mead that by denominating his project Fitzcarraldo Editions, he wagered on "a not very subtle metaphor about the stupidity of setting up a publishing house." Not surprisingly, Herzog makes a cameo in the micro-drama of coopting the name and establishing its new affiliation with Testard. As Mead tells it in the pages of *The New Yorker*:

> When Herzog's recent memoir, *Every Man for Himself and God Against All*, was being offered to publishers, Testard wrote to Herzog's German publisher with, he told me, "a publishing maneuver which I may have invented because it's so stupid—a lowball preëmpt." He went on, "I put in this impassioned pitch, with the biggest sum I could offer at that point, and ended the letter saying, 'If Werner Herzog has a sense of humor, he will say yes to this.' And then, obviously, he went somewhere else, for quite a lot of money." Testard quickly added, "I *don't* think Werner Herzog does not have

a sense of humor. I think he definitely does." (Herzog told me, in an e-mail, "I do not mind at all there was never any contact between me and Jacques Testard about him taking the name 'Fitzcarraldo' for his publishing house. He is welcome, since he seems to publish very fine books.")[59]

Testard's subsequent fortunes as a publishing impresario (however diminutive his operation may be in comparison with other houses) and a sometimes "Nobel whisperer," only burnishes the sacramental use of the name. (Speaking of his own, onomastics have the literary herald making haste in his struggle to outpace indicators [test/tard] while concurrently entering an imposing landscape [test/hard]. Either way). Given the four Nobel laureates on his list (thus far), among other illustrious author accolades, Testard would appear to have turned the company name ironical, since Fitzcarraldo Editions is anything but a "doomed adventure." Even so, the *romance* of the Herzogian allegory remains undiluted—ever available to draw upon as a bulwark against steep odds, choppy waters, and perilous terrain.

Lastly, it could be said Vegas-style that stories told at the Rogue Film School (of personal history and film production history) must remain at Rogue Film School. The revelations there are much in keeping with the tone, tenor, and temper that Herzog has cultivated for decades—in films, in writing, in interviews, in his cameos, etc. Herzog tells us his school is "not for the faint of heart." Indeed, as a sort of peripatetic anti-film school, the teachings at the core of the endeavor may be said to resemble spiritual truths (again [literary] instead of [literal] advice on how to make films): pick locks, forge permits, steal necessities, fake what you need to in order to get the job done. At one point, we are shown a device to slide under a car in order to move it out of the way—a parable of *Fitzcarraldo* in miniature. The very hubris of the criminally-minded advice gives the lie to the *spiritual* truths embedded (perhaps hidden) in the lessons: as if making a film (even a not-so-great-one) is a sufficient prophylactic against legal persecution and the routinized, all too easily accepted failures of everyday life. Though Herzog sounds dead serious when he encourages (and elaborates on achieving) such mischief, one would have to be deaf to miss the irony—even as

Herzog demurs on that register of human relation ("It's a serious communication defect," Herzog confides, "one I have wrestled with my whole life, ever since I was able to think independently. I have no sensory organ for irony and am I forever falling into traps."[60] — A predicament we may now share on account of his lacuna, since we continuously ask ourselves: does he mean what he says? If so, in what register of affect?). When he confers the advice: "Read, read, read, read, read, read, read. If you don't read, you'll never be a filmmaker" we assume he has radically shifted gears (from figurative to literal), and yet what if this apparent adjustment is a ruse too? The claim, empirically contravened in all directions, thus stands as a totem for what we should *want* to do, or what could intuitively aid making better films; and so it is not, in fact, a prediction much less a precondition, so much as an aspiration — a credo to underwrite the un(der)read. Still more, the proposition stands as a check on our capacities to interpret what Herzog says and the films Herzog makes, since the hermeneutic pressure of such admonishing advice is precisely to interpret things sagely by learning to be one's own semiotician of the spirit — including of spiritual truths (such as picking locks and forging permits). Reading itself becomes transcendentalized.

As I have retained and applied Stanley Cavell's orienting remarks, I hazard to presume familiarity with Paul Cronin's two books with Herzog,[61] Timothy Corrigan's comments on Herzog in *The Essay Film: From Montaigne, after Marker* and earlier in "Producing Herzog: From a Body of Images," and more specifically to draw out a dialogue with Brigitte Peucker's essential contribution, "Herzog and Auteurism: Performing Authenticity."[62] With respect to Peucker's work especially, I see some unexplored territory that emerges directly from her project, namely, how Herzog's brand of auteurism — involving the "performing" of authenticity, which we can take in this context to mean the feigning or faking of authenticity — aligns with his use, along with Les Blank's methods, of a pseudo-anthropological home-movie aesthetic (e.g., as exemplified by handheld camerawork, direct framing of those interviewed, lack of cinematic coverage, and imposed voiceover commentary, among other signal traits). To be clear and emphatic, these descriptions (faking, pseudo, etc.) are not meant to denigrate Herzog's work, especially his so-called documentary films, but to lend some assistance in our effort to understand what kind of film objects they are.[63] Notice that our having trouble calling his films "documentaries" is an indication that we are dealing with a special type or expression of the film medium—what I began, after Cavell, to suggest was an indication of Herzog exploring the "aesthetic possibilities" of cinema—a condition that requires a certain returning and re-thinking of established categories and descriptions of work.

We look to the end of Peucker's essay and her claim that Herzog is "[e]ver performing himself as auteur *and* as subject," since, for Herzog, "there may be no difference."[64] Both Peucker and Prager have pointed to the relevance of Theodor Adorno's *The Jargon of Authenticity* to thinking about Herzog's filmmaking.[65] Why? Because "Herzog's film practice welcomes all manner of artifice, provided that it promotes an 'ecstatic inner truth,' that it lends the film image the poetic qualities he admires."[66] Worthy of special mention is what Adorno cannily describes as a "pose of existential seriousness," which Peucker claims is "perhaps most easily located in the earnest, hushed voiceovers of so many Herzog films."[67] Quite helpfully, Peucker also sees reason to adopt—and apply—Adorno's notion of a "pathos of uniqueness" to some of Herzog's work, such as the aforementioned *La Soufrière*.[68] Why "pathos," though? Because the "uniqueness" in Herzog is something of a ploy—not a gift so much as a grift. As Peucker puts it: "*[The Enigma of] Kaspar Hauser*'s stunningly beautiful images—Kaspar's name spelled out in watercress and the flickering dream of the Caucasus— seemed at the time of the film's release in the United States to be wholly new images, although even then Herzog's posture of creating *ex nihilo*, was discernible as a pose."[69] Indeed, Jan-Christopher Horak was on the case in the mid-1980s, as Peucker reflects in hindsight: "Premised on the notion that Herzog creates a public persona that resonates with that of the visionary characters in his films, Horak's indictment of Herzog is in many ways convincing. As Horak argues, a consistent authorial persona emerges from Herzog's films, books, scripts, interviews, and from the films about him."[70] In short, according to Peucker (and earlier Horak), "[t]he discourse of authenticity surrounding Herzog's films was read as a marketing strategy." For Corrigan, like Horak, "Herzog's is a practice aimed unmistakably at calling attention to itself, mimicking an industry's tactics for self-promotion and representation."[71] Peucker is also sensible to repetitions in Herzog's body of work—the way self-citations can become calcified by means of recursion: "many formulations, even longish passages" in *Conquest of the Useless*, *My Best Fiend*, and Paul Cronin's interviews "repeat one another word for word. This, too, smacks of crafting a persona, of performing rehearsed texts."[72] In the wake of Herzog's memoir, *Every Man for Himself and God Against All*, where such repetitions also recur prominently and often isomorphically, let us observe that some of these instances are revisitations with a difference, featuring variations that may be semiotically *additive* rather than merely iterations meant (cynically) to enhance royalties and his reputation: as if, unlike Herzog's own directorial process — where he prefers as few takes as possible — each written return to a topic, a biographically-inflected memory, an invitation to think about the significance of his work or his influence, Herzog picks things up at a novel pitch, in a new key. Even when there are outright word-for-word duplications, the new, next, or surrounding context has a way of sounding (the) familiar in distinctive ways — ways that for the subtlety of variation, improvisation even, become freshly resonant.

Peucker's interest in Herzog's "performance of authenticity" and his "staging of the self" (e.g., in *Werner Herzog Eats His Shoe*) antagonize what she calls Herzog's "physical investment."[73] That is, how do we hold in hand (or mind) simultaneously Herzog's demand to enlist humans to move a ship over a mountain in the course of making a feature fiction (viz., *Fitzcarraldo*) while he also turns to Les Blank's camera for a performance of his own making (e.g., the director-as-sage, the persona-as-director)? Our question is answered, in part, by Herzog's insistence that he sees no difference between his documentary and fiction films — and so *Fitzcarraldo* is or contains a documentary (images of "presumptive assertion") while *Burden of Dreams* dramatizes cinematic storytelling (including its own memorable, ethnographically-inflected voiceover by Candace Laughlin). Peucker addresses the conflict/complement by saying that "the various forms of projection into the image are procedures that enclose that self within representation. As such, they can be read as fantasmatically protecting the real, temporal self within the imaginary, atemporal world of art."[74] The relationship between *Little Dieter Needs to Fly* (1997) and *Rescue Dawn* (2006) is illustrative on this front, since the earlier film is presented as a documentary that nevertheless contains abundant fabrications, while the latter film is presented as a narrative feature that nevertheless exhibits nondiegetic facts (such as Christian Bale's weight loss, handling dangerous snakes, eating live maggots). In the aftermath of filming *Batman Begins* (2005, dir. Christopher Nolan), Bale was on-set for *Rescue Dawn*, and learning of a proposed stunt. In his Welsh accent, Bale protested the director's harrowing cue: "I am not going to feckin' *die* for you, Werner!"[75] In Herzog's case, "Filmmaker, documentary subject, and fictional character merge through authorial self-projection; subject and object are blurred," as Peucker puts it.[76] On the nature of this mixing and blurring, Herzog says: "Everything is authentic Dieter [in *Little Dieter Needs to Fly*], but to intensify him it is all re-orchestrated, scripted, rehearsed."[77] With Peucker's reading— gathered with Adorno, Corrigan, and Horak—we can say the same for Herzog. Consequently, we are left with a "hybrid quality and mix of ontological registers."[78] Herzog perpetually "intensifies himself" by means of "re-orchestration"—including, as discussed, an obsessive return to and reduplication-with-a-difference of themes, concepts, phrases, metaphors, narratives, cinematic traits, and embodied characteristics (from how he holds his face when offering direction to the pace of his speech when he is ready to reply to skeptical, probing questions made by actors and interviewers alike).

As illustrations of this hybridity, consider the following variations on the autobiographical sublime, intentionally traced over several decades of filmmaking. In Les Blank's *Werner Herzog Eats His Shoe*, Herzog is the subject of a documentary about a stunt—indeed, the losing of a bet with Errol Morris. Yet the loss sets up a quintessential Herzogian move: make the figurative literal (eat a shoe) and then transform that performance into art ("eat a shoe"). The next year, when Herzog pulls a ship over a mountain, he is merely replicating the adroit shift from figurative to literal (and back) to figurative. *Metaphor* and *fact* are two Herzogian languages that are being endlessly translated from one realm to another—cyclically, with each new orbit reaching and risking an actually and potentially revolutionary result.

In *Burden of Dreams*, we hear a voiceover, but it is written by someone other than Herzog (Michael Goodwin), and voiced by yet another talent (the just-mentioned Candace Laughlin)— spoken in an observational, detached style befitting a trained anthropologist. We never hear questions posed to Herzog— and so miss the specific prompts (their grammar, their tone) that would help us better understand how Herzog responds;

furthermore, in virtue of this absence, we also lose a chance to study the *interval* between question and answer: a fraught temporal span (of wordless silence), however brief, in which we have further semiotic cues to study (e.g., Herzog's breathing, facial movements, bodily gestures, environmental sounds, and so on). The Conradian premise of seeking out and "finding Herzog in the jungle" might have been enough to give any subject the instinct, if not the motivation, to mythologize. The interview scenes with Herzog mark a striking evolution and refinement of his knowing conceptualization of his persona—in voice, sentiment, and demeanor. These are not typical "behind the scenes" interviews with the director, but the creation of an entirely new work of art. *Burden of Dreams* is not about the making of *Fitzcarraldo* so much as the (ongoing) making of Werner Herzog.

As discussed above in relation to and in contradistinction with Varda's *The Beaches of Agnès*, Herzog makes himself and his friendship with Klaus Kinski into a topic for reflection in *My Best Fiend*. In this way, excerpts from established films become evidence in the way that home-movie footage would otherwise be illustratively inserted. On this register, Rivette's observation— "that all films are documents of the history of their making"— finds a potent expression and, indeed, exemplification. The film transforms feature films into glimpses of a friendship, or at least a relationship—in effect, repurposing commercial, public films for the space of the personal, even private. For Herzog, Kinski's performances in his films become swatches and snippets for a family album. This film, perhaps more than any other of Herzog's, presents (however counterintuitive it may be) a more fitting sense of the "behind the scenes" just invoked since it affords an exposé by means of profilmic footage; one gets "behind" the screen by facing it head on, eyes open to the mysteries that lie in wait for Herzog to reveal. Such tricks are achieved by blending notorious Kinski performances with Herzog's familiar voice and thus the on-camera narration of thoughts and feelings as projections upon (cinematic) projections. Once again, the artful layering and remixing is a reorchestration—and renders forthwith a newly created artistic object. Not quite documentary; not quite fiction. Neither strict autobiography nor a fabric of self-appointed myths. Yet participating in all of them, in some portion, by way of some admixture.

Yet another variation on this theme: *Grizzly Man*, in which Timothy Treadwell's home movies are joined, as it were, with Herzog's own—his roving camera re-tracing Treadwell's steps, achieving in the process a kind of double or layered *ciné-*autobiography.[79] Consider especially those moments when "found footage"—indeed, with haunted, terrifying resonances (literally), in this case, since some of the sounds of a bear attack were "found" after Treadwell's brutal death—becomes, for Herzog, a trove of home-movie reels (some of them jealousy guarded precisely because of their evidentiary power, their aural violence).[80] Yet, we can re-describe the type of film Treadwell was making as more than merely "found," since it—like several of Herzog's own, other works—also lives at the intersection of home movie, video diary, essay film, and ersatz nature film. Even if "[b]ad faith is at work here" on Herzog's part, according to Peucker, it doesn't prevent us from recognizing that "Treadwell has a fully mediatized identity."[81] Like Herzog.

Lastly in this curated sequence we find *Into the Inferno* (2016), which stands out among contenders for at least two reasons: first, as a mature expression of Herzog's persona, especially as it has evolved in what might be called his "adventure films" or "travel documentaries" (e.g., from *Fata Morgana* to *La Soufrière*, from *Lessons of Darkness* to *Encounters at the End of the World* and *Cave of Forgotten Dreams*, among many similar others). Second, for the way the film encodes—and re-presents, self-cites—his earlier work on the topic, namely, *La Soufrière*. To be sure, the repetitions and resonances appear on many levels of sign, symbol, and selected extract, reminding us that, for example, *La Soufrière*, *Nosferatu the Vampyre* (1979), and *Lessons of Darkness* "all dra[w] on musical passages from Wagner operas (specifically *Das Rheingold*, *Parsifal*, and *Götterdämmerung*)."[82] Peucker describes the use of Wagner in *La Soufrière* as "mock-heroic," which means that Herzog's repurposing can arrive in any number of emotional tonalities—from portentous to pretentious, tragic to comedic, sincere to cynical.[83]

This quick digest, elaborated upon elsewhere in this book, hopefully illuminates some ways in which a knowing and accomplished metacinematic consciousness operates pervasively in Herzog's films—in myriad modes and in almost every one of his films, and often *across* them, in their vertiginously transtextual state, as a coextensive, unified oeuvre despite its variety. In significant measure, the manifold and affiliated "ontological registers" at work are made more evident by the intersection—and thus necessary interaction—of the home-movie aesthetic and a distinctively auteurist persona.

Herzog explores the "aesthetic possibilities of the medium" by returning us to a consideration of film's origins—to the catch-as-catch-can attributes of home movies—while innovating beyond them. Each of Herzog's films (especially those that court proximity to documentary-as-we-have-known-it) is not an independent dispatch from an amateur on holiday (offering, as he puts it, "footage shot with a cellphone at a spring-break beach party in Florida"[84]), but instead, an installment of conspicuous, ongoing project aimed at raising an audience's awareness of not just a single film, or scene within a film, but *the entire network* of images and sounds he has created. Faced perennially with such aggressive and expansive inter-and-intra-textual signification, there is no single or fixed formula for audience discernment, but instead, as Herzog deploys familiar methods differently in each film, applying some measure of false earnestness or parody, provocation or fabrication, as the case may be, we are positioned to respond. But how will we? What can we say to account for this eclectic assemblage and abundantly stocked matrix? By hybridizing self-citation and autofiction, Herzog uses and magnifies his persona (his "personal brand"), and by degrees reaches beyond the claims and achievements of documentary film—especially in the dispensations that have shaped the terms and conditions of the genre he inherited. And to what end? Toward the autobiographical sublime—a fitting Herzogian locution. Here the personal is all, but it is not at all personal. He has transformed—has molted, we might say, like the noble peregrine he admires—from Werner Stipetić to Werner Herzog; and not just molted, but mobilized his (next, new) persona and its (prolific, proliferating) "automatisms" for the peregrinations to which his wandering camera is disposed and continually repositioned. There is nothing left of the former person (but some bureaucratic identification papers, which themselves might have been forged), even while there is a still-evolving body of audiovisual mediations and meditations on the meaning and significance of the latter's persona.

IV

ANTI-SENTIMENTAL DISPATCHES

JOSEPH CONRAD RATIFIED OUR SUSPICIONS about the darkness that may lurk in the heart of man, and we are meant to be shocked and mortified by its expression. Yet isn't that "darkness" merely a quotidian feature of the natural world, a commonplace of the animal kingdom? Perhaps we should say that in the jungle Kurtz descended into nature—rejoined the order of things—became more animal than man. He transgressed the boundary that humans have at once invented and reinforced between themselves and the rest of the world's living creatures. Turning to a contemporary example of the oft-contested limit between animal nature and human nature, between darkness and illumination, we find in Werner Herzog's documentary film *Grizzly Man* (2005) the figure of Timothy Treadwell, the protagonist in a curious inversion of a Conradian tale: Treadwell ventures into remote Alaska to seek contact with animals he regards as docile, spiritual beings, who would harbor no ill will toward him. Treadwell's humanity— especially his disgust with the mortal, depraved species from which he hails—becomes a burden he carries and wishes to disabuse himself of. "The animals" are enlisted as his allies in the endeavor to shuck off the cruelty and ignorance of modern humans and their perverted understanding of their nonhuman brethren. Yet the partners Treadwell seeks to commune with in America's furthest, most expansive wilderness are not sled-dog puppies or baby penguins, but fully mature grizzly bears. Because Treadwell regards these massive, tall-toothed and claw-equipped creatures with the caution one might approach a teddy bear, we are left to think that he—like Kurtz—has taken leave of reason. Herzog describes Treadwell's footage as at once full of "human ecstasies and darkest inner turmoil"; by expressing himself in front of the camera, Treadwell "began to craft his own movie—something way beyond a wild life film." Even while readily and recurrently acknowledging the ferocity and power of the bears (their danger, their threat), Treadwell's anthropomorphic projection of sincerity, empathy, and knowing awareness upon these undeniably imposing animals gives him the aura of a man out of touch with the natural realities that surround him (and even that might or should animate him). In *Grizzly Man*, we encounter competing visions of animal life: Treadwell's trusting agreeableness and Herzog's skeptical dismissiveness. A sustained tension between Treadwell's harmonious vision of nature (of all creatures great and small) stands in stark contrast with Herzog's anti-sentimentalist, discordant view of the same, and will define a through-line of the comparison. As inheritors of the natural world—inhabitants in it, subject to it, subjects of it—we are forced to contend with these divergent modes of relation, these opposing claims to truth.

1. Hunger in the Heart of Nature

IF TREADWELL ULTIMATELY FACES THE BEARS' HUNGER, what can be said for his own? Treadwell's unmet desire is evident—but for what? To comfort the animals? To be consoled by them? His stated aim is to serve as their protector and "caretaker," even as the bears he presides over—or in Thoreauvian language, neighbors—live in a nationally protected wildlife reserve. Still, his attempted intimacy with the grizzlies illuminates the ways in which he transgresses laws that govern the bears' existence, and we are meant to believe, his own (which is to say, our own). These wild bears are not, for example, to be reasoned with, to be won over by tender falsetto voices—the kind of coaxing and cajoling one usually reserves for domestic pets or small children. At once, even Treadwell's name—a stage name he adopted in adulthood—seems an ironic commentary on the poverty of his approach. Unlike Herzog, he doesn't watch his step.

Treadwell's home-movie-style, self-narrated footage—that forms the basis of, and raw material for, Herzog's film, in the wake of Treadwell's demise, effectively a cache of found footage—fails to reconcile the ravaging realities we are accustomed to seeing in nature documentaries and reading about in the anthropomorphic sentiments of children's stories (along with their variants and adaptations on film). In Treadwell's self-produced video coverage, he seems to adopt a David Attenborough framework *without* a skeptical, scientifically-minded host at the helm who points up nature's patterns and laws, who presumes (and respects) the fissure between investigator and specimen. Instead, in Treadwell, we find a host who is a naïve mythologist of occult continuities between human and animal, and thoroughly captivated by a fantasy of animals' willing domestication (even while in the wild). Treadwell's desire—or is it more properly a psychopathology?—clouds his ability to assess the danger he puts himself and others in, while that same obscurity provides for viewers of *Grizzly Man* a clear lesson, or at least, a reminder that the hunger that rules nature cannot be dismissed because of a human regard for it; in this case, subjectivity does not trump objectivity; a person cannot remake nature after his or her own beliefs. The darkness is not, we might say, in nature, but in Treadwell: in his faulty cognitive and emotional relationship to what lies beyond him in the Alaskan wilderness.

Art is easier to remember than nature. Nature isn't narrative or mythological without human input; it is rather, in its independence, ephemeral and easy is to forget. Our ceaseless "return" to natural environments suggests we cannot fathom its qualities, its complexities, our position with respect to it; meanwhile, we know precisely where to find the Caravaggio in the museum. Herzog would appear to cinematically "tame" nature—some framed feature of it, some concatenated series of sounds and images—so that we might better claim a discernable and in time memorable encounter with a portion of it. Of course, the object of our recollections is but an artifact— and no natural thing in itself. Images that we hold from our wa(l)king experience must be contrasted with images that are presented to us at the movies—though both may be said to share space in one's mind. A first-hand, immediate experience will yield different images—call them embodied—than the sort derived from derivative, surrogate media (an extended mind of a sort). Treadwell, despite his seasons spent in the Alaskan bush, among the wild bears, continued to conflate the bivalent types such that the myths and two-dimensional facets of fiction blended dangerously with the three-dimensional realities of the mosquito-infested terrain of the Grizzly Maze. The confluence of these realms—ephemeral cinemascapes and durable extramental realities—create, for Treadwell and the rest of us, conditions for a paradoxical position: armchair traveling on foot. Familiar enough to go unrecognized, Treadwell provides an emphatic illustration of their fateful overlap, in his case, defined by a "fatal obsession."[1]

Even though Herzog adopts the task of trimming and shaping Treadwell's one hundred-plus hours of raw video footage into a gripping, well-paced documentary film, he doesn't do so as an ally of Treadwell's vision. *Grizzly Man* is, instead, an unflinching testament to the mortal danger of committing the pathetic fallacy, and a probing meditation on the ineluctable distance between humans and their "fellow" creatures. Indeed, Herzog treats Treadwell, one might say, with the skepticism one reserves for animals (or madmen) — hence the double entendre of the film's title; after all, Herzog made five films with Klaus Kinski — another human spirit who courted animality and madness (as well as divinity). Herzog recounts: "I have seen this madness before on a film set. But Treadwell was not an actor in opposition to a director or producer. He's fighting civilization itself. It is the same civilization that cast Thoreau out of Walden and John Muir into the wild." It may be the same civilization — an American one — and yet Thoreau's and Muir's experiments in nature were *continuous* with their obligations to the state, which in Thoreau's case included his defiance of it (e.g., by not paying his taxes as a mode of anti-slavery protest). To be sure, Thoreau, among the Herzog-anointed trinity, may have been fathoming the distance of the stars and the depth of Walden Pond, even while abiding close enough to the family hearth to join them for supper, if need be; his pursuit of the company of "wild" nature was a spiritual quest: he didn't ask nature to accommodate his idiosyncratic imaginations but sought to address nature honestly, by his own lights.[2]

By contrast, the darkness and danger of Treadwell's vision of nature arises for Herzog when Treadwell's treacly, mawkish sentiments pass from (what may be) an ill mind to otherwise sober minds, from his mind to what may be our own — including those who would, and did, fall victim to his convoluted conception of the world, natural and otherwise. When in the course of our affairs do we fail to give nature her due, and instead imbue her with an affection and communion she cannot possess? Treadwell's buoyant, light-hearted, variously goofy and earnest demeanor obscures, in Herzog's estimation, the violent, ineluctable hunger in the heart of nature.

Herzog is — and seemingly always has been — impatient with those who mistake in wild animals (and natural phenomena) a beneficent force. Whether noting, in *Burden of Dreams* (1982, dir. Les Blank), that in the jungle all he hears is "murder and strangulation"; or, at the end of *Echoes from a Somber Empire* (1990), that the sight of a smoking monkey evokes a paroxysm of concern about human and animal worlds overlapping; or, in *Lessons of Darkness* (1992), through Wagnerian-infused fugues, that nature's unimpeachable indifference to human endeavors seems only to make us more antagonized and alienated, Herzog—as he does in *Grizzly Man*—offers a corrective to (or perhaps a bulwark against) the sentimental doctrines that would see wild animals and wild nature as anything less than wild.

Since the footage that constitutes *Grizzly Man* was captured in the undomesticated landscape of Alaska, the vast, unarticulated natural sublime also entreats an interest in the Americanness of Treadwell's story and sentiments. Even as a place, Alaska—a location apart from the contiguous states, like Hawai'i—adds a further valence, an exoticism, to the American experience and imagination of the wilderness as such; the two places amount to "islands" beyond the imagination of those who road-trip across the continent—they are, in effect, further shores, and for that, largely beyond comprehension (for most Americans). In a time when the American West can seem as tamed and navigable as the Eastern seaboard, Alaska and Hawai'i retain much of their alluring pre-civilized wildness— partly owing to their remoteness, partly on account of the preservational and protective barriers imposed on uninhabited lands. For the twenty-first century citizen of the lower forty-eight, they are at once real places and possessed of rare mythological potencies.

Likewise, there is a robust ancillary realm of books and films that form a kind of background or shared context for such roving investigations into the American psychology of the West and wilderness, island existence, and life beyond the limit of human-dominated terrain, among contemporary examples: Jon Krakauer's *Into the Wild* and the eponymous film directed by Sean Penn (another tale of a young man's misbegotten adventures in Alaska); the subtext of man's relation to the bear—and his own wild nature—in Jim Harrison's *Legends of the Fall* and the subsequent film directed by Edward Zwick; David Mamet's treatment of Alaska, bears, and "civilized" men in *The Edge*; J. M. Coetzee's *Elizabeth Costello* and the impressive philosophical literature surrounding the novel, notably *Philosophy and Animal Life* by Stanley Cavell, et al., and Stephen Mulhall's *The Wounded Animal*. Though Herzog is (famously) German, he has lived for decades in Los Angeles, and has—as an inside-outsider—acquired a keen sense for critiquing the ironies, paradoxes, and fallacies that are imbricated in American culture. In films such as *Stroszek* (1977), *My Son, My Son, What Have Ye Done* (2009), and *Bad Lieutenant: Port of Call New Orleans* (2009), Herzog demonstrates a wily combination of drama and cultural criticism—embedding thoughts on the American experiment and American values at odd angles to the plot. The indirectness suits him—suits (film) art generally. However, it is in *Grizzly Man* that Herzog, arguably most perspicuously, became a competent critic of American thoughts about nature—even when, and perhaps especially when, reason seems to have abandoned the scene of encounter. Here, nature is a character and a context—as the Perúvian jungle is in *Aguirre* and *Fitzcarraldo* and *Wings of Hope*. Treadwell is the self-selected representative of a certain deranged image of the natural realm—a semiotic terrain he transfers from the backlots of a California dream to the human oblivion of the Alaskan bush.

2. Behold the Bear Before You—and Within

HEREWITH A RADICALLY BRIEF SYNOPSIS of *Grizzly Man*: Timothy Treadwell travels to Alaska to commune with wild grizzly bears, films himself doing so, approaches bears in the late fall (when they are hungriest), and is eaten by them. Werner Herzog learns of Treadwell's fate, the one hundred-plus hours of raw video footage that remains, and turns his attention to editing and shaping excerpts from that massive trove of moving images and their accompanying sounds into a documentary narrative feature of one hundred and three minutes entitled *Grizzly Man*. Though uncharacteristic of his standard shooting methodology, the core footage of the film was not made by Herzog—or his longtime collaborating cinematographer, Peter Zeitlinger—but the film does contain, as one has come to expect, Herzog's distinctive voiceover narration, which he wrote himself.[3] Structurally, then, the film is a helical hybrid of Treadwell's strand of real-time documentary imagery and Herzog's strand of after-the-fact commentary (a pairing that is further enriched by the addition of Herzog's newly-added interviews with others and an evocative and memorable score solicited from the celebrated guitarist Richard Thompson).

Herzog's attraction to Treadwell's story—in its facts and as filmed—is, as indicated above, pre-dated by Herzog's long-standing meditation on the human misalignment with natural forms and forces. When Herzog was filming his now-iconic *Fitzcarraldo* (1982) in "darkest Perú" (a phrase familiar from another bear story, *Paddington Bear* [1958]—a character introduced a year after Treadwell's birth), he confided to his journal: "In its all-encompassing, massive misery, of which it has no knowledge and no hint of a notion, the mighty jungle stood completely still for another night, which, however, true to its innermost nature, it did not let pass unused for incredible destruction, incredible strangulation."[4] The documentary filmmaker Les Blank, who was on location during the making of *Fitzcarraldo*, captured Herzog in what appears to be an off-the-cuff soliloquy about the place they find themselves in—physically as well as conceptually; these remarks find their way into Blank's astonishing and enduring *Burden of Dreams*: "Nature here is vile and base," Herzog intones. "I wouldn't see anything erotical here. I would see fornication and asphyxiation and choking and fight for survival and growing and just rotting away. [. . .] Taking a close look at—at what's around us there—there is some sort of a harmony. It is the harmony of overwhelming and collective murder. And we in comparison to the articulate vileness and baseness and obscenity of all this jungle. [. . .]" Herzog pauses only to summon his final statement on the subject: "We have to get acquainted to this idea that there is no real harmony as we have conceived it."[5]

Herzog speaks to Blank's camera with the kind of unvarnished, unaffected Bavarian soberness that we now think of as distinctively Herzogian (for this reason, as explored in the previous chapter and in the concluding one, parodies of the timbre of his accented voice and his distinctive diction abound, even including knowing self-parodies[6]). Given the framing implied by Treadwell's errant view, Herzog's intimation of "harmony"—or rather, its lack—stands out as overly, tragic-comically salient. For Herzog recognizes what seems to be an order that renders the natural world on its own terms (the "fornication and asphyxiation," for example), and then—quite at a distance—the harmony that we have "conceived" and thereafter *imposed* on nature.

And we haven't even left *terra firma*: Herzog seldom seems moved to speak about the vastness and indifference of the intergalactic space and time beyond our terrestrial realm; earth is plenty alien, and nature is no "friend" here, so there is little reason to presume any such cosmic benevolence when we leave the planet's gravitational field. Nature has its ways, but we are not privy to them; we are but witnesses to processes and spectacles, indentured victims of macro and micro phenomena beyond our control and comprehension—subject to fates that circulates in our blood streams, in the muscle fibers of our being: *de humani corporis fabrica*.[7] And most of the time, Herzog suggests, we are either blind to realities we cannot perceive and understand, or in denial about ones we do not wish to admit.

Herzog, therefore, perks up and takes notice whenever someone—foolhardy or not—braves the suggestion that a viable (and charitable) theory of nature has been found. Even in his *Encounters at the End of the World* (2007), what seemed a catalog of dispassionate scientific investigation concerning the qualities of ice in the Antarctic turned into a probing and haunting psychological portrait of the inner lives of the explorers. The scientists were more complicated and conflicted than they themselves thought; Herzog seems to have inadvertently assembled them for accidental brushes with psychoanalysis (a tendency and technique he himself despises). But the irony is telling, since we are left to wonder if humanity *in extremis*—set in radical isolation from others—conjures its own Conradian nightmares, these ones frozen in ice-sheets a mile thick instead of obscured by dense, verdant jungle foliage. Similarly, in *Cave of Forgotten Dreams* (2010), the mathematical and graphical renderings of the Chauvet cave become an odd moment of disclosure for the computer programmer caught unaware by Herzog's unflinching inquiry into the metaphysical aspects of the discovery; our scientist doesn't seem to realize what he is looking at, so Herzog intimates latent lessons. And Treadwell is, by far, an even easier mark than the geologist and the programmer, since he *consciously* aims to articulate a genial vision of nature, in particular, to depict just the sorts of "harmony" (in nature, and between man and nature) that Herzog finds as unpalatable as they are unlikely. Thinking analogically, Herzog's seems like a new atheist bent on debunking the claims of the spiritualist; yet, it must be remembered that Herzog himself is a proud pursuer of "ecstatic truth," and thus very much a contributor to faiths and fictions all his own.[85] Herzog, though, may have—after all these films and books, interviews and cinematic cameos— sufficiently domesticated in our minds that we no longer recognize his deviations as dangerous (even while Treadwell's saccharine divagations are repudiated for being precisely that). Periodically Herzog is cited as a man who may recklessly pursue his dreams—endangering others in the process, not unlike Treadwell—and yet, Herzog persistently and insistently pushes back: that his risks are measured, that he has no death wish.

Not surprisingly, then, in *Grizzly Man*, Herzog remains intensely at odds with Treadwell's willing march into the jaws of doom. Treadwell's vision of nature is too simplistic, too naïve, too much imbued with the soft edges, and peculiar projections of traditional nature documentaries. Scott MacDonald has written compellingly about the evolving traits of the "nature film," for example, contrasting the sophistication and poetry of Jean Painlevé with the anthropomorphism of Walt Disney.[9] More recently, in the BBC-produced *Planet Earth* (2006), an astonishing visual achievement in the history of nature documentaries, we hear the trusted voice of David Attenborough assess the fate of panda bears, as a panda pup dies: "A touching symbol of the precariousness of life."[10] Though the narrator admits that life is precarious, the event cannot be simply symbolic—or indicative—but must also be "touching." The intervention of Attenborough's affective description is not for the panda bears' sake, but for our own. And so a scene meant to depict—in rare form—what is happening "in the wild," becomes, through voiceover commentary, enmeshed in the *audience's view* of the far-off events. Instead of directly appreciating what happens (even if mediated by film), what most often occurs beyond human oversight (off screen, as it were), we are given a manufactured context in which to have a *feeling* about what happens—in effect, to *humanize* the overwhelming and indifferent churn of natural contingency. Nature, in this moment, as in so many others in documentaries, has been editorialized by humans and made to serve their dominion (and thus, we must presume, to counteract mortal anxieties even while experiencing unconscious comforts atop the food chain).

It may not be an overstatement to say that most nature documentaries (across a wide arc of time and despite evolving disciplinary techniques) cultivate maudlin forms of narrative description that emphasize how nature stands in compatible and analogical relationship to humans—as if we are the standard bearers of conduct and animals are, to some extent or another, imitating us! Erik Barnouw has given this long-standing and still reliably imposed filmic practice a most appealing diagnosis: treating animals in this way—not just anthropomorphically, but also condescendingly—entails believing they are nothing more than "burlesque humans."[11] Animals—especially the animals captured on film, for our entertainment—are there to illuminate the silly, exaggerated, faulty, and otherwise foolish things that *we* do. Arthur Dubs and Heinz Sielmann's *Vanishing Wilderness* (1974) is startlingly representative of the Disney approach: while admittedly accompanying exceptional footage taken over a five-year period of global expeditioning, the voiceover commentary erodes our appreciation of the visuals by issuing an endless stream of supercilious remarks about what is filmed—either limning animal life for humorous insights into human mores, or punning their way into cheap jokes at the animals' expense. In these unapologetically anthropomorphic depictions, animals are not mysterious, but merely humans in other (lesser) forms; when we laugh at them, the thinking goes, we can laugh at ourselves. Such constructions of image and word that we find in nature documentaries of this stripe might as well be animations—cartoons full of exaggerated gestures, embarrassments, and pratfalls. "Look at the way that bird attracts its mate. Doesn't that remind you of the awful outfit Felix wore and the embarrassing dance he did to impress Greta?" Even in the wild, these animals are at our service!

Treadwell has internalized this robust and influential tradition, playing into and amplifying its aesthetic and ethical claims, and we may say, furthermore and tragically, that he was personally and negatively affected by its influence—so much so that he lost his life for his faith in these faulty fabrications. If nature documentaries dwelled as much on how *dangerous* wild animals can be—instead of how playful we would like to think they are—then perhaps Treadwell would have been more cautious, and lived to tell another story (like Herzog). Though the bears that Treadwell "befriends" appear to announce their temperaments in their onomatopoeic name, Treadwell doesn't have ears for the *grizzly* part of these bears: those creatures who survive by tearing through the fresh flesh of other species.

Though Treadwell occasionally shows signs of aggression toward the bears—despite his faith, part of a bid to stand his ground and discourage a bear attack—he often follows up his unconsciously deployed survival instinct with a distinctively heartfelt apology to the confused bears: "I love you, I'm sorry," is a typical coda to his (mock?) fury. When he is petting a wild fox, we hear him address the animal "Thank you for being my friend," and then turning to us to note a "bond" between "this wild animal and this wild person." Another scene finds him in confessional mode (addressing an absent audience of humans while in the presence of the animals), still suffused with appreciation for the creatures: "Thank you to these animals for giving me a life. I had no life. Now I have a life." He tells us: "I was troubled. I drank a lot." The bears needed a "caretaker," so "I gave up drinking." While confiding to the camera his affection for the bears, Treadwell sometimes adds a revealing comment on his own (self-assessed) psychological condition: "I'm in love with my animal friends—and am very, very troubled." A mental health professional would be in a position to diagnose a cognitive pathology, but as we are in the realm of philosophy, literature, and cinema, we remain close to the text—what Treadwell says on film—averting speculation about how his theories of animal life might derive from an inner mental disquiet. As with many Herzog protagonists, the ambiguity of origins and states—feral, mad, mystic, sage, sane, and so on—hold our attention, push us back upon our own inner atmospheres and outer-facing judgments.

The pathology, if there is one, that feels proper to the domain and scope of this occasion is the pathetic fallacy—a literary term used to describe the attribution of human emotion and conduct to all aspects of nature, as it were *beyond* human emotion (*pathos*). The fallacy usually involves the kind of personification commonly found in poetical writing when, for example, animals laugh, clouds seem sullen, leaves appear to dance, or rocks stand indifferent. While these anthropomorphic attributions may find an effective role in poetic composition, the poems, by and large, are not meant to be taken up as *descriptions* of nature; rather, the poetic expressions are literary transformations made possible by metaphor and analogy, metonymy and pun. A parallel sort of "poetizing" can be found in the pseudonymous authorships created by Søren Kierkegaard, where we encounter a band of authors who are purported to be not instances or aspects of Kierkegaard, but independent creations (and creators) all their own.[12] Wherever this poetic use of allusion and analogy takes place—in poetry proper or in experiments of philosophical form—the fallacy takes flight when the metaphors are literalized, when we become forgetful of the distance between image and event, representation and empirical entity.[13] Treadwell is forgetful in this way, or perhaps he never appreciated the distance—and its significance—in the first place.

Treadwell's home-movie-style, self-narrated footage— not aiming for poetic eloquence but instead achieving a sort of memetic veneer of inherited forms (and norms) of wilderness filmmaking—fails to reconcile the ravaging realities of nature with the anthropomorphic sentiments of children's stories, including their variants on film (especially in nature documentaries of a certain Disney-inflected kind). Treadwell, a host who reads as a naïve mythologist of the occult communion between man and animal, the individual and the wild, is, then, not to be mistaken for a contender in our scientific considerations of nature, but as a sentimentalist better suited to quelling the fears children may have of nature—especially "wild" nature. Many of his videotaped dispatches arrive in the coddling tone of after-school programming meant to make scary things more approachable, not less. And we learn that Treadwell's brand of misrepresentation was appreciated by just such audiences: children appeared to love him.

Though we can find many analogues of Treadwell's dangerous distortion—whether in the centuries-old training of animals for the circus, or more recently, in the troubled captivity and treatment of orcas at Sea World (so alarmingly depicted in *Blackfish*, 2013, dir. Gabriela Cowperthwaite), we have ample representative precedents with grizzly bears themselves. We have an origin story of some significance and of direct relevance to the tragic vision promulgated by Treadwell, one in which the perspective of wild bears was formulated, and as it was for so many others, skewed.

For the vast expanse of human history (and even prehistory), the sheer presence of a bear would be sufficient to raise a person's defenses—to stoke a response of fight, flight, or freeze. A bear in the wilderness had a very narrow and very well-defined meaning: it was simply a threat. But, at least in America, this enforced and thus entrenched view—as much from natural selection as common sense—appears to have lost ground when Theodore Roosevelt shot a bear for sport, saw it suffer, and then, instead of finishing it off with a bullet, spared its life.[14] The President of the United States had, in this single gesture, seemed to cast off millennia of instincts—and in their place cast a spell; public praise for his act was outmatched only by the myth that grew around the scene. As they do, entrepreneurs rushed to create an object that would embody Roosevelt's act, and before long the public found its satisfaction with the teddy bear; the "stuffed animal"—a child's rendition of taxidermy—was at once good publicity for the President and a best seller for its creators.

After a fashion befitting a radical sentimentalization such as this bit of proxy-making, it was not with the bear-as-specimen in the natural history museum but the cuddly, anthropomorphized object of our empathy—the teddy bear— that another degree of human control over animal nature is annexed and sanctioned. The teddy bear, an inanimate object that found constant company with children irreverently whispered the depotentiation of its referent: for how could this soft, harmless, endlessly attentive and comforting companion figure sitting peacefully on one's bed be anything but a trusted friend? In our story of Treadwell—and as we assess the peculiar, uncanny, and strange etiology of a wider scenario of reception—the teddy bear may be marked as a candidate for culturally disseminating the pathetic fallacy. Without the teddy bear, would we have Treadwell? For Treadwell, there seems to be an inverted continuity between the wild bears in the Alaskan wilderness and the harmless, inanimate objects of youthful affection and imagined intimacy.

The progeny of the teddy bear are easy to spot because they have diversified and become ubiquitous—but for their prevalence we may neglect the unobvious implications of our complicit domestication of another aspect of wild, other-than-human nature. In a loose reverse chronology, spot Paddington Bear perched in the cloud canopy, who in recent film versions is called a "most unpleasant creature" only by a bear-hater; everyone else sits on the spectrum from amused to annoyed, and no one seems afraid to see a bear in London.[15] In Syd Hoff's *Grizzwold* (1963), a children's book about a grizzly whose land is destroyed, the displaced *ursus arctos horribilis* goes to town and plays with a boy; it doesn't work out (naturally)—not because he harms the boy (improbable) but because it isn't convenient for him to stay (understatement). The boy and the bear have different priorities, apparently. In Robert McCloskey's *Blueberries for Sal* (1948), a mother and daughter go blueberry picking, encounter a mother bear and her cub, and end up trading berries and frivolities; again, no one is injured or even mildly threatened. And don't forget the Berenstain Bears, "The Teddy Bears' Picnic," and the primary ur-text prior to the early twentieth century teddy bear: Goldilocks and the Three Bears. All of the above illustrate the general habit of anthropomorphism and sentimentality about animals—and bears as a signature instance—from Aesop's fables to Pixar, but perhaps especially since the political spin on Theodore Roosevelt's fateful first shot (and decision not to fire again).

Working from the origins of the teddy bear to the narrower meaning of its convoluted significance and motley allusions, it comes as a surprise—perhaps because it is so literal—that in *Grizzly Man* when we meet Treadwell's mother she is holding Timothy's own, beloved teddy bear on her lap as she talks about his life and death; she tells us "it was his childhood toy. [. . .] Teddy bears meant a lot to him." The mother's nervousness causes her fingers to pump the arm of the bear as if animating it, as if ventriloquizing with the stuffed animal, even giving the impression that the child's toy is offering a eulogy for its former owner, guardian, and friend. Furthermore, the sense in which this mother who has lost her son to a bear attack should be holding a bear in her lap seems at once a cruelty and an eerie confirmation of the subconscious salutary effects of such inanimate creatures. As the stuffed bear sits docilely in her lap, we can't help but appreciate how the objectified animal has become a proxy for her dead child—and so nature's murderous agent is transformed into a benign symbol of recovery. Later in the film, which is to say chronologically earlier, we see the same red-bandana-wearing teddy bear in Treadwell's tent, where Timothy rests his head on the bear as one might a pillow—narrating into the camera as a storm rages, comforted by his diminutive *locum tenens*: a grown man in the remote Alaskan bush, living with real grizzly bears, still carrying around his tiny teddy.

The people whom Herzog solicits for reflections on Treadwell's mental health take up a range of diagnostic positions. In the film, Sam Egli says Treadwell was "acting like he was working with people wearing bear costumes out there instead of wild animals. He got what he deserved." Speculating how Treadwell survived as long as he did—some dozen summers—Egli conjectures that "the bears thought there was something wrong with him, like he was mentally retarded." Yet that retardation or immaturity—that lack of grasp with (or of) reality, viz., that these are bears and not people-in-bear-costumes—is also rendered in Egli's generalized condescension to the possibility that *anyone* could meet with the bears and, as he puts it, "bond [with them] as children of the universe." Herzog notes that "the excitement Treadwell felt [about the bears] connected him immediately with children," a connection that reads as a double entendre: children loved him and he was childlike. Many times Treadwell's narration in front of the camera has the tone of a children's show—with him speaking in soft, nurturing rhythms as Mr. Rogers might. Treadwell himself candidly admits his innocent affiliation with the animals: "I run wild with bears, so wild, so free, like a child." Potential onomastics pile up, as when Teddy Treadwell (an amalgamation of the boy and his doll) might in the *nomen est omen* department link up with the misnomer of the man who didn't tread cautiously enough. Easy to imagine that he thought of his own name in connection with the sentimentalization of the bears. What to him may have seemed a birthright, a semantic anointing of his backwoods competencies and trans-species moral acumen, we are, for Herzog's counter-interpretation, sure that trespassing Timmy did not tread well.

The question of Treadwell's mental condition leaves some commentators to gesture toward borderline personality disorder—an important thematic overlap with the very notion of liminal spaces (terrestrial and cognitive). As Herzog comments early in the film: it was "as if there was a desire in him to leave the confinements of his humanness and bond with the bears. Treadwell reached out seeking a primordial encounter, but in doing so, he crossed an invisible borderline." The pilot, Willy Fulton, who flew Treadwell to his summertime "expeditions" said, in the time following his death, that Treadwell "lived on the edge." Herzog sought out local assessments of the standard relationship between bears and people, and learned that "[t]he line between bear and human has apparently always been respected by the native communities of Alaska." When Herzog interviews Sven Haakanson, a native Alutiiq, who holds a Ph.D. and is the director of a local museum, he said that "acting like a bear" is a form of disrespect: "Timothy Treadwell crossed a boundary we have lived with for seven thousand years." And Treadwell himself recognized that in his contact with the bears, he is continually on the "precipice of death." Yet, in the same breath, he claims "I found a way to survive with them. I'm different. Mostly, I love these bears enough to survive. This is my life."

Consensus opinion, whether casual or cultural, from friend or outsider, accommodating or castigating, suggests that Treadwell didn't just want to temporarily cross a boundary by becoming intimate with bears. He wanted, in the opinion of biologist Larry Van Daele, to "to become a bear"—to effect a trans-species adaptation. In a journal, Treadwell wrote that he wanted to "mutate" into a wild animal. In the film, Treadwell's ambition is described by others in religious terms as a desire to connect so deeply with animals that he would be "no longer human." The ontology of the dream remains murky—since the spirit of Treadwell in a bear's body would be merely a more spiritually advanced form of cosplay. Treadwell himself believed that bears have been "misunderstood" and that he could, at least, be their intermediary—a spokesman if not a four-legged citizen of the Grizzly Maze. "I know the language of the bear," he claimed, and he wanted to prove beyond the human/bear boundary "how I am one of them." We catch a glimpse of Treadwell's mission in the name he gave to his organization: Grizzly People. The name stands as a marker of his aspiration to undertake a deep and permanent transgression—indeed, an erasure—of the (natural) interface between bear and human. When he looked at humans he saw wild and aggressive creatures; when he looked at bears, he saw kin.

Grizzly Man is in many respects a psychological portrait made possible not just by the impressions of friends and experts, but also by viewers who have unrivalled access to Treadwell's personality on tape. Far from dramatic reenactments or biopics "based on a true story," we are granted access to Treadwell's first-person video diaries. Still, there is much that lies beyond the frame—as Herzog tells us. And not just important figures who do not receive the camera's attention, such as Amie

Huguenard, who was Treadwell's companion and, in the end, a victim of his outlook. Jewel Palovek, a friend and former lover of Treadwell's, tells us that "he was troubled," and she alludes to "highs and lows"—a euphemism, we are meant to assume, for bipolarity. "Treadwell *wanted* the highs and lows," she admits unreservedly as she describes his decision to stop taking antidepressants. "He definitely had a dark side." When the married biologist couple, Marc and Marnie Gaede, are interviewed, we can't help but notice a book sitting on the table between them: it is *The Dark Side of Man* (1999) — subtitled "Tracing the Origins of Male Violence." The book is by Michael P. Ghiglieri, a biologist and a protégé of Jane Goodall, who argues that male violence is "largely innate, a product of millions of years of evolution." On this natural scientific assessment, the animal is not so much in man (as a potentiality of our lapse from humanity), but that man is *still* animal.

The pro-animal quality of the Gaedes' remarks, taken in tandem with Ghiglieri's scientific promptings of man's inherently and abiding animal nature, seem to justify sentiments gathered from pieces of "hate mail" that Treadwell received, among them a note accusing him of creating an "anti-human eco-religion." By this point in our encounters with Treadwell, we surmise that he would have taken such an epithet as a compliment. Treadwell courted the dark side of nature by means of the dark side of man — that animalistic, violent, instinctive aspect. Yet, it is often hard to pick up on that darkness because of Treadwell's cartoonishly kind voice, his playfulness (as if not being an adventurer but merely *acting* as one), and his persistent recitation of soft refrains of gratitude and affection to the animals, such as "thank you" and "I love you." But, as Herzog demonstrates in a long take, near the end of the film, Treadwell's often childlike demeanor hid a cauldron of inner rage. In these late moments of *Grizzly Man*, it seems that a bear is wearing a human costume, and Treadwell is very eager to disrobe and tear the humans to pieces.

When Treadwell comes across the dismembered arm of a bear cub, Herzog offers a sober, unflinching voiceover — a counter-interpretation that shocks us out of Treadwell's spell: "Perfection belonged to the bears, but once in a while Treadwell came face to face with the harsh reality of wild nature. This did not fit into his sentimentalized view that everything out there was good, and the universe in balance and in harmony. Male bears sometimes kill cubs to stop the females from lactating, and thus have them ready for fornication." Crucially, we never hear how Treadwell himself accounted for such a scene—if he did at all. Rather, the ferocity of nature—especially when it was unleashed upon itself, as in this case, with a bit of prolicide and cannibalism—is inexplicable, beyond Treadwell's comprehension, and thus beyond his commentary.

When we do hear Treadwell's tearful reflections, they are more commonly tied to his perceived sense that the bears are under constant threat by humans—"it's not fair"'—and the expression of terse, generic summaries and ready bromides, such as "It's a painful world." To such claims, undigested in their simplicity and naïveté, Herzog offers sober, articulate, and definitive replies, intoned with a cool detachment bordering on indifference that channel the grave remarks he made in *Burden of Dreams* decades earlier (and included above): "Here I differ with Treadwell. He seemed to ignore that in nature there are predators. I believe the common denominator of the universe is not harmony, but chaos, hostility, and murder." Herzog may be over-correcting both in *Grizzly Man* and elsewhere, allowing little quarter for any sense of "harmony" in nature, but the contrast between him and Treadwell must be seen as a moment of gratifying dramatic tension: a genuine clash of worldviews, as if two bears were meeting on the Grizzly Maze, aiming to settle an eons-old debate. Who will prevail? We know the answer. To the victor the spoils, including Treadwell's tapes. Herzog survived to tell Timothy's tale, a lesson of how to manage the darkness of nature, how to navigate wisely through treacherous environments, and how to live long enough to gain a perspicuous sense of one's actual circumstances—including one's proper place in a universe of variously sized beings and unpredictable forces.

Though Herzog has little patience for Treadwell's extreme projection of the pathetic fallacy, he nevertheless remains studiously intrigued by Treadwell's case, a morbid fascination we likely share with our level-headed guide: "What haunts me," Herzog narrates late in the film, "is that in all the faces of all the bears that Treadwell ever filmed, I discover no kinship, no understanding, no mercy. I see only the overwhelming indifference of nature. To me there is no such thing as a secret world of the bears. And this blank stare speaks only of a half-bored interest in food. But for Timothy Treadwell, this bear was a friend, a savior." That "half-bored interest" proved sufficient, however, to destroy Treadwell's faith in the soteriology of bears, and to confirm his existential demise. When Treadwell appeared on *The Late Show* with David Letterman, the jocular host asked him with mock seriousness and artfully applied emphasis: "Is it gonna happen that one day we read a news article about you being *eaten* by one of these bears?" The audience laughed with the kind of nervousness reserved for death-defying spectacles. But the laughter was short-lived and the feared-for news was delivered soon enough: Treadwell was eaten by a bear, as was his friend, Amie Huguenard. Their deaths—full of screams and howls of pain—were captured on an audio recording (the lens cap still on the camera); as it turned out, an unheard cry then and into posterity. When Herzog listened to the recording, he told the keeper of this aural legacy, Jewel Palovak, "you must destroy the tape." (One of the most formally arresting passages in any of Herzog's films, the scene came in for parody in *Soldier of Illusion*—proving that in the Herzogian catalog, nothing is sacred, nothing is beyond satire: a testament, we should assume, to the quality and affecting power of the source material.[16])

Herzog regards Treadwell—in his life and in his death—not so much as a cautionary tale (though he is that too) as an indicator of something that may abide in all of us: a desire to transcend or transgress our humanness. Stanley Cavell has written that such a desire is part of our very nature as humans: "I mean to say that it is human, it is the human drive to transcend itself, make itself inhuman, which should not end until, as in Nietzsche, the human is over."[17] While Nietzsche sought the "over" or "after" man [*übermensch*], for Treadwell, transcendence was part and parcel of a movement toward the animal—not just to "make contact" with it but to become it, as if realizing our humanness at its highest level was found in achieving (full) animality. If Nietzsche sought progression, Treadwell seemed to court regression: retreating to the (pre-human) animal origins of *homo sapiens* instead of leaping—as if across an abyss—to the post-human.

After Cavell, one is left to wonder whether the human desire to transcend itself is a kind of cleansing of animal nature, of sin, of evil, of a "dark nature" that lurks in the heart of man. Yet after Treadwell, one is turned around, and made to think that no such escape is possible or even desirable. If Ghiglieri's research in *The Dark Side of Man* holds, then Cavell's account is a fantasy, while Treadwell's is our fate: if humans are going anywhere, it is backwards not forwards. Herzog concludes: "Treadwell is gone. The argument how wrong or how right he was disappears into a distance, into a fog. What remains is his footage. And while we watch the animals in their joys of being, in their grace and ferociousness, a thought becomes more and more clear: that it is not so much a look at wild nature as it is an insight into our selves, our nature. And that, for me, beyond his mission, gives meaning to his life and to his death." We are, then, not to pity Treadwell but to see his yearning to go beyond the human—through his pursuit of the *animal* world—as an indication of a general *human* quality. Treadwell's pathology—whatever it may be, alcoholism, bipolarity—masks the deeper truth of his struggle: that the hunger that lurks in the heart of nature is something we all possess. This unslakable yearning is something Conrad showed us through Kurtz; and it is something Herzog revealed to us—for us—through Treadwell. The paradox of humanity is its implied desire to transcend itself—to become, as Aristotle might put it, a beast or a god. Treadwell turned to the beasts. We stand by in horror and fascination perhaps because, as Herzog suggests, we have glimpsed a truth about "our selves, our nature."

V

The Humanistic Sublime

AT THE BEGINNING of *The Romantic Sublime: Studies in the Structure and the Psychology of Transcendence*, Thomas Weiskel declares: "The essential claim of the sublime is that man can, in feeling and in speech, transcend the human," and as such, he concludes: "The humanistic sublime is an oxymoron."[1] Does Weiskel state the matter so bluntly to hinder an inquiry or throw the curious off its scent? Was it perhaps an off-the-cuff conclusion that he would later wish to revisit and recuperate? Did he mean the pairing (also) gives rise to paradox? Harold Bloom, one of Weiskel's teachers at Yale, along with Geoffrey Hartman, said "Weiskel, as a critic, ultimately was in the tradition of Longinus rather than of Aristotle, which is to say that Weiskel was not a formalist, but was himself a sublime critic."[2] In that mode, Weiskel recognized that, as Bloom put it, "[s]ublime poets who are crucially humanistic in some aspects—Milton, Blake, Wordsworth, Shelley, Keats, Whitman, Stevens—must forsake the sublime when they foreground humanistic concerns."[3] Adding another sublime poet to the list, Herzog the humanist, we ask: must they? It is a testament to Weiskel's enduring authority as a scholar that one is inclined to take his word on the matter (however terse, however conclusively stated) and move on. And yet salient experiences caution a too rapid acceptance. With a hunch that the notion is already in service (if unidentified), has rendered perplexing phenomena sensible (if inchoately), we steady ourselves for a serious study of the casually marginalized philosophical idea. Phrase the opening salvo as a question with a touch of tension: does the humanistic sublime attest to phenomena we experience or do phenomena of a certain sort demand the concept so they may be named? Is the experience of the sublime a psychic phenomenon or something we recognize in nature and circumstance (in the latter case as if the sublime is an attribute of physical reality)? Perhaps the binary does us no favors and we ought to fathom a zone of overlap—of co-constitution.

An intrepid and philosophically-inclined Herzogophile will at once recognize if the questions betoken a lost cause; if so, it would be fitting—and serve as a further gird as much as an inciting goad. One can almost hear the newly-composed Herzog voiceover announcing the next essay film under his aegis, *The Mind of the Matter*:

> The humanistic sublime is a phrase of such intensity and unflinching power that it makes philosophers cry themselves to sleep at night. Unlike them, we won't turn away like sheep before the storm nor cower on our precarious footpath to prove its reality. Whether the sublime resides in the mind or in the mountain—or creates a connection between the two—we can live with this ambiguity. We will not let it drive us to insanity. The fact is we already know—and love—the sublime's shocking lessons, since we have dreamed of them.

If *we* write on—and read on—in pursuit of a chimera, Herzog arrived at the destination long ago and is waiting by the river, arms crossed, standing bemused as we show up haggard in sweat-soaked clothes. If the tandem concept, or some version of it, can be habilitated—brought back from scholarly oblivion—it would be a worthwhile venture (but no surprise to Herzog). Unsure what might count as victory in such a case, we take heart. It may be a conquest of the useless, but it will be a thrill nevertheless.

If an idea is a technology, if a concept can itself conceive realities, why not risk the recovery of a maligned one such as the humanistic sublime? Warnings are ceaselessly issued about the demise of the human and the humanities and the humanistic; they remind us of the onslaught of anti-romantic trends, such as postmodernism and post-humanism. A signal target of such an ongoing operation, the idea wouldn't be merely an oxymoron (as Weiskel politely if definitively reports) but a double negative—wrong twice over. No humanism. No sublimity. By the laws of math, though, the two negatives make a positive. We press on.

Even if the humanistic sublime only applies to a few instances in a lifetime, why not have it to hand? Why not keep it and let it broaden our options for categorizing and capturing and perhaps even, as intimated above, creating experience? There is a pleasure in calling things by their right names. But one *needs the names* as much as the *objects of experience* to be named. Studying and theorizing the humanistic sublime feels like a work of experimental translation—an operation conducted perpetually across a threshold. If the humanistic sublime is untranslatable, we will find out; if it is not, we shall discover that too.[4]

Such remarks frontload a defense in anticipation of headwinds, though with Herzog's films and his ideas about them close by, we are inclined to conclude they provide enough counterforce of their own that the supplement will be superfluous. A scaffolding that once reveals its interior creation can be collapsed without loss. If with a modicum of sweat still beading on the brow, how serenely we encounter this conundrum fit for a fan of Herzog's films, especially what may be deemed his "war films"—those works that antagonize the (purported) contradictory status of the humanistic sublime and instead yield a profound series of illustrations of the embattled syntagma.

Herzog's war films—as defined, described, and defended here—remove the impasse, or rather double-down on it, by transforming inherited notions of the triangulated relationship between those massive, unruly categories held together by the briefest, simplest words: man, war, nature. Though man at war, in the context of nature, may be the very epitome of man on the verge of annihilation, the *representation* of this circumstance needn't lead uniformly to transcendence. In short, instead of being the occasion to end or occlude or otherwise overcome the human, there are representations of war—as we find them in films by Herzog, incarnations that illustrate his peculiar invocation of the sublime—that seem favorably suited to manifest the notion of the humanistic sublime (and effect it among audiences). In part, the viability of a hybrid concept such as the humanistic sublime, much less its intellectual credibility as a unified phenomenon, is supported by Herzog's frequently invoked and widely discussed notion of ecstatic truth, the description or definition of which continually involves the presence, perception, and perspective of the human. The concept of the sublime (as a singular term and topic) is familiar from Longinus to Kant, Lyotard to Žižek, but Herzog's heterodox treatment of it is, as one might expect, not a strict inheritance of the category, since far from aiming to transcend the human, Herzog endeavors to situate the human at the very limit of its experience, at that place where its presence in nature—or at war—is at once fantastical and dreamlike and yet utterly authentic, a necessary part of an encounter and yet illusive, mirage-like, shimmering.

For those who endeavor to write about Herzog's films, he doesn't make it easy to undertake a speculative or academic investigation. He seems to have a very low opinion of such writing—and says so. In a series of controversies about the apparent resemblance between Herzog's *Bad Lieutenant: Port of Call New Orleans* (2009) and Abel Ferrara's earlier *Bad Lieutenant* (1992), Herzog said, now in something of a leitmotif that mocks critical comparisons, that obstructs the trials of interpretation—however genuine they may be, however varied the results: "I'm sure some of the more pedantic practitioners of 'film studies' out there will be ecstatic to find a reference in my film to Ferrara's here and there. I call upon the theoreticians of cinema to go after this one. Go for it, losers."[5] Despite his barbed incitements and derisive pronouncements, however, there is a veritable and thriving industry of scholars trying, I suspect with good intentions and with obviously prodigious intellectual resources, to make sense of his work and make it available to wider audiences. A scholar may wish, now and again, for a little less begrudging acknowledgment from his appointed subject, but then Herzog's resistance may be a productive—in turns motivating and orienting—part of the process of writing about his films: an obstruction that is, as so many are, generative.[6] Or as Paul Cronin suggests less optimistically: Herzog's "work, in fact, seems almost to defy analysis, and I can't claim to have read any substantial piece of writing from an academic angle that sheds sustained, engrossing light on [Herzog's] films, or teaches me anything radically new about them."[7] Cronin's bracing conclusion may beckon despair for the invested scholar hoping to make a worthwhile contribution to our thinking on Herzog's films, though perhaps Cronin's assessment can be treated as an invitation—hope against hope—to confront its principal implication, namely, that one should remain silent about the critical inheritance of Herzog's work. Is analysis a worthy part of experience? To what extent should we chasten ourselves to not spend the day in explanation? There is the object and then there is the *thought* about the object: making sense of this relationship murmurs its significance in quiet hours, though we blush when called to the dais.

Herzog's resistance or indifference to the analysis of his films could be taken up from the spirit in which he appears to create them—a spirit more concerned with native apprehension, instinctive insight, and the pulsing rhythms of an ever-changing present rather than terminological definition, taxonomical investigation, anatomic dissection, and systematic organization—to say nothing about his dismissal of the psychological origins and effects of cinematic creations. Because one of the central mantras underlying Herzog's advice at the Rogue Film School is the overly, almost comically emphasized repetition "read, read, read, read, read, read, read, read, read," and because he is himself so well-read (and an author to boot), it is hard to take his skepticism about academic analysis as a justification for charging him with being anti-intellectual.[8] Rather, it would seem he simply doesn't like to look back, endlessly revisit and rehearse what he has done, or think much about his works' meaning or impact. While we mull, he is already on to his next project. As Cronin notes in his preface to *A Guide for the Perplexed*: "Werner is, after all, a man who by his own admission lives with as little personal reflection as possible. He just isn't interested. Intuition is a more powerful guiding light than analysis ever will be, and the new film has always taken precedence over talking about old work."[9] If Herzog's lack of interest in theory is feigned (and given his apprenticeship to great books, there is reason to suspect a measure of dissimulation), we should enjoy its provocation to our conscientious research—or feel the spur to itinerant ramblings that might give rise to it. If his disregard is genuine and total, however, such indifference may mean we have work to do in his stead—despite his skepticism and ridicule.

The present investigation—addressing itself to the task, as before and since, of making sense of mysteries and incitements that may yet never cede ground to consecutive articulation—could benefit from a set of reminders drawn straight from the Rogue Film School: "Always take the initiative. Never wallow in your troubles; despair must be kept private and brief. Learn to live with your mistakes. Expand your knowledge and understanding of music and literature, old and modern. Keep your eyes open. Take your fate into your own hands. Don't preach on deaf ears. Learn to read the inner essence of a landscape. Ignite the fire within and explore unknown territory. Learn on the job. Don't be fearful of rejection. Develop your own voice. A badge of honor is to fail a film-theory class.

Chance is the lifeblood of cinema. Guerrilla tactics are best. Get used to the bear behind you. Form clandestine Rogue cells everywhere."[10] Got that? (He says to himself.) Advice to embolden one to take risks—to follow after thoughts boldly, to eschew complacency. The project may be doomed, but seen on a sufficiently long timescale, we all are. So make haste and be serious—but have a sense of humor and perspective that keeps pace.

The attempt to write speculatively about Herzog's films is further complicated by those scholars who remain committed to the existing—well-researched, well-defended—theories of the sublime (for example, and most prominently, the romantic, tragic, transcendental, ironic, hysterical, apocalyptic, and abstract sublime, among other variations) and would thereby regard any effort to explore or give credence to the humanistic sublime as fruitless, (merely) an academic exercise—and an empty one at that (perhaps "academic exercise" makes "empty" a redundant modifier). Countering dissent from the master filmmaker and from aesthetic theorists, and trying to do so without being defensive, there is, it would appear, something to be gleaned in both cases: either the humanistic sublime remains an oxymoron (and we can learn something from the nature of the contradiction as it is illustrated—demonstrated—in Herzog's work) or, inversely, Herzog's work lends credibility to the notion, and on account of his cinematic experiments we come to understand a novel dimension and, it would seem, redemption of the concept.

Despite Weiskel's expressed doubts about the viability of the humanistic sublime, let us take the bait and hazard an effort to recover it through a revisitation to Herzog's war films; primed to find evidence, we could then make a case for the concept's habilitation in the wider conversation about the cinematic and photographic representation of war (and perhaps also signal its application more broadly, beyond war). Hopefully it will become clear how Herzog's work puts in relief the degree to which the representation of war (in his films at least, and perhaps, in the light of these adduced traits, also in work by others) is uniquely suited to complement our postulated understanding of the humanistic sublime, since this kind of sublime is a phenomenon fundamentally defined by human agency and ecstatic potency, that is, somatic experience at the border of life and death, where one leaves one state and enters into another. Given the headiness of these claims and their antagonism to long-standing aesthetic notions, we are admonished to qualify such assertions with examples, to make evident the kinds of things that appear indicative of Herzog's work—as well as to draw support, as needed, from Herzog's own appraisals. For these reasons, we proceed inductively by a refractive analysis of some of Herzog's films while merging those remarks with Herzog's estimations of his aims and achievements. Fortunately for such inquiries, Herzog is a proficient interpreter of his own work—not in the customary art-critical sense (where form and content come in for aesthetic assessment) but in a peculiar and marvelously idiosyncratic cast. Consequently, Herzog's admission that he doesn't look back, that he is averse to study and analysis, is playfully undermined (or left underdetermined); a critic would be naïve, it seems, to believe Herzog doesn't do his homework—and occasionally our own.

We are, for example, lucky to have between two covers Paul Cronin's editorial feat *Herzog on Herzog* and its capacious heir, *A Guide for the Perplexed*, with which we might begin and almost end our pursuit of clarity on these matters. And for those tracking Herzog's perhaps reluctant or inadvertent attempts to "analyse" his films and books, the historiography of *A Guide for the Perplexed* is worth a word or two. Conjure a vision of Cronin and Herzog sitting in the latter's Los Angeles garden reading the text aloud to one another—trading thoughts on refinements, revisions, and redactions over the course of a dozen days. In *Every Man for Himself and God Against All*, Herzog lists *A Guide for the Perplexed* among his books, but the claim of authorship is complicated by Cronin's investments and interventions in the text. While *A Guide for the Perplexed* may be a definitive collection of Herzogian articulations, it is best to regard it also as a work of ecstatic truth: its truths earned by measures and modes of fabrication. In fitting fashion, then, the book is "all Herzog"—and none at all. *A Guide for the Perplexed* is a specter made of flesh and bone. Herzog—or rather Cronin—demonstrates the promise of Herzogian principles of truth through fabrication, evidence-based improvisation, and artful consolidation, by creating gripping intellectual and emotional arcs where there would otherwise be just notes or merely suggestions of them.

Partly, then, this chapter launches with the hunch that while we have *a lot* of serious commentary by Herzog on his own work and an appreciable and ever-growing secondary literature on his films, there are still things to ask after (indeed, to claim on his behalf, to make a case for by proxy). Though Herzog has said a great deal and has said it with captivating intensity and dramatic poise, he has also—perhaps for that distinctive style and its regular conjugation of profundity and ellipsis, grandiosity and mundanity, contradiction and eccentric phrasing—provoked further thoughts and questions. So, it is, then, importantly in the wake of a work such as *Herzog on Herzog*, *A Guide for the Perplexed*, and other efforts to inherit Herzog's films on critical terms, that my (or our) broader, ongoing inquiry finds fresh valences to pursue, as if to gain a better grasp of what happens when Herzog's comments are brought into the company of other texts, ones that can dynamically refract his meanings and methods in usefully illuminating ways.

1. A Kind of Sublime for War and Its Representation

IF WE HAVE SOUGHT A CONCEPT to engage or reflect or define our understanding—or more viscerally, our *feeling*—of war's visual and sonic representation on film, the humanistic sublime may be it. While the sublime in the romantic or transcendental sense is meant to convey an experience that gets us out of our humanness, where we feel instead connected to the eternal, external, absolute, or atemporal, the humanistic sublime by contrast orchestrates a return to, a remembrance of, or a reengagement with the human as such through an encounter with nature—with its necessary limits, often indiscernible but nevertheless real obstacles along with the fundamental extremes embedded in existence, mortality, and fatality. Where a confrontation with sublime facts of nature draws us outward—to the externalities that exceed our grasp—the humanistic sublime turns us inward such that we are changed: the scope and scale of our "inner landscapes" are enlarged, contact with the human factor in experience newly charged.[11]

In modern philosophy, the notion of the sublime is most closely associated with the philosophical writing of Immanuel Kant and Edmund Burke, though it comes in for memorable commentary by psychoanalyst Adam Phillips and the aforementioned Thomas Weiskel, and elaboration by Jean-François Lyotard in his *Lessons on the Analytic of the Sublime* and Slavoj Žižek in his *The Sublime Object of Ideology*, among others.[12] Kant formulates his account of the sublime in the *Critique of Judgment*, in a section entitled "Analytic of the Sublime," where he distinguishes between the mathematical sublime (which involves vastness and magnitude) and the dynamic sublime (which is meant to categorize the violent movement familiar to the forces of nature). The phenomena of the sublime, as Kant interprets it—or even creates it by conceptualizing it—leads to aesthetic experiences that transcend pleasure. In *Far from the Madding Crowd* (1874), Thomas Hardy delivers us a scene of such comportment:

> Heaven opened then, indeed. The flash was almost too novel for its inexpressibly dangerous nature to be at once realized, and they could only comprehend the magnificence of its beauty. [...] Gabriel was almost blinded, and he could feel Bathsheba's warm arm tremble in his hand—a sensation novel and thrilling enough; but love, life, everything human, seemed small and trifling in such close juxtaposition with an infuriated universe.[13]

The contrast of the moment is nearly unbearable: the intimacy of the hand—of human contact—and the wild energies of an agitated cosmic force shock with their asymmetries. The human response to either the mathematical or dynamic sublime may, indeed, create a sense of awe that confirms the limits of human understanding—the true horizon of comprehension. Before Kant, Edmund Burke, in *A Philosophical Enquiry into the Origin of Our Ideas of the Sublime and Beautiful*, argued that the sublime is the name we should give to feelings of terror and obscurity. He, unlike Kant, emphasizes the emotional intensity and pleasure derived from confronting powerful, awe-inspiring forces or situations (contrasting the sublime with the concept of the beautiful); Burke believes the sublime should be reserved for phenomena that evoke a sense of astonishment and reverence. Kant's rationalist approach to the sublime underscores our discovery of the limits of sensory experience, while Burke's attunement to somatic stimuli reserves a place (or affords a placeholder) for the way feelings of terror and obscurity catalyze visceral responses that are, in fact, pleasurable—if discombobulating. While Burke's and Kant's varieties of the sublime differ (especially on the point of pleasure), they structure the phenomena as dyadic—fundamentally a relation between the human and the natural (the latter being beyond the human). War, which has its obvious correlates in nature ("red in tooth and claw"[14]) is a category that calls out for possible triangulation such that we acknowledge war as "man-made" and yet of a scale and intensity that aligns more consequentially with natural forces. The *tertium quid* for war's particular force (its *might*; German, *Gewalt*; Greek, *dynamis*) would provide language for expressing our thoughts about the fearsome factors of fighting along with the aesthetically significant ones—especially in so far as the two realms interact.[15]

War makes us feel our finitude—how close we are to death from one moment to the next. And so war, as a phenomenon, is ultimately, intimately linked to any such conception of the humanistic sublime, since it is fundamentally an activity of humans at the edge (where dying is an imminent possibility, when survival means not falling into an abyss of nonexistence). War means continually, constantly living at the limit—a radical state of present-focused consciousness that prompts an awareness of the sublimity inherent in the existential parameters of the human condition—a condition, of course, that exceeds war, but is intensified by it. Unlike the spectator of nature, as depicted in paintings by Caspar David Friedrich, the soldier at war is immersed in nature—has become part of, returned to, its natural order, its rhythms, its logic.[16] Even a soldier's accomplices are "embedded." These soldiers, photographers, war correspondents, diplomats, spies, and bystanders are not dispassionately contemplating the scope and scale of steep mountains, deep oceans, wide deserts, and the expanses of interstellar space—from a distance; they are, in the crushing immediacy of their hyper-specific circumstances, pushed up to the very edge of their own all-too-mortal lives. Am I breathing my last breaths? Is this the last thing I will see and hear and smell on earth? What becomes of my body? What lies ahead for me after I am killed? What remains of me if I survive? Will my final thoughts confirm the value of my life—or torment me with their apparent inconsequentiality? These are the kinds of questions that must ring in heads of soldiers firing shots or photographers firing shutters. This is the sublime as humans know it when at war; this is the humanistic sublime.

In Herzog's war films, the defining characteristics of war are placed in the context of nature. At times, the two forces become complementary, coalescing into a single entity (e.g., when nature itself becomes part of the conditions or obstacles of war—"Don't you understand? The jungle is the prison?" says one inmate to another in a POW camp depicted in *Rescue Dawn* [2006]). At other times the two forces are strikingly divisible, parsed out (e.g., when nature is an ally in the midst of war—when the river becomes a means of escape, when the foliage camouflages one's otherwise vulnerable exposure).[17] Just as nature, like war, is possessed of beauty and terror, the conditions of either may save or savage a soldier's chances of survival.[18] Regardless of how the relation between war and nature occurs at any given moment, man (who has created war, but not nature) is pressed to fathom the limits of his natural, embodied attributes—of physical and psychological strength. Since Herzog's depiction of war highlights a different parallel, a different plait—namely, the interwoven relationship between the factual and the fictitious, the documentary and the narrative, the found and the invented— his films become a space of encounter that highlight how war is an activity that people choose to engage in or a created activity that men find themselves in; in these respects, war is an event, while nature is a circumstance.

For Herzog, heading "into" nature and going "to" war are related—parallel activities or initiatives—and his films show us how war is especially suited to revealing a humanistic sublime at such points of overlap and interaction, whereas man's encounter with nature per se stirs the notion of the (romantic or transcendental) sublime we find in the long, heavily theorized, and entrenched history of the concept. The humanistic sublime, by contrast, emerges from phenomena that are invented and provisioned by humans—such as war. As Brad Prager has noted: "Building on Immanuel Kant's idea that 'the sublime is not to be sought in the things of nature, but in our ideas,' Herzog asserts that sublimity is an effect of cognition—of an emotional relation to consciousness; its truths are endogenous to the spectator, rather than emergent on the screen."[19] The human encounter with war or nature *on film* turns the viewer inward and prompts introspection— recognition of inherent features of inner life that are vigorously neglected in the everyday lived apart from war. Like warfare itself, nature remains, or in these films becomes, even more pronounced as different from the human—as a foreign context that throws us back recklessly against our habitual disavowals of mortality.

There is the making of war and the image of war. As part of the human enterprise of *representing* war (often in the context of nature and its evident extremes), Herzog's radical—rogue—commitment to the conscious fabrication of cinema, even in so-called documentary works, underlies his stimulation of the humanistic sublime. For his films do not presume to be points or planes of direct access to war—as if the movie screen were a window onto a foreign, distant reality—but rather constantly remind viewers of a creator's intervention in the making of film (and, by implication, the making of war, and the manifestation of one's ideas about the meaning of war in its generality and its specificity). Herzog's war films, while artful and affecting, do not shirk the fact that the war we claim to see or know is made through the stylization of shots and their arrangement in the editing room—images often compelling coupled with prominent, affecting music and Herzog's ever-iconic voiceover. In this sense, war *remains* a human phenomenon *in medias res* (never wholly giving over to the war in nature, never presented as if from on high or outside, as a view of war in absolute terms *sub species aeternitatis*). Neither do the films become part of what we think of as History, as documents purporting to reveal unmediated facts and empirical data. Herzog's war films in effect present Herzog's wars—what he wants of them as a subject for thinking about humanity and the potential for its contact with the sublime. The war film for Herzog appears to make sense only as a parable of a human-at-the-limit, in serial scenes of coming to terms with the implications of that radical encounter.

In a documentary by Peter Buchka entitled *To the Limit and Then Beyond It: The Ecstatic World of Filmmaker Werner Herzog* (1989), Herzog speaks of an abiding purpose for inventing (ever more) moving images: "I often get the feeling that the cinema should create an image of humanity. [...] There always should be an image of humanity. Who are we? What is our inner history?"[20] For Herzog the project of imaging the world as an outward sign of inner, human experience is profoundly linked to our notion of mortality, of existential limits. "Here I get the feeling," Herzog notes, "that if we truly want deeper insights into ourselves we can only do so if we step back to the very edge of things."[21] Or, as the case may be, step forward, as if to the edge of an abyss—and then look down. We see Herzog literally doing just that in *La Soufrière* (1977), a documentary about "an inevitable disaster" that did not happen, when he steps up to the receding ledge of the erupting volcano and is thrown back by exploding chunks of molten rock. He cites this film as an example of a movement toward such points of transition between the present and absent, the human and nonhuman, the animate and inanimate: "Often in cinema, in the films that I make, it's only possible to obtain a truly deep insight when you push things to the outermost limits."[22]

In *La Soufrière*, the volcano is real—but it also a figuration of something, a natural phenomenon that makes possible certain registers of human introspection (otherwise unencountered, unaccounted for). We find this pursuit of direct experience in Herzog's own quest to visit the active volcano (daring himself to come face-to-face with natural conditions that are among the most inhospitable to humans) and, more intriguingly, in Herzog's curious wish to meet the one man among seventy-five thousand island inhabitants who did not evacuate. "And so I thought," Herzog recollects, "'This man is interesting.' His relationship to death is one that I don't know and one I find very interesting. Where is this guy? Let's go and find out."[23] Herzog's roving camera seeks out the holdout and questions are duly asked of him. Instead of concluding that the gallant loner should be dismissed for possessing an unsound mind, Herzog draws closer, recognizing in him attributes he finds in so many of his subjects: "I believe that it is an existential mindset. This rebellion against situations that are too big for us to handle. It's a mindset that enables us to preserve the dignity of our existence."[24] The "too big for us to handle" is a sentiment that links Herzog's subject to the history of the sublime, especially to Kant and Schiller, who believed that the sublime was essential to our apprehension and expression of human dignity.[25] Instead of the customary notion that sober rationality, detached calculation, and other attributes of refined judgment assure one's human dignity, Herzog says that it is the "insanity or such eccentricity, or something so extraordinary"—seen in so many of his film subjects and characters—that "is necessary to gain human dignity."[26]

In part, this description of Herzog's approach to the revelation of human dignity on film—often in the midst of circumstances that threaten human existence—is caught up with what Grazia Paganelli, in her book *Ecstasy and Truth*, calls "Herzog's tactile gaze."[27] She says this unique approach accounts for what we experience as Herzog's unmoored, interested camera (often achieved by proxy in the hands of cinematographer and long-time collaborator Peter Zeitlinger). Recalling how Herzog stated in his "Minnesota Declaration" that *"cinéma vérité* is devoid of *vérité,"* we never find in his films a documentarian's search for truth as something to be captured in (or from) the world (as if collecting specimens to prove a thesis), but rather an artist's sense that truth is something illuminated by invention—including from within, in a mode of responsiveness to the myriad thoughts and mercurial symbols that percolate to our attention, often seeming to appear in consciousness of their own accord, well beyond our control.[28]

Challenging the prevalent tensions between found and discerned, fact and fiction, documentary and drama, Herzog's cinematic provocations are, in these respects, similar to work by Paolo and Vittorio Taviani—from *Padre Padrone* (1977) to *Caesar Must Die* (2012)—who invest their fiction work with certain documentary effects; the hybridizations of encountered and invented facts in the films of Abbas Kiarostami, most notably in *Close-Up* (1990); and the palpable incitements of Casey Affleck's scandalously staged *I'm Still Here* (2010).[29] On the pretext and prevalence of such blending of found and made scenes, Kiarostami has commented: "We can never get close to the truth except through lying."[30] Or, more tenderly, the character Hossain Sabzian (played by Hossain Sabzian), the protagonist of *Close-Up*, says, while he is on trial for impersonating a famous Iranian film director: "It looks like fraud from the outside." When Kiarostami patiently and thoughtfully interrogates him, as part of a filmed cross-examination, Sabzian replies with heartbreaking sincerity, with what he believes amounts to a fitting counter-description—and moral justification—of his inadvertent stunt: "I'm interested in art and film."[31] In Herzog's films, and especially his war films, we find the *vérité* manifestation of his invention in moments of connection (or fissure) between the human and the nonhuman. It is precisely at these cleave points that Herzog replaces *cinéma vérité* with *cinema humanista*. As he says: "My goal is to explore and chronicle the human condition and our states of mind, and cinema is my way of doing this. I don't make films using images only of clouds and trees; I work with human beings."[32] Herzog might endorse ersatz director Sabzian's aphorism that "nature is a mirror in which to study ourselves," and furthermore agree with him that when such attention is translated into art—into film—we are, in our best moments, remaining loyal to our sincere "interest[s] in art and film," able to convey what Sabzian calls an "inner reality" and what Herzog commonly refers to as our "inner landscapes."[33]

Herzog's preoccupation with moments of contact—or disruption—between the human and nonhuman (that special interface that haunts us with each new breath), or with the transition into and out of human experience (as a matter of consciousness or its dissolution), illustrates how his films could be described, in part, as disparate, layered approaches to finding the terms and limits of the human shift to the other-than-human—call it nature, the nonhuman, or the alien, as screened in *Lessons of Darkness* (1992) or earlier in *Fata Morgana* (1971)— both of which include the physical detritus of war, and in the latter film we hear a terse but emphatic child-spoken chant: "War is insane." Paganelli claims: "There is no Herzog film that does not hide a sort of paradoxical nostalgia for what the world might have been before mankind, or else for what the world will be after it ends."[34] Similarly, Paul Cronin says of Herzog that "[h]e is a primeval sophisticate, a man of extraordinary erudition who yearns nostalgically for a pre-literate, pre-electric existence (or, even, post-literate and post-electric), where the wisdom of the illiterate—those able to memorize stories and poems, and recite them free of all props—predominates."[35] Perhaps also, if irreverently, a world *without cinema*, in which humans are convened to give expression to their earliest and most abiding instincts—creating meaning through storytelling and mark-making as a countermovement to entropy and eventual oblivion.

Paganelli and Cronin are sensible of such prospects, pointing up a paradox that also appears to be part of a productive tension at the heart of Herzog's imaginative initiatives in film. He seems inspired, at times possessed, by a vision of the pre- or post-human—of those very instances of contact and distance that define the human against all other forms, cosmic and terrestrial. Herzog's interest in the "before" and "after" of humankind emerges, then, as an expression of his curiosity about the peculiar presence of the human "in between" the time-before and the time-after (one's life itself being the brief span between infinitely extended durations of nonexistence). Herzog recalls: "I still like the shots at the beginning and ending [of *Where the Green Ants Dream* (1994)] very much, images as if from the end of the world."[36] Herzog, of course, later leans on the double entendre for his exploration of Antarctica, *Encounters at the End of the World* (2007) — the continent with the lowest human population on earth and, at a geographical pole, exists at the terminus of the known planet. "Nothing could be more human," Stanley Cavell has said, than "the power of the motive to reject the human."[37] In part the motive seems expressed in "the human drive to transcend itself, make itself inhuman."[38] Herzog's work offers an interpretation of what Cavell calls one of "the most inescapably human of motivations" — "the drive to the inhuman."[39] Herzog's visions, however, are the very opposite of nihilistic, cynical, or misanthropic lamentations for the nonexistence of the human; instead they direct us to regard the before and after (of the human) as occasions to reinvigorate an attention to the human — especially in its brevity, precarity, and exceptionality. Herzog's ecstatic cinema offers visual and sonic contact with the otherwise unseeable and unhearable; his work lends significance to the notion of the *counterfactual*. These works of imagined, stylized, impossible views of existence (before or after human presence and intervention) radicalize one's own status as a human capable of apprehending such perceptions — or making sense of them. We occupy a viewpoint (and earpoint) from nowhere and never — at the intersection of the pre- and the post-human — and from this odd placement catch a glimpse of our own transcendence (in the form of postulated and assured nonexistence). Since the traditional philosophical reading of the sublime could be cited as support for Cavell's claims, it must remain intriguing for us that Herzog shifts his representation of the sublime *toward* the human.

2. The Human at War in Nature

THE CONTRAST BETWEEN REAL AND IMAGINED DANGER, at whatever scale, confirms whether we can speak of the humanistic sublime, or any other sublime. We are told no phenomena possessed of genuine danger should be counted sublime—awful, perhaps; stunning and disorienting, to be sure, but without the merit of a sublime inflection. It is the very prospect of genuine danger that the notion of sublimity seems to eviscerate, thus underwriting Weiskel's claim for the oxymoronic status of a humanistic sublime. And yet that outcome doesn't seem to accompany the representations of war in war films and war photography. In case after case, visual and sonic representations of the human encounter with the destructive capacities of war—the threat of actual annihilation—often coupled with and compounded by the indifference of nature, suggest that *some kind* of sublimity may being experienced, makes itself known to soldiers and imagemakers on the front—and in some cases also to viewers of these moving or static representations.

Approaching an account that finds room for sublimity in the midst of danger (even if at second hand), Herzog's war films can be counted among those works that contribute meaningfully to our assessment not of referents (bullets and bombs) but of the representations of those real-world threats; these are films that revel in their artifice as a means for redressing our inurement to reality. Herzog's fictions and fabrications, then, bring us up against vital, corporeal, existential facts that are somehow obscured by the ubiquity of real (but unseen, unacknowledged) danger. Consider Herzog's account of the relationship between *Little Dieter Needs to Fly* (a 1997 documentary) and *Rescue Dawn* (a 2006 fiction feature), between Dieter Dengler and the actor who would play Dengler, Christian Bale:

> Although with *Little Dieter* I made a distinction between "fact" and "truth," in many ways the film is the truth I was bound to for practical reasons at the time. I remember watching it for the first time with Dieter. The lights went up and he turned to me. "Werner," he said without missing a beat, "this is unfinished business." The story of Dieter and Duane was always one I wanted to tell, this unbelievable and beautiful tale of human friendship. But to do this you either need Duane himself or someone playing him, and a feature film seemed the only way of reaching the depths of these truths that remained untouched by *Little Dieter.* In that

respect, the two films complement each other nicely. Though *Rescue Dawn* came second, in its fact and spirit, it really came first, and the paradox is that *Little Dieter* was strongly influenced by a feature film that hadn't yet been made.[40]

If we compare Herzog's war films with Terrence Malick's *The Thin Red Line* (1998), we find similar questions being asked ("What's this war in the heart of nature?" Private Train asks in the film's opening question). But Malick's more meditative interest in nature overtakes his reflections on war; the men become so many bugs, interchangeable creatures that climb anonymous hills like ants and die for achievements soon forgotten or forsaken. (In this way, Malick's view seems more Darwinian than Herzog's poetical take. Darwin made much of the metaphor of war in *The Origin of Species*—regularly referring to "battle within battle," how "the law of battle descends," how all species are engaged in "the great battle for life" and "the great and complex battle of life"—and he concludes his epochal book by suggesting that his labors are meant to explain the "war of nature").[41] The men in Malick's film go into nature to fight war, and nature goes on all around them, indifferently; something similar happens in Elem Klimov's haunting representations of nature's ceaseless flow around men at war in *Come and See* (1985). Some soldiers in *The Thin Red Line*—such as Private Witt (Jim Caviezel)—find peace, or illumination, from their awareness of natural phenomena, but Witt's enigmatic departure from the war's front lines still leaves him a casualty of combat. Herzog's craft or conjuring of ecstatic truth (through artful modes of construction and manipulation), contrariwise, returns us to the man-madeness of war, the humanistic quality of war in the context of nature. After all, war in cities or war in fields—battlefields—remains located in nature, as do the humans who fight and suffer to unknown ends. Herzog's revelation of a humanistic sublime doesn't make us transcend ourselves—or our circumstances—but brings us *back* to ourselves as human in these shared straights.

Paul Virilio claims in *War and Cinema: The Logistics of Perception* that we inhabit an era increasingly defined by "a growing derealization of military engagement." As part of the "aesthetics of disappearance" and the "logistics of perception," this derealization entails a concomitant depersonalization and dehumanization of the agents of war, combatant and his foe alike.[42] Very far from the hand-to-hand conflicts that formerly defined military engagement—necessarily creating an unsettling intimacy between enemies—modern warfare continually becomes more mechanized, accelerated, distanced, and anonymous.[43] In recent decades war films have regularly integrated the "active optics" of computer-imaging technology as part of the narrative of war-making.[44] But just as regularly, such films grapple with the human factor—as emotional and erring beings, and also as casualties-of-machines and victors-over-machines. We discover how war films, paralleling the derealization of military engagement, invert a viewer's sense of distance by personalizing and humanizing our relationship to conflict.

While a veteran may have only "seen combat" on a video screen from a thousand miles above his target, or ten thousand miles away from it, on film we are given a dramatic, embodied representation of his life before and after the weapon's launch. On film, the soldier and the frontline are proximate, a mere frame away; since we know that, in real time, the realities occupy distant realms, the forced cinematic intimacy delivers an ecstatic truth worthy of the name. We follow him to training camp, see him on the battlefield or remote control center (that is, on whatever "front" defines his contact) and, at last, we escort him home after the war, or after time is served. War films are—and it seems always have been—a forum for humanizing war, even as war itself has become increasingly a matter of seeking the *removal* of humans altogether (i.e., not just as targets intended for elimination but as the agents who are at a distance while pursuing those targets); the implementation of unmanned drones has become a signal feature of twenty-first-century conflict, and it accounts for an ever-increasing percentage of the total war apparatus. In Virilio's phrase, the "ubiquitous orbital vision of enemy territory" would create the conditions in which a soldier, sailor, or airman never sees the enemy as a person but only as a display of visual information on a screen.[45] More eerily, the decision to "act" on the displayed information may at some point cease to be a human decision but instead itself become an electronic pulse generated by the computer's program or some AI algorithm.[46]

The implementation of artificial intelligence in this nexus of human agent and computational (including screened) control would appear to engender and extend still further derealization and anonymity — a displacement of the human altogether.

Far from being a remote, arcane, or otherwise antiquated academic subject (even if intriguing merely in terms of intellectual history), the sublime is, in the present context, possessed of tremendous urgency primarily because war reminds us all of the absolute — whether we are fighting in a war or watching one represented on screen, whether the war is captured via livestream from the front, filmed on a backlot, or constituted by computer-generated imagery, the matter at issue is of ultimate significance: in effect, to be — or not. In the history of the concept, the sublime is fundamentally informed by our notion of limits — and more particularly, the vertiginous worry that we might exceed them, or already have exceeded them. Simon Morley has argued that Kant's notion of the sublime entailed a "negative experience of limits," which is to say, the sublime becomes "a way of talking about what happens when we are faced with something we do not have the capacity to understand or control — something excessive."[47] Morley continues:

> Behind Kant's discussion lay a keen sense of the independence of nature, whose sheer complexity and grandeur continuously exceeds any human ability to control or understand it. This sense of the sublime may be initiated by the terrifying aspects of nature such as Burke describes, or be provoked by an experience so complex that our inability to form a clear mental conception of it leads to a sense of the inadequacy of our imagination and of the vast gulf between that experience and the thoughts we have about it. We are made aware, Kant observed, that sometimes we cannot present to ourselves an account of an experience that is in any way coherent. We cannot encompass it by thinking, and so it remains indiscernible or unnameable, undecidable, indeterminate, and unpresentable.[48]

And yet it is precisely because, for most noncombatants, war is real via the surrogate of war films (and photographs) that we recognize how such screened proxies must constantly postulate a representation of the ineffable, must attempt to picture what otherwise would remain "indiscernible or unnameable, undecidable, indeterminate, and unpresentable." Even though the execution of war may closely resemble the conditions of the classical romantic (or transcendental) sublime—a constant engagement with the excessive—we remain preoccupied by the crucial difference between (the experiences of) spectator and soldier. The soldier is at war, and *ipso facto* in nature. And if the soldier will come to consciousness about the sublime—in the midst of combat—it will not be a remote and ethereal sublime but a visceral, gravity-laden, bloody sublime. The spectator's experience of a theatrical presentation of war-on-screen may activate the sublime—and though the film may be affecting, it is by comparison with the soldier's predicament, antiseptic.

Homing in on one of the most astonishing and unprecedented displays of cruelty to humankind, Michael Berenbaum has said that "part of [the Holocaust's] attraction to filmmakers, part of its attraction to an audience is: you're touching the absolute as you come closer to the truth of the Holocaust. And part of the failure of film, if it fails, is not to touch that absolute, not to go to the extreme."[49] Or by *limiting* points of contact, insisting on *indirection* and a peripheral vignetting, films may be more effective (and affecting) than if they aimed for the direct exposure of human suffering. Jonathan Glazer adopts the first method in *The Zone of Interest* (2023), and László Nemes deploys the second approach in *Son of Saul* (2015). Herzog experiments with cinematic indirection in *Fata Morgana* and *Lessons of Darkness* by turning our attention to the aftermath of battle—to the physical leftovers and paraphernalia of combat, to a bloodless post-mortem with a near absence of humans, and at all times with little to no clarity about victims or victors. Even his portrait of children at war— in *Ballad of the Little Soldier* (*Ballade vom kleinen Soldaten*, 1984)—operates mainly as a series of interviews with coverage of military training. To find a more customary "war film" one looks to *Cobra Verde* (1987), in which armed conflict is brought dramatically into view of the camera and features the suitably belligerent Klaus Kinski. Far from conversations about war or surveys of damage done, generic war films revel in the fatalities of hand-to-hand combat, of near escapes and losses counted, of blood spilled and foes vanquished. Herzog has demonstrated over the decades his adroit operation on several registers of the multifarious war film taxonomy and its nest of subgenres: from prison-of-war escape adventure to meditative aria, from bloody battle to loquacious post-traumatic therapy session.[50]

"Touching," or even modestly approaching the absolute on film, whether in depictions of Nazi crimes or the Jewish experience of suffering them, or more broadly in representing war as a phenomenon (in battles from Thermopylae to Bunker Hill, or genocides from the Peloponnesian War to Rwanda), nearing hate, evil, oppression, and discrimination at whatever gauge—and discovering compensatory measures in love, goodness, respect, and dignity—stimulates our humanity, our conscience, and our moral sense. War films provide a heuristic for noticing the asymmetry of this oppositional arrangement: the representational gesture on the one hand (of whatever style or generic mode—documentary, dramatic, explicit, indirect) and, defying, if not defeating the effort, the enormity of the object of interest (the war, the human suffering, the moral crisis, etc.). Even so, the precariousness of the very attempt to represent the expansive and illusive—an especially human effort in the face of relentless resistance—underwrites the poignancy of the humanistic sublime: a notion addressed to phenomena of the utmost importance and by turns thwarted by the scope of its objects.

War is an arena that requisitions the enlisted to admit their radical mortality, heightening consciousness about something that is always already present (but seldom apparent), coextensive with embodiment from moment-to-moment yet somehow persistently ignored, suppressed, or invisible. An infantryman who lived through D-Day and became author of the indelible *The Great War and Modern Memory* (1975), Paul Fussell reports a sentiment familiar to the attestations of many soldiers: war "gives you attitudes about life and death that are unattainable anywhere else."[51] As viewers of war films, then, we must feel the threat of our nonexistence by proxy—by association with some characters or disassociation from others. In these registers, going to see a war film is a choice—that encodes a desire—to approach the absolute, to gather some lessons about life and death that are "unattainable anywhere else," reflecting, we must assume, an inherent impulse to move into a realm of enhanced awareness about the reality and inevitability of our (one and only) death. In these ways, war films are unlike all other cinematic genres and subgenres in which the hero has many lives, leaves the firefight unscathed (save only a bloody scratch on a dirty cheek as a totem of bravery or physics-defying luck), returns to fight another day, survives without psychic torment, carries on/out a mission without reproach, applies himself to the next assignment with unguarded confidence, and so forth. War films—and their near variants, hybrids, and subgenres—by contrast, must be fundamentally about living one life and thus risking an encounter with the ultimate, *human* absolute: termination of all missions—without any hope for recourse or reassignment.

Maybe there is no humanistic sublime for Weiskel, or for Kant (in the presence of the mathematical sublime), but perhaps war—as the very definition of living at the brink of existential annihilation—is the appropriate place to speak of it. (Indeed, Weiskel's own premature death seizes the bystander with an inescapable illustration of the tragic sublime[52]). Because Herzog is attuned both to the European romantic tradition and its representational corollaries—for example, conspicuously in the paintings of Hercules Seghers and the plays of Georg Büchner—as well as to the creative nature of fabrication in documentation, Herzog's work in the genre of war films seems especially poised, at once urgently and latently, to offer some real insight into the meaning, and nonparadoxical status, of the humanistic sublime.[53]

Even if we narrow the field of Herzog's scores of films to a few instances of what might be called his "war films"—those films that wear war more overtly on the surface of the film (e.g., the war in Vietnam and the Persian Gulf War), we have an abundance of imagery and thematic innovation to consider. Moreover, the very attribution of the moniker "war films" to some Herzog films usefully complicates the genre as it might find expression in his other films: after all, war is the pretext, subtext, or even condition of filming in a prodigious range of Herzog's oeuvre, whether in *Ballad of the Little Soldier* (1985) (pretext), *Fata Morgana* (subtext), or *Fitzcarraldo* (1982) and *Cobra Verde* (1987) (condition). Three films from Herzog's formidable catalog—*Lessons of Darkness*, *Little Dieter Needs to Fly*, and *Rescue Dawn*—exemplify his representation of war and how his methods aim to constitute and convey ecstatic truth. In these works, Herzog—like Terrence Malick—creates a cinema in which the transcendence of the human is predicated on a hyper-realization of consciousness: a going-beyond the human that requires a form of immanence. By cinematic and conceptual means, and perhaps despite himself, Herzog makes a profound contribution to the lengthy and ongoing history of aesthetics.

In the first century A.C.E., Longinus said that "in discourse we demand that which transcends the human."[54] Literature and literary criticism must look to such overcoming. And so, while Longinus insisted long ago that "sublimity lifts [humans] near the mighty mind of God," Herzog doubles down on the ineluctable centrality of human presence to a point—to an extreme—that a humanistic sublime is no longer an oxymoron but redundant, arguably, the lowest and easiest kind of sublimity for humans to experience.[55] And yet, it still needs to be invoked. Herzog heeds the call cinematically. Even as we readily appreciate the values and virtues of the romantic sublime and the tragic sublime, especially as they are forms that have become familiar, almost banal in their ubiquitous invocation and iconicity, there is yet ample room for another valence. The humanistic sublime appears to be less available to linguistic description, even if the demand remains a stubborn ambition (partly because, as these remarks illustrate, the matter must necessarily gesture to the more potent inhabitations of the sensation as experienced in the plastic arts, and thus not necessarily in art criticism). Consequently, the humanistic sublime invites its appearance in other media—not just in novel and play, painting and sculpture, but in the visual, aural, narrative, experimental power of film.[56] Though Herzog has a penchant for featuring the preliterate naïf or the frenzied loner, his films—especially those falling under the aegis of war and its correlates—suggest themselves as creations of a well-read humanist who, nevertheless, wishes to challenge the tropes, logic, theories, and story structures that philosophy and literature have bequeathed.

3. Ecstatic Truth as Heuristic for the Humanistic Sublime

HISTORICALLY, THE SUBLIME has been discussed mainly in reference to natural phenomena and works of art, especially when they overlap. One of the many kinds of sublime objects that has drawn the attention of theorists—since the appearance of Friedrich Schiller's "On the Sublime" (1801), the first of many recoveries and adaptations of Longinus' notion from antiquity—can be found in landscape painting, a distinctive amalgam of nature and its representation. Though there are many definitions of the sublime, most describe or allude to phenomena that *exceed* human experience, including the ability to account for them—that are, after some form or fashion, unrepresentable (hence the daring innovations of romantic landscape painters such as C. D. Friedrich and J. M. W. Turner, who hazarded an iconography) or are unintelligible (hence the audacity of theorists trying to make the notion philosophically understandable and credible). Contemporary illustrations of the sublime hue closely to these artistic and philosophical traditions and their sturdy attributes; in many respects, various sublimes are recyclings and riffs upon antique notions (not unlike the reworkings of much modern philosophy). So notions of sublimity of whatever vintage—from Longinus to Schiller, through Burke into Kant and Hegel, and later Lyotard, Weiskel, and Žižek—typically retain their historical adjacency to experiences of awe, terror, disorientation, and horror, and, as Simon Morley has noted, to "something we cannot encompass by thinking, and so it remains indiscernible or unnameable, undecidable, indeterminate, and unpresentable."[57] Part of that line-up comments reflexively, as it must, on the very pursuit of philosophical, or more broadly, linguistic formulation such that the very project of defining and defending a sublime, or many (types of) sublimes, much less *the* sublime, is hampered by the limitations of prose expression; the semantics of a given language—right down to its workaday adjectives and adverbs—shape what is possible for picturing the event or processing the emotion. The thinker or theorist who attempts a portrait of the term (in one or more of its incarnations—in oil paint, in poetic allusion) risks coming up short, since the objects of one's investigations—necessarily—lie just beyond discernment. Given these admittedly unfavorable conditions for the thinking of and thinking out of the sublime, we revisit questions that will recur. If and how the phenomenon of war is, in fact, sublime: When? To whom? Under what terms and conditions?

War proposes itself as a candidate for the sublime in so far as it (again, necessarily) exceeds total comprehension and in many cases even partial understanding. By extension, filmmakers' attempts to represent these manifold and overfull phenomena on film—muscular efforts to confront the terrible fact (and facts) of war by capturing and creating new conditions for thinking about the elusiveness of what has been perceived—are themselves (necessarily) limited by the frame, strip, and digital pixel array; the lens type, editorial cut, and techniques of *syuzhet*. Every empirical instance of a war film feels destined to fall short of any such target as maximal comprehension, offering instead merely one of among an indefinite number of prismatic takes on an infinitely complex and irresolvable crisis. Even as such phenomena will exceed the historian's and the artist's gifted renderings, and in turn the theorist's *conceptual* framing, there is yet reason to reserve space for the human experience of the sublime—perhaps revised here to always include a provision about its perspectival qualities, its inherent limitations, its incapacity to fulfill its mission. In these respects, claiming that "war is sublime" is both apodictic and tautological; it is not a claim that stands in need of explanation. Rather, the lapses and lacunae that emerge in the transfer (and transformation) from event to representation are taken for granted, are understood and accepted as part of the compromised art of articulating the ineffable.

Several of Herzog's most celebrated films were made in the midst of wars (*Fitzcarraldo*, for instance), some invoke war's ineluctable presence in our lives (*Fata Morgana*), and some are explicitly "war films," such as *Little Dieter Needs to Fly* (a documentary about Dieter Dengler), *Rescue Dawn* (a narrative feature version of Dengler's story), and *Lessons of Darkness* (a documentary ostensibly about the aftermath of Persian Gulf War). In the context of these war films, so called, Herzog's notion of ecstatic truth reveals the new (or disavowed) kind of sublime we have been tracking: not the romantic, transcendental, tragic, apocalyptic, ironic, hysterical, or abstract sublime, as so many others have theorized, but instead, the humanistic sublime. If war films translate phenomena that exceed comprehension (and in many cases cause forms of post-traumatic stress disorder, hysteria, and madness); and if war is so complex that it leaves us, as Fredric Jameson notes, with the "suspicion that war is unrepresentable,"[58] then it would be advantageous to define and inherit a concept that directs us to the things—thoughts, images, ideas—war films, in fact, represent or make possible (because of those representations). A partial achievement is still an achievement.

In the case of Herzog's war films, we are given a chance to recognize our own anxiety about, or aspirations for, filmic representation: what do we suppose a director can *do* with his camera and cinematic cut to deliver the sublime on screen? Herzog appears to sidestep the question (a fitting foot-sure gesture) as he propounds a theoretical valence by which to experience his films. Face to face with an unintelligible phenomenon, such as war, ecstatic truth becomes preeminently significant, since it emerges at precisely the point where factual representation (that which corresponds to reality, or aligns with evidence, what Herzog calls the "accountant's truth") accedes to a representation that goes beyond the given: where truth is revealed through invention and fabrication, through lies and dissimulation. Importantly, given that he is arguably most famous for making documentaries, Herzog himself qualifies his own documentary approach by eschewing its nearness to ethnography: "A film like *Wodaabe* [*Herdsmen of the Sun* (1989)] can't seriously be considered ethnographic because it's stylized to such an extent that the audience is taken into the realm of the ecstatic," he cautions.[59] The ecstatic truth emerges, then, not from facts per se but rather from their selection, arrangement, and distortion (in so some cases, arrangement is a form of distortion, as with inventive plot sequencing). This kind of truth subverts a familiar, which is to say, ingrained wish or expectation that facts correspond to or constitute reality (usually understood as outer, empirical, observable reality) and instead awakens an experience of an *inner* reality (a properly Romantic-era appeal to the constitutive powers of consciousness). Hence the intimate and consecutive relationship between the representation of ecstatic truth and the achievement of a humanistic sublime—a sublime that is unapologetically a function of the human perception of its reality in all its limitedness and situatedness. War, like other extreme conditions, natural or otherwise, is a greater or grosser condition for the humanistic sublime; its scope and complexity reinforcing human incomprehension and thus eliciting the need for a concept sufficient to the task of description. The humanistic sublime, in retrospect, appears to be a notion in search of a worthy object—and war, in all its variety and terribleness, would seem to demand a concept subtle enough to capture its measures of gravity and grace, of depredation and heroic vigor.

For those who don't "see combat," the Herzogian innovation and implementation of ecstatic truth may become an ally (and useful proxy) for experiencing just this kind of profound — and distinctly human — sublimity.

If it were possible, the color-field painter Barnett Newman would likely be enlisted by Herzog for an iteration of the Rogue Film School, such was Newman's unchecked disdain for theory — even as, or perhaps because, he was a student of philosophy at the City College of New York. "Aesthetics is for the artists as ornithology is for the birds," said the "witty and truculent" Newman, whose moody insights are apprehended in his still-vital "The Sublime is Now."[60] Like Herzog, Newman theorizes competently in spite of himself:

> The invention of beauty by the Greeks, that is, their postulate of beauty as an ideal, has been the bugbear of European art and European aesthetic philosophies. Man's natural desire in the arts to express his relation to the Absolute became identified and confused with absolutisms of perfect creations — with the fetish of quality — so that the European artist has been continually involved in the moral struggle between notions of beauty and the desire for sublimity.[61]

An imaginary being invoked to frighten, a cause of obsessive fear and loathing, such is the bugbear — kin to Herzog's *ursus arctos horribilis*. Emerging from such a grizzly maze of cognitive conceptions (and deceptions), Newman strikes out to help us reset our relationship to the sublime. Among other examples, *Vir Heroicus Sublimis* (1950-51), "Man, heroic and sublime" comes to mind — with its five narrow so-called "zips" that vertically interrupt the massive red color field. In his encounter with the painting, J. M. Bernstein provides some crucial orientation: "To say that sensuous immediacy is capable of holding our attention, of engaging the embodied eye, of so suggesting meaning, is equivalent to saying that meaning does not unconditionally derive from intention, will, or desire — the mental, or, what this is sometimes taken as equivalent to, established conventions — and that it resides in the material/natural too."[62] It is gratifying to hear Bernstein suggest (even if he takes it back just as quickly) that "Newman can appear as almost a conceptual artist—although he never is."⁶³ Herzog occasionally prompts a similar conjecture, one that takes us back to questions of his "style" as a filmmaker, since the ideas Herzog adopts or importunes survive the films he makes— as if the films are serial (and fleeting) attempts to illustrate durable (if elusive) concepts. "Pulling a ship over a mountain" admittedly serves as a pithy plot synopsis for *Fitzcarraldo*, but it also feels capacious enough to embody an entire ethos—call it "Man, heroic and sublime."

In his quick history, Newman freely shares his contempt for the lineage starting with Longinus and stretching through Kant, Hegel, and Burke. Newman contends that the "impulse of modern art" was a "desire to destroy beauty."⁶⁴

> In other words, modern art, caught without a sublime content, was incapable of creating a new sublime image and, unable to move away from the Renaissance imagery of figures and objects except by distortion or by denying it completely for an empty world of geometric formalisms—a *pure* rhetoric of abstract mathematical relationships—became enmeshed in a struggle over the nature of beauty: whether beauty was in nature or could be found without nature.⁶⁵

Newman's solution to the bifurcation was to insist that in America, circa 1948, "free from the weight of European culture," artists like him were finding an answer "by completely denying that art has any concern with the problem of beauty and where to find it."⁶⁶ Such strident obstinacy feels familiar, though the wager is more cavalier than any Herzog would be willing to place. Even so, and sounding like an Emersonian circa 1848, Newman and his ilk haven't given up: "We are reasserting man's natural desire for the exalted, for a concern with our relationship to the absolute emotions. We do not need the obsolete props of an outmoded and antiquated legend. We are creating images whose reality is self-evident and which are devoid of the props and crutches that evoke associations with outmoded images, both sublime and beautiful."⁶⁷ Newman, like Herzog, is seeking and creating new images, demanding them for our own good. Yet

Herzog remains very much an artist in a Renaissance tradition: aware of archetypes and eager to respond to them by making impressions of his own. Herzog is no aesthetic anarchist, but rather an archivist of our dreams and fascinations—a visionary bent on using the film screen as a membrane through which we make contact with the exalted (even if, more than occasionally, we find it in company with the delirious and downtrodden, those suffering from extreme thoughts and severe conditions).

Since Herzog regularly grants himself license to depart from the actual, literal, or real elements of the experience of war—say by treating Dengler's first-person account of what happened to him as an occasion to plant or reformulate biographical "evidence" as well as to reconceive historical records and on-the-ground resources—he is able to better express the *human* factor in war, to reveal what he calls our "inner landscapes."[68] By abstracting or poetizing the individual's experience, and for that matter the war's narrative in general, Herzog reaches for something at once "far higher and far inward," beyond the limits, namely, a work of art that in his words "intensifies" and "elevates" the human.[69] In these ways, the pursuit of the ecstatic truth—going beyond the facts of an individual's human experience and of collective or agreed upon historical records—serves humanity by convening conditions favorable to a higher perception of itself, indeed, as Kant suggests, to a recognition of human dignity. In Kant's view, "Man's dignity is the ground of the judgment that man himself is sublime."[70]

While Herzog has been criticized, for the most part playfully, for his creative interventions in the sometimes journalistically hallowed territory of documentaries, including those with war as a subject—even as one might add justifiable concern for a troubling slippage, or even equivocation, between ecstatic truth and the Trump era's post-truth/alternative facts rendition of reality—there is reason to believe that his instinct to subvert fact in favor of fantasy and dreams might, paradoxically, be an advantageous way to represent *further* realities of war. The dividend is nothing other than a moment of contact with the humanistic sublime—not something we commonly expect in run-of-the-mill genre representations of war (reliant as they often are on a down-to-the-buttons accuracy) nor from the bloodless CGI blizzards of various comic-book-based intellectual properties. As a result of

Herzog's wily fabrications and canny inventions, we seldom end up with overworked clichés, much less maudlin morals, but rather with rarer emotional and cognitive responses that take us well beyond scenes of battle and their recycled cacophony of harrowing effects. Having been told lies, as it were, having let a war story become a science-fiction story—a dream or a mythical tale from some alien planet in which these forms of life once did battle with one another, in which this is how it looked and this is what the humans tried (and failed) to say to one another before they perished—there is an unsettling sense that we are in a better place to speak of the *truth* of war: that it is a truth that exceeds direct representation. It is a truth, in the wake of Herzog's war films, that appears both profoundly sublime and ineluctably human.

Presented with a film such as *Fitzcarraldo*, one would think Herzog's natural métier is the romantic sublime, but then that was not a story about a man's contemplation of nature (in its terrifying remoteness) but rather his engagement with it, in it, knee-deep in the mud. Les Blank and Maureen Gosling's enduring documentary *Burden of Dreams* (1982) even more surely returns us to the space of a different sublime—a romantic redux in which our fearless director isn't in awe of nature, but, paralleling his title character, aims to encounter and overcome it—to literally pull a ship over a jungle-laden mountain. Even so, some scholars have selected yet another sublime to describe Herzog's work: Alan Singer argues for an ironic sublime, despite Herzog's apparently genuine claim that he is incapable of understanding irony.[71] Depending on definitions, filaments of the romantic and ironic sublime could yet underwrite how Herzog's work—by and large, and in particular instances—creates the cinematic conditions for an experience of the humanistic sublime. Herzog himself has theorized—though he would resist the suggestion that he is theorizing (as he does just below)—that the prime impulse and main achievement of his work entails a search for ecstatic truth. (We ask, as Emerson does, "Is not the sublime felt in an analysis as well as in a creation?")[72] Like the humanistic sublime, ecstatic truth is a compact concept that needs elaborate—and despite its notoriety, seemingly perpetual—glossing. In a speech entitled "On the Absolute, the Sublime, and Ecstatic Truth," Herzog describes the term this way:

> The reason is simple and comes not from theoretical, but rather from practical,

> considerations. With this quotation [viz., the epigraph of *Lessons of Darkness* featuring counterfeit lines by Pascal] as a prefix I elevate [*erheben*] the spectator, before he has even seen the first frame, to a high level, from which to enter the film. And I, the author of the film, do not let him descend from this height until it is over. Only in this state of sublimity [*Erhabenheit*] does something deeper become possible, a kind of truth that is the enemy of the merely factual. Ecstatic truth, I call it.[73]

Herzog's effort to prepare his audience by "elevating" its point of entry into the film is itself an expression of the customary ways of speaking about ecstasy.[74] Etymologically, *ekstasis* means "to take out or remove [*ek*] from the regular position or standing [*stasis*]" and bring into a different state (say, rapture) beyond ordinary perception. More figuratively, *ekstasis* can be understood as "bewilderment" and "amazement"; "distraction or disturbance of mind caused by shock"; "displacement or derangement of the mind."

Etymology elucidates yet another affiliation between the ecstatic and a term that launched these studies, namely, paradox. Workaday definitions of paradox suggest a "statement that contradicts itself," while oxymoron arrives as a commentary on two terms that are contradictory; both definitions promote *contradiction* as the central (logical or philosophical) offense; conceptual dissolution appears to be caused by the very act of conjugation (e.g., the "humanistic" and the "sublime" on their own are stable, but when grammatically fused the interaction proves logically fatal). Even so, the Greek language encodes a redemptive philosophical lesson, since we are told that a paradox can take us "out of" our common ways of thinking. The prefix *para* ["beyond" or "outside"] is added to the root of the infinitive verb *dokein* ["to think"] to form *paradoxos*, which can be translated as "contrary to expectation"—rather than simply wrong (or contradictory). Latin later adapted the term as *paradoxum*, which emerged in English in the sixteenth century as paradox. Weiskel's appeal to oxymoron (rather than paradox) may have exceeded such etymologically-derived evidence—since the Greek denotes "keenly foolish" or "pointedly stupid" [*oxymōros*] instead of the more circumspect, "out of phase with preexisting ideas" or "contrary to expectation" [*paradoxos*]. Neither of the Greek origins bespeak contradiction as singular attribute (there are other ways to be foolish than through contradiction—a Latin compound that means "speak against" [*contra* + *dicere*] or "assert the contrary"). When looking to a tandem phrase such as the "humanistic sublime," a scholar of Romanticism could pick up on a tension or opposition between conflicting forces or ideas and yet not conclude the two words placed together are logically self-cancelling. Looking back at the opening salvo, had Weiskel claimed instead "the humanistic sublime is a paradox" (in the sense just mentioned) productive reciprocities of the preexisting Herzogian lexicon would have been much more readily forthcoming. The "humanistic sublime" would then join "ecstatic truth" (and "accountant's truth") in a library of pairings that cause a perpetually productive intellectual and affective frisson. An etymological investigation in the spirit of Herzog's quest, as conducted here, takes an accusation of paradox or oxymoron as an invitation to further dialogue—not as a rationale for its cessation.

Quite pertinent for our ongoing exploration with Herzog, etymologically and otherwise, *ekstasis* also involves entering into a trance; (additionally, the word can be defined, as Wieskel does, as "transport," which makes it an uncanny conceptual sibling to the Greek meaning of metaphor [*metapherein*], "transfer"). In an all too compelling contingency, Herzog speaks of his long-standing fascination with hypnotism—especially the nature of human cognitive experience and physicality when a person is under a trance—transferred, as it were, to another plane of relation to oneself and the world one inhabits. Testing his amateur avocation in the field, he had all the actors in *Heart of Glass* (1976) act while under hypnosis. But Herzog's abiding interest in the technique, which he has himself emphasized as fundamental to his cinematic experimentation, is, he insists, not theoretical but practical. While appeals to the sublime can seem highfalutin, fact is, Herzog appears committed to the connection between the pedestrian and the out-of-the-ordinary. Yet, as should be expected, the path from here to there will require some detours—footsteps taken, as well as flights of fancy.

The varieties of ecstasy as seen in Herzog's films—induced through meditative shots and complementary editing; haunting and evocative music (early on with his frequent collaborators Popol Vuh and more recently and memorably with Ernst

Reijseger)[75]; bravura physical and somatic techniques, including athletic trials (e.g., in *The Great Ecstasy of the Woodcarver Steiner*, 1974)—are meant to create access to domains of truth otherwise inaccessible to us. By contrast, the "accountant's truth" is prevalent and ubiquitous, and it summarily reinforces a strict, we could add, common sense, faith in the alignment of fact with observable reality—what philosophers regularly call a correspondence theory of truth. Indeed, even as admonishments about the threat of fake news and alternative facts proliferate, the *blasé* cast of these storms of misinformation give them little to no purchase on the revelation of sublime insights; sustaining and honoring Herzog's own lexical innovations, the proper name for fake news and its ilk is not ecstatic truth but instead *the accountant's lie*.

Ecstatic truth is, by contrast, a truth that emerges from fabrication, conflicting accounts, obscurity, and coming up short. And it is exactly this kind of truth, in manifold varieties, that we find in a humanistic sublime. The continual pressure to exceed the human, as for example, in a ski-jumper (even as one wants to revise the term to the sobriquet sky-jumper), Steiner's radical, literal, elevation beyond the normal plane of existence, is transformed into the promise of a rare moment of contact not with the ethereal heavens, but with the earth itself, when he returns safely to the slope. When Steiner leaves *terra firma* we witness aerial moments of terrestrial disconnection, albeit brief durations of tremendous mental concentration and physical exertion on his part. A leap into another territory of existence, sure, even into an *ex/*istence fit for *ex/*stasy—living, if for a few seconds, beyond his own, our own collective, *familiar* humanness. Like Dieter Dengler, Steiner needed to fly. Elevated to this (higher) degree, Steiner has—in fitting Herzogian fashion, literally and figuratively—transcended the human *while remaining human*; from this exceptional height, in which he has made an exception of himself, his humanness is not diminished but rather intensified—placed as he is at the very threshold of destruction. After all, our view of Steiner aloft, and his view of us down below, may be the last such shared vision; when Herzog films him in flight, Steiner—like an astronaut still under the sway of gravity—experiences a radical, hovering last moment of human awareness before returning to planet earth, while we study in slow motion the subtlest gestures of muscle and mind that may bring him back to us in one piece.

This moment of disruption in the continuity of everyday, accountant's-truth-based human life creates conditions for perceiving an ecstatic truth (his and ours, or ours because of his); in this glimpse, we can reclaim more intensely, more attentively, the facts and features of human dimensionality (gravity, finitude, perceptual and conceptual limits). Unlike a romantic sublime (of a Teutonic sort) that "concerns power and sets man and nature in desperate opposition," what appears to be a suitably Herzogian humanistic sublime makes nature (or Nature) a *facilitator* of the human perception of ecstatic truth.[76] Without the grandeur of nature—especially of its inherent extremes, conditions often hazardous to fleshy, mortal creatures—humans would be less able to comprehend their circumstances, states of consciousness, and modes of revelation. Admittedly, at times Herzog's humanistic sublime may court affinity with a nineteenth-century *English* romantic sublime "in which nature is not merely thrown over but appears as the medium through which the mind discovers and presents itself, in eddies of separation and reunion"—much as we see in Steiner's departure from earth and his eventual, successful return.[77] The proximity to Herzog's erstwhile experiments with Steiner (on the slopes and in the editing bay) are palpable, and yet Herzog would resist employing nature for merely instrumental purposes—even if for the heightening of human consciousness; he prefers to focus instead on the human situation *within* a natural context. Whether nature is agent or accomplice, medium or substrate, and what those differences portends, remains open. Nature, whether it is figured as the densely verdant Perúvian jungle or the bleached vastness of Antarctica, is secondary to man's scenario—even so, tautologically speaking, humans are themselves natural phenomena. The question, then, is how to come to consciousness of our humanness when lost or otherwise indistinguishable from our natural environment—an environment that claims us well before we have any awareness of its existence. Though frigid winds howl on the other side of the one-hundred denier thick tent in *Encounters at the End of the World* (2007), or for that matter, *Grizzly Man* (2005), Herzog's primary focus is not outward conditions but "inner landscapes"—the emotional, intellectual, moral, aesthetic, and psychological terrain of the remote human explorers. At such apocalyptic moments, we perceive the glacier within.

Herzog, unlike most of his cinematic contemporaries, has not become immune to the allure of the sublime—treating it, as they often do, only with ironic detachment and modern condescension as a "moribund aesthetic."[78] But, almost as a traveler from antiquity, Herzog has retained "the obsession, so fundamental to the Romantic sublime, with natural infinitude."[79] As part of his inheritance, and *transformation*, of this tradition—reaching as he does to Longinus, Kant, and other thinkers of the sublime—Herzog pushes the notion into a modern medium, cinema, and finds in this novel form a way of relating man to nature that other modes of representation (from novel to verse, from effigy to fresco) express differently. As a visual space of moving (in at least two senses of the word) representations—often with diegetic sound, score, and voice embedded—the cinema screen suggests an alternate reality: conditions ready-made for perceptions of another "world" before us (brute reality as a phantasm) or within us (a dream, or nightmare, as an otherwise until now undisclosed reality).[80] The war in nature is already apparent in our own interiors, still we need visionaries to show us—to summon us—to the stakes of such revelations.

4. POW / POV

IF HERZOG REPRESENTS the humanistic sublime for the characters or subjects in his films (either as part of their experience retold in a documentary mode, however manipulated; or, by means of dramatic reenactment)[81]—it is a question in itself whether he succeeds at this conjuring. Yet, we seek to add a further valence to the postulation: to ask and reply to the question whether, as intimated, those ever-so-Herzogy cinematic representations stimulate an experience of the humanistic sublime in his viewers. Hence, the prospect of the sublime on screen and the sublime within—a distinction without a difference? Or must we stop short, cautious that the humanistic sublime is a vantage only a prisoner of war, a soldier in combat, or some similarly threatened figure can occupy? Even so, might film—select Herzog films in particular, or especially his war films—create the conditions for viewers to perceive an encounter with the absolute, existential limits, and the sort of ecstatic truth Herzog claims such cinematic works will or should avail? Though we look to films that announce their alliance across the regions of documentary and drama, first-person testament and fictionalized narrative, the interaction between them leaves open the extent to which Herzog's pursuit of ecstatic truth may yield a perception of the humanistic sublime very far from the site and sight of war. From *Wings of Hope* to *Into the Abyss*, we don't have to strain to identify candidates who modify the appeal to war as subject. War may be especially proficient at activating the humanistic sublime in us, but its representation via ecstatic truth suggests the Herzogian library of the humanistic sublime may be very extensive—reaching well beyond any prerequisite for war and its vital conflicts.

Herzog's documentary *Little Dieter Needs to Fly* participates in a sturdy subgenre of war films defined, in part, by the protagonist's status as a prisoner of war: if in captivity also preoccupied with escaping it. Most of the many well-known representative examples of the subgenre are feature dramas—*Grand Illusion* (1937), *Bridge on the River Kwai* (1957), *The Great Escape* (1963), *King Rat* (1965), *The Dirty Dozen* (1967), *The Deer Hunter* (1978), and more recently, *Hart's War* (2002), *Defiance* (2008), and *The Way Back* (2010); and for narrative similarity, though not war content, one also thinks of *Cool Hand Luke* (1967), *Papillon* (1973), *Escape from Alcatraz* (1979), and *The Shawshank Redemption* (1994). But *Little Dieter* is (again, ostensibly) a documentary, and since Dieter Dengler is its subject, the viewer already knows he survived his ordeal: the drama of the film, therefore, will be how he survived and, perhaps—as we meet him in late maturity—how he has weathered the effects of being, since liberation, a former POW. Almost a decade after *Little Dieter*, and five years after Dengler's death, Herzog staged a narrative feature, *Rescue Dawn*, starring Christian Bale as the Vietnam-era Navy pilot who was shot down over Laos. The relationship between these two films is complicated, and complicating, since Herzog sees them as coextensive: not separately as a documentary and a feature, but as two dramatizations of a unified narrative told by Dengler. Herzog says: "We were very careful in the reenactment and stylization of Dieter's reality. He had to become an actor who is performing himself."[82] For Herzog, the camera doesn't bear witness to Dengler's story but rather contributes to its fabrication. Herzog explains:

> When we made *Little Dieter*, it was very clear to me that we were making a fiction

film. But from the moment we realized that it would take so long to find the money and the actors, we decided to make a documentary, but a documentary that was both staged and stylized, with invented moments, but without touching the heart of the story. So the documentary came first, and then the fiction film *Rescue Dawn*. But in my mind, just like in the mind of Dieter Dengler, *Little Dieter* was always a fiction film. [. . .] In simple words, I could say that the documentary is a remake of the fiction film but, of course, neither is a remake of the other because they're so different. And yet they complement each other very well.[83]

Though *Little Dieter* would have to be a remake of *Rescue Dawn avant la lettre*, Herzog spares no (traditional) film theorist's feelings by pointing up the customary, one might say naïve, notion that documentary filmmaking is "more true" than fictitious narrative; or even more troublingly, that documentary filmmaking, by virtue of its form or the intention of its creators, (somehow) provides unmediated access to the otherwise obfuscated and unknown (despite the medium at hand). A couple of years after *Little Dieter*, Herzog stated in his "Minnesota Declaration"—a kind of send-up of Lars von Trier's "Dogme 95" creed—that "*Cinéma Vérité* is devoid of *vérité*."[84] So truth is on Herzog's mind—in this pair of films, as elsewhere in his work—just not the kind of truth commonly associated with *cinéma vérité*: namely, a kind of revelation of reality-as-it-is, a disclosure of true but otherwise concealed things. Herzog's truth in *Little Dieter* and *Rescue Dawn* is ecstatic. It is not, as he says, "the truth of accountants," but a collaboratively discovered mode of cinematic storytelling.[85] One doesn't point a camera in a certain direction to get a true picture of things; rather, one shoots in the direction of one's interests—pursues obstacles, finds paths that prove false, collects footage without knowing if or how it will matter—and later, often well after the moment of encounter, in editing, a director discerns lines of (often surprising) connection and congruity. These are the assemblages that are more than the sum of parts; as such, they do not generate the truth of a referential realist, but a truth that emerges from within the film itself, achieves expression on screen, and lastly in relation to the interiority of its viewers. We are many degrees removed from the fateful immediacy of Dieter in his wartime jungle prison.

What is perhaps most illuminating about *Rescue Dawn* as a cinematic object is its relationship to narrative invention and storytelling compared with its predecessor, *Little Dieter Needs to Fly*. The two films offer a clinic in different ways of telling "the same" story. Or rather, as Herzog has noted, the distinguishable approaches are complementary, and, one might add, mutually reinforcing. The constitutive elements of both films—montage and music, plotting and pacing, diegesis (as narration) and mimesis (as reanimation)—are variously, sometimes conversely, represented in the two works. Consider how *Rescue Dawn* begins with the same documentary aerial footage featured at the start of *Little Dieter Needs to Fly* (an archival sequence of napalm being dropped from airplanes onto Southeast Asian villages). Yet this found-footage framing device comes to different effect when it is followed by after-the-fact "documentary" coverage of a man, Dieter, who participated in such a campaign, especially when compared to a dramatic visualization of a man training *before* the fact (as is the case with Christian Bale's Dieter in *Rescue Dawn*). Both presentations of archival footage are offered without diegetic sound and are set to music. As such, the graphic footage anticipates and contextualizes the personal story to follow: this, we will learn, is a story of a boy who was bombed and who grows up to find himself bombing others. As Dwayne (Steve Zahn) says after hearing Dieter's story about how he "needed to fly" upon seeing a pilot eye-to-eye while the latter laid waste to his beloved Bavarian town: "A guy tries to kill you and you want his job."[86]

The structure of the two films, among other things, highlights the nature of point of view (POV). In *Little Dieter*, we are meant to see and hear Dengler's experience narrated first-hand and reenacted by the man who underwent the trials he describes; in *Rescue Dawn*, without the presence of the historical Dieter Dengler (the realist referent of the action), the narrative takes on a more familiar chronological progression as well as a group portrait (since Dengler is shown, first, in the company of his fellow Navy comrades, and then, in captivity with fellow American prisoners of war). Where the audience is addressed directly in *Little Dieter* (by Dengler), those same stories are consolidated in *Rescue Dawn* for the purposes of a dramatic representation by professional actors—with exposition revealed mainly through conversations between characters. Despite the shift in perspective (or POV), when the two films are taken as a tandem—as a pair of complementary and continuous works—we discover how their temporalities proceed first through documentary measures and then by way of fictional re-creation. In *Little Dieter*, the story begins with a sixty-seven-year-old and ends—hours later—in *Rescue Dawn* with Dieter on board the aircraft carrier, at the very beginning of his liberation. *Little Dieter*, structurally, possesses three basic segments: (1) documentary footage of Dengler in his then present-day life in California, that is, living the life of a liberated survivor; (2) Dengler retelling, recollecting, and recounting his experiences years earlier as a POW in Laos; and (3) Dengler returning—again, in his present-day, post-liberation state—to the site of his capture and incarceration: going so far in his embodied repetition that he reenacts the conditions and torments he suffered, including (pantomimed) torture. In *Rescue Dawn*—after the initial footage of aerial bombing (a sort of audiovisual overture that links the documentary and the feature)—familiar narrative conventions take over and the film moves chronologically from Dengler as a child, to him entering the Navy, being shot down, taken prisoner, escaping, and finally being rescued. Approached together, *Little Dieter* and *Rescue Dawn* illuminate aspects of each other, including how Herzog's multi-perspective, multi-genre experiment succeeds in providing a rare cinematic composite.

Where in *Little Dieter* we see a military training video presented with Herzog's sardonic voiceover (in a mode of narration as moral re-evaluation), in *Rescue Dawn* the documentary voice-from-above is replaced with Spook's (Toby Huss) sarcastic diegetic commentary created *in media res*, without the benefit of hindsight. When scenes in *Little Dieter*—such as when Dengler on the site of his former imprisonment reenacts making a fire, describes in detail how he was tortured, or shares techniques for opening rudimentary handcuffs—are played beside scenes in *Rescue Dawn*, where these same narrated and reenacted elements are dramatized, we can more easily perceive the modes and effects of narrative invention. One almost understands this contrast as a proper gloss on the meaning of the filmic proviso "Inspired by True Events in the Life of Dieter Dengler." Herzog "breathes life" [Lat. *spirare*] into the story, animating the events, which are said to have happened—to be true. All events in a life, after this fashion, are true, since whatever happens is, in this sense, true. Yet it is our *telling* about them that "gives them breath." If they are "untold" events, they would seem to lapse as readily as one's fallable, ever-fading memories. In the manner of propulsive invention, by contrast, we discover a new reality, a new perspective on events (and the facts that given them shape). Facts that are "inspired," Herzog invites us to recall, are not the facts as we have experienced them. The *inspired* fact—a fact that is a hybrid or mutation with fabrication—is the kind of fact we should hope to accompany us to a different kind of experience: not of the truth, but of ecstatic truth.

War, for Herzog, is intimately bound up with questions of orientation and disorientation—hence the crucial role that POV plays in framing Herzog's subjects (in documentary work) or characters (in dramatic work). Casting a glance across decades worth of Herzog's films, we note how he is neither preoccupied with the romantic lives of his subjects and characters nor with their personal identities, but with something more like the relationship between a man and his knowledge of where he is or belongs (often in the context of forbidding natural contexts: jungles, volcanoes, ice sheets, oceans, deserts—and sometimes, in cities, with computers, in the convoluted context of contemporary societies). This existential outlook reveals itself in the interaction between the imprisoned Eugene's (Jeremy Davies) embroidery on the back of his tattered shirt that asks *Quo Vadis* and later, after a successful escape, the deliriously-free Eugene pleading response to the demand: "You tell me where to go. You tell me where to go," asking his fellow man rhetorically, if desperately: "Where am I going to go? Where am I going to go?"[87] Similarly, soon after Dengler arrives in the prison camp and starts planning his escape, Dwayne points out something obvious but unseen: "The jungle is the prison. Don't you get that?"[88] War among men, we appear always to forget, is *also* always a war with(in) nature—with its particular forces of menace and imposed disorientation, of overwhelming scale and might. One may survive the bullet only to be eaten by the bear.

5. Illumination from Darkness

THE QUESTION OF ORIENTATION arises early in *Lessons of Darkness* (1992), where in Herzog's self-authored voiceover we hear: "The men appear to be trying to communicate with one another. Offering signals." After a close study of *Little Dieter* and *Rescue Dawn*, however, we can appreciate how *Lessons of Darkness* offers yet another approach to the relationship between man and nature during war, namely, through the conceit of science-fiction. There are no soldiers in *Lessons of Darkness*, though we hear stories about them and what they have done (e.g., testimonials about the tortures carried out by Iraqi soldiers). No battles are waged, unless the attempt to quell oil fires is a kind of battle; and even then, out of boredom or perversity, the oil wells are relit so the "battle" to extinguish them might continue. No injuries are inflicted on camera, and no deaths are shown. But above all—there is no protagonist. The film is largely comprised of long takes of landscapes: with ground-level views of men at work in oil fields ablaze and with aerial shots (which Herzog achieved by hiring a daring helicopter pilot) of the cityscape and surrounding land (remote, desolate, forbidding). How does this series of images and sounds amount to a representation of war? We are meant to believe that the city we see is one that existed in splendor before the war began, but we learn (from Herzog's subsequent confession) that the floating views of Kuwait City were filmed *after* the war ended. This is neither a city from before times, nor one reconstructed after a war, but a city that survived the onslaught. Such a deception (achieved through the redescription and recontextualization of documentary footage) gives us another occasion of Herzog's method of transforming facts to give up a truth that would not otherwise obtain—the kind of truth he calls ecstatic because it stands outside of, or beside, the given. Customarily we have a name for the kind of representation that is a redescription or fabrication: a lie. And yet, Herzog's filmic alterations are not aimed to deceive but to enlighten. Rather than propaganda in the service of persuasion (and the manipulation of power), Herzog lets the phantasm speak for itself, do its own work. Rather than misinformation, illumination.

In *Lessons of Darkness*, among other films, Herzog engenders epiphanic effects through the fictionalization of fact.

Though the images are themselves strictly documentary—in the sense that there *are* oil fields burning and men trying to snuff them out—the editorial construction of the film (including music and voiceover) undermines the apparent givenness of the action. Even the subjects of the documentary cannot be trusted to be speaking their own words, a violation of documentary conventions and "conventional realism" that Brigitte Peucker has pointed out: "As in *Fata Morgana* (1971) and *The Great Ecstasy of the Woodcarver Steiner* (1974), *Lessons in Darkness* [noting her variant translation of the title] features frontal shots of war victims delivering scripted poetic monologues, one of which voices the recurrent Herzog theme of the insufficiency of language."[89] That is, the war victims speak Herzog's scripted lines, not their own narration of private emotions and historical events. Furthermore, the added voiceover written and read by Herzog, along with the muted diegetic sound replaced with the presence of bold nondiegetic music by the likes of Richard Wagner, contributes to the chances that a viewer will be stimulated or provoked to have a view of things that are not there per se, and instead will be moved into a space defined by mirages, hypnosis, hallucinations, and dreams.

As Herzog doesn't conform to the visual and narrative conventions of traditional documentary practitioners, so too does his use of music depart from the standard supporting or even explanatory role. When he laid down tracks for *Wodaabe: Herdsmen of the Sun* (1989), he said the use of Bach/Gounod's *Ave Maria* "creates a strange ecstasy" and "using that aria means the film isn't a 'documentary' about a specific African tribe, rather a story about beauty and desire."[90] Herzog tells us: "The music helps carry us out of the realm of what I call the accountant's truth, and without that specific recording, the images of this amazing and bizarre male beauty contest wouldn't touch us as deeply"—which is to say the film as a work of art would not have found its connection to the human phenomenon that Herzog aimed to represent.[91] In *Lessons of Darkness*, the prominent use of music is similarly affecting—from Arvo Pärt's *Stabat Mater* to Gustav Mahler's *Symphony No. 2*, from Prokofiev, Schubert, and Verdi (*Messa da Requiem*) to a range of works by Wagner (*Das Rheingold*, *Parsifal*, and *Götterdämmerung*). These are not musical pieces that naturally—that is to say, historically or contextually—align with the oil fields of Kuwait. And yet, it is precisely that discontinuity — that sense of unnatural or cultural asymmetrical juxtaposition — that awakens an ecstatic apprehension of the unaltered, lens-based footage.

The perception of our inner landscapes through encounters with Herzog's films — especially, as it were, their representations of outer landscapes — reinforces, uncannily, how inner landscapes are necessarily human. The interaction of these two kinds of terrains, in Herzog's rendition of them, informs our understanding of war — how his films "about war" (however obliquely) do not stylize violence and destruction but instead poetize them. Watching these films — *Little Dieter*, *Rescue Dawn*, and *Lessons of Darkness* — doesn't feel voyeuristic, masochistic, or cathartic, but instead more like occasions for contemplation and insight. Cinema admits its sacred potential. Viewers don't feel punished or frightened by Herzog's war films so much as illuminated by them: as if words and images, music and voiceover addressed us at odd angles — not with direct, gruesome depictions but with sideways provocations that make inner human experiences (of fear, awe, panic, grief) differently available to us. "Has life without fire become unbearable for them?" Herzog asks in voiceover as the silent "creatures" relight squelched shoots of vertically jetting oil; in posing that question, he makes uncanny and unknowable what might be going on inside those distant figures.[92] What *are* they thinking? Not surprisingly, though, such questions revert to viewers, who must contend with their own inner landscapes — including the dialogue between concealment and disclosure, self-delusion and self-revelation. Herzog reminds us at such moments of contact that we too are in need of asking ourselves why we watch — or want to watch — these films, including war films? Part of our reply suggests that we want to *understand* something about the human experience of war in particular, and humanness more generally, that has remained inchoate and indecipherable. This will not be achieved by spectacle, but instead by seeing the spectacular elements of the anti-spectacle. Herzog's technique, or habit, of recontextualizing documentary footage by reordering it, applying nondiegetic sound, using fanciful intertitles ("The War," "A Pilgrimage," "The Drying Up of the Source," "I am so tired of sighing; Lord, let it be night")[93] and mock-serious voiceovers (courting religious profundity and science-fiction fantasy), are attributes he brings to war films from cinematic experiments across genres, many of them motivated by a quest to unsettle the logic of entertainment and truth. Given the evidence of his work in *Lessons of Darkness*, *Little Dieter*, and *Rescue Dawn*, Herzog's creative practice illustrates how war films may be particularly suited to the expression—and arousal—of ecstatic truth.

6. Is War Sublime?

KANT DEFINES THE "TERRIFYING SUBLIME" as that which induces or activates or otherwise "moves" us to feel fear—but *without danger*.[94] A firsthand experience of war, therefore, cannot be sublime but simply and straightforwardly terrifying. To survive war—to literally *live through* its mortifying terror and threat—cannot be a sublime fact for combatant or civilian noncombatant. No matter how much death a soldier or bystander sees, no matter how close he comes to his own extinction, surviving is not sublime because death is a genuine, even plausible, effect of martial engagement: one may have *approached* the brink of nonexistence and lived to say something (or remain silent) about it, but it was not a fabricated precipice, not a false encounter with the absolute. And so the reality of war's danger, on this view, denies its claim to the sublime. We may conclude, therefore, that war is not sublime while countering with the contention that war's *representation*—on film, among other places—can be sublime. Of course, many representations of war confuse matters as they suggest that war *is*, in fact, sublime—from Private Witt's apotheosis in the remote jungles of Guadalcanal in *The Thin Red Line* to Swofford's (Jake Gyllenhaal) apocalyptic oilfield phantasmagoria in *Jarhead* (2005, dir. Sam Mendes). But these are *depictions* of soldiers apprehending aesthetic impressions of war's conditions; these are sublime visions produced for viewers. The proxy structure is precisely why, for example, *we* may take Private Witt's experience in the jungle depicted in *The Thin Red Line* as sublime, and why he—or rather, some historical soldier situated in that combat zone—cannot: he is in mortal danger and we are safe spectators. The representation of war, even combat, *can* be sublime for viewers since we are brought up close, face-to-face, with the force and effect of war—the bullets, blood, pain, and hunger—and yet are physically left as we were found. What has changed, or may have changed, is our understanding of war (and we assume, of ourselves).

We have, in short, been "moved" (again, in Kant's parlance); we find that our feelings [*Gefühl*] for war have altered because of our intimacy with its representation on screen; Kant cites one's experience of tragedy as stirring the person—allowing him to be "gently moved"—to discern "the dignity of his own nature."[95] Herzog's harrowing—terrifying—depictions of escape from a POW camp in *Little Dieter* and *Rescue Dawn* engage Kant's "terrifying sublime" (for the viewer) since we see our emaciated escapees summiting the terrain only to confront a rangy expanse of "inescapable" jungle: this is a moment of awe and terror for the viewer, one that agitates an awareness of one's deepest *human* nature. The insight is possible in part because, in Burke's description, one has experienced something "analogous to terror."[96]

Still, there is something dubious in such an account, since it seems to miss or misrepresent what appears to be the *genuine* experience of a sublime that happens both for soldiers in combat (and prisoners of war) *as well as* those who look upon the representations of those experiences (as depicted on film, but also as conceived in literature—from the *Iliad* to *The Things They Carried*). We need, therefore, a way to correct such a misalignment, to speak about what the literal act of genuine danger (for soldiers) and the figurative acts of filmic representation (for viewers) stimulate. As war so often brings its combatants to the threshold of nonexistence, accomplished war films bring viewers to the (terrifying but not dangerous) point of contemplation of the humanistic sublime. For after all, it is the human encounter with its own limits—coming right up to the edge of ultimate and irredeemable erasure—that becomes the terrifying fact for the soldier. And the viewer could be said to participate in a (shared) recognition of this fact, even if via cinematic surrogate. The soldier lives a sort of perpetual death shudder, always aware that by the hand of another agent (usually another anonymous soldier, a manned craft, an unmanned drone dropping an explosive, or a strategically placed improvised explosive device), or some other contingency (including "friendly fire"), he might not return home. Viewers, in turn, become sensitive to this life-lived-at-the-limit. The emotional or cognitive effect of these states of mind—at times trancelike, at other points dreamlike—is a perception of the grave and fragile nature of human corporeality. In effect, war films remind viewers that there is no escape from the enemy, no way to dodge the bullet once it has been released. We are all, it turns out, victims of finitude—even before we succumb. When a war film becomes an allegory for mortal struggle as such—to love, to live, to survive—it activates a viewer's sense of the humanistic sublime.

By now, it is analytic to claim that Herzog frequently features nature prominently—that it is an essential context and in many cases, a figure fit to be its own outsized character. In the documentary *To the Limit and Then Beyond It*, Herzog aimed to set the record straight on this score: "Someone once called me a nature lover. Just because I'd filmed in the rainforest or desert. But ultimately this is completely wrong. Actually I think that nature is stupid and obscene."[97] The denigration—exaggerated to the point of comedic punchline—nevertheless, begs the question, since no matter how "stupid and obscene" nature may be that very indifference (compounded by its far-reaching power) makes it all the more essential to human experience, shaping consciousness and thus perception from one moment to the next. In his war films, despite his dismissiveness, the presence of nature is highlighted almost as a third aspect of war (two enemies at odds . . . and nature—variously for or against these warring parties, aiding or obstructing them as the case may be). Nature conceals the soldier from the enemy (camouflages him) but may as easily leave him stranded and starving—exposed to the elements or the crosshairs of enemy scopes. And yet even with a sharpened focus on nature's presence in human affairs, particularly during wartime, Herzog's war films present the sublime as a feature of human life and a confirmation of human dignity, especially as such human attributes are heightened—made newly explicit and affectively suasive—in relation with or in opposition to nature.

To make these claims about the meaning and relevance of ecstatic truth more concrete, consider Herzog's contempt for the blasé sentimentalism and generic pathos common to so many accounts of nature. In *Conquest of the Useless*, Herzog's journal from the making of *Fitzcarraldo*, he writes at odds with any inherited and unqualified acclamation for nature and its ways: "In its all-encompassing, massive misery, of which it has no knowledge and no hint of a notion, the mighty jungle stood completely still for another night, which, however, true to its innermost nature, it did not let pass unused for incredible destruction, incredible strangulation."[98] He conveyed a similar sentiment in an eloquent but apparently off-the-cuff soliloquy about the jungle featured in *Burden of Dreams*: "Nature here is vile and base. I wouldn't see anything erotical here. I would see fornication and asphyxiation and choking and fight for survival and growing and just rotting way. [. . .] Taking a close look at—at what's around us there—there is some sort of a harmony. It is the harmony of overwhelming and collective murder. And we in comparison to the articulate vileness and baseness and obscenity of all this jungle. [. . .] We have to get acquainted to this idea that there is no real harmony as we have conceived it." Many years later in *Grizzly Man* (2005)—far from the Perúvian jungle, in the midst of an immense arctic wilderness—Herzog offered another counternarrative (this time presented in voiceover) about maintaining a strict anti-sentimental, anti-anthropomorphic relation to nature's forms and forces. Ratifying his earlier remarks, Herzog says the fundamental characteristic of the universe is not "harmony but chaos, hostility, and murder."[99] When Timothy Treadwell looks into the eyes of the grizzly, he sees a cuddly teddy bear, but Herzog sees only the animal's hunger and the prospect of a painful death.

And yet, while Herzog continually reminds us of, and remains adamant about, the depravity and indifference of nature, he also amplifies our propinquity to the strange fact of the human presence in nature. In *Cave of Forgotten Dreams* (2010) the revelation of a man's handprint—not a representation of a generic human hand, but an impression from a singular, crooked pinky finger—radically reinforces the particularity of this prehistoric person so much so that we are tempted to include him in human history. The man with the anomalous digit is not a remote, indiscernable, and anonymous ancient cave dweller, but comes alive in his singularity as a situated and individuated human consciousness. The handprint—a gesture familiar from a child's kindergarten art class to contemporary installation muralists—articulates his continuous relationship with our sustained instincts (the Latin roots of *articulus*, *articulare* as "small, connecting parts" and "joints," give proximal shape to portions of the human hand, phalanges in particular). Suddenly the dexterous Chauvet artist is not a transitional figure between animal and human but human in fact, a proto-Michelangelo. Such is the phenomenon of a phantom limn.

Like their cousins, etched petroglyphs, the cave paintings of horses, aurochs, mammoths, cave lions, leopards, bears, even rhinoceroses, near the handprint become their own signs of life—evidence of an ancient moment in which a mental image is translated into a picture. These artful human markings evince a desire—however untutored, however much before or beyond a "history of art"—to mix action with invention, to distill an unbounded natural immensity (whether it be beast or cosmos) into a convenient set of symbols and systems, codes and illustrative contours, to place action in context, to narrativize inner experience in relation to merely sequential outer events. The quest for such elegant concentrations of mark-making and meaning generation continues.

Herzog's notion of ecstatic truth, similarly, stands in continuous relationship with the humanistic sublime, insofar as the former appears revelatory of the latter. While the ecstatic truth is not something a soldier can access in the field of battle (since his first-person presence in combat is coextensive with immediate—factual and true—mortal danger), it may be that very scenario of proximity to death that prompts the soldier's apprehension of the humanistic sublime. But for the viewer who is not in real danger, who very often is being shown (mere) representations of temporally and spatially distant events—or outright fictions—film may serve as an agent of the humanistic sublime.

Even as protected voyeurs we are, in a sense, subjecting ourselves to the extremes of human experience. We go into combat by proxy—and though we walk out unharmed, we are not unmoved. The degree to which we are *moved*—in *feeling* and *understanding* in Kant's phrasing—registers the way the ecstatic truth transforms our encounter with cinematic representations; they do have an effect on us—not on the order of the soldier's wounds but as an invitation to fathom his humanity, and our own. In Kant, we find the crucial link between the ability to experience the sublime and the ability to fathom human dignity.[100] In effect, an apprehension of sublimity is a sign of one's aptitude for perceiving the worth of humans—generally and specifically. Paradoxically, then, an encounter with a nonhuman (or natural) landscape (whether it be in a jungle or from a vantage atop a mountain, amidst an immeasurable ocean surface or facing a blinding arctic sweep) may instigate a feeling of, or for, humanity. As W. H.

Auden tells us in *The Enchafèd Flood*, the sea—or "the great waters"—is "the symbol for the primordial undifferentiated flux, the substance which became created nature only by having form imposed upon it or wedded to it."[101] The combat zone as its human counterpart—an immense if wholly manmade condition that coalesces the extremes of human creation, gives them form, purpose, and sacral significance—may be similarly generative of such recognition and appraisal. Consequently, whether intentionally or not, Herzog's war films—and many of his other works of documentary and fiction—draw on the same structure and presumption: putting viewers in a position to experience the sublime by means of ecstatic truth *in order to* fathom the confounding strangeness of human existence (its expansiveness, finitude, isolation, and rare moments of insight)—and therefore its value, its demand for respect, its inherent dignity (against all odds).

The symbiotic connection between ecstatic truth and a perception of humanness (in its variability and peculiarity, its vulnerability and precariousness) is exactly why Herzog defiantly pursues the *manifestation of truth through fabrication*—instead of the presentation of truth through documentary pieces of evidence and the presentation of facts.[102] Herzog is a poet-filmmaker who falsifies in order to give us truths. What we garner from them, if anything, is a measure of our attunement to his films and our attraction to their lessons. By Herzog's special means and resolute faith in his methods, he "consciously muddle[s] that classic distinction between narrative and non-narrative form"[103]; he eschews the "accountant's truth" because it fails to deliver us face-to-face (as voyeurs, as adventurers, as rogues, as mortals) with the limits of experience—the very constraints that become the conditions for the revelation of the humanistic sublime.

7. Sincere, Not Cynical Images

SOME VIEWERS MAY TAKE HERZOG'S INVOCATION of ecstatic truth as part of some quasi-religious or pseudo-liturgical ambition (to say nothing of its embattled philosophical credentials— as a notion precariously situated in the vicinity of alternative facts). As Herzog's fame continues to dilate and his persona becomes more prominent and varied—especially in the form of voiceovers that can seem increasingly sententious—his work has become the subject of parody; as a result, speculation may rise whether *his own* work has become parodic (such that he has been taunting and mocking us all along). Because Herzog performs his own voiceovers, he is vulnerable to attack from those who would hear them as (merely) a mode of play—a ludic conspiracy against seriousness. Since empirical (or historical) Herzog and the filmic (or commodified) Herzog coalesce in the sound of his singular voice—with its particular tones, rhythms, accents, and diction—his work becomes subject to the criticism of cynical viewers.

Onlookers may wonder if Herzog is also satirizing religious experience. Is he pulling a stunt on a postmodern capitalist society, which appears to have no fixed commitments to divine reality—besides a faith in almighty currencies? Does he want us to buy into his films' profundity only to later declare he was joking—no such serious matters were at issue after all? Evidence from his oeuvre suggests otherwise. As early as *Fata Morgana* (1971), importantly in *Bells from the Deep: Faith and Superstition in Russia* (1993), and onward to the hypnotized actors of *Heart of Glass* (1976), Herzog has appeared engaged in serial attempts to, at the very least, represent—if not contrive outright—a kind of religious experience: where mirage or mysticism or hallucination gives rise to insight. (Of course, all the while fabricating the "documentary" material to suit the expression of ecstatic truth.)

The figure and sensibilities of Ludwig Wittgenstein percolate through these pages in so far as the Austrian philosopher and his nearby Bavarian neighbor at times recommend a kinship—in among other ways, experimenting with the status quo of their respective professions (for Wittgenstein, conducting a philosophical practice mainly through conversation and, when written, sustaining the presence of an interlocutor, or more than one, inscribing remarks as aphoristic nodes set in a matrix of inter-referential entries; for Herzog, mixing fabrication with fact, removing a distinction between dramatic art and documentary). Both have a proclivity for drawing serious things to the edge of silly, turning sincere investigations into games people play (however grave the consequences), gripped as they are by prevailing habits, concepts, and frames of reference. In keeping with such constraints, we overhear an illustrative confession: "I am not a religious man but I cannot help seeing every problem from a religious point of view."[104]

Herzog might have said it, but the line is attributed to Wittgenstein. Herzog's early Catholicism aside, we could say that Herzog, like Wittgenstein, was drawn to the transcendental in the everyday—for the Viennese *wunderkind*, in the forms of music and mathematics, later engineering and logic, still later, the grammar of consciousness. In this moment of comparison between famous personalities, we note how a "religious point of view" differs from a *philosophical* one: the two standpoints demand different standards of demonstration, solicit varied calls for criteria. The philosopher prefers "reasons," while a religious vantage may tolerate more patience, afford a broader scope for proof.

Unable—powerless—before "every problem," Wittgenstein dramatizes the world-expanding qualities of a "religious point of view." Metaphysical is a sometimes dangerous word, one that can foreclose understanding rather than expand it, so we resolve to recognize a human instinct or desire for, or simply a positive responsiveness to the presence of *myth*: for perceiving it and contending with it. Modern day mass marketing would harness such a desire for *expression through consumption*, while Herzog commodifies the same for contemplation. His product is mystifying the everyday, not harnessing its obviousness for mercenary ends. A clear vision needn't render refined truths, but reveal the way myth *holds* our dreams and dearest values, *encodes* our delusions and self-defeat. Myths lives in us, mingle with our solitary dreams—signal a special *human* element in the brain; Herzog stands stalwart as a sentry ready to defend the human from all comers, all detractors. He appreciates and celebrates how the private imaginary has its images (incrementally accreting over the years) and how it also grows by compulsive acquisitions of cultural and natural offerings—for in due time, the outmost becomes inmost. What feels like a self—(pre)occupied with a special narrative—is a webby, tentacular phenomenal, ever-linked and endlessly revising its positions and possessions. Myth and image are interactive, negotiated at the level of individual mind and social encounter. The film lives in me ... and I in it; I can longer, nor ever could, negotiate a separation; fiction enters the bloodstream and oxygenates the respiration of consciousness, including the thoughts and images that appear of their own accord. The mirror (of myth) isn't held up so we can *finally* have a perspicuous view—but so we can see it is shattered. The fractured mirror is the myth itself and leaves us none the wiser—and yet we have sought to face it, wished to succumb beneath the weight of desire for transcendence, despite conditions that merely tease—tempt us to compulsively, obsessively seek the impossible. The myth is not a means to an end but the end in itself—a labyrinth of thought that grips us and won't let go (like the "demented fury of a hound" that holds fast[105]). In view of it, we face our faults and failures, our precarious position on earth. The way of culture is distraction and dissipation (work, spend, work, spend, expire), but Herzog touches our shoulder—and sometimes grabs both—to shake us awake. This is your circumstance! Wake up before it's too late!

Though the scholar and novelist Alan Singer has suggested that Herzog's sublime is best treated as an "ironic sublime," there is good reason to resist cynical readings of his work. Even so, we should preserve a sense of humor about his films—documentary and narrative features alike—since they often contain moments that are extremely funny. And self-seriousness would simply set up further abashment and defeat: Herzog's impatience with film criticism provides the case in point. Still, our principal mode of engagement with Herzog's films should not be as if they were produced by Christopher Guest (*This Is Spinal Tap!*, *Waiting for Guffman*, *Best in Show*) and other mockumentarians, but rather by a visionary whose vaunted schemes and knowing interventions are meant to prompt our genuine insight into human desires, aspirations, and dignity. Herzog's work should neither be dismissed as pretentious art films nor as playful and sometimes caustic amusements about human folly, since his primary mode of address—and appeal—is to immanent human life as transformed through encounters with alien and uncanny figures, extreme scenarios, and vast landscapes.

Why *not* conceive of Herzog as a confidence man? One can neither claim that he intends the kinds of effects attributed to his work nor prove that his films have, in fact, delivered such effects. But the accumulated body of his images—and their inherent sounds—suggest he doesn't *set out* to mock or otherwise satirize his subjects, undermine his themes, or compromise his questions. If Herzog wanted to ridicule his subjects, for example, he would aim for as much objectivity as possible; he would adopt the methods and rhetoric of *cinéma verité*, suited as they are for unintended exposure and immeasurable embarrassment. We have seen this approach taken up *in extremis* by Sacha Baron Cohen (*Borat, Brüno, Borat Subsequent Moviefilm*). While Herzog could ridicule the authentic behaviors of the people he films, he chooses to move radically in the other direction by boldly, willfully, and provocatively flaunting the fabricated nature of his cinematic creations. Consider an emblematic prevarication in *Bells from the Deep*: "I wanted to get shots of pilgrims crawling around on the ice trying to catch a glimpse of the lost city, but as there were no pilgrims around I hired two drunks from the next town and put them on the ice. One of them has his face right on the ice and looks like he is in very deep meditation. The accountant's truth: he was completely drunk and fell asleep, and we had to wake him at the end of the take."[106] But the ecstatic truth is wholly different: not a portrait of soporific inebriation but of men seeking the reality of myth, the power of faith—depth from the depths. Consequently, and quite consequentially, by aiming to reveal ecstatic truth, Herzog makes his subjects, in effect, immune to satire. Fabrication as prophylactic against cynicism. Since the state of the men is made ambiguous (dipsomaniacs? spiritual seekers?) they are not on display in a documentary fashion—not there to give up the literal truth of the situation or be criticized for it; they are subjects who can neither be investigated nor disparaged. Instead, such cinematic scenes become imagined expressions— hallucinogenic vignettes—of some version or vision of the world that Herzog has invented.

And when we cast our attention at Herzog's treatment of landscapes, the situation is the same. Whether drawing on the innovative Dutch painter Hercules Seghers, the German romantic tradition in painting, or the *Heimatfilm* tradition in Germany (e.g., as seen in *Heart of Glass* and *The Great Ecstasy of the Woodcarver Steiner*), Herzog creates images of landscapes that resist our condescension to them. What we see of mountains, fog, mirages, jungles, deserts, rivers, oceans, ice, and caves are offered as solicitations; viewers respond as they wish, trying, perhaps, to see what can be seen, studying the effects such moving pictures have on them. In these respects, Herzog has liberated the images (and their accompanying sounds) to communicate as they can, though, for convenience, we continue to think of them traveling under the shorthand, auteurist moniker "Herzog." In that mode of address—where images and sounds are devoted to human perceptions and their attendant sentiments—such filmed landscapes may kindle the humanistic sublime among audiences. Under Herzog's tutelage, the cynical sublime is precluded, becomes a domain left to other directors.

8. The Salvific Effects of Regressive Irony

EARLIER I NOTED Herzog's self-described inability to understand irony. Whether or not this is true (or a fabulation fit to serve an entrenched-if-ever-evolving persona), there *is* a kind of irony that usefully contextualizes the achievements of Herzog's *films*, namely, an irony that is suited for someone who is sincere in his effort to create and emphasize the images (and sounds) themselves. Timothy Corrigan calls "regressive irony."[107] And there is good reason to appropriate Corrigan's attribution of regressive irony in Herzog's work as a way of explaining the effectiveness with which Herzog's images—expressed through his films—establish the conditions for an experience of the sublime in viewers, in particular the humanistic sublime. "[T]his kind of irony," Corrigan postulates, "would align Herzog with other contemporary directors like Terrence Malick, Chantal Akerman, or Nagisa Oshima who each in their very different ways have attempted to move beyond the literate irony of Godard and others using irony to reconstruct images as significance."[108]

According to Corrigan, Herzog and the others "[…] juggle and undermine a variety of points of view, human and non-human alike, so that the stability of any perspective gives way to the indeterminant point of view of the physical image it and of itself" and thereby achieves the eponymous "regression": "Like a child's sense that the physical world is all an imagistic extension of self, this narrative and imagistic irony becomes a 'regression' in that the material presence of the image moves to usurp the symbolic, socially determined distinctions of any single perspective."[109] This is, to use Herzog's own description, not very French, and certainly not cynical. Herzog's films, instead, appear not only to court an anti-auteurist effect (by displacing the fantasy of the director-as-sole-creator with "intentions") but also to invoke in and invite from the audience a kind of pre-linguistic and pre-historical perspective—something that will situate the viewer at his or her "interpretive limits and capacity." As Corrigan says, "[t]he difficult irony implicit in this action is that it forces perceptual desire to confront its real object—the unsocialized acquisition of the world as material image, not language."[110] When Corrigan describes the effects of regressive irony on the audience, he seems to presage the way Herzog's films create the conditions for an encounter with the humanistic sublime: regressive irony "works to place the spectator on the edge or at the brink of an acquisition of the world through images themselves."[111] Where the cinematic (and cynical) irony of the *Nouvelle Vague* and neorealists encouraged viewers to look away from the film to find meaning (a nascent postmodern move indicative of metacinematic methods), Herzog wants the images and sounds themselves to captivate viewers' attention such that meaning tracks that same concentrated interest— as with the *internalized* behavioral effects of a trance. *Fata Morgana* begins with an airplane landing serially upon a tarmac. Depending on whether regressive irony takes effect, a viewer will either become hypnotized by the recurrent images and sounds—and therefore availed of them in a way in which the ecstatic truth activates the humanistic sublime—or, instead, look around nervously at other theatre-goers wondering if he is the subject of a psychological experiment or a practical joke.

When Herzog says "film is not the art of scholars, but of illiterates," there is a reasonable temptation to read the remark as a critique of academics—with him, in effect, saying cinema is not available for the kind of analysis (and significance) scholars want to give it, or make of it.[112] Meanwhile, the naïf— unencumbered by book learning and often contradictory concepts—merely faces the screen and "gets it." However, Herzog doesn't mean that film is anti-intellectual, rather that it has the power—when the images and sounds are sufficiently arresting—to be *pre*-intellectual, to find us (however well or poorly educated) where our humanity makes contact with the eternal. Film—in its visceral, visual movements, its sonic sensibilities—has the representational resources to muster primal, instinctive, intuitive truths ... from everyone. So when Herzog says, "[w]e have to articulate ourselves, otherwise we would be cows in the field," he doesn't (only) mean through linguistic invention, but also through the pursuit of new images—images that might penetrate *through* our linguistic apparatus and the mass of "worn-out images" that surround, numb, and distract us.[113] Herzog is perpetually "searching for a new grammar of images and expressing this desire in the films [he] has made."[114]

Regressive irony offers an alternative way to assess cinematic spectacle. Film images are no longer places to get lost, to be distracted, but conditions in which to make contact with something on its own terms. In a mood of availability to the visual and aural, of exposure to perceived images and their sonic accompaniments, one gains orientation from immersion, one is freer to feel (and occasionally fear) the rapture of imagistic possibilities, open to influences that would shape one's understanding of sheer existence. With Herzog, the transformation of spectacle from a moment of distancing and distracting (that makes us allergic to the phenomenon before us, beyond its reception) into a scene of intimacy (where viewers feel elected, implicated, even seduced) can also occur through oral storytelling, such as when Dengler narrates an account of the beheading of his dear friend, Dwayne—and the aftermath of that incomprehensible sight. Sitting on the bank of the Mekong River—with no professional actor and no computer-generated imagery at hand—Dengler tells a story of coming to the limit, facing his own death, living at the very precipice of annihilation. After Dwayne's nightmarish murder, "I couldn't care less if I would live or die. But then, later on there was this bear—this beautiful bear that was following me. It was circling me. [. . .] Of course I knew this bear was there: he was waiting to eat me [Dengler pausing, tears welling up]. When I think about it, this bear meant death to me. It is really ironic that the only friend I had at the end was death."[115]

Whether the bear was real, like Treadwell's teddies, or was a roving figment of Herzog's imagination, when Dengler calls this ultimate moment "ironic," it is a regressive irony—an irony that returns him to the unexpected but fundamental gift of coming face-to-face with the patient bear—death awaiting. As *Little Dieter Needs to Fly* begins with an epigraph from Revelation 9:6 stating "And in those days shall men seek death, and shall not find it; and shall desire to die, and death shall flee from them," and as Herzog concludes the film paraphrasing Dengler—"Death did not want him"—Dengler's tale continually confronts the viewer with the fact of his survival.[116] That is a fact in the accountant's book of invoices: he survived. But how Dengler survived, and what it meant to see Dwayne beheaded—to live after him—

requires an orientation by means of ecstatic truth. Dengler didn't ask to be sent to the limit of human existence—to hallucinate, to see mirages, to have dreams, to suffer nightmares—but his account of his ordeal, regardless of his intent, kindles for us—by way of Herzog—a fundamental encounter with the humanistic sublime. The viewer in Dengler's company is changed from voyeur to vicarious victim, from passive viewer to active inhabitant of the precarious human province. In the safety of our seats, we nevertheless have gone some distance toward ourselves—in our shared humanity: have seen and suffered, in our minds, the trials Dengler narrates.

What exactly is the use of the protracted reenactment of Dengler's captivity in a prisoner-of-war camp? Why did Herzog put Dengler through this harrowing revisitation, in effect, this re-living—this repetition of his ordeal? Dengler clearly seems upset by the reenactment (it is, for him, "too close to home"), but for Herzog and his viewers, the return to the jungle—Dengler's presence, frame by frame—counter-narrates his seemingly assured death in Laos. Just like the stockpiles of food in his California home, and his paintings of open doors, Dengler's very existence creates a mood of wonder in the audience. How is it possible to endure this kind of torture *and* survive it? The wonder is further intensified by a kind of bracketing that creates the illusion that *having once survived*, Dengler has *forever* survived; living becomes a transcendental achievement akin to resurrection and eternal life. These are neither phenomena nor lessons that can fit neatly into the accountant's ledger.

Regressive irony tracks both *Little Dieter* and *Rescue Dawn*, but is especially evident when they are seen together—availing their symbiotic and reciprocal powers. When Dengler was a child, perhaps five years old, he watched as his small Bavarian town was bombed by Allied forces. Dengler himself recounts the formative quality of this raid, especially seeing a pilot up close: "From that moment on, little Dieter needed to fly." His desire to fly seems to have obscured the fact—even to him, as he doesn't mention what seems to be a complication, indeed, an irony, worthy of mention—that as a pilot himself, he was sent to bomb small towns in Laos, home to small children looking out at (American) fighter planes. Of course, Dengler only has a chance to unleash a few bombs before he is returned to his former (childlike) status under attack, this time a prisoner rather than a bystander, an intrigued if terrified onlooker. Once again, but this time in the jungle, the planes flying overhead become a sight causing fear—and eliciting hope; all these years later, they remain objects of threat—and salvation. Dengler's authenticator name was "Rescue Dawn," a time of day associated with the natural sublime but also a state of affairs—the need to be saved from danger—that reaches back to his childhood in Bavaria. Since Dengler survived four plane crashes *after* his escape from the Laotian camp, the theme and the structure of this relationship lingers throughout his mature life.[117] Having crashed to earth with him once, *Little Dieter* and *Rescue Dawn* haunt us with the fact of these further crashes on the horizon. No details beyond the tally need be given for us to shudder with alarm and incredulity. How is it that humans endure such accidents and fates?

Thinking of the empirical or historical Dengler and *Little Dieter* (as a Herzogian conceit), we can appreciate how they both anticipate and complicate *Rescue Dawn*, the feature film made almost a decade later featuring Hollywood star, Christian Bale in the lead. With professional actors and alternative modes of showing (rather than telling or narrating) Dengler's story, the filmic representation operates in a different register. *Rescue Dawn* reveals attributes of Dengler's story that were untouched by *Little Dieter* or beyond its cinematic milieu. *Rescue Dawn*, especially as created and viewed in the wake of *Little Dieter*, beckons us to appreciate how fiction-based-on-fact is necessarily a kind of dream. Reenactment on screen cannot mean re-creation, but something more like an incantation: as if a cinematic summoning of a spirit, mood, or phantasm—a calling out for help that allows us to hear a definitive reply.

9. The Dream of Humans

IN A SPEECH GIVEN AFTER a screening of *Lessons of Darkness*, Herzog spoke in a Heideggerian idiom about the nature of truth—yet with his films as illustrations, the sentiments underwriting his etymological conjecturing were directed to the nature of cinema as well:

> Nor is the Greek word for truth, *alêtheia*, simple to grasp. Etymologically speaking, it

> comes from the verb *lanthanein*, "to hide,"
> and the related word *lêthos*, "the hidden,"
> "the concealed." *A-lêtheia* is, therefore, a
> form of negation, a negative definition: it is
> the "not-hidden," the revealed, the truth.
> Thinking through language [*im sprachlichen
> Denken*], the Greeks meant, therefore, to
> define truth as an act of disclosure—a gesture
> related to the cinema, where an object is set
> into the light and then a latent, not yet visible
> image is conjured onto celluloid, where it
> first must be developed, then disclosed.[118]

Herzog's nuanced exposition—though purportedly unrehearsed, improvised—suggests how the cinematic medium itself is a form of "disclosure" and thus a participant in, or a condition for, the expression of truth [*alêtheia*]. If cinematic reality has been likened to a dream—a trick humans have invented to solicit and entertain the senses beyond their somatic limits, into the sphere of the sublime—is it possible that truth itself is a human dream? And by relation, or implication, could the very notion of the human be part of this vision—a dream only humans can have, a kind of hallucination in itself?

Herzog has noted that the erosion of the foundations of civilization "means that human dignity has also been destroyed" and by extension "that people's dreams have been destroyed."[119] If we cannot dream, it would seem, we cannot be human (or at least cannot be humans with dignity). Herzog counters the destruction by appealing to the film medium itself, for cinema is "something that can make our dreams whole again."[120] Cinema may be an ephemeral trick of light, traveling with invisible if deeply felt sounds, but it can also offer a substantive expression of human dignity and the grounds for its acknowledgment in oneself and others. Cinema is about possibility; it is a condition through (or medium in) which humans have an opportunity to inhabit humanness in its fuller range of potentials. When we look at a great white shark, it is hard to imagine the creature is made for anything but prowling the seas and consuming fish. The grizzly bear's teeth and claws signify a similar narrowness of existential purpose. But humans? Hairless, clawless, with small teeth; erect with bellies exposed; needing years of tender loving care to survive infancy; and equipped with strangely large brains (proportionally). What are we here for? To dream up meaning? What would the fulfillment of human form look like? A recollection by J. M. Bernstein offers counsel on such questions:

> There were times in the 1980s [… when] I thought the world was getting smaller, meaner, nastier, more impossible. And the discourse of postmodernism seemed to me crazy; it seemed to me crazy because it seemed as if it was talking about the thought that history was over, that the important things were over. And my deepest intuition is that a wholly human, wholly secular form of life has barely begun. That we are at the beginning of history not at the end. Because history up to now, as Marx would say, has been the history of necessity. The history of figuring out how merely to survive, and then of course, the history of religions, of illusion. And we are now just beginning to create a wholly human world, one in which the world is made by us. But if we don't believe that, then it won't happen.[121]

While humanism has been under attack for decades—the dream of the Enlightenment called out as retrograde and worse; the accused culprit of cultural narcissism and climate catastrophe—Bernstein shocks us with the thought a humanism existing a bit beyond necessity hasn't yet found expression. Instead of being revanchist, longing for some lost golden age (that never was), Bernstein makes us nostalgic for the future: the human isn't "fallen" but has not yet ever fully been itself. Herzog's brand of "seeing plain" acknowledges the "history of religions, of illusion" by mobilizing a human yearning for their presence through art.[122] His films are so many new reports of meaning-and-mark-making—yet without a divinity, without guidance for practical effects; his lessons do not teach us what to do: they create conditions in which to study ourselves, to fathom the humanness that lurks, yet remains inchoate, incoherent. Herzog's moving images move us to believe—to believe in the dream of humans.

In film after film, and especially in his war films, Herzog appears to transcend the human *in order to fathom it*, to create a cinema of dreams in which the human makes its appearance in the form of absence, eradication, or threatened disappearance; one might go so far as to describe this approach as the mission of ecstatic truth. If literalness precludes a sense of irony, then it also gives rise to an awareness of human existence: what is literally there before us, as us. Direct approaches to the presiding state of affairs are compromised by habit, ritual, and the blindness caused by familiarity. We often do not see what is always already before our eyes—and within. Hence Herzog's turn to fiction, fabrication, and dreams as a means of attuning us to the peculiarity of the ordinary and the proximity of the extraordinary, including their overlap in the ever-present but ceaselessly occluded fact (and delayed promise) of eternal nonexistence. Among other topics or themes, Herzog has found that exploring life lived at the limits—in war between men, or "war" between man and nature—we are given dreams to consider and revise, dreams that may define and enrich human consciousness or not. Herzog's dogged pursuit of limits, and those cinematic subjects who share his passion for them, has given us filmic evidence for the manner in which the sublime can amplify, not diminish, one's humanness.

Herzog's films, including and especially his war films, direct us to our world, though often by making that world strange, or estranging it from us so that we may perceive it anew. After all, Herzog contends that "film is not analysis, it is agitation of mind."[123] An encounter with Herzogian cinema, therefore, should not be sought as a confirmation of what we already know or believe, but instead faced as if addressing a foreign being or upon entering an unfamiliar land. Herzog's methodology—liberated from any fastidious loyalty to the accountant's truth—invents worlds from the traumas and terrors that surround us. Herzog himself refers to the circus as the "one place left where you find artists."[124] Like a circus performer himself, Herzog challenges conventional (especially cinematically conventional) notions of narrative, character, causation, and consecutive logic. With Herzog as a circus performer (an appellation he would likely feel complimented by and proud of), we could attend to the endowment his films possess for illuminating the exotic aspects of the everyday— and through acts of fabrication—holding up odd creations for our sustained reflection. The freak catalyses our stake in the normal. As we would give our attention to the provocations of magic and science-fiction, so we should, along these lines, also confirm our awe in the human circumstance—in all of its abundant diversity and across its manifest deviations.

By acts of artistry, Herzog creates new relationships to existing phenomena, to immanent life, to the unlooked at and unlooked for—seemingly weighing each moment with a freshly appointed transcendental significance (as if continuously on the verge of revealing how the trick was achieved and then cleverly denying us a glimpse of the technique—likely for our own benefit). One may be justified in regarding such circus-like artistry-of-agitation as part of Herzog's initiative to create "adequate" images—since the existing ones, like ourselves, are "tired"—or we are tired of them.[125] After all, these "worn-out, banal, useless, exhausted images" do not stimulate our thinking about our human predicament but leave us complacent and indifferent to it. The proliferation of inadequate images "limping and dragging themselves behind the rest of our cultural evolution"—has become its own kind of camouflage.[126] As noted at the outset of these investigations, we long to "see plain"—and despite all of Herzog's dissimulations and artful digressions, his enforced paradoxes and playful puzzles, his films appear exemplary for their seemingly native knack for awakening us to the extraordinary in the familiar, the transcendental charge in the otherwise low-hum of the everyday.

Though Herzog doesn't theorize, or doesn't want to admit that he has (even as his thoughtful inheritance of Greek philosophy and Romanticism above would have us believe otherwise), he has formulated in several ways—in his films and writing and interviews, and in his pedagogical perorations at sessions of the Rogue Film School—an approach to cinematic creation that lends itself, and adds credence to, the revitalized and even invigorated notion of the humanistic sublime. When Herzog says he is "profoundly unreconciled to nature," he reminds us how he continually estimates the human as a measure apart or allergic to total natural reality.[127] We are in nature *differently* from natural things, perhaps strictly because we can fathom a conscious relation to—or alienation from—nature. Our propensity for disenchantment avails us to recognize the breach (the interstices between forms of life) and thus imagine the restitution of what is, in fact, a unity without exception. The human is ever and always coextensive with nature, and yet the *thought* of nature can place humans at odds with it, liable to indulge apparent (but unreal) differences and moments of separation. With Herzog's films we discover the human capacity to perceive this alienation—perpetually invoked as a version of the question "What is this war in nature?"—and to acknowledge this awareness as a point and proof of human continuity with nature. The human is, then, simultaneously special and irrelevant, singular and every bit as natural as the flux of matter we find ourselves enmeshed within. The tension inherent in this insight—of fissure and extension—so emphatically illustrated by Herzog's war films, intimates how the humanistic sublime is no longer an oxymoron but a method, an outlook, an effect, and a quintessential register of the Herzogian realm.

VI

Perúvian Metaphysics

"If we opened people up, we'd find landscapes."
—Agnès Varda

---

1. The Edge of the Known World

We begin near the beginning of Werner Herzog's roving cinematic experiment. In Perú.¹

This is the country—the rivers, the mountains, the jungles—that, after a few salient forays in filmmaking (*Signs of Life*, 1968; *Fata Morgana*, 1971), provided Herzog with the conditions for making his first epic, *Aguirre, The Wrath of God* (1972), shot on the tributaries of Ucayali, and a decade later, his career-defining *Fitzcarraldo* (1982), both starring the electric and enigmatic Klaus Kinski. Perú is where Les Blank filmed Herzog filming *Fitzcarraldo*, culminating in the metacinematic marvel, *Burden of Dreams* (1982). Herzog has made additional films in Perú—including *Wings of Hope* (1998), discussed in more detail below—and imported a version of his Rogue Film School to the Tambopata Reserve on the banks of the Madre de Dios River, where he oversaw a willing cohort in the creation of their own short films *in spiritu Herzogus*.² Even more recently, Herzog's devotion to and identification with Perú achieved full apotheosis in the naming of a new orchid species in his honor: *Sarcoglottis Wernerherzogii*. "It is worth nothing..." the biologists write with a false start and comic inversion, though they mean, "It is worth *noting* [...] that the hypochile characteristics of *S. wernerherzogii* are unique in the genus."³ An organic double, then, for Herzog's own uniqueness within *his* genus. The plant lives not far from terrain familiar to Herzog's infiltration: in the Historical Sanctuary of Machu Picchu and the Choquequirao Regional Conservation Area, both near Cusco. In this act of naming—a signification of sentimental and practical significance—Herzog is now part of the very biological constitution of Perú.

When on Christmas Eve 1971, Herzog missed a flight from Lima to Pucallpa, it proved fateful. The plane was struck by lightning and disintegrated in midair. The sole survivor, seventeen-year-old Juliane Koepcke, still strapped to her seat, fell ten-thousand feet—all the way down to the Amazon rainforest. Though there are accounts that others survived the crash, they died before rescue. Injured and alone, Juliane spent eleven days navigating the forest and rivers before being found and transported to a hospital. Herzog, postponing his date with destiny, or rather, extinction, tracked Koepcke down in the wake of his *Little Dieter Needs to Fly* (1997), another true story of a plane crash and an escape from the jungle—in that case, a prisoner of war camp in Laos. In Koepcke's harrowing experience, Herzog not only caught a glimpse of his own accidentally avoided demise, he also admired the existential overlaps between these death-defying figures. As Dieter Dengler returned with Herzog to the forests of his captivity, Koepcke joined the director as they retraced her steps in the Perúvian Amazon together. They even found portions of the plane's wreckage. Herzog's film—*Julianes Sturz in den Dschungel* [*Juliane's Fall into the Jungle*]—was released as *Wings of Hope: Alas de Esperanza*—the name given to the fateful flight's memorial in Pucallpa. In fact, after being in the newly-built Lima airport together—just steps away from one another, one of them about to board the plane, the other about to be kept off—in December 1971, Herzog was soon filming *Aguirre* in the jungle, "a few streams away" from where Juliane was struggling to stay alive after the crash. In *Wings of Hope*, they reunite a quarter-century later to reflect on their improbable survival.

I first drafted these remarks ahead of my inaugural visit to Perú, with a lifetime of (merely) watching the place on film, but especially in Herzog's films. In so far as I have observed the humanistic sublime—perceived it, written about it, attempted to theorize it—I have done so in response to its cinematic realization. I have long wondered about the relationship between such effects as epiphenomena of Herzog's particular approach to moviemaking, his cinematic precipitates, and the place itself—what Perú itself offers and evokes, on film and on foot.

Shall we *speak* of the humanistic sublime or try to *experience* it cinematically? I suppose we should know what to look for, so a terse excursus appears in order. And Herzog, especially in *Burden of Dreams*, and in many of his own documentaries, is prone to reflect on matters as much as to behold them or attempt to create them. Like Juliane, "a sea of jungle sprawls around" us, "further than thoughts can reach."[4] And yet it is the *thought* of movies, as Stanley Cavell says, which propels us to think about them—what they are, what they make possible; what mysteries they embody, what lessons they convey; how our lives are interwoven into the sights and sounds we encounter on screen.

In the final moments of *Fitzcarraldo*, as Fitzgerald (the "White God" dressed in white) reflects on his bold foray to bring opera—Enrico Caruso, in particular—to the jungle, he remarks to Don Aquilino (José Lewgoy): "I will tell you something. At the time when America was hardly explored. One of those early French trappers went west from Montréal. He was the first white man to set eyes on Niagara Falls. When he returned, he told of waterfalls more vast than people had ever dreamed of. No one believed him. They thought he was a madman or a liar. They asked him 'What's your proof?' He answered [here Kinski turns in our direction]: 'My proof is I've seen them.'" Fitzgerald pauses, shrugs, and apologizes: "I'm sorry. I don't know what that has to do with me."[5] Since we were in the jungle, crossed the deforested isthmus, and faced the rapids with Fitzgerald and his crew, we know what this has to do with him. He has seen something—done something—that *defies even our dreams*. The passage between the rivers, over a hill, or if you wish, call it a mountain, amounts to a transfer between realms: the domain of the believable, factual, identifiable, plausible on the one side and the actual if ineffable on the other side. "That slope may look insignificant," Fitzgerald says, "but it's going to be our destiny."

As someone born one mile away from the onrushing waters of Niagara Falls, steps from the perpetually rolling, appositely-named rapids, I have many times made pilgrimages to the edge, visitations conditioned by the lands of the Onguiaahra tribe of Iroquois that traces its ancestry there to the fourteenth century—a time when the Falls existed in primeval solitude, untroubled by human infrastructure, receiver only of its admiring gaze. The river was then (only) a liminal space between two lands (not yet countries), a vigorous current of water that would later generate currents of electricity—currents of sublime charge twice over. In pre-Columbian days, energies only flowed from falls to outstretched lake, but in later ages humans made formal, stable crossings—bridges and checkpoints—that embody the daily transgression of borders and waterways, connecting despite the impasse. Border patrol makes the natural political.

In the same era that the Incas inhabited Machu Pichu, finding orientation to the sun and the sacred mountains that gathered and shaped its light, indigenous people of the Niagara Escarpment beheld these liquid vertical cliffs, these mountains of moving water—some seven-hundred-fifty-thousand gallons falling over the stoney brink every . . . second. With such abundance and such a steep descent, the Niagara gorge was excavated—gravity-propelled water gouging it out from limestone, shale, sandstone, and dolostone. The water that cut this shaft created two lands (today two countries, three or more if you count various indigenous tribes), and is now known by an anglicization of this name—for we are told Onguiaahra became Niagara—variously translated as "the strait" or as "the thundering water."

In time, inventive and industrious engineers such as Paul and L. L. Nunn found their way to the north side of the Canadian Falls at Niagara, where they designed and built one of the world's largest alternating current hydroelectric substations—Nikola Tesla looking on admiringly from the other side of the border, his patented design realized once again at scale.[6] Whether called to mind, or faced immersively—while mist descends tenderly on one's face—the haunting, electrifying reality of sublimity's three-dimensional effects is persistently held in abeyance at Niagara Falls. The visitor confronts the churning onslaught only briefly, while the dark waters hasten their passage ceaselessly by day and night and through all seasons. If you haven't yet visited those cataracts and their downriver whirlpools (so fearsome they resemble a portal to the netherworld, an observable Devil's Hole), what is your sense of their potential as images—or as actualities? To generate voltage in man and matter? Perhaps the humanistic sublime Herzog schemes to visualize and give voice to is, by his own standard, merely—but importantly—an image, most auspiciously by virtue of his ambition, a *new* image (even if, always already a *film* image). The proximity of the letters in the near anagramic "image" and "mirage" encourages us to doubt that what we have seen is real, could find its reality as a *moving* image, the film strip like the ribbon of river—or merely as a thought about it.

Herzog inhabited, then crossed, the isthmus between the Urubamba and Camisea rivers,[7] filmed these waters and lands, but the experience didn't remain his own—the subject only of autobiographical notes and unreleased film footage. Rather, the aftereffect of his "vast" vision—the story that remains beyond what "people had ever dream of" lies in the film *Fitzcarraldo*. Herzog and Kinski alike are infamous as "madmen," but they have supplied for us this film as "proof" against their private fantasies and misbegotten adventures. *Our* proof of these sublime actualities is that we have "seen them." They have come not from in-person encounters along violent waterways, across treacherous hills and mountains, but through contact with the film medium and its special potencies, here mobilized and tested by Herzog and his team.

Thus the idea of pulling a ship over a mountain ("the essential metaphor of my film," Herzog tells us), to take only his most famous example, is sufficiently generic to be a notion that will travel—to the rivers of the American West, to Europe, to Africa, perhaps one day to Niagara Falls and the Niagara River. Let bringing opera to the jungle reside as another fundamental trope: that fantastical collision of the human voice—passionate and cultivated, performative and affecting—and the vast, earless immensity it addresses. "When the whole world is transformed into music," Herzog says, "the result is opera."[8] Opera in the jungle, but turned the other way: the jungle in opera.

And so, along at least these two axes, if not others, the specificity of Perú announces itself because the film—whatever an author's ambitions for it may be—inhabits this *genus loci*. In Herzog's films, then, our preoccupation must be with the way an idea meets a place, a dream materializes—"[e]very natural fact is a symbol of some spiritual fact," as Emerson puts it.[9] Capturing Perú on film may itself be an act of subliming the actuality of the land, so the further question is whether a humanistic sublime is something Herzog manages to draw out or add to the landscape to which he addresses his lens. In such cases, the humanistic sublime would be a supplement to the Perú of our lived experience, a special effect Herzog summons from the peaks and valleys, from the rushing rivers and their human inhabitants.

On this occasion, I am inviting a return to thinking about Herzog's films on Perúvian *terra firma*—that is, in a double sense, both as the site of these films and the context of our reflections on them. More particularly, or I suppose more expansively, I wish to underwrite how Herzog's films made in Perú conjure a filmic representation of the humanistic sublime. In the previous chapter, I contended that Herzog's "war films," such as they are, activate and maintain contact with this variant of the sublime. But there is reason to see these Perúvian works as not just foundational to Herzog's expression of the phenomena, but also as a series of special dispensations of it.

What have we come to understand as Herzog's version of the humanistic sublime?

2. Sublimity's Stake in the Human

IT WAS THOMAS WEISKEL who said "the essential claim of the sublime is that man can, in feeling and in speech, transcend the human."[10] At the outset of *The Romantic Sublime: Studies in the Structure and the Psychology of Transcendence*, that it is, without deliberation, he concluded: "The humanistic sublime is an oxymoron." An earlier, corrective report on Herzog's war films as candidates for expressing—and thus recuperating—the credibility of the humanistic sublime (see chapter V) are now joined by remarks on a handful of films made by Herzog on location in Perú, a half-century of instances to further ratify the noncontradictory status of the notion. Instead of finding confirmation of Weiskel's conclusion, we come out on the other end, transformed, feeling that the humanistic sublime is something we have experienced, something the cinema of Herzog has made visceral and thus discernable. An immanent sublime.

The concept of the sublime, generically speaking, is familiar from Longinus to Burke and Kant, from Schiller and Wordsworth to Lyotard and Žižek, but Herzog's heterodox treatment of it is, as one might expect, not a strict inheritance of the category or concept, since far from aiming to transcend the human, Herzog endeavors to situate the human at the very limit of its embodied experience, at that place where its presence in nature—or at war, and in other such extreme circumstances—is at once fantastical and dreamlike and yet utterly undeniable, a necessary part of such run-ins, and yet illusive, miragelike, shimmering. "Today the [film] rushes seemed like something I had dreamed, or rather," he says, writing from Iquitos, "like something someone else had dreamed."[11] Reality is an imagination; imagination is a reality—like a boat lodged high above the water, resting at the top of a tall tree.[12]

How telling of our sometimes misbegotten usage of the word, then, that sublime things are often associated with excess, the transgression of limits. Etymologically the *sub-limen* is that which "comes up to the lintel but doesn't go beyond it." In proximity to the sublime, we add the subliminal—that which remains "below the threshold." Yet it is those boundary conditions—the interstitial spaces—that provide the frisson from which we come to *perceive* the sublime (in us, as it were). "The nature of my storytelling," Herzog told Terry Gross, when promoting his memoir, "sometimes requires to go into extreme situations, yes, but I think to look deep into our human nature, to look deep into the darkest recesses of our soul or the hidden things deep in our soul, you have to put human beings at some sort of an edge."[13] The edge of Niagara Falls, the precarious cliff, the unstable shoreline, the murmuring volcano, the iced-over mountain peak, lethal injection, and at last, the territory of all such conditions: human consciousness (stable, fragile, clear, clouded). Ordinary life places us *in media res*, far from these stark contrasts, hence our immersion within—rather than emergence from—the undistinguished everyday. Crossing a border, by contrast, calls us to attention. Transgression—in fact or as imagined—*heightens* consciousness, gives it a lift, a new vantage from which to observe itself.

In Peter Buchka's documentary *To the Limit and Then Beyond It: The Ecstatic World of Filmmaker Werner Herzog* (1989), Herzog makes the following remark about an abiding purpose for inventing moving images: "I often get the feeling that the cinema should create an image of humanity. . . . There always should be an image of humanity. Who are we? What is our inner history?"[14] For Herzog the project of imaging the world as an outward sign of inner, human experience is profoundly linked to our notion of mortality, material ends. "Here I get the feeling," Herzog notes, "that if we truly want deeper insights into ourselves we can only do so if we step back to the very edge of things."[15] Or, as the case may be, step forward, as if to the brink of an abyss. The humanistic sublime, then, is not a humane one. "Man is an abyss, and I turn giddy when I look down into it," wrote Georg Büchner, author of *Woyzeck*, one of Herzog's perennial authors.

Herzog seems inspired, at times possessed, by a vision of the pre- or posthuman, or of those very instances of contact and distance that define the human against all other forms, cosmic and terrestrial. His interest in the "before" and "after" of humankind is actually an expression of his curiosity about the peculiar presence of the human "in between" the time-before and the time-after—human life as necessarily interstitial: an embodied span between oblivions. Herzog has remarked: "I still like the shots at the beginning and ending [of *Where the Green Ants Dream* (1994)] very much, images as if from the end of the world."[24]

"Nothing could be more human," Stanley Cavell has said, than "the power of the motive to reject the human."[16] In part the motive seems expressed in "the human drive to transcend itself, make itself inhuman."[17] Herzog's work offers an interpretation of what Cavell calls one of "the most inescapably human of motivations"—"the drive to the inhuman."[18] And yet Herzog's visions eschew a nihilistic, cynical, ironic, or misanthropic wish to dwell on the nonexistence of the human; instead they are oriented to the use or presence of the before and after of the human as an occasion to radicalize, revitalize, and reinvigorate our *attention* to the human "caught," as each of us are, in the "unfathomable abyss of time."[19] His is an unsentimental vision of nature—and our predicament within it. "This expedition is doomed," we hear in *Aguirre*.[20] We are all, it turns out, "conquistadors of the useless."

Fittingly, in Kantian aesthetics, we have another (seeming) oxymoron to complement the humanistic sublime: "purposeless purposiveness," which fulfills the so-called "analytic of the beautiful." The beautiful, we are told, is beyond instrumental use. "The judgement [of the beautiful] is called aesthetical just because its determining ground is not a concept," Kant writes, "but the feeling (of internal sense) of that harmony in the play of the mental powers."[21] Alas, the beautiful is the useless—i.e., the purposeless—and for that reason we are poised *constitutionally*, as humans, to recognize its aesthetic attributes. The purposelessness—the uselessness—of art is what makes it art! The work of art isn't instrumental in the material sense; it appeals to a different registration of value. Notice how we don't seek out Herzog for facts about reality but for intuitions about the reality of what exceeds our grasp in what we *call* reality. Perceptual distortions, psychological rifts, religious inclinations—these are fraught energies that hover on the surface of the film frame, that track the sentences he inscribes. We do not know what to *do* with Herzog's work—and since it is art, that incapacity is as it should be.

What then of the power of those moments in Herzog's films when the viewer *seems* to be seeing something she could, perhaps should, not see: a primeval region in which humans are no longer or never were? Take the opening shot of *Aguirre*, in which humans emerge out of a steep forest-laden mountain—as if we find ourselves witnessing a creation myth in the making. "We descended from the clouds," says Brother Gasper de Caravajal (Claus Biederstaedt). They are, in fact, traversing the stone steps of Huayna Picchu, a nine thousand-foot mountain that rises above Machu Picchu, the Inca city that is ever so nearby but never shown in the film.

An imagined, stylized view of existence *without* human presence and intervention radicalizes one's own status as a human viewer who suddenly finds herself on screen or beholding it. We occupy a viewpoint from nowhere and never—namely, the pre- and posthuman—and from there catch a glimpse of our own transcendence (in the form of postulated nonexistence). Since the traditional philosophical reading of the sublime could be cited as support for Cavell's claims, it must remain intriguing for us that Herzog shifts his representation of the sublime *toward* the human. Recall Harold Bloom, lighting out into the territory Weiskel prepared in *The Romantic Sublime*, declaring how "Weiskel's power as a theorist of the sublime is condensed in his implication that the Hebraic or Christian sublime, the Homeric sublime, the daemonic sublime, the natural sublime—all evade oxymoronic status [unlike the aforementioned humanistic sublime]. They may also," Bloom continues, "evade precise definition, indeed may blend into one another, but none of them is so problematical and paradoxical as that *seeming* self-contradiction, a humanistic sublime."[22] Given Bloom's clout—and credentials that endow the matter at hand—we needn't pass up an *argumentum ad verecundiam*. News of the apparent antimony is welcome (across this and the previous chapter), yet there is authority too in Bloom's reminder-cum-admonition about the potent(ial) gauzy divisions among inherited terms. Still more, we wonder where the human fits into this expanded list of candidates—each of them vying agonistically not just for clarity but perhaps also for supremacy.[23]

As discussed, the humanistic sublime may be an advantageous syntagma for thinking about Herzog's war movies. Yet with so many of his films at our disposal, which is to say, at our command, there remain myriad ways of categorizing and arranging them to make similar claims. On this occasion, in this place, I am aiming at a perception of films Herzog made in

Perú—in its jungles, on its mountains, upon its rivers. How does the humanistic sublime reveal itself to us in these local films? What is unique and revelatory about the human encounter with limits as they are known in this country, across this land, on these waters? Such rhetorical questions are especially suited for those familiar with both territories—the terrestrial Perú and the cinematic Herzog. Still more, the questions call out for context: how Perú is exceptional and emblematic of other terrains featured in Herzog's films—and those made by others (some of them in Perú). The attraction of Herzog's films commonly encourages— and rewards—a sustained focus on works drawn strictly from his catalog such are the intertextual matrices to be productively sketched (as if he spoke a language that only makes sense in isolation, cut off from the rest of cinematic history, a world all his own). This can't be so. In fact, Herzog's distinction—and the Perúvian difference in his cinematic escapades—is that much more salient when the shot widens, when other lands and varied cinematic vectors are taken into the frame.

3. The Herzogian Cinematic Social Imaginary

ZOOMING OUT FROM Herzog's Perúvian filmmaking trials, we also catch sight of his films shot or set in Brazil and Colombia (*Cobra Verde*, 1987[24]), Guyana (*The White Diamond*, 2004) and Bolivia (*Salt and Fire*, 2016), and are invited to recognize the wider cinematic context of his work—how it stands on its own and in relation to numerous, diverse representations of Central and South America, Antarctica, the Amazon, and the jungle (actual and mythic). To be sure, a more than Amazon-size anti-jungle, like Antarctica, also calls out for its continuity with the Andes mountain range and its completion of the extremes we observe from Iquitos all the way to McMurdo Station (*Encounters at the End of the World*, 2007). We are in the hands of a director who has filmed on all seven continents; still, the capaciousness of his dauntless drive may yet conceal the subtle interactions between those traits that feel common across vast expanses of sea and desert, boreal forest and tropical jungle.

Despite his association with disparate geographical territories, he offers no national cinema (an origin story that finds him on the shortlist of formative forces in the New German Cinema is developmental rather than definitive) and despite his decades of imbrication in American culture—his ascension as a permanent star in its firmament—no cinema with an American accent has emerged. Rather, keeping his own company and counsel, Herzog's films and books speak directly to the planetary human circumstance: a shared existential condition that obliterates political borders and collapses the proximity of one hominid to another across time and space. Herzogian images—whether visually constituted or codified in the visceral language of his sentences—are transnational and transtemporal. In this durable mode, Herzog boldly sustains his role as a poetic antagonistic to a detached scientism: from his offerings, we find a thinly veiled but firmly held contempt for the reduction of human life to its constituent parts. In counter response, he attends to emergent and supervening phenomena—mists and flares, electric shocks and deranged outbursts, the ungovernable, the freakish, and the berserk; humanity situated uneasily at its extremes—and thus very far from being reducible to anonymous creatures (the sort that fill statistical databases and afford numerical and evaluative extrapolations therefrom, however dubious). Herzog proceeds by his own odd, combinatory measures: he focuses on specific phenomena (an individual person, an identifiable natural feature, a peculiar cultural practice or more) and discovers in them emblematic aspects of generic traits: this is close reading fused with genre investigation. He has a knack for training our senses on phenomena (the close reading) that give rise to thoughts that exceed them (the turns and trends of genre).

By virtue of Herzog's intrepid exploration of the world and its strange inhabitants (that is, bringing to our attention how the ordinary is itself very strange, or may be estranging once attended to), and by the merit of his cinematic eye and distinctive voice, he offers us, if we are inclined to accept it, a recognizable Herzogian cinematic social imaginary. "Everyday life," he tells us in *Burden of Dreams*, is only an illusion behind which lies the reality of dreams." His regular screen presence; his iconic voiceover (when not on screen); a mood of existential seriousness that vies with a strain of tragicomic impishness; and a reflexive tension that ebbs and flows. For these and related reasons, we easily identify his films and moreover can quickly spot parodies and homages that draw upon that social imaginary, as when the teenage boys in *Me and Earl and the Dying Girl* (2015, dir. Alfonso Gomez-Rejon) not only watch segments of *Burden of Dreams* (when Herzog's reflections on the "collective murder" and "asphyxiation" of the jungle are played diegetically with the boys-as-audience within the mise-en-scène), but as amateur filmmakers—budding actors and directors alike—mount a genre-shifting remake entitled *Burden of Screams*. Gomez-Rejon adds a further, nested flourish when he chooses Brian Eno's "The Big Ship" as the nondiegetic soundtrack to Greg's hospital-room, audience-of-one film premiere for Rachel. In the eponymous novel by Jesse Andrews, who also adapted the screenplay, the homemade film Greg and Earl set out to make, against all odds, is entitled *Earl, The Wrath of God II*. In the novel, the boys analogize their difficulty making films with their tutor: "Like Werner Herzog in the South American jungle, we faced almost unimaginable setbacks and difficulties." When asked what their film is about, the boys reply, as if channeling Herzog's sensibility: "It's a documentary about human stupidity."

Given the time stamps of *Aguirre*, *Fitzcarraldo*, *Burden of Dreams*, *Lessons of Darkness*, *Little Dieter Needs to Fly*, *Wings of Hope*, *Grizzly Man*, and *Rescue Dawn*—ranging from 1972 to 2006—a dilated compare-and-contrast with films by others proves revelatory. Readers can exercise the pleasure on their own terms, for example, by learning that Francis Ford Coppola was a fan of *Aguirre* and the 1972 film informed the creation of *Apocalypse Now* (1979). Though we can thrill to the metacinematic mise en abîme afforded by Coppola's cameo as a TV director—telling the soldiers in the midst of battle "It's for television. Don't look at the camera. Just go by like you're fighting."—the scene can also be read as a Herzogian moment in which a director imposes himself in the sprawling narrative underway.

Two years later, Steven Spielberg's first entry in the Indiana Jones franchise, *Raiders of the Lost Ark* (1981) begins by Indy swapping a bag of sand for a golden idol in a jungle-laden Perúvian temple. After Jones iconically outruns a rolling boulder, and loses the prized statue to rival Belloq, he is seen being chased by indigenous Indians—an action shot that has become a meme of the blockbuster era and veritable shorthand for action-adventure. In *Indiana Jones and the Last Crusade* (1989), Indy, ahem, Dr. Jones, lectures in a classroom at the University of Chicago, where he tells his students: "Archeology is about facts. If you want truth, go down the hall to the philosophy department." But this must be a screenwriter's odd epistemology because the more salient contrast would be "if you want fiction, go to the English department," since fact and truth are typically a happy tandem. What gives? Is this a screenwriter's joke on his audience (of children) who are paying admission but aren't paying attention, or who can't make heads or tails of the clever-seeming distinction?

A protégé of Spielberg, Robert Zemeckis directed *Romancing the Stone* (1984) from Diane Thomas' screenplay, a film that begins with an ersatz Western (based on one of novelist Joan Wilder's romance novels) and then announces a frame story from the present day on the Upper West Side of Manhattan. Timid, talented, love-starved Joan (Kathleen Turner) runs headlong into a 1980s terror trope: the abduction of a North American by South American thugs. Trying to save her sister, Joan flies to Cartagena, a Colombian city on the Caribbean. (Actual dangers in Cartagena pushed production to Mexican sister city, Veracruz.) Hostilities between local tribes informed how *Fitzcarraldo* was shot — and the real danger that lay at the edge of the film frame. In *Romancing the Stone*, safely re-settled further up the Caribbean coast, the jungle is an accomplice to slapstick: falling, sliding, swinging, being overwhelmed by rain and mud and foliage. One shot stands out: a fifteen-second, locked-frame, wide shot — running from 00:21:15 to 00:21:35 — that is the first daylight scene since Joan's arrival in Colombia, following immediately after her bedraggled nighttime arrival (and its noir edge of menace). The shot runs in sync with a nondiegetical score that blasts a horn section, adds era-appropriate percussion marking a tropical locale, and even includes some '80s electric guitar flourishes. The almost static visual blast of verdancy and stark blue skies finds its lone movement, as in the opening shot of *Aguirre*, from pilgrims along a path, this time in a rickety bus passing horizontally along a cliff-hanging road in the upper right quadrant of the frame. Nothing like the cinematic potency of this shot is attempted in the rest of film . . . save for the film's final one, in which the canyons of Colombia are traded — during the end-credit sequence — for the canyons of the Upper West Side, a landed yacht sailing down West End Avenue, down the street from Columbia, the most elegant and cosmopolitan representation yet of dragging a ship across the island of Manhattan.

The jungle comedy continues in the New York-isle to Caribbean-isle double-dealings of *Club Paradise* (1986, dir. Harold Ramis), in which we meet a motley cast of dreamers and misfits. A representative scene: while a massive snake slowly slithers up and squeezes his wife, Linda (Andrea Martin), husband Randy (Steven Kampmann) postulates aloud—in a rendition of existential mansplaining: "You know what's funny, honey? I like it out here. It's primal and, well, it's honest. You don't survive in the jungle in a tie and a suit. You survive with pure animal instincts. [The camera cutting back and forth between his oblivious self-satisfaction and his wife's pending peril.] God, my senses are alive. When I'm out here, I ask the really big questions, like 'is it man against nature?' or is it 'man in harmony with nature?'—The latter I think. [Sounds of Linda choking]. You know what I'm talking about, honey?"[25]

In the same year, but in a different tone, *The Mosquito Coast* (1986, dir. Peter Weir) puts us in the company of Harrison Ford, by this point already established in three of his eclectic franchises (as Han Solo, as Indiana Jones, and as Deckard in *Blade Runner*, 1982); Jack Ryan launches in 1992; and a year after his Philadelphia cop swapped "cults" and cultures for an off-the-grid romance among the Amish in Weir's *Witness* (1985). *The Mosquito Coast*, based on the 1981 novel by Paul Theroux, begins with Allie Fox lecturing us about the decay of American culture in the age of Reaganomics. With consumer capitalism's aggressive ascent and the ongoing threat of nuclear annihilation, Allie, an inventor, sells his farm and uproots his family, heading for the jungles of Central American (scenes for which were shot in Belize; the farm, in Georgia). As if to invert the discovery of high-temperature atomic energy, Allie aims for refrigeration—going so far as to name his machine Fat Boy (an amalgam of the two bombs dropped on Japan in August 1945). With his technology, Allie hopes to bring refrigeration—ice!—to the jungle. Only a handful of years earlier, we heard Fitzgerald, an ice producer, describe an entrepreneur gambit as a means for funding his mission to bring *opera* to the jungle: "imagine, one day […] ice in every warehouse, on every ship." The parable in *The Mosquito Coast* ends with Allie having his worst nuclear nightmares realized when an attack by Central American guerrillas leads to an explosion that destroys his machine (which, in Herzogian fashion, had to be hauled up the slopes of a hill), his cooled village (now burned down), and for an added measure of poignancy in the era of Love Canal (which sits along the Niagara River), the poisoning of the river that lay at the feet of Jeronimo.

With a screenplay by Robert Bolt (*A Man for All Seasons*) and directed by Roland Joffé, *The Mission* (1986) dramatizes

Jesuit proselytizing in eastern Paraguay during the unsettling transfer of land from Spain to Portugal. Since the Portuguese permit slavery, the mission to convert the indigenous Guarani to Christianity is imperiled. Other transatlantic "mission" films also include Terrence Malick's *The New World* (2005) and James Gray's *The Lost City of Z* (2014), both of which visualize first encounters between Europeans (more specifically, Englishmen) and tribal cultures of the Americas. While the source stories for both films are purported to be based on actual persons and events, the adaptation to the screen forces a robust stylization—a poetic fictionalization that, by way of Herzog, can be generative beyond the confines of history. Indeed, all three of these films—by means of cinematography, score, and atmospheric sensibility—convey a serious relation to the transformation of scattered biographical fragments into something more like piercing, transcendental effects. They dramatize the cognitive and somatic agitations that happen when foreign bodies "make contact"—and capture the fallout from those transgressive intimacies and crossed boundaries.

As if to magnify the storytelling accommodations of the sometimes named, many times unspecified South American jungle, John McTiernan's *Predator* (1987) delivers a *mille-feuille*: alien arrival; unidentified species of jungle monster that reveals itself to be a heat-seeking intergalactic predator; Soviet-era espionage; and war film. Even for these veteran soldiers (some of them bona fide, forged in the Southeast Asian jungles of Vietnam), the jungle (here shot in Mexico) presents formidable obstacles to match or complicate the pursuit and attempted destruction of the undocumented migrant from outer space.

While predators may arrive in the jungle from cosmic distances, others are said to hail from those very multitudinous environs, King Kong being among the most enduring exemplars of exaggerated animality and threat native to such places. Peter Jackson's eponymous film from 2005 splices together Melville, Conrad, monster movies, a mixed bag of iconography for jungles and "natives," and no shortage of metacinematic tricks by way of vaudeville antics (including a frame story involving the theatricalization of beauty unrecognized, in the form of *Mulholland Drive*'s Naomi Watts, and, later, the gargantuan beast in plain sight). Kyle Chandler looks his dashing best as an Errol Flynn-cum-Cary Grant preppy swashbuckler, who arrives with his own nested romantic adventure in the can: *Tribal Brides of the Amazon*. With a Herzogian mission inscribed on the manifest, the steamship *Venture* (all too on point) is bound for a remote island upon which the crew plans to make a movie; *Heart of Darkness* is cited and made partner to these "adventures on a tramp steamer." "Just like us," says an eager Jimmy (Jamie Bell), who is reading Conrad's 1899 novella, in a bit of superfluous exposition. The boy wonders in the audience's stead: "Why does Marlow keep going up river?" then quizzically asks his shipmate of their own endeavor: "It's not an adventure story?"—"No, Jimmy, it's not," correcting the lad and countering Conrad. While the steamer persists in seeking the unknown on high seas, we soon enough see how the white whale will be swapped this time for a black gorilla—the roving and lethal leviathan of the island (discovered in due time to be a real softy with a thing for blondes who have a knack for pratfalls). And so it is, with the Māori crewman Māteatu on board and wild license taken in the depiction of local tribes (an amalgamation of myriad peoples), we make landfall in the vicinity of *Typee* and *Omoo*. Call it metaphysical romance.

From a formidable gorilla to a courteous bear, our quick re-screening in the light of Herzog's Perúvian experiments continues with the must-be-mentioned Paddington hailing from "deepest, darkest Perú," most recently caught on film in *Paddington* (2014) and *Paddington 2* (2017), both written and directed by Paul King. In these films, the usual drama of white people heading south of the border, into the jungle, is replaced by a Perúvian (bear) heading for London (albeit one of the most ethnically and racially diverse spots on earth, the result—ironically—of the once-sweeping empire's scope). The direction is notably reversed in *Paddington in Peru* (2024, dir. Douglas Wilson)—that is, returned to the familiar genre structure of white people out of context, starting with *Robinson Crusoe*, continuing with *Tarzan*, and culminating comically in this third outing, in which the Brown family (not White, not Black) seeks Aunt Lucy in the Perúvian mountains.

On to another expedition, this one from a Disney film entitled *Jungle Cruise* (2021)—a further bit of intellectual property that started out as a ride at Disneyland, just like the *Pirates of the Caribbean* franchise. Directed by Jaume Collet-Serra, *Jungle Cruise* returns us to Don Aguirre, and a variation on his legend. Though the characters head for Brazil and the Amazon, the film was shot in Hawai'i—giving us renewed license to think about the cinematic anonymity of jungles, as if any overwhelming green space with ample waterways and heavy rains will suffice. These sly trades and proxies—Mexico for Colombia, Hawai'i for the Amazon, etc.—confirm the ongoing virtues of a willing suspension of disbelief, as when, in another genre, Sicily took hold as the home for the nineteenth-century American West. In *Jungle Cruise*, one can't miss how MacGregor Houghton (Jack Whitehall) went to Fitzgerald's tailor and milliner: a white suit, a white hat. The steamboat skipper, Frank Wolff (Dwayne Johnson) calls to mind the captain of Fitzgerald's ship—Orinoco Paul (Paul Hittscher). A shot of Wolff—later revealed to be Aguirre's adopted brother, Francisco Lopez de Heredia—at the helm with MacGregor at his side (again, dressed all in white) seems a match for similar shots of Fitzgerald beside Orinoco Paul as they look out with concern from the captain's deck, wheel in hand, trying to navigate the river.

Lastly, another comedy, this time with references to Perú that arrives with a light touch, feels adjacent to Herzogian preoccupations even beyond his genres: the zombie film *Life after Beth* (2014), directed by John Baena, who gave us that remarkable take on selected stories from Boccaccio's *Decameron*, *The Little Hours* (2017). During a heated discussion about the surprise "resurrection" of a recently dead family member, we see a documentary playing on a television set. With voiceover narration by Nick Offerman, we learn about Machu Picchu. Later in the film, when the gun-loving older brother panics about where the family might flee from the zombie attack, his first thought (doubtlessly informed by the documentary) is Machu Picchu. Coming full circle in this quick survey: as with *Me and Earl and the Dying Girl* (also starring Nick Offerman, there as Greg's father—with a penchant for exploring uncharted cuisines and exotic tastes), such touchstones may be random, but they are salient enough to intimate some kind of, perhaps subliminal, Herzogian influence (like the notion to flee to Machu Picchu— we pick these things up from the ambient media-saturated ether). Because Herzog is, in fact, a prominent auteur—one familiar to any of these film-school grads (NYU! AFI!) and industry-trained directors (such as Baena, Gomez-Rejon, et al.)—we need only look to the likes of Zak Penn, Harmony Korine, and Joshua Oppenheimer to appreciate Herzogian homage and references. Yet, as this sampling of movies illustrates, the generic jungle social imaginary—created largely, in these cases, by Hollywood or other entities originating from the northern hemisphere—runs in parallel, and occasionally makes contact, with Herzog's own incarnation of images.

Given the evident gender distribution of the generations enthralled to the man, it is worth a breath or two to consider (per the needs—existential, spiritual, practical—of "creatives," perhaps especially among the young) the extent to which Herzog's fan base skews male. The clientele seeking succor with the sage suggests as much. And so while launching a tour of the environmental atmosphere in which we receive Herzog's films (the jungles and rivers that populate his cinematic canvas), there may be a layer of interest in those people who principally do the receiving—and in turn the homage-making and allusion-setting—of his compositional offerings. What denotation, if any, in the discovery of an Herzogian demographic? In the 1960s, Herzog certainly didn't put on retainer Munich's finest marketing analysts so they could run the data on how to create such an audience. Such importuning effects are unpredictable . . . until they aren't.

The creative teams at *Adult Swim* would appear to have Herr Herzog on speed dial—calling him down from his sunny Los Angeles lair to give voice to animated characters in *The Boondocks* (2010) and *Metalocalypse* (2012), in the former playing "himself," in the latter for nine episodes as Ishnifus Meaddle.[26] At first glance, we guess that *Meta-localypse* is a show about how reflexive art will be the death of it, yet we soon enough learn that *Metal-ocalypse* follows the death metal band Dethklok; however, the show's reliance on parody and pastiche (mainly of heavy metal cultures) lends renewed salience to the title's interpretative slippage (at the level of spelling). Whether Herzog is called up—and upon—by these producers, or those working on *The Simpsons* (Matt Groening), *The Mandalorian* (Jon Favreau), *American Dad!* (Seth MacFarlane), *Entourage* (Doug Ellin), *Rick and Morty* (Justin Roiland and Dan Harmon, also for *Adult Swim*), *Parks and Recreation* (Greg Daniels and Michael Schur), *Documentary Now!* (John Mulaney) & co., there is reason to wonder what these men—among the aging of all ages—seek in seeking out Herzog. Paternal advice in an era of inept, self-involved fathers? Poise when masculinity itself, we are told, has curdled into toxicity? Appeals to higher laws—and forces—that acknowledge a hunger for the numinous against the persistent commodification of reality, materially and otherwise, into commercially viable ephemera; that indemnify the embattled state of democracy and the rule of law? Authority in the midst of a moral abyss? Visionary insight for a superficial age? Compensations for the perceived decay of character in modernity and the corrosive effects of individualism . . . by turning to thoughts of a postliberal (and posthuman) society, indeed, to the recovery of certain preliberal traits?[27]

The run of questions refracts how the West, after millennia spent building institutional and conceptual hierarchies, has entered a phase that encourages their dissolution, tolerates the erosion of social structures that once supported the constructive inheritance of patrimony and decorum. There are now fewer shared rites of passage. Meaning making has been divorced from genuine danger and in that separation forsaken the special capacities of life lived *in extremis* (in a war zone, say, or in preparation for war; humans bonded against whatever foe or ordeal), to create a durable, sanguine, buoyant community.[28] Herzog is, in an almost anachronistic way, a man. (Though to some his man-ness may be dismissible—a feature of his persona that exposes immaturity or marks him for retirement— still others find his resolute, if unacknowledged, masculinity appealing).[29] Herzog layers and enriches his special status (however one deems it) with qualities that also seem rare: darting to an adventure on a moment's notice, bearing up stoically while under extreme strain, finding depth in the quotidian, living at a remove from mass culture—slightly ahead or well behind it. No wonder Herzog despises the "culture of complaint," psychoanalysis, film schools and film criticism—these comparably effete if not hare-brained preoccupations. Though he boldly speaks of "inner landscapes," Herzog's inward turn is not made in pursuit of the private self or to resolve feelings about one's father; indeed, the longings that underwrite this paragraph would seem misguided to him. The attention given to his work by men cannot be lost on him, yet there seems little he can do for them. Save a man from a car crash, yes, but work with him through the trauma of the accident after the fact, no thanks.[30] And the sentiment may go the other way too: no need for a surrogate father or faux-paternal advice, just a chance to refract hilarious Herzogian memes through the latest *zeitgeist*, perhaps the only spiritual *geist*—that is, *quest*—we should be so bold to expect from succeeding generations. (Intriguingly, authors of the "secondary literature" tell a different story of Herzog's appeal to the gendered, leaving us to surmise that "creative" and critical responses to his work circulate through the culture unevenly.[31])

Given the implied seriousness of Herzog's role as a role model (perhaps especially for aspiring [male] filmmakers), what to make of his role playing as actor and voice talent—often in the key of silly? By expanding the scope of his performances beyond directing epic adventures and earnest documentaries, by jobbing himself out to bit parts, does he (inadvertently, unintentionally) dilute or damage the potency of his pre-existing brand? As a measure of authorial reflexivity (and we could add copyright control), he has contributed more to making his voice parodic than anyone else; for their persistent missing of the mark, however slight, the perennial and proliferating parodists make Herzog *more* not less essential. Even so, since his voice has expanded its registers, he now risks audiences hearing his voice *first* as unserious—as the go-to sound of mock profundity (instead of simply profound). Yet, the dynamic range of Herzog's self-authored voices (including those accompanying his incarnations on screen), intentionally or not, casts a new light—and sensibility—on the full scope of his work: what if it's *all* mock serious, done in the same key (and we merely took him, once upon a time, for sincere)? The question destabilizes Herzog's legacy; it also creates an active charge—a bivalent prism in which his work hovers precariously between two states. To the extent that any celebrity has control—a cybernetic capacity to navigate the currents of the cultures that person finds themselves buffeted upon (off-shore winds propelling more elegant and efficient lines to oceanic influence; choppy headwinds turning one back, or capsizing the venture altogether)—Herzog's meta-inflections (viz., aesthetic traits that circulate through, and circle back within, his work *and* persist as features of his public persona) may find him unable to land a critique on shore. His moviemaking musings as much as his literary and vocal stylings tend to beach themselves far from the centers of critical power. Scanning the horizon, we feel sure it is Herzog's vessel—helmed by a man of repute, of notorious perspicacity and inveterate ingenuity—that will save us. Alas, he fails to see our flailing arms signaling him to our salvation. Herzog too is a mirage.

With *Fitzcarraldo*, one would think Herzog's natural *métier* is the romantic sublime, but then that was not a story about a man's contemplation of nature but rather his engagement, better his entanglement, with it—including his obsession with the idea of bringing opera into the matrix of the jungle. As Fitzgerald tells those in earshot: "This god doesn't come from cannons, he comes with the voice of Caruso." And when he is pitched at a moment of high crisis—with his crew having abandoned ship, Fitzgerald says, as much to reassure himself as to confirm his faith in music: "Now we really need some Italian opera very much." The next shot is of a gramophone perched atop the ship-in-motion boldly projecting Caruso into an indifferent jungle. Exemplars of Western civilization shipwrecked, ragged, and facing an unknown fate yields yet another new image: *Robinson Caruso*. The juxtaposition generates sublime moments—as when monkeys climb upon the gramophone playing Mozart in *Out of Africa* (1985, dir. Sydney Pollack); what euphoria and longing these musical phrases deliver to the foot of the Ngong Hills, and yet they can be so brazenly silenced with one swipe of a monkey's diminutive hand.

Les Blank's enduring documentary *Burden of Dreams* (1982) even more surely returns us to the space of a different sublime: Herzog not in awe of nature, but, paralleling his title character, aiming to negotiate with it—to literally pull a ship over a jungle-laden mountain. As he notes, eschewing 20th Century Fox's offer for him to find a "good jungle," or simply pull a scale model of a ship over some lush foliage in San Diego's Botanical Garden, Herzog writes: "not for the sake of realism" must it be a real ship "but for the stylization characteristic of good opera."[32] For someone famous for faking and fabricating things—for extracting ecstatic truth from otherwise recalcitrant mundanities—Herzog has reasons why it was essential to his vision that he pulled a (real) ship over a (real) mountain. We must reconcile, time and again, Herzog's drive for literalness (in this case, real things at scale) with his willingness, indeed, his proclivity for fabulation and his persistent inhabitation in the realm of dreams.

Further to the point of such stylization in the service of truth, something similar could be said of Herzog's invocation of the "wrath of God" as neither Calvinist nor millenarian but a bit of good stagecraft; he is the dramaturg of his own brand of brooding intensity. As Juliane Koepcke, a biologist, tells us: there is, in fact, very little to fear in the jungle, little of real danger. (She has Perú's jungles in mind). The grandness of Herzog's gestures, then, and the extremities of his grammar are suitably in proportion, part of a campaign of mutual reinforcement.

Fitzcarraldo offers a cinematic portrait of literalness in the guise of fiction: a real ship for a bit of make believe; *Burden of Dreams* presents a stylized, that is, an ersatz ethnography of the lengthy, elaborate shoot with Herzog its most unreliable informant; he doesn't speak in a parlance of clichés but with a pained effort to give voice to poetical exaggerations. The birds don't "sing," they "screech in pain"; the trees "are in misery." Such is natural history told from the perspective of a mystical Bavarian seeker with a penchant for tricksterism. Projected from Herzog's mouth these things, which when we say them aloud sound idiotic or parodic (even of the man himself), come across as perfectly plausible, comically on point, and laden with spiritual truth.

Herzog himself has described—he won't admit to theorizing—the prime impulse and achievement of his work as a search for what he calls "ecstatic truth." (We can ask, as Emerson does: "Is not the sublime felt in an analysis as well as in a creation?")[48] Like the humanistic sublime, ecstatic truth is a compact concept that needs elaborate glossing and benefits from compelling illustrations; in a speech entitled "On the Absolute, the Sublime, and Ecstatic Truth," remarks invoked in the previous chapter, Herzog characterizes the mission of summoning the sublime. He tells us that the fabricated opening intertitle of *Lessons of Darkness*—lines by Herzog attributed to Blaise Pascal—were inserted from "practical" rather than "theoretical" considerations. By means of this trick, Herzog claims, "I elevate [*erheben*] the spectator, before he has even seen the first frame, to a high level, from which to enter the film. And I, the author of the film, do not let him descend from this height until it is over. Only in this state of sublimity [*Erhabenheit*] does something deeper become possible, a kind of truth that is the enemy of the merely factual. Ecstatic truth, I call it."[33] Herzog's self-assigned effort to prepare his audience by "elevating" its point of entry into the film is itself an expression of the customary ways of speaking about ecstasy.[34]

We are by now familiar that etymologically speaking *ekstasis* means "to take out or remove [*ek*] from the regular position or standing [*stasis*]" and convey one into a different state—rapture, delirium, euphoria—beyond ordinary perception. More figuratively, *ekstasis* can be treated as synonymous with "bewilderment" and "amazement"; "distraction or disturbance of mind caused by shock"; "displacement or derangement of the mind"; but perhaps most pointedly for our exploration with

Herzog, it also means entering into a trance. (Additionally, the word can be defined, as Thomas Wieskel does, as "transport," which makes it an uncanny conceptual sibling to the Greek meaning of metaphor [*metapherein*], "transfer"). Herzog has a long-standing interest in hypnotism and the nature of human physicality when a person is under a trance; for example, as referenced in an earlier chapter, he had all the actors in *Heart of Glass* (1976) act while under hypnosis—and later claimed that the techniques he used to hypnotize actors then informed his approach to rendering his own voiceover thereafter.[35] Juliane of the jungle describes herself, in *Wings of Hope*, as having been in an extended trance.

Unlike a romantic sublime (of a Teutonic sort) that "concerns power and sets man and nature in desperate opposition," attributing a humanistic sublime to Herzog's creations makes nature (or Nature) the proper antagonist—and better facilitator, in Kantian parlance "the condition for the possibility" of the human perception of ecstatic truth.[36] Without the grandeur of nature, humans would be less able to comprehend their condition, states of consciousness, and modes of revelation. There are moments, in facets of what we have seen, when Herzog's sublime aligns productively with a nineteenth century English romantic sublime "in which nature is not merely thrown over but appears as the medium through which the mind discovers and presents itself, in eddies of separation and reunion"—much as we see in skier Walter Steiner's departure from earth and his return to earth in *The Great Ecstasy of the Woodcarver Steiner* (1974).[37] The prominence of rivers in the Perú films gives vivid context for discussion of any such "eddies," how waterways would appear to embody the *fort-da* of attraction and repulsion, restraint and propulsion. The watery energies of rivers, moreover, contrast with the gravity, rootedness, and slow-but-still-moving growth of landed flora.

And yet, Herzog's erstwhile experiments with Steiner (on the mountain, and in the editing bay) resist employing nature for instrumental purposes—even if for the heightening of human consciousness—but instead focus on the human situation *within* a natural context. Nature, whether it is figured as the densely verdant Perúvian jungle or the bleached vastness of Antarctica, is secondary to man's scenario—and yet, tautologically speaking, humans are themselves natural phenomenon. The question, then, is how to come to consciousness of our humanness when lost or otherwise indistinguishable from our natural environment—an environment that claims us well before we have any awareness of its existence. Picasso described paintings of his studio in the south of France, including "L'Atelier de la Californie" (1956), as portraits of his "inner landscapes," and from this familiar phrasing, we glean from him a double sense: the interior workspace filled with stretched canvases, paints, and brushes giving rise—or reflecting in the finished works themselves— Picasso's own emotional and imaginative interior. Though the frigid winds howl on the other side of the tent in *Grizzly Man* (2005) and *Encounters at the End of the World* (2007), Herzog's primary focus is not outward conditions but inner landscapes— the emotional, intellectual, moral, aesthetic, and psychological terrain of the human explorers, situated as they are, with a only a thin membrane between the infinite expanses of outer space and the indefinite depths of inner space.

For Herzog, Perú turns inside out Emerson's pregnant logic that "the inmost in due time becomes outmost"—making it, instead, the *outmost becomes inmost*.[38] The material world of extremes (from tundra to jungle, taiga to desert) offers a province, an atmosphere in which to recognize his (inner) dreams and articulate his (private) visions. Without the imposing grandeur, at times terror, of nature, humans would be less able to comprehend the fragility of their circumstances within it— including revelatory states of consciousness. In an unsentimental mood, like Herzog's, farmer and classicist David Grene extols the sublime virtues of the hunt: "All in all, hunting is something entirely on its own. For enjoyment and revealing yourself to yourself it hasn't its equal. Trollope says somewhere that he believes three-quarters of the field of riders in any hunt are frightened to death half of the time. He's probably right. But it is very great thing to have your enjoyment so combined with the sense of being on your mettle, which naturally involves being frightened."[39] If analogies will hold, in his films, Herzog often appears on a hunt (questing being the operative metaphor), while viewers pursue his images—both enterprises engender productive energies and occasional contact with sublime forces. Hence a dialectic emerges between the "inner" and those forces that enable a passage "out of" oneself (an *ekstasis*). To perceive an *indifference* to the human accentuates the *fact* of the human. Facts may be stubborn things, but an ecstatic relation to them may also sublime them such that they are made newly revelatory—beyond our sense (or sensation) of them. "It is not words only that are emblematic," writes Emerson, "it is things which are emblematic." As noted earlier, "[e]very natural fact is a symbol of some spiritual fact."[40] Herzog's nearly sixty-year, global pursuit of "new images" appears in the service of this symbolization—devoted to a movement that happens within the human to transform evidence into emotion, brute materiality into spectral consciousness. Emerson continues: "Every appearance in nature corresponds to some state of the mind, and that state of the mind can only be described by presenting that natural appearance as its picture."[41] Concluding, at last, as if with Herzog and Heraclitus his neighbors on the shores of the Urubamba and Camisea, Emerson asks: "Who looks upon a river in a meditative hour, and is not reminded of the flux of all things?"[42] Emerson's rhetorical question, like an encounter with an "outer landscape" admits its inversion: the question answers itself in the affirmative, the atmosphere of one's interiority cannot help but concede the influence of the climate beyond it.

Imagine Wim Wenders' surprise when he bumped into a jacket-and-tie wearing Werner at the top of a tower in Tokyo. Interviewing his New German Cinema colleague, Herzog speaks of those "who recognize the need for adapting and maintaining sparse images." In Wenders' *Tokyo-Ga* (1985), Herzog tells his friend that "we need pure and absolute images," but "it's hard to find transparent and pure images here on Earth" (as if images from a cosmic elsewhere were set in contrast with his worrisome finding). These Herzogian adjectives—sparse, pure, transparent, absolute—resist in their very nature the disclosure of the concrete. And yet, for Herzog, the *creation* of such images requires a confrontation with the particular: it is only then that by way of camera-work, editing, voiceover, scoring, and similar cinematic techniques that we may be struck by images that are not mere hand-me-downs, relics of a culture bent on aggressive recycling.

Comfortable using a word like "absolute" in all seriousness, Herzog, unlike so many of his contemporaries, proves to us that he hasn't become immune to the allure of the sublime—treating it, as they often do, only with ironic detachment and modern condescension as a "moribund aesthetic."[43] But, almost as if he were a traveler from the past (or an extraterrestrial spot in the Milky Way), Herzog has retained a fascination with "natural infinitude."[44] As part of his inheritance, and *transformation*, of this tradition—reaching as he does to Longinus, Kant, and other thinkers of the sublime—Herzog pushes the notion into a new medium, cinema, and finds in this form a way of relating man to nature that other modes of representation (from novel to verse) express differently. Herzog's war films have been especially capable of translating the conceptual apparatus behind the theorization of the sublime into the "practical" (his word) experience of the sublime by cinemactic means; so too his Perú-based endeavors. As a visual space of moving (in at least two senses of the word) representations—often with diegetic sound, score, and voice embedded—the cinema screen suggests an alternate reality: it conditions the perception of another world somehow newly apparent before us (brute reality as phantasm) and in turn, within us (as dream, nightmare, or an otherwise until now undisclosed dimension of consciousness). The war in nature is already apparent in our own interior, still we need visionaries to show us—to summon us—to the stakes of such revelations. Perú has perennially provided Herzog a context for achieving them.

Herzog claims that "film is not the art of scholars, but of illiterates."[45] The temptation is to read this as a critique of academics—in effect to say cinema is not available for the kind of analysis (and significance) scholars want to give it, or make of it. Yet Herzog doesn't mean that film is anti-intellectual, rather that it has the power—when the images are sufficiently powerful—to be *pre*-intellectual. Film—in its visceral, visual movements, its sonic sensibilities—has the capacity to convene primal, instinctive, intuitive truths (yes, cosmically significant lessons). So when Herzog says, "[w]e have to articulate ourselves, otherwise we would be cows in the field," he doesn't (only) mean by way of linguistic invention, but also through the pursuit of new images—images that might penetrate *through* our linguistic apparatus and the mass of "worn-out images" that surround, numb, and distract us.[46] Herzog is perpetually "searching for a new grammar of images and expressing this desire in the films [he] has made."[47] He mines his own inner landscapes to find these forms—where veins of familiar ores and common elements make themselves evident in outcrops, where difference has been etched away by the winds and waters of time to reveal unified strata of imagination. "It's not only my dreams. My belief is that all these dreams are [...] yours as well [...] and the only distinction between me and you is that I can articulate them [...] and that is what poetry or painting or literature or filmmaking is all about—it's as simple as that. And I, I make films because I have not learned anything else and I know I can do it to a certain degree and it is my duty because this might be the inner chronicle of what we are.[48] The inner chronicle of inner landscapes must be made cinematic—if only to be shareable as images. For a man seized by the burden of dreams, Herzog claims that when he sleeps, he doesn't dream. "Maybe that's why," he says, "I compensate by making films."[49]

4. Cannibal Metaphysics and the Recirculations of Thought

ONE OF THE IMMENSE BENEFITS, for me, of bringing my long-standing study of Herzog to Perú—to going "on the road" with it, and soon after walking on foot—is having such investigations complicated, enriched, and extended by savvy South American colleagues (and other visitors to the appointed colloquium). I think here of Victor Krebs, our intrepid host, and also of Lorena Rojas Parma, Daniele Lorenzini, and especially, in closing, Gabriela Balcarce, who, after hearing an earlier version of this chapter, turned my head by recommending prospective affiliations with Eduardo Viveiros de Castro's *metafísicas caníbales*. Thinking of relevant anthropological points of reference, I had learned of Philippe Descola from his visit to the School of Criticism and Theory at Cornell University, and have benefited from contact with the wider circle of what could be styled "Cavellian anthropology," or anthropology with Stanley Cavell in mind (e.g., Veena Das, Andrew Brandel, Michael Puett, et al.). Here, then, let me send out some initial speculations—rhizomatic reports—about the way the foregoing dispatch on the (Herzogian) humanistic sublime may be compellingly underwritten and further unfolded by, for example, what Viveiros de Castro calls the Amerindian perspective (and its cosmology), multinaturalism, and "cannibal metaphysics as comparative metaphysics."[50]

While my working list of sources on the sublime—from Longinus to Burke, Kant to Schiller, and Wordsworth to Lyotard and Žižek, along with Herzog—remains bona fide, certainly among the most enduring transtemporal and transterritorial voices on the subject, they all, building upon one another or reflecting on the notion in light of the rest, form a more-or-less continuous tradition. Among many identifying traits, the necessary recourse to, and negotiation with, various dualisms—self/other, individual/community, human/animal, nature/culture, interior/exterior, immanent/transcendent, ordinary/sublime, etc.—becomes a principal preoccupation of one's inquiries. Admittedly, in a spirit eschewing such binaries, there may be an attractive appeal to some kind of spectrum or gradation, for example, as part of an attempt to find continuity between realms (rather than firm delineations), hence the role of liminal spaces, since the very prospect of transgression depends on the preexistence of a discernable boundary or definable border. Rather, we may wish to linger in the threshold, in the arena of matricial overlaps. While we debate nuanced adjustments to anthropocentric reasoning (is there another?), Viveiros de Castro delivers not a Copernican but an Amerindian revolution, in which we are "turned around"—availed to appreciate how the animal is looking back at us. It is not just, or no longer that we must "[g]et used to the bear behind" us, as Herzog says, but rather that we must meet it face-to-face—or even, more radically, in a collapse of inherited categories, such that we speak of the bear within us.[51] We behold, we inhabit yet another social imaginary. As editor and translator of *Cannibal Metaphysics*, Peter Skafish glosses Viveiros de Castro's "basic idea" for a "post-structural anthropology":

> Amazonian and other Amerindian peoples (from the Achuar and the Runa all the way up to the Kwakiutl) who live in intense proximity and interrelatedness with other animal and plant species, see these nonhumans not as other species belonging to nature but as PERSONS, human persons in fact, who are distinct from "human" humans not from lacking consciousness, language, and culture—these they have abundantly—but because their bodies are different, and endow them with a specific subjective-"cultural" perspective. In effect, nonhumans regard themselves as humans, and view both "human" humans and other nonhumans as animals, either predator or prey, since predation is the basic mode of relation.[52]

Clearly, it is not just Herzog's films that would be aided by such insights; consider how much more interesting the film *Predator*, mentioned above, becomes. Who is alien now? Yet, even if we stick to Herzog's own narrative pursuits in his Perúvian films, and his remarks given to Les Blank in *Burden of Dreams* and on other interview occasions, we quickly see "Herzog's jungle" in different terms—and not just inverted ones. Herzog, like the other and earlier metaphysicians of the sublime, needn't have his discourse discarded, rendered at odds or obsolete. Rather, we could, more generously, see what a notion like the humanistic sublime is *aiming at*. Emanating from a Western context—in Herzog's case also complemented and complicated by his earlier turn to Catholicism—the peregrinations of the postmodern seeker are familiar. Herzog has company in his pursuit of new and adequate images—those that would compensate humans for their losses, among them the evacuation of the divine from the mortal plane. Who can blame the metaphysically destitute for manufacturing realms that offset inherited forfeitures?

The "theory" of recent decades—even across the last century-and-a-half—has forced its promulgators to take sides on the question and status of the human. As Wilfred M. McClay notes, gravely: "We now live in a different time, one in which Matthew Arnold's idea of culture is disdained. In our age, it is the very category of 'the human' itself that is under attack, as philosophers reject the hierarchical distinction between humans and animals, or humans and nature, and postmodernists of various stripes proclaim the disappearance of the human 'subject.'"[53] McClay's lament arrives in the mood of an elegy, and yet the perceived deprivations—in the accumulating erosion of Western categories, among them the glories of an ancient, medieval, and Renaissance humanism—may yet benefit from contact with opposing strains of thought (as antique in their own ways yet likewise not at all antiquated). For instance, as I picked up Weiskel's philosophical declaration that the humanistic sublime is, or must be, an oxymoron, I found—I argued, let us say—that the twinned terms are suitably complementary (and Herzog's films and writing demonstrate ways for representing them and thinking about them in a coherent, if ever-unfinished fashion); the contradiction was regarded as an invitation to innovate—to see the struggle between allergic partners as a bid to achieve homeostasis, to use opposing energies productively. So now that the humanistic sublime makes contact with the post-human and transhuman, and the sorts of revisionist onslaughts that would dissolve humanism's long-standing hold on our imaginations, there is reason to think *with* the so-called opposition, in part by asking: what are we missing? Holding severe worry at bay, consider that a cannibal metaphysics may be *additive* when fathoming the structure and stakes of the humanistic sublime. Rather than visiting the vital riches of an Amazonian basin teeming with verdant life and a multitude of crawling species, one marvels that it was enough for Emerson, while touring Paris, to see bones assembled into skeletons and specimens gathered in vats of formaldehyde to declare: "I feel the centipede in me—cayman, carp, eagle, & fox. I am moved by strange sympathies."[54]

In the Jardin des Plantes, Emerson seems to have been surprised by the effect these cabinets of natural history were having on him: "The limits of the possible are enlarged, & the real is stranger than the imaginary. [...] Here we are impressed by the inexhaustible riches of nature. The Universe is a more amazing puzzle than ever as you glance along this bewildering series of animated forms—the hazy butterflies, the carved shells, the birds, beasts, fishes, insects, snakes,—& the upheaving principle of life everywhere incipient in the very rock aping organized forms."[55] The paleontologist with literary sensibilities will smile at that final phrasing, such that the inanimate "rock" would imitate by way of proto-human feats of "aping" the varied and marvelous organic forms. But then it was Emerson who said that "language is fossil poetry," so all is, in fact, continuous from his vantage.[56]

Standing there at the edge of the glass cabinets and the vitreous jars, Emerson might well have been describing the contours and contents of South American jungles with the first-hand fantastic experienced by Charles Darwin, who was—in this very same season—touring South America by way of the *Beagle*. While Emerson jotted his notes in a Paris museum, Darwin was in Uruguay (Maldonado, a coastal city not far from Buenos Aires); Darwin would make it to Lima, Perú two years later (in mid-1835). Though Emerson lacked the tumescent effects of a three-dimensional jungle incursion (with its olfactory onslaught of humid, redolent air), he was sufficiently sensible to these hermetic displays—imported and arranged—to say "Not a form so grotesque, so savage, nor so beautiful but is an expression of some property inherent in man the observer,—an occult relation between the very scorpions and man."⁵⁷ The human, then, is not diminished by the range and diversity of these earth-dwelling compatriots, but enlarged. Moreover, the scope penetrates the dermis such that the continuities dive inward. The centipede is not out there, in the jungle (whether mythic or factual) but, at last, in me—as I read the latest work of natural history by a hearth a few thousand miles away from the home of these seething, dynamic entities.

Cannibal metaphysics, like Object-Oriented Ontology, goes some way towards flattening persistent hierarchies that have come to define Western metaphysics; they both diminish the stature of the human in the taxonomy of specimens, an effect that can render the human indistinguishable from its material cousins. Where once the humanistic sublime was described as a human encounter with nature (admitting the divisive binary), now there is a twist, a reversal: nature "looks back" at the human—beckons it to the point of recognition and subsequent dissolution. Outer/actual landscapes cultivate an inner/human response (not one thing, but rather a singular feeling-emotion-thought). Earlier renditions affirmed how the humanistic sublime *dislocated* something in us, and by extension in Western metaphysics (hence Weiskel's quick dismissal of it as an oxymoron; the pair doesn't fit together; the assembly of terms isn't compatible given the contours of categorial inheritances). On such a reading, when we experience the humanistic sublime, in effect, we are out of alignment: the sensory realm stiffens, time shifts, space mutates. But these reallocations and ruptures—however intense or for whatever duration—indicate that a "human" human is trying to make sense of the encounter (say, between the perceivable everyday and the immensities that exceeds one's perceptual grasp). To some degree, Western metaphysics denies our attempt to do just that; it *leaves us* dislocated—at odds with ourselves, unable to integrate what we have experienced—especially in measures of the grand Other and otherwise, alienated from the picture of Western logic that we took (and we were told to take) for granted. Enter the Amerindian perspective, which has been sensible to *just* this kind of radical reorientation. Quite consequentially, then, Skafish's description of Viveiros de Castro's project lends credence to the (until now unarticulated) conceptual affiliation between the humanistic sublime and the post-human. When *all* animal entities are "human," we, at last, can glimpse domains beyond this motley assortment of creatures. If the appeal holds, humanness—across material forms—re-announces itself. We find ourselves; the dispossessed are re-located.

Making multiple pilgrimages to the Museo Larco, one of the world's most exhaustive collections of pre-Columbian ceramics, we confront—and are mesmerized by—cultural artifacts that speak to the interaction between a metaphysics of the sublime and a cannibal metaphysics. These handmade creations are not merely representations beyond themselves—referents meant to call to mind a lost horizon of history—but appear as the very embodiment of ideas and beliefs. In ancient Perú, in the Cupisnique culture (which flourished between 1500 B.C.E. to 1 A.C.E.), the gods were represented by animals. In time, these (animal) gods would *take on human form* yet possess the powers of the feline (some of them deemed supernatural). Sculpted faces are commonly formed by the combination of human and feline features. One even comes across the union of three animal attributes such that a feline-bird-serpent is recognizable in "human" form. The notion of "complementary duality" (arising during the Andean, fusion period from 800-1300 A.C.E.) arbitrates the potency of fluidity: water, semen, breast milk. Enrichment and fertilization become master tropes of sacred culture and are embodied in ceramics. There is an allowance for a surplus of pleasure in the form of non-reproductive sex (depicted figuratively in clay by human acts of fellatio and masturbation). This "jungle metaphysics" is not dislocating, but integrative, not wasteful, but distributive; points of orientation perpetually shift, overflow is efficiently rerouted. "Asphyxiation," familiar from Herzog's *Burden of Dreams* disquisition, becomes circulation, "collective murder" becomes the movement of life forces—including into the underworld and back out again to the level of the living. Upon the arrival of conquistadors in 1532, the "extirpation of idolatries" (such as sacred animal power) began. Humans would now rule without recourse to animals. The free flow of energies would cease, interrupted as they were by conceptual limits and partitions. The human stood alone. Little surprise that the imported metaphysics would alienate and make the jungle alien. The *ostranenie* afforded by the pre-Columbian lies precisely where the pre-human greets the post-human. We remain in the middle, in the muddle of living not quite a human life, and not quite an animal one either. Stuck in the thought of the individual, the self, and the rights of man we are estranged from the beings swarming around us and swirling within. The view from Perú allows for measures of awe and epistemic humility. We may know something but the catalogs of ignorance remain vast.

Such a comically abbreviated tour of a few features observed in the found objects handsomely housed at the Museo Larco is nevertheless meant to signal the evident regularity with which Herzog's films—whether fictions based on factual stories, such as *Aguirre* and *Fitzcarraldo*, or factual accounts given a lift through artifice, such as *Wings of Hope* or Blank's *Burden of Dreams*—dramatize the presence of nonindigenous people in a Perúvian context that reaches back thousands of years; and, of course, the natural historical conditions of these precincts retreat even further, into the deep time tens and hundreds of millions of years prior. Just as Juliane Koepcke provides a biologist's corrective to the (Western) stereotypes of a jungle outwardly, almost personally, intentionally hostile to humans, so a cannibal metaphysics—situated in part in the physical artifacts of indigenous peoples, such as those held and beheld in their ceramics—may counter, if not also correct, inherited categories that preclude a fuller understanding of the places Western, modern philosophy has traveled.

FOR THE LAST HALF-CENTURY, and especially in his formative first decades as a filmmaker, Werner Herzog found in Perú an outer or actual landscape that appears—when put on film—to activate something crucial about his inner landscapes ... and ours. Perú, as he put it, is "an unfinished country," "a sleepy country at which God's wrath has cooled"—a Herzogian compliment that underscores why the place is susceptible to offer such ecstatic visions.[58] A real world became a dream and a dream-on-film transformed into a new reality for humans to behold, fathom, and make integral with their own varied interiorities. No wonder Herzog concludes: "I love the jungle—against my better judgment."[59] Few of us have visited the Perúvian jungle, and yet Herzog's images of this place have become cinematic realities for generations of moviegoers and filmmakers across the globe—from tundra to taiga. (As sketched above, consider how frequently and prominently Herzog—in person or by virtue of his persona, through reference to or reformulation of his quixotic quests—is invoked in movies made by younger generations of filmmakers). As of my arrival in Perú, I have entered a new phase, as it were with two realms of reality to contend with: one longstanding, of Herzog's films, especially the Perúvian ones, playing over and over again across the decades of my life, in different cities, where, as Cavell says, "[m]emories of movies are strand over strand with memories of my life"[60]; and another, the place itself, announcing its presence from moment to moment. Both conjure their sublimities. Both become indelible entries in a metaphysical memoir.[61] After decades of mediated experience, I am grateful, like many other wayfarers who preceded me, to have made first contact. And obliged to those who listened to, and commented on, these reflections of a visiting Herzogian pilgrim, traveling somewhat on foot, to a country of captivating natural beauty—one that should be known as a permanent home for the humanistic sublime.

VII

Rogue Agent in an Ambivalent Universe

In this concluding sheaf of folio pages—claims percolating, conclusions deferred—we continue to encounter our mercurial hero, a keen student of classical languages and literatures. As Herzog assesses the matter: "To me, the deciphering of Linear B is one of our greatest cultural and intellectual achievements bar none."[1] We believe him, then, when he says:

> Reading signs, reading the other team's tactics in soccer, reading the world, all that never let go of me. It is a theme in *Kaspar Hauser*, where the young protagonist is projected into the world, as if from a distant planet, without any understanding of houses, trees, the clouds in the sky; without language, without understanding the people around him.[2]

If in our moral moments we are Spartacus, in our existential predicament, we are ever Kaspar Hauser asking: "What is this sign and how do I read it?" We are emergent beings set upon this earth doomed to negotiate the interaction between outward signs and inner thoughts, the contours of space and time and the emotional conditions for intuiting them. In our isolation and disorientation, eager to pursue translations but thwarted by circumstances, we may be fated to read, as Garrett Stewart styles it, hier-*rogue*-glyphs.[3]

And though we have, like many other Herzog fans and critics, labored to secure some fixed interpretation of our leather tramp, we come up short: deviant translations abound. Instead, like an ancient and inscrutable script, Herzog remains of vital interest because the *thought* of Herzog is generative and elusive, not because it is definitive. Here, then, we continue and conclude this session of musings by making contact with recent moments of generativity—by Herzog himself and by others (including nonsentient entities), those whose own relations to our rogue agent remain robust. On this occasion, disquietingly, the mission includes contributions from what amount to slabs of silicon; of course, I speak of artificial intelligence (section 4). But before we skip ahead to the edge of leading technologies, let's make recourse to one of our familiar, if still mysterious, mediums: television (section 1). For it is there, in the tube, now a screen, that we find parody mixed with nostalgia, homage coupled with genre mash-ups, and throughout, a specter of our fleet-footed filmmaker. Nestled in between these investigations, we allow an echoic vignette on truth and authenticity (section 2) before picking up a yet further—albeit a throwback—technology, a book, one by Herzog's own hand, his memoir, *Every Man for Himself and God Against All* (section 3). There we find Werner in his preferred mode: among books and making them. How many devoted Herzog cinephiles have been startled by the master's prognostication that his *books* will outlast his cinematic creations? Will it be so—and *if* it is so, we should have been reading them all along and closely, hence our interstitial engagement with the man and his pen.

1. Of Metatexts and Doppelgängers

Documentary Now!—with exclamation point duly in place—is both the name of an esteemed, if fake, public television news magazine *and* the name of an IFC-produced mockumentary television series about documentary films made for the (fictitious) public TV program that shares its name. In this scenario, the mise en abîme has *Documentary Now!* in its fifty-third season, hosted most recently by the acclaimed actress Helen Mirren *and* (somehow simultaneously) finds IFC's *Documentary Now!* kicking off its fourth season with a two-part feature entitled "Soldier of Illusion" (2022; s4:e1-e2). The opening credit sequence begins the braid of the actual and fabricated by interweaving a string of famous documentaries (*Man with a Movie Camera*, *Don't Look Now*, *Harlan County USA*, *Roger & Me*, *Hoop Dreams*, *Man on Wire*, etc.) with the show's evolving (but alas nonexistent) brand identity. Call this counterfactual cinema: fake documentaries that evoke the style of real documentaries while entrancing us with a parallel history of parodic films; we want the originals *and* we relish these false pretenders, these simulacra of our earlier objects of admiration.[4] A capable and compelling incarnation of metatelevision, the IFC series certainly rewards documentary devotees, since the more familiar one is with the real history of documentary cinema (especially its iconic standard bearers), the more the matryoshka satisfies.[5]

The pleasures of parody begin with the double episodes' title, since Herzog has made his status as a "soldier of cinema" a subtheme of his life's work.[6] While there is a touch of Herzog as a camera-for-hire (the mercenary seeking funding from disparate sources and improbable allies), and commodifying his talent for easy adaptation in myriad contexts (from *The Simpsons* to *Jack Reacher* to *The Mandalorian*), he doesn't strike us as a "soldier of fortune." Rather, if he is avaricious for anything, it is for showing humans their insignificance, how they are ruled by error and accident, and yes, how most of what we hold dear can as easily be styled an illusion. The soldier of illusion—and its near equivalent, the rogue agent—are fitting analogs for that tried and true hero of Herzog's universe: the conquistador of the useless. For if we are soldiering on, conquering new terrains—of outer and inner landscapes, peddling frauds along the way—we are also, alas, fated to encounter the fata morganas that dissolve our enterprises; the windmills on Crete are real—*and also* a cinematic mirage (the paired terms rendering a redundancy).

The brand we call "Herzog" has long absorbed its affiliations with the quixotic; we note recurrently how he doesn't appear to have an ax to grind so much as a thought to spare, indifferent to our best attempts at dismantling a sentiment that unsettles our logic, or building a system in his stead. Not breaking a sweat of nervousness but only of vigorous onward movement, Herzog follows his own path, whether motivated by clear resolution or cloudy whim, enunciated claims or guileful craft. He is, in this measure, a conquistador of the quixotic.[7] "All of us carry in us a quest, some sort of quest, and I think every grown up man (or woman) should do something like moving your ship over the mountain. It's absolutely natural [...]. You've got to do it."[8] Moreover, the metonymic soldier, while carrying the weight of someone ready for combat, or always already waging it, conveys yet another fitting metonym of Herzog's quest: walking on foot. Hence, foot soldier. And lastly, there is the coincidence of illusion as a shorthand for cinema itself—a medium of attractions and distractions, of moving images that seem real yet are as thin as the screen they are projected upon—

again, those windmills. A soldier of illusion, then, can be added to our list of phrases aimed to capture what Herzog has been up to all these years, inscribing it in a column not far from our central phrase and figuration: rogue agent.

As in chapter III, our object here is Herzog as persona, though dilated to accommodate a new era of examples and refracted texts. How is it that he has manifested characteristics — vocal inflections, mystical diction, a dead-serious demeanor — that are so attractively and contagiously worthy of imitation, including playful re-interpretation? Indeed, as Mark O'Connell has noted, with a shelf of films standing in the near distance, the filmmaker's "real masterpiece is the character known as Werner Herzog. This is not to diminish the scale of his cinematic achievement, to paint it as somehow the work of a shallow self-promoter, but rather to insist that the power of his work is often inseparable from, and in fact, reliant upon, this persona."[9] For more than half a century, and across all of these pages, we have been tracking Herzog's pursuit of new images, but, as O'Connell rightly declares: Herzog himself *is* such an image, and if the ledger is tabulated, perhaps also his best one. Herzog-as-character has supervened upon his many fine forays; for all of his artful transformations of facts into fabrications, he too might be surprised by the results. Herzog's persona has gone rogue: it has come to serve us — supply what we need, no longer (just) what he wants; this entire book, despite evidence gathered and theories articulated, may be counted an illustration of the phenomenon. In a deromanticized and disenchanted age, we romantics and seekers, we dreamers and metaphysicians clamor for a cipher. Herzog is the image we have sought; his persona — varied and still evolving, yet emphatically iconic — provides lasting and satisfying compensations.

The now commodified and recognizable "Herzog" has become — rather, let the copula state it more boldly, *is* — an idea, which is to say, a dream, a hallucination, an apparition, a specter. His salient qualities as a *cipher* capitalize on the word's varied definitions: as a method of transforming a text in order to conceal its meaning; and as a form that has no weight. Mysterious and ephemeral — and add affecting — it will draw us closer to a gloss on the sublime itself. Such qualities are especially suited to personas, which are (etymologically speaking) thin masks betraying what lies behind them. If Herzog is compellingly attractive, he is also adaptable — easily put to use (for serious as well as comic purposes), a jester fit for the times, and it is clear: serial generations. Every age has its prevailing doom (in recent decades, the murmur of world wars and cold wars, nuclear threats, terrorism, climate instability, pathogenic menace, cultural decadence, capitalist excess and severe asset asymmetries, political attacks on liberal democracy and the rule of law, the derangements of social media, the pervasive if coy emergence of generative artificial intelligence)—though it would seem ours has a share in all of these facets—and so every age cries out for its right agent of counterforce: someone to remind and encourage, to recover imperiled virtues and hold fast to them, to envision alternate possibilities or make room for them. Herzog has become such a figure—a figment of our imaginations set to work on the problems of the perilous present. Why some personas feel plausibly imitable and others, perhaps others that are ostensibly quite similar do not, is a mystery of human affairs. (Even so, who is like Herzog?) Pinpointing what we like about such galvanic, mesmerizing figures—what attracts us to them, what makes them useful to us—including at the level of seemingly superficial characteristics, proves a challenge.

Herzog himself cites the techniques of hypnosis, commentary upon which he devotes a chapter in his memoir, *Every Man for Himself and God Against All*:

> In fact, anyone can hypnotize. The cause of the mystifications is that we know very little about the mechanics of the brain switching off in hypnosis and sleep. All we really know is that we have to proceed methodically. There are simple techniques, fixing the eyes of the subject, say, with the point of a pencil. That is accompanied by a certain intense and suggestive way of speaking. In my later film voiceovers and commentaries, I was to draw on this way of speaking.[10]

The sound of Herzog's incantatory voice, then, lies at the rhythmically beating heart of any such audience attraction: "[t]here is at least a memory of my role as hypnotist in the timbre of my voice in documentaries."[11] And yet, Herzog, as is his way, counters mainstream opinion (e.g., by minimizing the power of his voice) and then concedes it. Note, in this passage the movement from pushback to double-down on the pertinency of his vocal inflections, his distinctive sonic registers—and how those qualities, in fact, cultivate imitators, which he now (in late maturity) seems happy to welcome.

> What matters, though, is not the voice itself but what the voice has to say. It is the content that spooks the audience. What I write and record could never appear, say, in a National Geographic film. At the end of my film on volcanoes, *Into the Inferno*, you see the streams of lava erupting from the interior of the earth, and my voice reminds the listener that deep under our feet there is glowing magma "that wants to burst forth and it could not care less about what we are doing up here. This boiling mass is just monumentally indifferent to scurrying roaches, retarded reptiles, and vapid humans alike." Sentences like that demand the appropriate intonation. I accept then that my voice in German has the South German twang of my first language, Bavarian. And I accept too that I speak English with a strong accent, maybe not quite so strong as Henry Kissinger's English but still sufficiently so for there to be a number of imitators on the Web who in "my" voice read fairy tales or give advice for living. There are dozens of imitators, but none of them has really caught my sound. My voice has found a great community of fans, which combined with my view of life asks to be imitated. I am a grateful victim of such satirists.[12]

Punctuation clues us into Herzog's careful attunement to provenance: there are many Herzog voices out there (viz., imitations), and yet they are not "my" voice. As with so many other vocal parodies, there is a need to combine sonic qualities with grammatical specificities. For instance, to an American ear, shifting from vocal parodies of Herzog, Henry Kissinger, and Arnold Schwarzenegger will be positively aided by diction and syntax. Moreover, practicing, as it were, the connection between the sound of a person's voice and the sorts of things that person says, over time, reinforces the deeper registration of that voice for one's own subvocal literary enunciation.[13] In everyday experience this attunement reveals itself in the contrast between the nearly isomorphic way in which one can replicate Herzog's voice when reading him (e.g., in his memoir) as against one's strained efforts to vocally imitate his voice (as he says, no one quite catching his sound). The version of Herzog's voice in one's head, therefore, can feel like the "grateful victim" of Herzog's own hypnotic powers: the mimesis is uncanny.

Meanwhile, when someone elects to imitate Herzog's voice—to tell a story or a joke, to apply it like a distinctive typeface to a given aural occasion—the results, subject to greater variation are also, therefore, subject to higher chances at falling flat. One can test this against one's own experience, but it seems that because one's personal/private Herzog (the mimetic voice operating mentally) is a closer match to Herzog's own voice, the mood remains serious; this is the voice, for instance, that accompanies one when reading *Every Man for Himself and God Against All*. When the voice becomes an affectation—a transformation applied by others—the results are regularly, even necessarily, more humorous. The pantomime, in turn, reflects back on our reception of Herzog: our imitation changes his status.

Again, O'Connell: "Though he is often a subject of parody, it is rarely noted how powerfully amusing—how seriously funny—Werner Herzog is. In a way that strikes me as characteristically German, he is often funniest when he's at his most serious."[14] Though O'Connell says it is seldom perceived, he captures a prevalent account: that it is Herzog's *seriousness* that is the activating agent for what makes him funny. Yet, in light of the logic just sketched, O'Connell's clever take is incomplete. When we listen to Herzog deliver his film voiceovers, the result is hardly ever laugh-out loud funny; rather, and this may be a function of those hypnotic qualities he propounds, what he says and how he says it rarely seem ridiculous. When Herzog's voiceover is placed in conversation and comparison with the distinctive qualities of that other iconic voiceover artist, Terrence Malick, we see how his Texan contemporary— and sometimes counterpart—draws from deep wells of (fictitiously-rendered) first-person and personal fragments filled as they are with poetic longing and a perpetual tilt that crosses from the immediate to the cosmically distant and back again; the Malickean approach also readily invites imitators—and satirists—but the structure of the voice/image interaction is of a different type than Herzog's method: not least the fact that actors perform the vocal insertion, whereas Herzog's voice inhabits the space at the screen's edge, around the film frame: Herzog is our guide not our protagonist (however much he "acts" his own sonic/iconic identity); he comments on scenes in sober, almost dispassionate and nondidactic exposition; he is authoritative but not preoccupied with persuasion. Malick's voiceover—circuited through actors in character—aims to make sense of the moving visual content he supplies (to intensify the emotional, erotic, or existential struggles on offer), whereas Herzog problematizes the obviousness—of the otherwise apparent meanings—of the images. With Malick's Heideggerian-inflected ontology, the voiceover and the film dissolve into one another, while Herzog's voiceover arrives from the puzzled mind of a proletarian autodidact.[15] Perhaps suited to such sensibilities, much of the time Herzog's seriousness strikes me as melancholic, as emerging from a man of profound sorrow, of a somber and serious man who (as he says of himself) cannot understand irony.[16] (Admittedly, such an impression may be true of his persona, yet false for the historical Herzog.) O'Connell turns our ear back to that iconic moment in *Burden of Dreams* when Herzog delivers his memorable monologue on the state of the jungle—and along with it, the state of men's souls in the midst of the cosmos:

> Taking a close look at what's around us, there is some sort of harmony. It is the harmony of overwhelming and collective murder. And we in comparison to the articulate vileness and baseness and obscenity of all this jungle, we in comparison to that enormous articulation, we only sound and look like badly pronounced and half-finished sentences out of a stupid suburban novel, a cheap novel. And we have to become humble in front of this overwhelming misery and overwhelming fornication, overwhelming growth, and overwhelming

lack of order. Even the stars up here in the sky look like a mess. There is no harmony in the universe. We have to get acquainted to this idea that there is no real harmony as we have conceived it. But when I say this, I say this all full of admiration for the jungle. It is not that I hate it. I love it. I love it very much. But I love it against my better judgment.[17]

First, note that the structure here matches the excerpt from the memoir just above: a proposal and then a reversal (or as above, a reversal and then a proposal). Here "there is some sort of harmony," and then the *type* of harmony we have is one defined by "overwhelming and collective murder," vileness, baseness, obscenity, misery, fornication, and—wait for it—"overwhelming lack of order." And so, yes, a type of harmony is lavishly, grotesquely defined by its disharmony. I raise a rhetorical point since we have been tracking such tendencies throughout the essays of this book: the way that Herzog's profundity regularly feeds on contradiction; he courts clarity then undermines it.

And so to the second point, while keeping the first in mind, namely that whether reading the display quote above ("Taking a close look at what's around us") or watching and listening to Herzog on camera in Les Blank's film, I don't find myself laughing. Herzog's seriousness in this case, and many similar others (including when he is "just" providing a voiceover, as in say, memorably *Grizzly Man*), is not funny, and definitely not seriously funny. Rather, it is parody that gives seriousness its lift-off, perhaps not surprisingly by virtue of the contrast parody provides. In other words, Herzog is seriously funny when others use Herzog's voice—or brand, and even sometimes Herzog himself (as actor)—to achieve parody.

Capturing a satisfying Herzogian-inflected image or sound is, by now, an old and reliable pastime. Talented forebears should be given their due, if also to provide tutorials on how it is done. One notable early contributor to the library of entertaining examples comes from the novelist Cathleen Schine, who in 1983—with *Fitzcarraldo* and *Burden of Dreams* still fresh in the public imagination, and clearly in her own—offered up dour (and yes, fabricated) excerpts "From the Diary of Werner Herzog."[18]

July 9, 1977. Idea for new film. *Fritz: Commuter*, nightmarish tale of German businessman obsessed with bringing professional hockey to Westport, Connecticut. No going back for me now.

October 6, 1977. There will be no compromise. Film must be shot on location in Westport. From the lurking danger of this landscape must come the authenticity that separates the filmmaker from the cows who do not dare to cross the street. My crew quits.

November 5, 1977. Make first expedition to Westport. Fascinated by fierce commuters found riding primitive Conrail line. I love this people. I love the spirit, full of a profound weariness of the feet. Alone and unarmed, I hire the trainload of passengers as extras. [...]

September 23, 1978. The devil plagues my production. Highest pollen count in history of Fairfield County. [Laurence] Olivier [hired as lead actor] develops hay fever. Ordered off set by doctors. The suffering here is overwhelming, a rotting, unspeakable suffering. There are no butterflies in this place, only moths. There are no flowers, only pollen. No joy, only death and chaotic sneezing. Documentary crew films as I and 300 commuters hack with machetes at eerie 10-foot stalks of goldenrod surrounding the station, Westport-Saugatuck, forsaken even by God, if he exists.

January 2, 1979. Scrambled eggs runny. I take walk. [...]

February 1, 1982. I am cursed. My film is cursed. My destiny is cursed. My film is my destiny. We are all three of us cursed: The

> engineer in charge of moving the train quits. Announces it is impossible to drag railway cars down Main Street on Memorial Day. I must go on without him. This is the central metaphor of my film, my vision—commuters straining at the ropes, hauling the reeking, brooding train through crowds of tiny, evil Cub Scouts. Without this central metaphor, my film is lost in the stinking emptiness of foul mediocrity. [...]

Schine's capable—and very funny—"selection" of diary entries manages, in a mere quarter-page spread in a local newspaper, to imitate Herzogian diction and syntax, the weight of self-imposed projects, the struggle to cooperate with one's fellow man, existential despair in the midst of the everyday, and the humor that underwrites all moments when seriousness goes too far—to the limit and then beyond it. Collapsing into laughter is one's only recourse. So with *Documentary Now!* and its Herzog parody, *Soldier of Illusion*—recast from its IFC television rendering in quotation marks (in two parts) to its unified status as a *Documentary Now!* (pseudo) documentary film and henceforth typeset in italics—where we can appreciate how the episodes' writer, John Mulaney, like Schine before him, mobilizes his extensive knowledge of Herzog's oeuvre in relation to our own to generate comedy.

We need to be literate in Herzog Studies, in some measure, in order to get the jokes. Mulaney, for instance, shows no clips of Herzog's actual work, but instead, satirizes a number of his films—calling forth our memories of these films (many of them desperately serious) to re-present them by way of an aggressive mimesis and distorted repetition. The films called in for duty include—*Burden of Dreams*, *Grizzly Man*, *Into the Abyss*, *Little Dieter Needs to Fly*, and *My Best Fiend*—all of them documentaries featuring Herzog's unmistakable voice and voiceover, and all of them with Herzog's on-camera presence as well. Feature films also inform staging and *mise-en-scène*, including *Aguirre, the Wrath of God*, *The Enigma of Kaspar Hauser*, and *Fitzcarraldo*. If we took these films seriously the first time (and during many screenings since), perhaps in Mulaney's hands, we can laugh at them when repurposed for the purposes of comedy.

Mulaney confidently enters the fray of debate, nay controversy, about how to capture the spirit of an Herzogian cinematic enterprise. Is the giveaway thematic? Or an aspect of cinematographic style? A matter of casting? Or dialogue? Since *Soldier of Illusion* is presented as an analog of *Burden of Dreams* (the latter a documentary about *the making of* a Herzog film), Mulaney picks up on the strange (ironic?) fact that Herzog's most emblematic films—perhaps also, the films we like best, including those made by Herzog—feature *him* in their diegesis (see remarks to this effect by Žižek in chapter II). In *Burden of Dreams*—as in so many of Herzog's own films, and again in *Soldier of Illusion*—Herzog is the main attraction (as interpreter of himself and *Fitzcarraldo*) of the feature presentation he is creating in real time (simultaneously as the interpretable object, the subject of his quest, and the proximate cause of his own self-inquest).

Retreading features of this handful of Herzog films, however, wouldn't be half as funny if Mulaney hadn't hit upon the notion to couple the Herzogian ethos—including a radical seriousness—with a genre that would slice through any imported pretensions, namely, the late 1970s/early '80s American sitcom. We are reminded of Mulaney's stand-up joke: "I'm a terrible driver. I know nothing about cars. I meant to learn about cars, but I forgot. Nothing that I know can ever help out with your cars ever. Unless you're like, uh, 'Oh, I got a flat tire. Does anybody here know a lot about *The Cosby Show*?'"[19] Mulaney's overfamiliarity with *The Cosby Show* and its ilk is on full display in his virtuosic insertion of a plotline involving the production of a sitcom pilot. The structure of *Soldier of Illusion* is quintessential Mulaney: "blending a highbrow loftiness with a certain lower strata of trash TV nostalgia."[20] Here we have famed German cinema legend Dieter Daimler (August Diehl), playing a variant of Klaus Kinski, who goes mad with a rage-and-resentment fueled tear when he loses a primetime Emmy Award to none other '80s teen icon Michael J. Fox.

Soldier of Illusion finds our rogue agent stylized as Rainer Wolz (played by Alexander Skarsgård with a combination of calm intensity and knowing self-involvement) in the midst of shooting a 1982 documentary about the indigenous people of the Ural Mountains—transformed into the titular inset documentary-in-the-making by Wolz: *A Journey Into The Way of the Dushkir People of the Ular Mountains*. Mulaney pushes a Herzogian ambition to new heights when we learn that Wolz is hard at work on not one but *two* projects: the first a "film chronicling the Dushkir people during their Tusian sheep breeding season" just mentioned. And the second? "A CBS sitcom called *Bachelor Nanny*." [Cue laugh track] The full title of the doubly ambitious, overlapping endeavor:

Soldier of Illusion

A Journey Into The Way of the Dushkir People of the Ular Mountains and The Making of the CBS Pilot "Bachelor Nanny"

Mulaney's prodigious Herzogian expertise is on full display in the crucial moment of this juxtaposition: where Wolz's "serious" film (viz., *A Journey Into The Way...*) would appear to be hampered, compromised, and otherwise undermined by the ludicrous time-filler, *Bachelor Nanny*, Wolz is, instead, shown to be as serious about the pre-production of his TV show, one featuring "[t]he story of a single guy who, after agreeing to take in his sister's twin newborns, has to juggle both babies... and babes." Critic William Hughes even detects a sentimental strain sufficient to declare that "*Soldier of Illusion* reveals itself, not as a parody of Herzog, but as an exploration, even a celebration, of his commitment to his creations."[21] Admittedly, Hughes is tracking a trend in *Documentary Now!* across its four seasons, such that "[t]here's been a shift away from parody deep in the show's DNA, into something more akin to a kind of comedic synthesis of the real and the fake." Cue Herzog as exemplar of the contest and intermingling of "the real and the fake" since forever, and you have the ideal candidate for homage at this stage of the show's evolution. In fact, Helen Mirren (playing Helen Mirren) raises the matter in her introduction, noting how the layered production shows how "truth and fiction blur" along with "man and nature." Compare the majestic *Fitzcarraldo* to the insouciant *Bachelor Nanny*—such a sentence has never before begun this way—and you get Hughes' point, dead on: "[i]t was absurd and tragic for Herzog to risk life and limb (his own, and others') for a doomed stab at dramatic grandeur; seeing the exact same level of dedication applied to a multi-camera sex farce airing opposite *Three's Company* elevates the entire thing into something both silly and sublime."[22]

We can duly factor the contrast into our own deliberations on the real/fake, authentic/factitious, truth/lie, silly/sublime, ordinary/ecstatic, man/nature, highbrow/lowbrow, film/TV, and the further running list of Herzogian tandems. With Herzog-as-auteur or Herzog-as-actor, and with varied incarnations of Herzog-imitated-by-others, we note the serious as it dissolves — or sometimes boldly inverts — into the unserious. Thus a further dyad for the list: a serious/silly binary is a fitting (and funny) dichotomy for our age, a durable pairing that informs or refracts "late modernity," "surveillance capitalism," "Western decadence," and other categories we use to explain our predicament. Reaching for a *tertium quid*, I invent or invoke the binary *sincerely*, since it is apt for measuring the manner of delivery (whether sincere seriousness or mock seriousness; sincere silliness or sardonic silliness), *and* since it has for some time provided elucidations about our era, a time we share on earth with Werner Herzog.

Mirren introduces the rogue filmmaker in the field by noting his "uncompromising vision," and thus picks up on the stubbornness or (again per Mirren) "single-minded vision" often associated with Herzog's projects. A running question in *Burden of Dreams* is the extent to which Herzog is genuinely endangering actors and extras in his pursuit of his objectives in fiction. When Rainer begins to speak (Skarsgård in command of his own claim to the timbre of Herzog's accent), we hear invectives that go too far (insulting "the ignorant stones") or using tropes in unrecognizable ways, as if coining his own sayings (bemoaning "the vinegar of the pompous"). (Herzogophiles will be charmed anew by Mulaney's prodigious casting since, of course, it is Alexander's dad, Stellan, who embodies "Verner Vollstedt" in the HBO series, *Entourage*[23]). Mulaney's writing and Skarsgård's performance parodically illustrate the oracular fashion in which Herzog speaks — and how it can be heightened by puerile comparisons, as in a scene set in a cave: "In silence, we can hear the anguish of the men mining boron decades ago. And maybe, we can hear our own heartbeats. [Beat. Gesturing to his right.] We could build a jacuzzi set here." When hiring a former child actor, Kevin Butterman (Nicholas Braun, Skarsgård's compatriot in *Succession*) to play Gordy Sinclair, the best friend of *Tonight Show* mainstay, Gary Jacks (Kevin Bishop), we learn of Wolz's casting strategy: Butterman exudes "the desperate longing of a broken man." When Wolz himself despairs after Gary Jacks is arrested and sent to a Russian gulag, Wolz describes the imperiled project: "We seemed destined to be another carcass on the shores of Hades."

Intercut within the making of *A Journey Into The Way... and The Making of the CBS Pilot "Bachelor Nanny,"* we are also treated to clips from ersatz "Herzog" films (complete with outtakes, fabricated world-building details, release years, and running times), among them Wolz classics:

The Trials of Master Pfreim (1979, running time: three hours)
The Bavarian Widow Cole
The Cruel Pubescence of Anst Dangler
The Stigmata of Aldo the Dwarf (1962, featuring Dieter Daimler)

Documentary Now!'s Mulaney treatment, like other knowing meta-critiques, illustrates in hilarious detail—this time with a live audience and applause sign (made of wood and illuminated by fire)—how humor erupts from these now-familiar and ever-distinctive features. Herzog's Bavarian dialect mapped slightly out of alignment onto English, then matched with inventive diction, coalesce into an instrument for insight: *whatever* he says has a chance to *sound profound*. And funny. Meanwhile, quite startlingly in our day, Herzog's speech is not peppered with filler words that weaken his resolve: like, you know, literally, actually, kind of, sort of, or the confirmation-seeking, upwardly inflected "right?" Sure his mystical pronouncements *sound* genuine, but so does his shopping list and directions for getting to the grocery store. Lines from ancient Greek philosophy or German Romanticism, a cereal box or a commercial for laundry detergent; high and low culture, rarefied intellectual domains and pop marketing find their shared level.

Saturday Night Live drew from Herzogian resources for audio book auditions to read Britney Spears' memoir, *The Woman in Me*. In the star-studded line-up of celebrity voice talent invited to the test, Herzog (played by James Austin Johnson) reads lines from the book with a diction and intonation meant to muster the German filmmaker for the soundstage: "'N Sync was what people called back then so pimp. They were white boys, but they loved hip hop. [Stopping, turning to the camera, breaking from his narration]

I'm entranced by this Floridian vernacular."[24] Three sentences: first, name-checking from the 2020s the exoticism of 1990s teenage pop music, then an unexpected overlap—or contest— of cultures, and finally, mock-Herzog's use of serious words spoken seriously—"Floridian vernacular"—to comment on an unserious phenomenon. So if he were, in turn, to speak of Fruit Loops or Pop Tarts, the mundane would be charged with an odd, new energy. The ordinary would be estranged— forcing us to approach it on new terms. His capacity to forge hitherto unmade combinations is one of (genuine) Herzog's gifts to us. And also among his repertoire of pranks. For if his voice, his talent for speech, his quest for (invigorating) imagery and worthy objects of attention is generous and generative, it also often invites us to approach that razor's edge of silliness upon which we slice ourselves (ever-sharp machetes wielded wildly in the mist). In Herzog's seriousness, he has courted, rare among his contemporaries, the comedic equivalent of "breaking"—for Herzog's speech can feel serious right up to the moment it becomes something else: self-mocking, lost in a fog of indecipherability, incomprehensible to even the more sincere and devoted among his listeners.

Let me knowingly test out the playful formula with the dead-serious implications. Herewith we recall that Ludwig Wittgenstein once said: "[f]or if today's circumstances are so different, from what they once were, that you cannot compare your work with earlier works in respect of its *genre*, then you equally cannot compare its *value* with that of the other work."[25] Wittgenstein, a veritable icon of (philosophical) seriousness and distinctively European sophistication (Brahms and Mahler performed in the family home; Klimt and Schiele were beneficiaries of his father's largesse) was also known for being a dedicated fan of detective novels and the silliest of American movies (among them Westerns)—a patrician in dungarees.[26] Perhaps we have hit upon some feature common to these boys from Bavaria and Austria, a knack for penetrating intensity (necessarily) alleviated by distracting ephemera, as if after reading the *Tractatus Logico-Philosophicus*, the only satisfying recourse for recovery would be an off-the-stand issue of the latest *People* magazine.

Sachrang, where Herzog was raised, is nestled close to Austria ("The border to Tyrol was no more than half a mile away."[27] "I am a Bavarian. Bavarian is my first language."[28]).

Herzog, like Wittgenstein, often speaks in parables and puzzles drawn from everyday language, religious inheritances, pithy apothems, and cultural miscellany; these philosophers of the commonplace—and the heady—make the simple complicated and the complicated simple, speaking and writing in ordinary language that is disarming (if often still intellectually demanding, enduringly mystifying). Wittgenstein, who in his life published a slim book and a few book reviews, is the instigating cause for bookcases full of critical commentary by others; a modern-day Socrates, someone who so unsettled established philosophical habits, beliefs, and practices that posterity became obsessed with parsing the subtleties of what (little?) he said and wrote. Taken seriously, such remarks are haunting, life-altering. Taken up as ponderous or tendentious, they are silly. "If a lion could talk, we would not understand it," noted Wittgenstein.[29] So too perhaps with Wittgenstein and Herzog. The enigma has company, as when the sensibilities of the poor, fatherless Bavarian-living-on-the-border meets the wealthy, cultured Viennese, and the two see eye to eye.

Upon a superficial scan, we wouldn't be inclined to say that Herzog creates religious films, and yet when reviewing—and tallying themes, styles, and obsessions across the decades—it can appear that Herzog might agree with Wittgenstein, who said: "I am not a religious man but I cannot help seeing every problem from a religious point of view."[30] In this apparently godless universe, or one equipped with an ambivalent (noninterventionist) god, both men—philosopher and filmmaker alike—have ears for the "bells from the deep." During a session of the Rogue Film School, Herzog provided for the class live audio commentary on the eponymous film, describing how those Russians, face down on the ice, searching for salvation, for absolution from a distant chord were, in fact, drunk—passed out. And yet *Bells from the Deep: Faith and Superstition in Russia* (1993), nevertheless, resonates with a kind of (genuine) religious depth. In Herzog's films, the immanent real is imbued with the gravity and grace of the numinous. Framing, long-takes, voiceover, and the imposition of nondiegetic music—these are part of the Herzogian toolkit for transcendentalizing the familiar, the earthly, the otherwise ordinary (and thus unseen, unheard, unattended to). Who can hear such callings?

For one and all, there is ever a question of vocational fit: what is it one is *called* to do? The answer may reveal itself in native talent or by way of an accident. Indeed, we may be called—permitted—to perform in ranges beyond our skill set. What then? "She should've been a _____," the common judgment goes—as if time had exposed one's proper realm, but history or fate or some other force had chosen otherwise (however unexpressed, left latent). Herzog had simply set out to make a film (I am thinking here of *The Great Ecstasy of the Woodcarver Steiner*), when he had to solve the problem of supplying voiceover talent. Inserting himself into the position might have been a one-off, a go-to place for Herzog fans to listen to the director narrate a film, never to be repeated. Instead, it was a test—an audition not for an audiobook but— for a life-defining alteration in the fabric of his films. "This was a step the full gravity of whose implications I did not see right away," Herzog tells us, "[i]t led to my finding my voice, my stage voice, if you like."[31] Rather than Stanley Kubrick, Herzog would edge closer to David Attenborough—a voice, and in time, also a presence on screen.

The accident of Herzog's desperate problem-solving gave rise to a distinctive approach to filmmaking—and by logical extension, a distinctive kind of film. We could quickly, provocatively conclude that as a result of this single—if substantial, and in time pervasive—shift in technique, Herzog became his own genre: one that includes his films *and* his persona. And we could go further to claim that the (Herzog) genre also hosts subgenres and cycles that accommodate his range of experiments (adventure narratives, TV shorts, public service announcements, documentaries of mixed veracity, topic-based think pieces, biographical portraits, retrospectives, found-footage experiments, concert videos, etc.)

Still more, parodic work, such as *Soldier of Illusion*— what can be deemed a late entry into the satirical uptake of the Herzogian brand—provides confirmation that Herzog is also an idiom: artists, comedians, cartoonists, fellow filmmakers, and more can work in the key of Herzog. And yet working "in the mode of Herzog" would be self-contradictory and thus self-defeating, since part of Herzog's challenge is his inimitability— despite all evidence to the contrary: to the way his work forces us to take it on his terms and *not our own*. As the Rogue Film School perpetually emphasized, it is only by working on one's own projects that one finds a way forward. Still, the notion that every filmmaker—or even many of them—could be "original" is absurd. After all, the Rogue Film School itself was a paradoxical expression of Herzog's long and fervently held intolerance for film schools (and along with them, famously, academic criticism of films and film theory, the worst of all). Yet, there is one exception to the self-defeat—namely, when "Herzog" takes on "Herzog"—as is accomplished by *Soldier of Illusion*. Mulaney and team deploy an *idea* of Herzog (as a genre with identifiable traits that can be marshaled and applied) to specific elements of a Herzogian *idiom* (e.g., head for the mountains or some extreme in nature; make contact with an indigenous culture; include humans behaving in ways that defy easy explanation; struggle with the practical and logistical elements of filmmaking itself; include animals that point up human foibles and idiosyncrasies; compare-and-contrast disparate phenomena so they end up "speaking" to one another, as if offering unvarnished commentary; deploy an evocative score (Wagner played over burning oil fields); insert a formidable voiceover saying things that make viewers question their relation to what they see and hear, what they believe as it connects to the circumstances in which they watch and listen, and so on. Funny, then, that when Mulaney reached out to Herzog with an invitation for him to appear on the comedian's live talk-show, *Everybody's in LA*, Herzog responded by saying "I have to keep away from the comedians."[32]

Among the many reactions Herzog may be said to activate in his audience is the question of how much the historical, born in Bavaria, living in Los Angeles, Werner is genuinely "himself" on screen, or more pervasively, "in voice"—an unseen presence that fills the frame yet remains invisible. Perhaps our reasonable error, being trusting, gullible souls, is taking him at his word. Little Werner has transubstantiated into "Herzog"—the brand, the genre, the idiom. Herzog himself—in the figure of his own physical person *and* in the nature of his own idiosyncratic quests—has provided an image for us all to ponder, reflect up, and measure ourselves against. The doubleness that often tracks his characters' pursuits (e.g., Fitzcarraldo's mission, Herzog's mission to film the feature *Fitzcarraldo*) shows up in our own viewing of his films and interviews. Here is a person who, like Thoreau, aimed "to front only the essential facts of life"—and stirs us to question whether we have done anything similar, or want to—including questioning those "facts of life."[33] Perhaps they too are in need of critique, have introduced layers of obscurity between oneself and right perception. After all, for some, for many perhaps, it is satisfactory (and satisfying) to watch *Fitzcarraldo*, where a vision is pursued relentlessly (with Herzog set in apposition to the eponymous hero); for others, it is a pleasure to listen to Herzog's metacinematic comments in *Burden of Dreams*. This tandem is gratifying. For others, though, such experiments may be a prod to seek one's own "original relation to the universe," as Emerson put it.[34] Not to absorb or abscond with Herzog's dream of the world, but to have one of one's own—and live in it.

Herzog's doubleness—his persona and its varieties—helps us see the constructedness and illusoriness of ourselves, that is, *our* selves, our *selves*. No wonder we are entranced with a human who seems to have quieted the vices of vanity in himself. Herzog, it would seem (and it is just fine if this is but another appearance) has figured something out, so why would we willingly miss the chance to learn from him by looking away, by condescending to his findings? Character is a name we give to represent our virtues and virtuousness, but *a* character is something we "play"; the same word pivots between our highest ideals and their most illusory states. Similarly, a self is a role, a project, a story; hence unreal but also in progress and thus revisable (able to be seen and re-seen). Do we all have personas as well as selves? Having a persona—perhaps especially an evolving or refractive one—reinforces the ephemerality of the self. The *creation* of a persona must entail a *death* of the idea that one is who one *thinks* one is—or, more literally, that one is precisely that: who one regards oneself *as* is in fact what one *is*, which to say no *thing* at all, but a collection of gestures and ideas and characteristics. Whether they are willed into existence or accidental may stir a riddle.

For the rationalists among us, we recall Alan Watts describing human incarnation as "symptomatic" of prior causes and effects: this logic seems to strip existence of its mystery, and yet, it also liberates us from the painful, problematic illusion that we have control over the constitution and care of the self—especially in so far as we take that name, "self," as anything more than a system-in-flux; we aren't selves so much as shifting patterns of energy that are (for social convenience) referred to by a name—an appropriately tenuous label for an erratic network of potentialities that make themselves known—then disappear. For the comedians among us, *Soldier of Illusion* finds Wolz standing beside a camp fire, announcing to his compatriots: "Tonight we kill our egos by burning ourselves in effigy," whereupon he drops his hand-carved wooden Rainer into the consuming flames. (Those caught up in the wider cult of Herzogian mass culture can think of that other consumable: a six-inch high *Star Wars* action figure of The Client—made as if to make real, by proxy, a Herzog who is "a half-foot in the finite."[35] Herzog's persona embodied in plastic, a durable petroleum-based artifact that may outlast his films, his writing, and humanity itself.)

All to say that whether Herzog intuited or was instructed in certain strains of Buddhism, Hinduism, and Stoicism, his stance of anti-analysis, anti-psychoanalysis, anti-therapy, anti-theory, anti-navel-gazing, anti-vanity, etc. places him in proximity to these anti-theoretical traditions. There is in them a preference for action over any deep reasoning about truths and traumas. Herzog's latent/lapsed Catholicism stokes a point of intrigue here, since he may have stumbled upon appealing— and appealingly similar—methods of orientation elsewhere: in Perú, in Ghana, in Tokyo, among other places, in company with other people.[36] Still another dispositional inflection arrives from ancient Christian contemplatives such as the desert fathers with their penchant for asceticism, hermeticism, and mysticism (especially the practice of *hesychasm*—from the Greek for rest, stillness, quiet, and silence). Ironically, in this context or set of contexts across broad timespans and varied traditions, *meditation* suggests slowing down to think (to think things over and through), and yet that isn't what Marcus Aurelius' *Meditations* or Dzogchen meditation counsel: they are observational, not judgmental; perceptual, not analytical. Hence, "seeing plain"—seeing and hearing and observing and doing.[37] What else do soldiers do but do? What else are boots for but walking? The rhetorical questions send us back afresh to the ways that Herzog destabilizes the singularity and solidity of identification (including treating one's thoughts as one's own—indeed, as a collection amounting to a self) and instead takes up residence in his ever-shifting, ever-evolving persona (or however many of them there might be).

A change of name is such a method for calling these attributes to mind, thus by no more than fiat—a whim, however deeply felt—Werner Stipetić becomes Werner Herzog.[38] In a retrospective mood, he writes: "[...] I was torn between the two surnames. When I entered my first screenplay in a competition (it was for *Signs of Life*), it was under the name Stipetić, but later as a director, I thought I'd better stick to Herzog. To this day, I feel some relief in knowing my origins are somewhat swathed in mystery. Which surname is the *nom de plume* and which isn't?"[39] The terminological trade breaks what can feel like an alchemical bond between a name and its referent; Emerson tells us "[g]ood and bad are but names very readily transferable to that or this."[40] Admittedly, the claim weighs in on a nascent nineteenth-century moral relativism, but when the stress of interpretation is placed on "names," there is a shocking admission of the contingency of ascription. The new name is a mask but also a marker of ephemerality: it is always provisional, never something that rewards an *indulgent* inwardness. Herzog postulates that, despite its apparent superficiality, a nominal exchange may be a prophylactic against malicious cosmic forces.[41]

Still, expectations for understanding—and practicing— such programs can, in fact, be or become hard, even impossible tasks, ones that each and all come to know as their own Sisyphean "conquests of the useless," including the quixotic pursuits of random extremes, stranded as we are on remote shores or lost in dense jungles of our own making. With our stage names, how apposite to find ourselves upon nature's stage—subject to its caprice, defined by its laws and limits? All the while surveying general human conditions, shared circumstances, we have been encouraged (especially by his films and the critics who study them) to consider Herzog's essential particularity—his own very Herzogness. Notwithstanding, it could be that all along he has been trying to illuminate something specific about human imagination as such, which to say, how we are all subject to the very same forces and thus availed to same opportunities for searching (and perhaps also, subsequent elucidation). Though we watch what Herzog has imagined—cultivated from the found objects of civilization, conjured from his encounters with its inhabitants, we ask: What can we imagine? And why don't we do a better job of imagining it? The historical Herzog, living serenely in Los Angeles, has managed to punctuate his life such that the idea of Herzog—as seen and heard on film, as glimpsed in his books—is also a reality. Should we wish to adopt it, the strategy appears ready for the taking. And yet: to what end? Imitation of others can become its own kind parody; in time, so focused on others—especially exemplars—we lose track of ourselves.

As *Soldier of Illusion* makes evident, parody works best when it is internal to the system under investigation—thus, Herzog on Herzog. Moreover, the greater the context, the greater the potential insight leveraged from the interaction, thus: more than a half-century of Herzog's work can gamely be referenced in the span of these short episodes. Consequently, the television text becomes a repository of prismatic and refractive significance. Note by contrast, how Mulaney's points of cinematic homage are numerous (at least eight separate films, as adduced above), whereas most other episodes of *Documentary Now!* find room to engage only a single prior instance (in some cases two). Of the twenty-seven episodes thus-far created, only the one devoted to Herzog draws on more than two films. The deviation underwrites claims already under investigation here, namely, that Herzog has escaped the bounds of his films and that his films are more than just filmed works of art, instead standing as totems of signification awaiting our interpretation; and still more, that Herzog's films—despite lines of coincidence and affiliation between them—are too disparate to be reduced to a single, iconic work (as has been done for other auteurs, such as Robert J. Flaherty, Errol Morris, and Spalding Gray).

In the case of Les Blank's *Burden of Dreams*, Herzog emphatically left the editorial suite for the diegetic space of another's film. A mockumentary film like *Incident at Loch Ness* (2004, dir. Zak Penn) appears to blend aspects of *Burden of Dreams* and *Soldier of Illusion* in so far as it trades on Herzog's actual presence in the documentary space (like Blank's film) and mounts a parody of Herzog's work (like Mulaney's episodes). As a reminder: *Incident at Loch Ness* begins with a flashback where we are, in fact, watching a different film—a documentary called *Herzog in Wonderland* directed by the esteemed cinematographer John Bailey (also playing himself), in which Herzog is interviewed ahead of his pursuit of his next documentary, *Enigma of Loch Ness*. Genre hijinks ensue, including a familiar contest between Herzog and Penn that calls to mind the fraught relationship between Herzog and Kinski. At the end of *Incident at Loch Ness*, doubt is introduced that this film—as well as *Enigma of Loch Ness*—could be fictitious. Just because people are "playing themselves"—Werner Herzog as himself—doesn't mean the documentary is presented in earnest. The concluding joke trades on the audience's struggle to determine the diegesis within the multiple films on offer, even if prior knowledge of the Herzog/Penn co-production might have confirmed, or led us to suspect, that we were headed for a multi-layered fabulation. The hoax teaches its own kinds of lessons, among them the disorientation that magnifies when an historical person becomes a persona, when, say, Werner Herzog "as himself" becomes dislocated from an aspiration for an origin—a meta-Werner.[42]

2. Truth, Authenticity, and Cinaesthetics

WE HAVE HEARD MUCH ABOUT PEOPLE BEING, or claiming to be, "authentic"—about having or disclosing an "authentic self"—and as a measure of cultural criticism in response to such sentiments, Theodor Adorno chiding the "jargon of authenticity."[43] But what would "authenticity" mean with respect to cinema, in a past age or in our own? For instance, as Filipe Martins, editor of the volume *Aesthetic Authenticity in Cinema*, generously invited us to consider, how might such authenticity be expressed or function as a matter of cinema aesthetics—cinaesthetics?[44] Or as some next-gen incarnation of auteur theory? (The death of the author risks a sin aesthetics, so we have to scramble.) Replies to such questions and quagmires would do well to take stock of the triangulated network of concepts on offer—namely, cinema, authenticity, and aesthetics—by terminological investigation and also by way of illustrative examples. Yet what is the *motive* behind such an exercise (as for example, embodied by the present book: a good faith investigation of Herzog despite his dubiousness about the merits of such a venture)? One could choose from a few compelling ones, but established discourses about the demise, decay, or death of cinema stand out as do the skeptics who would imagine there is no such thing or attribute as authenticity to seek after (especially when speaking of the individual "self" and by extension the cinema such an alleged self would somehow create or possess). Hardly news, we live at a time when the very definition of cinema is contested—as medium, as artform, as mode of expression—and authenticity may seem very far from its mainstream offerings, such as the computer-generated frenzies of various Marvel, DC, and

Disney dispensations, and now the onrushing emergence of generative artificial intelligence and its onslaught of deepfakes and unapologetic plagiarisms. In many cases, and as part of the proximate background that haunts these proceedings, we hear whispered suggestions that cinema has not so much died as, to some extent, become televisual—and/or that television has become more cinematic.[45] What then, we ask anew, of cinematic authenticity? Or more generally, "*aesthetic* authenticity," which can seem even further from daily concerns and popular entertainments than (an increasingly marginalized) cinematic tradition? And yet the powerful syntagma suggests we should want to make sense of it, as if coming to clarity about such a notion would be illuminating for what we take to be a gift of cinema itself, including, with some measure of sanguinity, its future.

The contours and questions of the foregoing paragraph— and several to come—were prompted by Martins and the occasion of his *Aesthetic Authenticity in Cinema*, a project for which he proposed that authenticity may be aligned with species of realism, including naïve versions.[46] In a word, what is authentic is real, or "comes off" as realistic. Sometimes we hear of "gritty realism"—implying, perhaps, that there's a spectrum from "gritty" to "refined." Finding examples of extremes and the increments in between poses an amusing challenge. Are diegetic locations enough to make the call: where the midtown grime of *Uncut Gems* (2019, dir. Josh and Benny Safdie) marks it as gritty, while the lustrous accommodations of *The White Lotus* (2021-23, creator Mike White) make it refined? High-end hotels can't hide the moral debauchery, double standards, and ethical breaches that make the resplendently-appointed scenes as "gritty" as some big-city, backstreets, contraband thriller; those rarefied island getaways appear just as compromised as the sordid Manhattan stockroom trades, the five-star betrayals just as tawdry. *Cinematic* realism (or cinematic *realism*), then, may be a mismatch for a quick or satisfying definition of authenticity because the context of the diegetic space shifts the very conditions for what counts as realism, as realistic. And when one adds the passage of time, what appears realistic to one generation seems campy or pantomime to another. The spell of (cinematic or televisual) "realism" is unpredictable in its potency and duration.

If we turn to ask about formalism, which in some precincts—especially the experimental and avant-garde cinematic traditions—celebrated standard bearers can feel very far from "realistic," and yet may still derive, in all earnestness, from an artist's "authentic" vision. Indeed, it could be a filmmaker's uncompromising deployment of the medium—e.g., by way of structural techniques—that places the result beyond the appreciation of most moviegoers. Hollis Frampton's *Lemon* (1969) is nothing but an encounter with its eponymous fruit, and yet what film student is not (at first and perhaps for a long time after) confounded by the concentrated, durational portrait? Even with a studied long take, one doesn't rush to declare the film a "realistic" encounter with a lemon. A filmmaker may cultivate certain styles that become recognizable such that in time we affiliate formal techniques with a given artist; such a habit, though, can make authenticity the enemy of innovation. As betokened early on, style as constraint.[47] When a celebrated auteur deviates from a style—or styles—for which the filmmaker is well-known and perhaps highly esteemed, the artist may be derided. (Acknowledging the risk, where is Herzog's rom-com?) Formalism, then, resists a quick determination of authenticity, or should, since we miss the surprises that await when an auteur moves on from signature traits and repetitions that made fame possible in the first place.

Then there is truth as it finds its associations with realism, formalism, and perhaps especially, authenticity. As the convenors of this conversation note, "there are less naïve realisms that accept the inevitability of performance and artifice, even though, at the same time, they also seek to preserve, or even intensify, some form of truth or authenticity."[48] The inclusive disjunction at the end—truth or authenticity—underwrites an appreciation of their synonymity; and yet, after the editor accentuates Herzog's cinema as an exemplar of this type of realism—an auteur who "highlights the subjectivity and poetic effort involved in cinema, including documentary cinema," we note quotation marks in another claim soliciting our reflection: "[a]ll art seeks some kind of authenticity or 'truth.'"[49] Suddenly, and not long after we had handy equivalents, truth has become "truth." The apparent debasement—an effect of ironizing, perhaps, or the result of a prevailing skepticism—can be explained, in part, by reference to the just invoked Herzog, who confides:

> I have, with every one of my films, attempted to move beyond facts and illuminate the audience with ecstatic truth. Facts might have normative power, but they don't constitute truth. Facts don't illuminate. Only truth illuminates. By making a clear distinction between "fact" and "truth," I penetrate a deeper stratum that most films don't even know exists. The truth inherent in cinema can be discovered only by not being bureaucratically, politically, and mathematically correct. In other words, I play with the facts as we know them. Through imagination and fabrication, I become more truthful than the bureaucrats.[50]

Some filmmakers and literary theorists might simply ask in reply: "Why not call it *fiction*, then, since fiction is the art of 'moving beyond facts?'" But that wouldn't be as much fun, which is to say intellectually stimulating. So we allow Herzog to prank us while we play along with the quotation marks around "truth," as the punctuation finds its bearings—and semiotic import. The inclination to regard facts as interpretable (rather than as given, singular, etc.) and as the conditions for distortion is tied to Herzog's early encounters with fabrications that have real-world effects. "There were some things in my studies that I found utterly absorbing," he tells us.

> For a class on medieval history, I wrote a paper on the *Privilegium Maius*. This was a flagrant forgery from 1358 or 1359; in fact, it was a set of five clumsy mutually reinforcing forgeries, one supposedly going all the way back to Julius Caesar and Nero. […] The false documents led to the establishing of legally binding conditions and ultimately to the creation of the state of Austria. The falsification was already recognized by the Renaissance poet Petrarch, but in historical terms, it was crowned with success.[51]

Note the layering of eventual Herzogian themes: how fabrications may yield truth or true effects; how forgeries can be efficacious (Rogue Film School students will recall lessons on forging permits); how fictions beget fictions, illusions all the way down—and yet, with a bit of an undiagnosed Freudian flourish: admit what is truly at issue, lurks latently, and then lay the tracks for a veritable return of the repressed. Herzog calls the *Privilegium Maius* "an early instance of fake news," and describes how its qualities informed his future life as a raconteur of the fabulous:

> I developed in my work a method that—not that I knew it—had never previously been used. Because my films to this day are preoccupied with questions of factuality, reality, and truth, in the sense of what I am pleased to call "ecstatic truth," I offer no more than a short account of it here. I declared, even if it was illogical, that the "privilegium" was a true account and knocked props into the ground to view the documents from all possible perspectives while always using a contemporary argumentation of the time—power politics, social change, understanding of the law, balance of military power—and at the end, one could take out the props and one still had a supportable tissue of argument. In other words, the falsification, the fake news, turned in its structure to truth because history had anchored its changes there, as in an evolving truth.[52]

Call this a petrified wood theory of historical truth, or, befitting Herzog's devotion to the classics, perhaps a ship of Theseus theory of how the incremental investment of falsities leads ineluctably to truth—at least to habits of thought and action that are sufficiently integrated to no longer cause alarm. In his anecdote about the *Privilegium Maius* and his explanation of its effects on his outlook, Herzog is, in effect, providing a clinic on how tiny fabulations can become grand, world-shaping myths—demonstrating how the more lies the more potency.

If Herzog is obscuring his rightful claim to "fiction" (or fictionalizing) he is, let us say more genuinely, scrambling the customary or inherited conversation about authenticity;

he is, if with a wink, undertaking a revaluing of values. The Nietzschean percipience is poignant, since it was Nietzsche, another beloved provocateur declaiming from mountain tops, who gave us "On Truth and Lies in a Nonmoral Sense"—and elsewhere gestated a crucial credo of contemporary authenticity talk in his commendation-cum-admonition to "become the person you are."[53] Note, in what follows, how Nietzsche drops the quotation marks around "truth," or never had them.

> [Humans] are deeply immersed in illusions and in dream images; their eyes merely glide over the surface of things and see "forms." Their senses nowhere lead to truth; on the contrary, they are content to receive stimuli and, as it were, to engage in a groping game on the back of things.[54]

Nietzsche's attention to "dream images" makes him seem positively Herzogian *avant la lettre*. And the scene takes us back even further to the protocinematic quality of Plato's cave, such as it depicts in striking, uncanny clarity the first principles of cinematic projection, illusion-making, and, for Plato at least (and allegorically speaking), confirmation of the human *distance* from truth. The flickering light of the projection flame, though made of the same substance as the sun, fails to provide adequate illumination for the perception of truth. In Plato's allegory, after all, we were (merely) present to the dance of shadows, more precisely, enslaved to them. Nietzsche appears to metabolize the Platonic heritage in his line of questions made twenty-three centuries after the fact: "Where in the world could the drive for truth have come from?"[55] Before Freud gave us the sex and death drives, Nietzsche descries a "truth drive" in humans, something that, ironically, gives rise to a passion for dissimulation.[56] Now the quotation marks are replaced or rather, put in place:

> [*T*]*hat* which shall count as "truth" from now on is established. That is to say, a uniformly valid and binding designation is invented for things, and this legislation of language likewise establishes the first laws of truth. For the contrast between truth and

> lie arises here for the first time. The liar is a person who uses the valid designations, the words, in order to make something which is unreal appear to be real. [...] He misuses fixed conventions by means of arbitrary substitutions or even reversals of names.[57]

Again the cinematic affiliations declare themselves as we make a wider consideration of the whole fateful business of moving images (and accompanying sounds). Are they not all—from sincere documentary footage to the digital-effects tempest of CGI-laden fantasy—aimed at making the "unreal appear to be real"? Film of whatever strip(e), or arriving with whatever intention, is under Nietzschean analysis, fundamentally a matter of proxies. We do not look *through* a window into the world that documentary filmmakers inhabit, but rather *at* a screen upon which the reflected and refracted findings of the filmmaker are presented (according to the structures and effects of filmstock, digital sensor, lens type, color grading, *syuzhet*, voiceover, score, screen size, computational software, and more).

Moreover, our artful philologist points out the emergent habits of invention as they pertain to the "legislation of language." Alas, another medium of surrogacy. We do not behold the object so much as handle its reality by means of names and the art of naming ("We separate things according to gender, designating the tree as masculine and the plant as feminine. What arbitrary assignments! How far this oversteps canons of certainty!"[58]). Once something has been named, we can easily—with but a typographical flourish—make a *punct* with punctuation, invert or reverse its definition: in one stroke, truth becomes "truth."[59] Metaphors become the currency of human perception and human knowledge: "Truths are illusions which we have forgotten are illusions; they are metaphors that have become worn out and have been drained of sensuous force, coins which have lost their embossing and are now considered as metal and no longer as coins."[60] Using metaphors to describe metaphors—a bit of bold Nietzschean metaphilosophy to exhibit how the reversals and reflexivity in our thinking about any such thing (or attribute) as authenticity, realism, formalism, and truth are compr(om)ised by our embodied perceptual apparatuses, our thoughts as mediated by language and fleshy circuits, and perhaps most emphatically, our (perverse) *pleasure* in being deceived. For if we have a "truth drive," we sublimate it in our fascinated, fastidious movie watching—attending to unreal realms that comfort and illuminate by dissimulation. Cinema has lost its embossing, hence our deliriously, generously applied willing suspension of disbelief. We love to be lied to; in this scheme, it is how we fathom truth. No quotation marks needed.

What began as an acknowledgment of the polysemy of authenticity now seems tied to a forced admission that it will remain a term of art designed and implemented to suit our disparate purposes. In today's parlance, authenticity is a buzz word—that is, a word with a charge (and occasionally a sting) but also without any fixed, formal, or agreed upon definition. The word makes an impact—we feel its sizzle when applied—but also cannot account for what it entails. We have arrived at a picture of our world, or our circumstances within it: the material dimension ruled by time and space; our imagemaking tools; our languages; and the human perceptual states—somatic, cognitive—that contend with the first three categories.

The celebrity memoir—not ghost-written, not "as told to"—activates an interested fan's pursuit of an author's authenticity. Are these stories and anecdotes true? How sincerely told? To what extent are the memories embellished—or for that matter, pure fiction? What, in fact, is an *authorized* autobiography?[61] Since the 1970s, we have been treated to Herzog's private journals, memorably in *Of Walking in Ice*. Periodic dispatches, such as *Conquest of the Useless*—an excavation of an artifactual diary—arrived later, out of phase with the time of its deliberations (the late seventies and early eighties production of *Fitzcarraldo*). Yet, as if on cue, a pandemic-era distraction made available, we have been gifted Herzog's memoir in motion—that is, an up-to-the-minute reflection on a life that percolates with present-day commentary and even includes a digest of (provisionally?) "unrealized projects." Like Woody Allen reading aloud from scraps of papers with one-line sketches for future films, Herzog gives voice to some visions—though we may not be ready to sign up as executive producer just yet: "I want to make a film with Mike Tyson about the early Frankish kings."[62] Other strands are less esoteric and more tantalizing, especially after spending a few days with Herzog's novel, *The Twilight World*: "I want to make a film about Onoda on the island of Lubang [...]."[63] Herewith, then, from Herzog's own pen, a book title—*Every Man for Himself and God Against All*—that would appear to capture a vast swath of the Herzogian perspective, a sheaf of pages aimed to explain and excite in shifting measures.

3. The Exceptional Everyman

WHY DOES WERNER HERZOG STILL FASCINATE US—perhaps increasingly so with each passing year, each new decade? In unheroic times defined by physical dissipation and mental distraction, Herzog is a formidable icon of clear-sighted focus, self-sufficient determination, poetic straight-talk, visionary ad/ventures—shouldered, provisional, failed, recuperated. Of questions asked, quests taken. He identifies a point of interest and then pursues it relentlessly to see where it leads; it often delivers him nowhere—hence these conquests of the useless, these fruitless forays. But for us that endeavor is, nevertheless, illuminating, inspiring, emboldening—for we are not just questing and questioning after the useless, but *finding* it, *answering* its call—and thereafter "con-questing" it: taking command of the results, come what may, as one's ownmost domain. The burden is bold and romantic, but why should we spare or squander our limited time and waning energies for anything less—even if the ends end up being worthless? —Risk all to yield mighty truths.

Herzog is the flip side of Noah Baumbach and his cast of proxies—characters from *Kicking and Screaming* to the present: anxious, effete, deferential, perfectionistic, neurotic, negative, ineffective, frustrated, full of longing and regret, melancholic, pessimistic, self-doubting, self-hating, self-defeating, self-sabotaging, buffeted by events, easily wounded. A modern man. Ben Stiller's characters in Baumbach films (and beyond). Meanwhile, Herzog is serious, often mock serious. And so when he is parodied, it seems the mock seriousness is mocked—a double negative reminding us of the positive? Seriousness regained? The intensity of Herzog's disdain—while couched in a calm manner—makes his brand of equanimously delivered critique all the more penetrating. Herzog alternates between a man who wears a perpetual smile, who is at ease with himself (a Bavarian Buddha) and a man who rarely smiles—plays things straight—deadpan even (a Hollywood villain). He is wise to any slippage from serious to self-serious, when profundity risks becoming false profundity. Irony bites at his heels. At times Herzog's logic becomes convoluted—silly, worthy of ridicule; he seems to be dissembling. He takes on odd—sometimes offensive—causes; he champions figures whose behavior and values many find contestable, if not detestable. But then, if we are savvy or lucky, or both, we join him in the joke—revisit our own prejudices with his fresh critique at the ready—and thereby absolve ourselves of being unsuspecting marks, unwitting accomplices to false idols.

Picking up the thread noted above—about the potential irony that *Burden of Dreams* may be Herzog's most emblematic film—we notice a diachronic theme in Herzog's own reflections in that film, and ever since, namely, a special talent for giving expression to impenetrable elements of the human condition, dormant attributes that rarely find articulation, and yet, Herzog concomitantly contemptuous of any such thing as "self-analysis," including psychoanalysis. The latter mode of interrogation strikes him as an offensive waste of time, noting with customary hyperbole: "I'd rather die than go to an analyst […]."[64] When a writer for *The New Yorker* suggested to Herzog that "characters of your films seem to be externalizations of forces within you," he shrugged: "I don't like, and I've never liked, introspection."[65] Such clarity, such keen self-awareness metastasizes the meta moment. What haunts us still, all these years later, about Herzog's impromptu, yes, analysis, in *Burden of Dreams*—his obvious gift for metaphysical musings, his cantankerous observations, cosmic pronouncements, poetic diction, and self-assuredness—is seemingly disavowed, as if the oracle didn't wish to take credit for its insight. (The same contempt for analysis, not incidentally, tracks closely with Herzog's avoidance of any such thing as film theory or the elaborate criticism of films. "To this day, I can learn only from bad films," he tells us. "The good ones I watch in the same spirit in which I watched when I was a kid. The great ones, even when I see them many times, are just an enigma."[66]) In *Every Man for Himself and God Against All*, Herzog expounds on his confession with just the sort of analysis we crave but are told to avoid.

> I'd rather die than go to an analyst, because it's my view that something fundamentally wrong happens there. If you harshly light

> every last corner of a house, the house will be uninhabitable. It's like that with your soul; if you light it up, shadows and darkness and all, people will become "uninhabitable." I am convinced that it's psychoanalysis—along with quite a few other mistakes—that has made the twentieth century so terrible.[67]

As Herzog's audience—his readers, his movie fans—we are told one thing (often couched as a personal preference, say, his rejection of self-analysis) even as we are presented with elaborate, capable exhibitions of its opposite.

Yet another paradox to mull: Herzog's analysis of analysis is profoundly astute. Still and all, there remains a desire for more, for Herzog to go on: for him to develop the thought about how *illumination*, in the case of the self or soul, causes trouble, while his serial intrepid film and writing projects appear to do nothing more, which is quite enough, but shed light on the shadows and dark corners of existence. As he tells us: "I've never been afraid to look into an abyss, but I wouldn't want my worst enemy to see what I saw then. [...] There is such a thing as one's own household of emotions."[68] In these unexplored regions, paradoxes proliferate likes jungle vines at midnight. As David Trotter, author of *Paranoid Modernism*, has said, Herzog's "unquenchable intellectual curiosity is, however, accompanied by an almost complete incuriosity about what it is in our equipment as human beings that enables some of us, at least, to recognize an ecstatic truth when we see one."[69] The King Edward VII Professor of English Literature Emeritus at the University of Cambridge strikes at the heart of the enterprise, for what is the point of seeking out and defending "grand visions" unless one learns, or at least labors, to assess one's findings? As goes the film critic, so goes the literary critic, another of the "pedantic theoreticians"[70]—and yet, such insults and (in Freudian language) repressions will not resolve matters, much less move us incrementally closer to admitted objectives or the realization of furtive plans. Herzogian psychic architecture avoids rooms full of worthy appurtenances, while his lightly-packed duffel is by the front door—nature's extremes awaiting his tour.

With the tactical achievements of *Land of Silence and Darkness* in mind—"the generous, precise attention it gives to the workings, for better as well as worse, of the 'human society' so despised by the ecstatic truth bro"—Trotter offers a lament: "This is the Herzog crux: that a filmmaker able as few others are to sense and grasp the uniqueness of what is happening in front of his own eyes should have expended so much effort in recycling the more ornate elements of Romanticism's extensive detritus."[71] With a hint from David Grene that "Romantic" has become one of those "affectionately contemptuous terms"[72]—an outcome he acknowledged and bemoaned—it very well may be that Herzog's absorption and subsequent remobilization of German Romanticism engenders a desirable European exoticism among non-Europeans, including Americans of a certain sensibility.

Denizens of the New World, despite Emerson's admonishments and corrective counsel to the contrary, still gullibly defer to the inherited hierarchies of an archaic and outmoded Continental past. There is a longing for what America never had, cannot have, and will not emerge endogenously. From an American perspective—and over a long arc, stretching from the founding period to the foundering present-day—European civilization has been a subliming force, one able to render the brusque American mute and resentful. A bewildered Wittgenstein once asked "What can we [Europeans] give the Americans? Our half-decayed culture? […] From us they have nothing to learn."[73] In practical terms—industrial, commercial, cultural, political, military—European alternatives and attractions have faded or (for a prevailing incuriosity) remain unknown on the west side of the Atlantic. Out of this void, Herzog seems apparitional, some kind of emissary from another place and time—delivering himself and his bespoke blend of gravity and buoyancy, the portentous and the puerile—and ready to teach. The exotic Herzog, arriving as an alien presence among American dupes, entrances with benevolent echoes of a foreign past, the seductions of lost age.

Though Herzog has been alive during the steepest inflection of technological achievement in human history, and thus has witnessed its attendant exuberance, he may yet serve as a harbinger of our romantic *future*—going offline/off-screen, being out of doors, trading in virtual proxies for personal contact with bona fide humans, dwelling intently in the quotidian, including in its attendant boredoms and occasional exaltations. In a retrospective mood, casting an eye across the wide and varied expanse of Herzog's films and writing, we descry a model, a guide, for a nascent neo-Romanticism. If there is a facet of Herzog that conveys the tireless man—a *Bayerische Motoren Werke* made mortal—there is also the stuck-in-traffic Angeleno who dreams behind sunglasses and the wheel as the asphalt melts beneath his tires. He is that rare "import" to the Valley with a gift for discussing Longinus and Goethe off-the-cuff—a professor of Greek manqué who finds himself making films. "I'm not an American citizen," he confirms. "I'm a guest in your country," he tells Nick Schager, "and I love to be here and I like America for its astonishing qualities to overcome crises."[74] An outsider inside—an intimate outsider—Herzog counts his status as a gift: "Looking at it halfway from the outside, sometimes you can see the perspective clearer, and the contours you may see a little bit clearer, than being inside the forest, where you only see trees. You do not see the forest."[75] Herzog's neo-Romanticism entwines sober assessments with a talent for enchanting the mundane.

As William H. Galperin has framed a backdated portrait: consider the extent to which "the Romantics turned their—and our—attention to the quotidian."[76]

> What's also interesting, then, about the various histories fashioned by Wordsworth and Austen is that they forgo memorable content in deference to something of which memory is no more than a feeble index. Stanley Cavell, in one of his many meditations on the ordinary, describes this unmemorable content as "something there," something "open to our senses," that "has been missed" and whose discovery amounts to what he hyperbolically calls an "ecstatic attestation of existence."[77]

Galperin references here Cavell's late twentieth-century Presidential Address "Something Out of the Ordinary," delivered in Atlanta, Georgia to the American Philosophical Association, a venue filled with professional philosophers, a talk that Cavell begins autobiographically with memories of living "the first seven years of my life in a house placed three or four miles from the site of this hotel."[78] Physiologically and psychologically such years are designated "formative," and so the point of launching his remarks on this measure of the everyday is fitting. Of course, given Cavell's talents for using ordinary language to unsettle our grasp of high theory (including the findings of so-called "analytic" philosophy), we note first the title of the talk which, when translated to Greek and then back again into English underlines that something "out of" the ordinary is, in fact, *ex*/tra/ordinary. And yet, that ecstasy [*ekstasis*] is found nowhere else but in the range of human experience we call commonplace. The audience of (mostly) analytic philosophers must have looked on with bemusement while their President spoke first of John Dewey, then Ralph Waldo Emerson, picked up with Nietzsche (who with sincerity called himself Emerson's "soul brother"[79]), continued with J. L. Austin, Wittgenstein, Kant, Hegel, and Heidegger before turning to that alluded to "something out of the ordinary," an expression of ecstasy in the everyday in the form of Fred Astaire singing and dancing his way through *The Band Wagon* (1953, dir. Vincente Minnelli), a Hollywood musical. Wonders never cease.

As if to ratify the occasion—and Cavell's sanguine recommendation to revisit (with new eyes and ears) this mid-century cinematic marvel, Galperin notes: "[a]s the experience of re-seeing suggests, the emergence of the everyday as a distinct category comes to consciousness as a history of missed opportunities."[80] Such as it is, then, not a history Cavell wishes to extend, but rather to amend by such interventions as the calling forth of Astaire in the company of philosophers (of a certain analytical stripe) who are all but certain to overlook (i.e., not look over, peruse) and remain deaf to such communications when they are sent from the margins—even when those places are housed in Harvard University's home for philosophy, the (now, that is, in hindsight) ironically-named Emerson Hall. WHAT IS MAN THAT THOU ART MINDFUL OF HIM we find inscribed in the frieze atop the building (question mark duly deleted). The still-salient sentiments of Psalm 8:4 etched in stone, along with a Daniel Chester French bronze on the first floor of a presiding Emerson (occupying a chair he would never hold in his lifetime, nor in his afterlife as a spirit in these halls), put us in a mood to notice what most everyone else is inclined—by training and modern temperament—to walk past without detecting. As was his way, Cavell takes the occasion, its selected texts—and his accidental audience—seriously. Herewith the Cavell passage containing Galperin's point of focus:

> Now the utterance or delivery of Astaire's song and proto-dance has singled me out for a response of pleasure which I propose to read in terms of the concepts of psychic hovering, of dissociation from the body, within a state of ordinary invisibility, which (though you have to take my word for it now), subsequently finds resolution in an acknowledgment of origins which reinstates a relation to an intact body and causes a state of ecstasy. In my wish to share this pleasure I judge a scene of walking and of melodic syllabification as appropriate expressions of the ordinary, as the missable, and the taking of a portrait of a shod foot as an ecstatic attestation of existence. Such proposed touchstones of experience do not, I trust, immediately put the future at stake between us, but they are measures, yet to be assessed, of what the stakes might be.[81]

As Cavell has made evident in *Emerson's Transcendental Etudes*, and earlier in *In Quest of the Ordinary*, the caricature of the Romantic mindset—from Coleridge and Wordsworth on one side of the Atlantic to Emerson and Thoreau on the other—places the human at odds with itself, ever seeking to "transcend" its pedestrian predicament.[82] And yet, the poetry and philosophy, the painting and sculpture of the era are replete the "missable" ordinary, in effect, reports amounting to serial "ecstatic attestation[s] of existence." In his own time, by means of his own media (film in the popular imagination, books among his self-appointed students), Herzog sustains this rendition of the Romantic tradition. A documentary film (say, in the vein of *cinéma vérité*) would have us think we have direct access to some evident truth; consequently, we become inured—we either look away or don't take stock of what we are seeing. By operating at odd angles, by seeking life at the extremes, ecstatic truth becomes a practice of re-seeing. The quotidian is newly layered, a space in which the given is mixed with the imagined, the empirical anointed with a dreamy haze. The mind at rest in such meditative moments is liable to achieve a penetrating perspicacity. These are among the paradoxes that track the Herzogian enterprise—his *inquest*. Truth plus lie equals illumination.

What else is a memoir, which *Every Man for Himself and God Against All* purports to be, but an attempt to fashion an analysis (that word again) of the self (and that one too) whose memories are at issue? "If facts had any value," Herzog tells us in *A Guide for the Perplexed*, "if they truly illuminated us, if they unquestionably stood for truth, the Manhattan phone directory would be the book of books. Millions of established and verifiable facts, but senseless and uninspiring. The important truths remain unknown."[83] We turn to Herzog and his memoir, asking: have you gone beyond the facts? Do we know what you dream about? For whom you cast your ballots? Why you cry into your pillow at night?[84] Put another way: *Every Man for Himself and God Against All* is the kind of memoir one should expect from a thinker who detests self-analysis. There are a hundred tantalizing autobiographical moments, by-the-way details drawn from a life of global trekking, and myriad psychological, cinematic, and cultural observations in the book that nevertheless remain at the level of aphorism and abbreviation, that stir the imagination but stop short of a fuller dimensionality, that remain steadfastly allusive and elliptical. Unlike another contemporaneously-released memoir, Barbra Streisand's sprawling, nine-hundred-ninety-two-page *My Name is Barbra*, chock full of frank surmises about the contours of her life, Herzog appears like the stenographer of his own picaresque. *Every Man for Himself and God Against All* is "in its self-mythologizing way the record of a charmed life"—including the fateful near-misses that had him avoiding the death kiss of scorpions, a firing squad of guerilla executioners, freezing to death beneath an avalanche—and surviving an 'insignificant bullet' that hit him during an interview in the hills overlooking Los Angeles.[85]

Every line of the present book, and all the others written about Herzog, is shadowed by his contempt for the activity of criticism—and especially theorizing. We write against prevailing winds—leaning forward slightly to keep up the momentum of such lines in resistance to any next gust of Herzogian doubt that may cause them to dissipate. And so we critics aim to refine the thought still further, to follow those rich patches of provocation and contradiction, and even to track the barren spans. Along such paths, self-analysis reveals its relation to self-awareness, critical judgment yields momentary and productive alignments of sense even while leaving other adjustments unresolved. Do such effects hold for Herzog? Of the life and mind of the critic, one overhears Gina James' remarks about her mother, Pauline Kael, at her mother's memorial service: "A lack of introspection, self-awareness, restraint or hesitation gave Pauline a supreme freedom to speak up, to speak her mind, to find her honest voice. She turned her lack of self-awareness into a triumph."[86] The depiction of Kael, in fact, presents an option, but it emerges inverted: Herzog appears triumphantly self-aware while lacking a further instinct for self-criticism. Maybe this is a recipe for mental health! Still, awareness, for most of us, at least, calls out for (some kind of) analysis; we need to know what to do with our perceptions, much as we must write to determine what we think on a matter.

Like Herzog's films, his memoir calls us to consider what kind of object it is—what sort of literary or philosophical creation it amounts to. From the start, we gather that Herzog is in control of his narrative: he will tell us what he wants, and only just so much about it. There are a few moments when he narrates his own self-censure, for example, in the chapter "Wives and Children" ("To speak about my wives violates my natural discretion."[87]), but for the most part, he conveys no sense of struggle about what to say—no second-guessing, no hesitation. It is said or it is not said. Of the unsaid, of course, we have no idea what lies within but remains unarticulated—only that there is more that could be said. As with his authored cinematic voiceovers, so in this extended memoir-as-voiceover, Herzog's penchant for the epigrammatic, for the vignette, reinforces the enigmatic qualities of his claims and observations, his memories and his commentaries.

The memoir, a story told very much on his own terms (as is maybe the wont of all memoirists), has an echoic quality—as if his earlier conversations with Paul Cronin, presented first as *Herzog on Herzog*, then in an expanded and definitive form as *A Guide for the Perplexed* (the text created by Cronin, much scrutinized by Herzog, reviewed by the two together) were sieved for selected fragments, then more plainly connected to life events. What to call this move: the biographizing of philosophical remarks? Many of the stories we find in *Every Man for Himself and God Against All* materialized in an earlier form in *A Guide for the Perplexed*, such that Herzog appears enmeshed in a project of re-vising (that is, re-seeing) and revisiting his earlier thoughts. The practice is familiar to Herzog fans given the sheer extent of repetition in his spoken and written output: twice-told tales are most regularly thrice- or for that matter thirty-times told. Repetition, however, needn't be a liability, nor dull, a sign of stale or stalled thought; rather it can instruct us about what is most important to Herzog (what he cares about enough to speak of more than once) and repetition can, often does, arrive with salient refinements of syntax and context, textual reference and semiotic allusion. Beholden to the diurnal structure of planetary habitation, our diaries [Lat. *dies*, days] and journals [Late Lat. *diurnalis*; Old French, *jurnal*] confess our lessons upon the spinning rock, our incremental and sudden apocalypses [Gr. *apokalyptein*, uncover, disclose, reveal]. No one can begrudge such iterative, cyclical chances to reclaim the dawn—undertake, after Thoreau, one's morning work. In proximity to Kierkegaard's book devoted to the topic—*Repetition*—he confides in a letter that "Every morning I shave off the beard of all my ludicrousness."[88] A hitherto unrecognized (sur)face of reality is duly revealed by way of the freshly sharpened blade, but it will need tending, as with shaving, a return is built into the act itself. In a single night, the jungle overgrows a hard-won path; in the next day's light, an artfully wielded machete slices through the obstructing foliage (that would otherwise reclaim revelations). Freud diagnosed *homo sapiens* with a repetition compulsion, but the prognosis is more severe: it is a fate.

With Herzog fulfilling a new book contract, and an opportunity to address familiar notions from slightly different angles, we measure his pressure applied unevenly but appreciably on the literary, philosophical, autobiographical, and historical dimensions of his experiences. Though readers can ask—and track—the extent to which *Every Man for Himself and God Against All* was influenced by the content and composition of *A Guide for the Perplexed*, we can also wonder how different the new memoir would be if *A Guide for the Perplexed* didn't exist. Admittedly, any revisitation of earlier writing invites the critical literary function of revision.

Given a second (or third or fourth) chance, how might we write differently—in tone, in the selection of consolidated stories, in the manner of rehearsing them: deciding which tales to tell (again) and which to pass over? Knowing what he knows now—having, in Herzog's case, made additional films and read further stacks of books, traveled to previously untoured places, suffered the losses of dear friends, etc.—how would he, should he, tell or re-tell a story, retail it—especially one already on the books, as it were?

Herzog's film about his friend Bruce Chatwin (1940–1989) is, like *My Best Fiend* (1999), more exemplary as memoir than *Every Man for Himself and God Against All*. Following in lockstep with earlier observations about the transformative and attractive powers of Herzog's presence in *Burden of Dreams*, something similar occupies the running times of these two auto/biographical films. Yet unlike *Burden of Dreams*, in *Nomad: In the Footsteps of Bruce Chatwin* (2019) and *My Best Fiend*, Herzog has license to discuss himself—his feelings, even perhaps at moments, slipping inadvertently into some measure (for him, for us) of satisfying self-analysis. It matters further that both biographical film portraits were made after their subjects had died—Klaus Kinski at the start of the same decade (1991) and Chatwin a couple years earlier (1989) —thus creating an even longer retrospective gap for Herzog: three decades. Herzog challenges conventional wisdom by saying he would have said *exactly the same things* at Chatwin's memorial in 1989 as he would in the film made thirty years later, but would he? Could he? Herzog's catalog of ways that Chatwin influenced him even after his untimely early death suggests otherwise— and yet, as a measure of "seeing plain," it may be that once Herzog perceives a matter, he knows it the best he can and ever will; repetition becomes a sign of astute perceptions made and committed to—hence the lack of need to retrace and second-guess, to mull and equivocate. Herzog says what he means at the time and ever after. The leather rucksack at the center of Herzog and Chatwin's relationship—as if an orphaned child in need of new custody, or at least as a very potent metonym— creates a reliable existential and conceptual feature that Herzog (and we) can trace across his many film shoots, adventures, and, yes, even introspective reflections since Chatwin's death. Repetition is a totem of fidelity. The faithful needn't revisit or revise in order to take their next steps.

In a further flourish of the homophilic bond he claims with Chatwin, Herzog eulogizes "in the footsteps" of his beloved, departed friend. In part this means Herzog aligns himself with the ethos of the nomad—yet another variation of the rogue agent we have invoked and stylized for our intrepid filmmaker. Here *rogue* and *roving* coalesce as mutually reinforcing gestures—the first allowing for detours off established tracks, the second encouraging the hiker to seek new vistas. Fitting too on etymological grounds, since *rogue* migrates from the Latin *rogare* [to beg, to ask] and comes to English as *roger* [a beggar]; in further linguistic turnings, our mendicant vagabond is said to be arrogant [Middle French], aggressive [Old Northern French], a deceitful vagrant full of "excess" and "exuberance" [Old Norse]—a haughty interloper and a scamp. Such a mini-lexicon suits—and reflects—Herzogian methods and itineraries all too well, since how peaceably Herzog inserts himself into flora, fields, and fora that may not know what to do with him. His "foreignness," in many regions of the earth (a variant on the European exoticism already noted), creates an expected tension for viewers: will he be welcomed as a stranger (the roving rogue asking tough questions, begging, if on his own terms, for answers) or will he be shut out?—refusal only emboldening our drifter, compelling him to seek yet further means for approach and entry, for entertaining and persuading.

If *My Best Fiend* resolved into a double portrait of antagonists (where Kinski's wild madness heightened, by contrast, as he would for most any person, Herzog's calm sanity), *Nomad* is more like a visitation from a saintly and sage ghost. Herzog had tremendous respect for Chatwin while he lived, including his many books that cataloged his physical and cognitive nomadism, but in death Chatwin would appear to be a patron saint of Herzogian enterprises, far and wide, and also—if against his conscious judgment—those that take one inward. In *Nomad*, Herzog's retrospective account of Chatwin cannot help but make Herzog introspective. Because Herzog feels such intense affiliation with Chatwin's demeanor— not just his presence, but also his cast of mind, his values, his literary achievements—any time Herzog gives voice to such virtues the act refracts upon his own. What we admire mirrors what we wish for ourselves. Our esteem embodies ours aspirations. Herzog, who perpetually extols the virtues of "walking on foot," found his soul brother in Chatwin and kept up the peripatetic pace in the wake of his demise. Picking up Chatwin's rucksack and carrying it forward became Herzog's literalization of a spiritual fact, a confirmation of his shared and treasured values.

We can pick up *Every Man for Himself and God Against All* in still another way: as a document that Herzog intends to be a composite of fact and myth—and in this confluence aims for ecstatic truth, much like many of his films. Herzog is, to some degree, uncharacteristically careful in *Every Man for Himself and God Against All* to specify what derives from his own memory and what is borrowed from others; he admits that something he has just told us or is about to tell us in fact may have happened differently. The hedging at times can feel like a bit of indemnifying coverage to avoid legal controversy and yet the move also comes across like a bit of self-licensing for fictionalization—to sharpen or soften edges as need be to constitute or reconstitute a memory, or better, a myth-based-upon-a-memory ("I'm not sure if this is a memory or not"[89]; "I don't think it was a dream, although it's always a possibility"[90]; "Was it even from this world or another entirely?"[91]; "Did I misunderstand something as I was reading it or did I actually invent this quote myself a very long time ago and keep saying it back to myself until I took it for fact?"[92]).

In his memoir, in another repetition of note, Herzog repeatedly narrates his struggle to remember, seemingly eschewing a willful invention as a safeguard for lacunae and distortions. The calling forth of (cognitive, perceptual) lapses aligns with many of Herzog's films, those in which we aren't sure if something happened. Like Tarkovsky at times, the films themselves can appear to be dreams or memories—forgotten dreams? faded or appropriated memories? but whose, from where? As it turns out, such hyphenation (viz., myth-based-upon-a-memory) feels like a more honest—a genuinely self-critical—gloss on the task of memoir writing as such. Facts and the factitious intermingle. Something similar happens at the beginning of *Conquest of the Useless*, initially subtitled *Reflections from the Making of Fitzcarraldo*—recently updated in a more poetic yet strangely more accurate way as *Fever Dreams of the Jungle*—where Herzog suggests in a brief preface: "These texts are not reports on the actual filming— of which little is said. Nor are they journals, except in a very general sense. They might be described instead as inner landscapes, born of the delirium of the jungle. But even that may not be entirely accurate—I am not sure."[93] Given that psychologists insist our memories are faulty, subject to errors of omission, alteration, and even insertion (fata morganas of the mind), why would we want to rely on them as our exclusive sources? Poetizing the past seems the better route, and may be, despite claims and clamoring otherwise, the only pathway available to us. Herzog came to this conclusion long ago—and is sticking with it.

Despite Herzog's critique of academic patois and the labyrinthine logic that can push criticism off course, he has successfully marshaled a tone, syntax, and technical vocabulary to create his own kind of everyman's metaphysics—a stew of German Romanticism, classical Greek heroics, and boot-strap individualism (with but a savory dash of the potent, possibly ruinous spice of film and media parlance). The result is speech and prose that often *sounds* like philosophy—with jargon-laden gems such as "ecstatic truth" and the sublime, and even containing, at times, whispery filaments of a philosophy of life (as Emerson might say, orientation on the matter of where and how one ought to live). Yet, despite what appear to be ancient sources and antiquated values, Herzog's realm is, in fact, postmodern in so far as pushing on any door too hard reveals empty spaces and missed connections, profundities that are *papier-mâché*. Herzog doesn't explain or defend positions, he expostulates in the moment. Some themes repeat to the point of *seeming* like theories or have the ring of a deductive syllogism (again, "ecstatic truth" may be the champion of this network of mini-manifestos, and yet it too deforms or even dissolves under pressure).

Still, Herzog's composite techniques are taken to be a virtue of his intuitive, penetrating, seer-like powers of discernment. He recognizes our bullshit and calls us on it. But there is little in the way of actionable advice (aside from reading a lot, avoiding film schools and academic film theory, and adopting a handful of mock-guerilla tactics for making films circa 1970). "In my unease with what is practiced in film schools all over the world, I started a thing called the Rogue Film School, a countermethod, a guerrilla school or hedge school where the only two things I actually teach are the forging of documents and the cracking of Yale locks"—staying clear of any Ivy League pretensions.[94] Lovely to line up these words as analogs or complements: rogue / countermethod / guerilla / hedge—that last calling forth "weasel" and "equivocate," "elude" and "eschew." The school's motto is "Not for the faint of heart." Fair enough. It might also enlist the slogan "Truth by Means of Tergiversation."

As we encounter Herzog's varied output—a vast-and-still-evolving catalog—that continuously heralds our attention as much as it demands a response to its semiotic functions, we find ourselves gathering names we think suitable to his given labors: filmmaker, writer, screenwriter, memoirist, artist, and master pedagogue of his own (anti-)school—with strains of the raconteur, fabulist, and modern-day mystic percolating throughout these categories. Still, the most suitable compound may simply be imagemaker, since in each of his roles he provides for us strange, startling, disorienting images. Thus, in coming to a critical assessment of his cinematic and writerly output, we may be wrong to assess his films on strictly cinematic grounds, and his written work on strictly literary or philosophical terms (however counterintuitive this double suggestion may sound), but rather should look to them, listen to them for the particularity of their images, their metaphors, and what they do to us. There is more than a touch of reception here, even reception *theory*: the idea that we would find lasting value in Herzog's works mainly by their effect upon us—a perhaps startling pragmatics, given all the apparently high-flown romanticism saturating the frame—and yet, when studied patiently, with a prompted amplitude of attention to experiential factors, the recommendation seems of piece with a person, such as Herzog, who ignores theory and eschews the supercilious. Here, then, the *imagemaker as illuminator*, whether written in light or lines of prose. Garrett Stewart's postulation of "cinematographic sentences" seems apt for capturing Herzog's effects—ones that cross categories in ways that suture his commitment to ecstatic truth and trade under the currency of the humanistic sublime [see chapter V]. As Stewart writes:

> In literature as well as film, parts are as serially determined as the whole. In making our way along the cognitive chain of meaning, phonetic lettering flashes past into gathering word forms even as these so-called parts of

> speech, one after another, cede syntactic space to a sometimes unexpected next-in line across the resting spots and run-ons of adjusted sense. This is the *drama* of writing—and its kinetic art: the never-stabilized ways of the word whose temporality cannot therefore be dissociated from the flicker effects of screen motion. The fact that the emergent screen image, the photogram-impacted gesture, can never be returned—in unaided ocular experience—to the file of cellular frames that induces it, whereas in prose a suspected syllabic echo in segue, or an ironic slippage between script and phonetic enunciation, can always be double-checked before spooling forward: this fact does not disable the transmedial comparison; rather, it can only help sharpen our sense of prose resources in in their cinematographic ambition.[95]

Herzog's own sense that his writing may outlast his films—that his posterity lies in the written word rather than the projected image—seems preposterous until one fathoms how his films are a form of inscription and his prose is a mode of imagemaking enabling and deserving "transmedial comparison." (Encounters with his scripts ratify the hunch, since they are rich in evocative imagery and often stint on dialogue.) Herzog, under these mixing and transfixing categories, may be said to *write* movies—offering, as he does, a schematic map for unrealized images; these *ciné*-cartographic visions exist in his screenplays and treatments, notes taken on set, memoirist recollections, and permeate his essays, public talks, and podcast interviews. The visual, sonic, and thematic evocations of *The Twilight World* are especially gratifying, since the novel has not yet been adapted to the screen; with the benefit of Herzog's catalog of movies readily held in mind, we read his cinematographic prose rich in compelling descriptions that summon scenes as yet unfilmed. We can make a found footage assembly of pre-existing Herzog clips and fill in gaps with projections all our own; a dialogue between the literary and the cinematic creates an interstitial territory for pre-existing and imagined images to conjugate. A sequence of close-ups of varied species in the run-of-the-mill style of a nature documentary gives way to a profound allegory—a human admiring the qualities of his earthly neighbors, learning from their exemplifications. Herzog's list of spectacular camouflages and defenses, in keeping with the metaphors at hand, subtly yields to our protagonist's survival strategies—including the dreams that keep him alive.

> Onoda will repeatedly think about the way creatures defend themselves in nature, how they make themselves invisible like moths taking on the blotches of tree bark, fish whose coloration matches the pebbles on the riverbed, insects that resemble the green leaves of trees, spiders like diabolical harpists plucking irresistible melodies from their strings and thus cause the webs of an enemy species to vibrate just as though an insect had become caught up in them. Consumed by curiosity, the queen spider approaches the web, and her doom. Or the snake whose rattle distracts the rabbit from the mortal danger approaching. The deep-sea fish whose light signal lures smaller fish that thus allow themselves to be trapped. And how do such creatures protect themselves? By playing dead, like the beetle that lies on its back. By the spines of cacti and thorn trees or the quills from animals like the porcupine, the hedgehog, the spiny fish that at the same time are able to inflate themselves to such a degree that they are too big to be swallowed. Safety in poison, as is the case with wasps and snakes and stinging nettles; by shocks, as from the electric eel, and by malodorous secretions, as is the case with skunks; by a thick veil of ink from octopi. Misdirection, ruse, mimicry — all elements that Onoda wants to learn from nature, whether honorable or otherwise. The only criteria are effectiveness in battle and achieving one's objective. Instead of a full-frontal attack with banners waving, he wants to make himself invisible, become

an impalpable dream figure, an elusive and
deadly mist, a rumor, a report. Through him
the jungle is to become more than a jungle,
a landscape with a deadly nimbus of sudden
demise.[96]

The filmic embodiment of these visions does not exist. And yet for Herzog's cinematographic sentences, the shot-list is set, the thematics of form articulated. A double sense of adaptation flowers: as Onoda takes notes, we fathom a transfer from one medium to another. Whether Herzog translates these lines into motion pictures or not remains to be seen; either way, for the pedagogical force of his extant films and the tutelage of his taut prose, we can take pleasure—even experience awe and a touch of the humanistic sublime—from his linguistic sketches of this otherwise unmade movie.

Over the course of the deliberate dispatches in this volume—beginning with a title whose forward slash makes synonyms of the figures on offer and stretching forward to these subsequent remarks—we have roamed and ruminated on our rogue filmmaker and rogue writer, our rogue persona and rogue mystic, our rogue artist and rogue imagemaker. With each new valence, fresh permutation, the book title's forward slash marks an onward limit and confirms its transcendence, captures continuity as well as a mode of interruption—a dialogue across domains, a volatile transfer threshold. Alas, we arrive at the culmination and coalescence of all these postulations: our rogue illuminator. The one who writes cinematic prose, who makes films that operate as literary expressions. At this late stage, we note how the present book contributes to the further constitution of Herzog's persona—a virtuous circle in which more attention to the man and the manner and the matter intensifies and complicates the object itself. Indeed, Herzog's especially protean persona suggests that it too is a rogue agent— capable of enlarging and splintering, multiplying and emitting still further versions of itself. Though there are many lines of critical comment—observations meant to enrich our collective sense of Herzog's persona—the net effect may simply be to entrench it as a multivalent phenomenon (quite apart, as noted at the outset) from any firm, fixed, or final designation. Herzog remains a mystery to us, cloaked in "shadowy forms from the fogs of the Nibelungs,"[97] which is just as well, since his service has been transcendentalized, made an adaptable conception available to all for bespoke adjustment and application (even by that new transcendental mechanism: artificial intelligence—however much we fear that its dictations will dissolve sense). "Herzog as _____" may yet be a reliable phrasing, a method even, for any number of investigations. Take our assigned job description: Herzog as "rogue filmmaker." It encodes the very thing it seeks; it is an ascription that begs the question with a tautology.

Merve Emre makes a wise admonition when she writes that "[t]he search for truth is always in danger of toppling into either pretension or madness."[98] An astute reproach. For his own part, Herzog dismisses pretension (especially of the academic sort: he still drinks beer from the bottle and loves nothing more than to barbeque a steak[99]), yet he courts glimpses of madness, perhaps especially in others. Kinski is the easy mark here. "Herzog's attraction to Kinski," writes Mark O'Connell, is "perverse but undeniably fruitful" and "the ultimate manifestation" of Herzog's "commitment to difficulty."[100] Even more insightful, though, is the sense of Kinski as "an avatar of impersonal violence—like the Amazon, or the meteor that wiped out the dinosaurs, or the grizzly bear that killed Timothy Treadwell in *Grizzly Man*—and a wild creative force to be literally directed toward the purpose of art."[101] While O'Connell reminds us of Treadwell, we can keep an alternate ledger going: those among Herzog's subjects who deviate from cognitive and behavioral norms—who are loners or rebels, the damaged or disavowed, the awkward or inarticulate, articulate but ultimately nonsensical, brave but foolhardy. (The last description is revised for Herzog, since his bravery—manifest in however challenging the appointed mission—is meant to confirm his caution. His longevity may be an accident, yet if it is, it is a salient one.) "Madness" so-called would be observable in disparate instantiations. And yet, O'Connell mixes categories in a very Herzogian way—with meteors and men coming in for the same treatment. "Impersonal violence" presents as a perfect fit for describing the indifferent gaze of a starving bear about to eat a human supper, but what of the person who commits "impersonal violence"? We are again returned to deliberation over the coupling of words that variously undermine and reciprocate, contradict and reinforce.

The Herzogian lexicon gets cluttered when some words are seemingly used as synonyms, while others appear to cancel each other out, and still more amplify one another in complementary fashion. Fact, myth, truth, dream, image, reality, fiction, abyss, madness, sublimity, inner landscape, and so on. "I like to sleep whenever I can," says the indomitable filmmaker, always walking on foot, or wanting to.[102] But "I have no dreams."[103] By this Herzog means, he doesn't dream *in his sleep*. Yet "I do have daydreams when I'm hiking," he says, adding cryptically: "I walk entire novels sometimes but never go off course."[104] Herzog would appear to slip into a moment of self-analysis — trying to explain to himself, or us, why he doesn't dream when he sleeps: "Sometimes when I wake up, I feel bad that I didn't dream, and maybe that's why I compensate by making films."[105] Herzog's films become these waking/walking "novels" materialized on screen. "My films come to me very much alive, like dreams, without explanation."[106] The psychoanalysts would be able to say how daydreams and night dreams differ — what they reveal, what they obscure. Herzog concludes his sketch of types of dreams and peregrinations — including "wild episodes of sleepwalking" — by noting his avoidance of drugs, since "there's so much turmoil inside me anyway."[107] The paragraph ends: there is no indication of what the turmoil might entail.

The word "dreams," and not just for Herzog, often serves as a shorthand for a personal vision, including aspirations one holds dear. It is in this sense of the word that Herzog confides in *Burden of . . . Dreams* and writes in *Every Man for Himself and God Against All*: "I said that if this film failed all my dreams would be at an end, and I didn't want to live as a man without dreams."[108] In a similar sense, he writes: *Cave of Forgotten . . .* , again, *Dreams* "remains my only work in 3D. For me, it was the fulfillment of a dream."[109] The amphiboly makes the fulfilled (rather than forgotten) dream ambiguous: either the dream is the seemingly unremarkable technical fact of having (finally) shot in 3D (does this count as a dream?), or it is the almost cosmically grand fact of being granted access to a space of hominid habitation some thirty thousand years ago (to be the "next man" who walks into the cave, the one appointed to reclaim the last man's "forgotten dreams"). Syntactical ambiguity aside, we shall presume the latter. In *Where the Green Ants . . .* , yes, *Dream*, "I invented my own myth of green ants," Herzog says, because "I would never be able to penetrate the thought of the Aboriginal people and their concept of dreamtime."[110] These three films all take up variations on the notion of dreams and dreaming—of having dreams, including "fever dreams"[111]—but they also point to the connection between the unconscious or inadvertent conjuring of images and the creation of images, myths, and other types of representational content. Herzog shares an insight into the moment when the dream of *Fitzcarraldo*—as a film—came into being, first as a thought or set of images: "In my head, everything began to cohere: fever dreams in the jungle, a three-hundred-ton steamship carried over a mountain, turnstiles manned by Indigenous peoples to wind it up as it was done in the Stone Age, the voice of Caruso, grand opera in the jungle."[112] To this daunting scenario, Herzog concludes that he "saw it as my duty to follow a grand vision."[113] *Fever Dreams in the Jungle* has now been repurposed as the new subtitle for *Conquest of the Useless*, so intimately tied are these demented perceptions of the numinous and the pursuit of aesthetic ecstasies.[114]

At the intersection of grand visions and bold realization, a Herzog-adjacent fever dream for your consideration: when the *flâneur* walks through Paris' Bois de Boulogne, recommended to the path by an esteemed predecessor, the lush green late-summer leaves give way to a series of inflated four-storey-high white sails, tall wooden masts upholding the billowing arches frozen in place, and from a distance, the faint sound of falling water invites the intrepid interloper to board. This is Foundation Louis Vuitton, Frank Gehry's napkin sketch of a monument to—well, what would a fan of *Fitzcarraldo* see but—a steamship emplaced upon an river on the brink of darting a new set of rapids amidst an enclosing jungle. The interior is luxury Robinson Crusoe—all tree-nests and lookouts (there's the Eiffel Tower!), a layered approached to life in the canopy. If Gehry was not inspired directly by Herzog, the architect has spent time exploring, constructing, the same evocative imaginary—having brought some measure of it into existence in a Parisian park (as he did earlier with his smaller ship on the Hudson River, the IAC building, sails pronounced, pulling the vessel forth). The layers of *arche* texts emerge seamlessly from the Gallic mists.

In the latest installment of the tradition of Herzog's visionary commitments, we have Thomas von Steinaecker's documentary film, *Werner Herzog: Radical . . .* , once again, *Dreamer*. Through a series of newly-enjoined interviews, the documentarian seems intent on giving us fresh takes on Herzog's maverick marvelousness. The *Observer*'s chief film critic, Wendy Ide concludes, however, that "interviewees tie themselves in knots of gushing superlatives, but the real insights come from the man himself."[115] To a certain generation, perhaps Herzog's own, the "radical" of the film's title evokes a robust affiliation with the revolutionary foment of the 1960s, a decade when Herzog's quick-study of cinema techniques in Munich gave rise to the formation of a production company in his early twenties. Given the deliberateness of Herzog's ventures, however, perhaps it is better—more fitting, more fortuitous—to gloss the term by way of its Latin roots, *radix*: that which forms the root and alludes to inherent elements. A radical dreamer, in this sense, would pursue the meaning of dreams (those waking visions, those spectral mental eruptions) in so far as they admit essences or force us to contend with the ineffability of their representation in words and on film. "Under the keel nine fathom deep / From the land of mist and snow / The spirit slid: and it was he / That made the ship to go," writes Coleridge in "The Rime of Ancient Mariner." "The spirit who bideth by himself / In the land of mist and snow," is the sort of visionary who would claim—looking back across a catalog of more than seventy works—that *Land of Silence and Darkness* is "surely my deepest film."[116] "I have had some rare moments in my films," Herzog admits, "how I did it I can no longer say, in which something extraordinary came to me as by God's grace, some mysterious unfathomable beauty and truth, moments lit up as though from within."[117]

There is a perennial debate (among those who care) about whether Herzog is irresponsible in his pursuit of grand visions, endangers his own life or the lives of others. In his own defense, Herzog waves away such preoccupations, reassuring those concerned with a sober insistence that he never takes unnecessary risks. Indeed, the very momentum of Herzog's life—including the kinds of projects he has pursued—invites our consideration of what may be deemed a *necessary risk*, as if one has to do certain things in order to remain oneself, to not go mad from the frustration of harboring unfulfilled desires, the realization of one's dreams. "Is a dream a lie, if it don't come true," Bruce Springsteen asks in his ballad of broken heroes and derelict dreams, "The River," "or is it something worse?"[118] Worse, Herzog would hazard. In his foreword to *Every Man for Himself and God Against All*, he asks his own questions:

> What then did destiny have in mind for me? How did it keep changing the direction of my life? At the same time, many things remained constant—a vision that never left me and, as with a good soldier, such qualities as loyalty, duty, courage. I always wanted to defend outposts others have already abandoned.[119]

Like Hiroo Onoda, hero of Herzog's novel *The Twilight World*, Herzog seems himself alone, embattled, a committed partisan in defense of what others leave behind—perhaps including the having of dreams and the very instinct to pursue their fulfillment. He asks later on, "[h]ow can something unimaginable be possible? I never closed my mind to that question."[120]

A chapter in the memoir is entitled "Mythical Figures," yet is about people Herzog knew—family, friends, neighbors. "My heroes have a lot in common." There is Siegel Hans, a local figure from his childhood who achieved "mythic status"; "[h]e was like a phantom."[121] There is the ski jumper Jan Boklöv, "a stubborn visionary character. He was marked down by the judges at every event, but he carried on incorrigibly and so has earned his own place on my list of secret heroes."[122] Of his own paternal grandfather, Rudolf,[123] a classics professor, Herzog tells us he "had the imagination and the feeling for landscape" that could perceive things across time, adding that "it's in the nature of legends to have a long life irrespective of the facts. My grandfather had a gift that I hold in high regard; he could read landscapes."[124] We can't overlook the time a toddler Herzog (then little Werner Stipetić) encountered the omnipotent and omniscient divinity of all things in the family home: "Once I bumped into God there."[125] He "smiled at me. He leaned against the doorjamb wearing washed brown overalls with dark oil stains on it, and I knew I was saved. It was God." Or, we are told, "[m]uch later, I heard the man happened to have come by from the little electrical hut in the gorge by the waterfall [...]."[126] This granting of mythic—nay divine!—status to familiar people is a recognizable part of Herzog's power to estrange and enliven the mysteries of the everyday. At such moments, Herzog comes across as a griot—a combination of historian, storyteller, praise singer, poet, and prognosticator—someone who transforms found facts (and in select films, found footage) into myths.

Herzog's mythologizing of himself and others exposes an underlying yearning in him that took hold in his youth. When he was thirteen and living in Munich, he recalls: "I started to feel a kind of emptiness. There was a yearning for transcendence, sublimity, that left me restless."[127] Not long after he had himself baptized a Catholic. As if to dispel coercion, he writes: "I was a Catholic of my own will."[128] A few years later, on the south coast of Crete at sixteen, Herzog finds himself ...

> Bedded in a cosmos without compare, above, below, all around, a speechless silence, I found myself in a stunned surprise. I was certain that there and then I knew all there was to know. My fate had been revealed to me. And I knew that after one such night, it would be impossible for me to ever get any older. I was completely convinced I would never see my eighteenth birthday because, lit up by such grace as I now was, there could never be anything like ordinary time for me again.[129]

With the skill of a novelist, Herzog translates the felt immediacy of embodied existence into the prose of sensational sentences: embedded by alliteration to begin with followed by three momentarily free-floating adverbs anticipating nonverbal silence—then tracked by the odd prepositional locution of "surprise" as a noun, as a state, to be inhabited—he conjugates a linguistic 360 pan from a subjective POV without reverse shot of the somehow dissipated subject. "Lit up by such grace" as an inner illumination, Herzog had entered his own reality—beyond the time and space of mortal men. In Perú, he reports on his response to seeing Quechua women in the Ticlio Pass, having driven from Lima into the Andes Mountains: "They stood that way for a long time, perfectly still, as though made from a different kind of reality. I did not remotely understand this display of something so utterly alien. I was excluded from the reality around about me but still felt deeply immersed in its mystery."[130] Herzog notices a theme and a pattern:

"A distant echo of divinity or transcendence is evident in many of my films. Even some of the titles, it seems to me, bespeak that: *Every Man for Himself and God Against All*; *Aguirre, the Wrath of God*; *The Lord and the Laden*; *Huie's Sermon*; *God's Angry Man*; and *Bells from the Deep*, a film about faith and superstition in Russia."[131] And of course, God plays a prominent role in Herzog's musings in *Burden of Dreams*, the title of which derives from just such an excursus at the conclusion of *Conquest of the Useless*, Herzog's "reflections from the making of *Fitzcarraldo*." There he writes: "I looked around, and there was the jungle, manifesting the same seething hatred, wrathful and steaming, while the river flowed by in majestic indifference and scornful condescension, ignoring everything: the plight of man, the burden of dreams, and the torments of time."[132] With an assonance that sounds as mindful as the personified—and impersonal—environment, Herzog appears to treat the jungle as a surrogate for God, yet, once again and not for the last time, the logic is scrambled, for an angry God cannot be an apathetic God. Hatred, wrath, scorn are attitudes of extreme interest rather than nonchalant indifference.

Herzog's self-proclaimed "hunger for transcendence" travels with his homespun theology.[133] For the man who says "I was by nature an autodidact," an avid lifelong reader who nevertheless shows contempt for academics, the self-canceling words may simply be a symptom of his "shoe-leather mysticism."[134] Herzog's own mother, Elisabeth Stipetić, offers a knowing summary of her precocious son's origins:

> All the time he was at school, Werner never learned anything. He never read the books he was supposed to read; he never studied. It seemed he never knew the things he was meant to know. But then, in fact, Werner always knew everything. His senses were extraordinary. He could pick out some note or sound and ten years later remember it exactly. He would talk about it and use it in some way. He's completely incapable of explaining anything. He knows, he sees, he understands, but he can't explain. That's not in his nature. With him, everything goes in. And if it comes out again, then it'll be in some altered form.[135]

Let our first respondent be Herzog himself: "It's not an easy matter, quoting one's own mother, and I don't think she's always right. I do think I've learned to explain a thing or two, maybe. But I have a deep aversion to too much introspection, to navel-gazing." Yes, yes, we know about the resistance to self-analysis, but how about the disobedient and dissolute student who nevertheless exhibited his own kind of keen intelligence? Herzog simply *knows*, but he cannot *explain*. An emblematic moment of the American consciousness makes its appeal at such moments, as Emerson wrote: "I shun father and mother and wife and brother, when my genius calls me. I would write on the lintels of the door-post, *Whim*. I hope it is somewhat better than whim at last, but we cannot spend the day in explanation. Expect me not to show cause why I seek or why I exclude company."[136] What of Emerson's lines read aloud by Herzog as a voiceover for his own home movie:

> Whoso would be a man must be a nonconformist. He who would gather immortal palms must not be hindered by the name of goodness, but must explore if it be goodness. Nothing is at last sacred but the integrity of your own mind. Absolve you to yourself, and you shall have the suffrage of the world.[137]

Certain strains of nonconformity announce themselves in sentiments borne by the title of Herzog's memoir, especially a double sense of "every man *for himself*," namely: every man is *on his own* and every man must be *his own advocate*. As "common-sense is rare as genius,—is the basis of genius," we underscore how infrequently we encounter the person of radical self-possession.[138] As a gloss on Herzogian nonconformity, then, another series by Emerson: "It is easy in the world to live after the world's opinion; it is easy in solitude to live after our own; but the great man is he who *in the midst of the crowd* keeps with perfect sweetness the independence of solitude."[139] Not far from the madding crowd, but *in it* is where the contest with oneself lies. Richard Eldridge has argued that Herzog's films explore the achievements and failures of personhood, in his preferred parlance, selfhood.[140] "Our first journeys discover to us the indifference of places," observes Emerson, from his own hard-won experience:

> At home I dream that at Naples, at Rome, I can be intoxicated with beauty, and lose my sadness. I pack my trunk, embrace my friends, embark on the sea, and at last wake up in Naples, and there beside me is the stern fact, the sad self, unrelenting, identical, that I fled from. I seek the Vatican, and the palaces. I affect to be intoxicated with sights and suggestions, but I am not intoxicated. My giant goes with me wherever I go.[141]

We can abandon lands and peoples, but the stream of thoughts we call "self" is a steadfast companion. We seem to have a society in our skull. And so the task of the nonconformist is neither overthrowing nor revolution, but something like an interior *agon*, a conversation with oneself that yet can listen and learn from others. Madness descends upon minds in isolation, suckled on the sweet whispers of narcissism. Yet comity—in books or in the beleaguered presence of one's fellow man—can restore and recalibrate. When genius calls, we should be lucky to have practiced common sense sufficient to know how to honor it—to heed such a vocation.

For his own sake, Herzog notes: "I got myself under control by means of absolute self-discipline. A good part of my character to this day is determined by sheer discipline."[142] Looking at the mainstream behavior and mental states of so many of his fellow humans, he demurs: "The so-called culture of complaint disgusts me."[143] Herzog doesn't want to hear about excuses. At the same time, he is not advocating a simple-minded, self-made-man approach, but something more straightforward and honest: a simply-give-it-try method. The results may not be the best (O'Connell describes Herzog's "vast and variegated" body of work as "radically uneven"[144]), but they are results nevertheless. They are real and undeniable—and solicit our critical attention. To be sure, dismissive of imposed self-defeat, when Herzog's genius calls him, he will pack his rucksack, hiking boots, penknife for lock-picking, and be gone. And yet, his nonconformism—the intellectual anti-intellectual who writes books, the anti-institutionalist who founds a film school, the loner "capable of silent brooding" who somehow repeatedly marshals and leads a film crew, the anti-analyst of the self who nevertheless defends his own private visions as if from an embattled outpost—admits of the love and support of family.[145]

Referring to the title of his memoir, Herzog admits: "Perhaps it makes me sound like too much of a lone warrior. Whereas, in fact, I almost always had helpers, family, women. [...] Without them, I would have been just a shadow of myself."[146] While acknowledging the actual, factual assistance of others, which Emerson, no doubt, would ratify, we see also Herzog's depersonalized sense of self. Sure, there is an admission about being a self-starter (and we could add, a self-finisher) as well as being a person supported by others, and yet—in a distinctly Emersonian, nay Romantic sense—honoring one's genius radically undermines self-importance. As Emerson testifies: "To believe your own thought, to believe what is true for you in your own private heart is true for all men,—that is genius."[147] "Every man for himself" suddenly reads like the beginning of a syllogism that will end with "means every man for others." Self-discipline—a non-narcissistic commitment to pursuing one's dreams, visions, and the exploration of inner landscapes—becomes a radical devotion to one's fellow man. A person who has been thinking aloud on film for more than a half-century of course involves himself, but the result, in Herzog's case, is very far from the practice of gossipy autofiction and much closer to some hybrid medium-cum-ethnologist. He sees and interprets, but not for himself. In the spirit of Herzog's beloved *Georgics* by Virgil, also on the reading list at the Rogue Film School: *Sic vos non vobis mellificatis apes*.[148]

When Emerson visited England on one of his transatlantic voyages, he met with, among many other illustrious writers, the novelist Elizabeth Gaskill. And perhaps even more saliently, she keenly attended his public lectures in Manchester in 1847, including one on that ur-Romantic, Goethe—Herzog's Frankfurt neighbor to the north.[149] The lecture entitled "Goethe; or, the Writer," would soon be featured in Emerson's *Representative Men* (1850), but in these years prior, Gaskell was an audience to the American's take on his exalted forebear. Emerson spoken of Goethe, Gaskill listened—in the years immediately prior the publication of *North and South* in 1855. In Gaskill's reception of Emerson, sinews of connection to the visionary sensibilities of the age and its most innovative exemplars become evident: Romantic, transcendentalist, and otherwise. Still again in our mode *avant la lettre*, the Herzogian soul sores through such atmospheres of thought, as Emerson writes of Goethe:

> There is a heart-cheering freedom in his speculation. The immense horizon which journeys with us lends its majesty to trifles and to matters of convenience and necessity, as to solemn and festal performances. He was the soul of his century. If that was learned, and had become, by population, compact organization and drill of parts, one great Exploring Expedition, accumulating a glut of facts and fruits too fast for any hitherto-existing savans to classify,—this man's mind had ample chambers for the distribution of all. He had a power to unite the detached atoms again by their own law. He has clothed our modern existence with poetry. Amid littleness and detail, he detected the Genius of life, the old cunning Proteus, nestling close beside us, and showed that the dulness and prose we ascribe to the age was only another of his masks.[150]

The French *savans*, savant in English nomenclature, is equipped with and exercises the poetic mind. Hence the territorial roaming, the expansive vistas taken in, the keen capacity to find pattern and purpose among otherwise listless lists, inventories of empty parcels. As Herzog speaks of our need for "adequate images," of truths that bypass the constraint of facts—indeed, to discern truth through the art of assembly, distortion, and dramatic fabulation, so Emerson claims:

> Society has, at all times, the same want, namely of one sane man with adequate powers of expression to hold up each object of monomania in its right relations. The ambitious and mercenary bring their last new mumbo-jumbo, whether tariff, Texas, railroad, Romanism, mesmerism, or California; and, by detaching the object from its relations, easily succeed in making it seen

> in a glare; and a multitude go mad about it, and they are not to be reproved or cured by the opposite multitude who are kept from this particular insanity by an equal frenzy on another crotchet. But let one man have the comprehensive eye that can replace this isolated prodigy in its right neighborhood and bearings,—the illusion vanishes, and the returning reason of the community thanks the reason of the monitor.[151]

In myriad scenes and sentiments, the dialogue and descriptions in *North and South* carry with them a certain strain of Emersonian—nay Herzogian—impatience with constraining custom and inherited values that would subdue one's most ardent passions, one's most abiding calls of conscience. The novel's title is itself loaded with implied oppositions: industrial and intellectual, embodied and cognitive, patrician and plebian, fine-speaking and rough-talking, mannered and uncouth, obedient and rebellious, at home and alienated, and most pointedly here, as we note lines of affiliation between our nineteenth-century essayist and our twenty-first-century visionary, a skepticism about the utility of theories—of having them or making them. Mr. Bell, a fairly obscure Oxford Fellow, speaks frankly with his dearest, oldest friend, Mr. Hale (whose abdication from clerical duties strikes one as a fictional flourish of Emerson's withdrawal from the same obligations, and only a short time after he crossed over officially into them). In this scene, one imagines Herzog speaking Mr. Bell's lines, saying them from the heart, perhaps especially in their Emersonian cast of mind:

> Mr. Bell blew his nose ostentatiously before answering. Then he said: "[God] gave you strength to do what your conscience told you was right; and I don't see that we need any higher or holier strength than that, or wisdom either. I know I have not that much; and yet men set me down in their fool's books as a wise man, an independent character, strong-minded, and all that cant. The veriest idiot who obeys his own simple law of right, if it be but in wiping his

> shoes on a doormat, is wiser and stronger than I.
> But what gulls men are!"[152]

When Mr. Bell finds himself in communion with the mill-owning industrialist, Mr. Thornton, the two discover common ground:

> "Nothing like the act of eating for equalizing men. Dying is nothing to it. The philosopher dies sententiously, the pharisee ostentatiously, the simple-hearted humbly, the poor idiot blindly, as the sparrow falls to the ground; the philosopher and idiot, publican and pharisee, all eat after the same fashion—given an equally good digestion. There's theory for theory for you!"[153]

To which Mr. Thornton replies in accord:

> "Indeed I have no theory; I hate theories."[154]

Some while later—echoing her paramour, Mr. Thornton, and without knowing it—Mr. Hale's daughter, Margaret, sounds another Herzogian note: "I don't analyze my feelings."[155] Such moments, plucked as they are from the white heat of Victorian Romanticism, offer bracing reminders of the tradition we find ourselves within when reading Herzog's books and watching his films. As he mocks theorizing and self-analysis, Herzog also has no patience for the institutions that would set out to form him and subsequently bind him. "It has been clear to me early on. This is my destiny," he says of his fate as a filmmaker. "I have no alternatives, no choices. I've never learned a profession. You have to carry me out from a set one day feet first. That would be the best."[156]

The self-"less" ventures familiar to Herzog's earliest expenditures of will and imagination recommend him to our attention as a distinctive incarnation of, variation on, the autodidact. Herzog has ever been the student "out of school" seeking his own *curricula extra*. Emerson says "all education self-education," which can mean all education is an education of, or for, the self (a lesser reading), and/or that all education is a matter of self-starting and self-sustaining (a more vigorous and viable reading—one befitting Herzog's temper). Thus we find Herzog founding a film company before he owns a camera. Something similar recurs in other figures about whom I have served up cinematic and critical portraits: Brunello Cucinelli, who philosophized in neighborhood cafés, abandoned university studies in engineering, and started his eponymous clothing company with a single sweater; and Jill Freedman, who never went to art school or took photography lessons, yet set out with a borrowed camera to photograph the Poor People's Campaign in 1968 because the urgency of the moment outstripped the need to first have technical mastery of her machine, the history of the art, permission to "take" pictures.[157] Each of these strains of autodidacticism resolve themselves into a response to the very contemporary (so-called) crisis of expertise. What is the service of a capable amateur? In the time it takes Casaubon to struggle—and fail—to write his *The Key to All Mythologies* in *Middlemarch*, Herzog made six films, staged an opera, wrote a book, and provided a voice for *The Simpsons*.

The poetic extremism exhibited by Emerson and Herzog is meant to underwrite and reinforce their lived affiliations with and dependencies on others. A plea for nonconformism isn't the same as a call for anarchy and isolation, but rather a prophylactic against giving up on one's dreams, especially when such dreams can feel so fragile or implausible—so easily thwarted by the gods and the will of other men. What else is a conquistador of the useless, then, but a person in pursuit of objectives who hopes they will be "somewhat better than whim at last"? If, as Herzog himself postulates, the making of films may be a form of compensation for the lack of nighttime dreams, then it is ever so much more important that he holds fast to his daydreams and visions—those "gleam[s] of light" that flicker and all too easily fade into oblivion.[158] The bold words, then, are a form of cheer dispensed on one's own behalf—a pep talk for the spirit. Emerson's illustrative anecdote—perhaps laden with a clever memoirist's license to dramatize—would seem at home in the sequence of Herzog's own tales of self-formation:

> I remember an answer which when quite young I was prompted to make to a valued adviser, who was wont to importune me with

> the dear old doctrines of the church. On my saying, What have I to do with the sacredness of traditions, if I live wholly from within? my friend suggested, — "But these impulses may be from below, not from above." I replied, "They do not seem to me to be such; but if I am the Devil's child, I will live then from the Devil." No law can be sacred to me but that of my nature. Good and bad are but names very readily transferable to that or this; the only right is what is after my constitution, the only wrong what is against it. A man is to carry himself in the presence of all opposition, as if every thing were titular and ephemeral but he. I am ashamed to think how easily we capitulate to badges and names, to large societies and dead institutions.[159]

How often do Herzog's heroes—possessed by daunting goals and terrible odds—fail, suffer comeuppances, or end their screen time *in media res* haunted by paradoxes and irresolvable *aporia*, or, if prevailing, somehow winning the wrong prize. Herzog's adventures—on screen and in print—are somewhat about the application of ideas, but mostly about the conceptions themselves. The idea is the thing. And when Herzog and his team do occasionally surmount their obstacles—such as, famously in *Fitzcarraldo*—the achievement itself reverts back to trope. Once the ship arrives in the new, next river, it is summarily cut loose—emancipated—leaving the human plan to ruin, running it to ground. The actualization of an idea transforms into a figure of the mind. As Mark O'Connell claims, Herzog's "resistance to self-analysis leads him [in *Burden of Dreams*] to refer to the central motif of *Fitzcarraldo* as a 'wonderful metaphor' of whose meaning he has no notion."[160] Even when the dream becomes a reality, it can't sustain itself there, and so must find a new home in still further dreams. In *My Best Fiend*, Herzog confirms his allegiance to the significance of the act—a three-hundred-ton ship pulled successfully across a mountain, from one river to another—"It's a great metaphor. For what, I don't know to this day. But it's a great metaphor."[161] These days, more than four decades since his reflections on the matter with Les Blank, Herzog holds the same note:

> You see, when you move a ship over a mountain, it is doable. And I knew it was doable, although quite hard. But I think it is such a big metaphor. Like, in literature, you have it, for example, the white whale, Moby Dick and the hunt for it or Don Quixote attacking the windmills with his lance. So there are big metaphors, a big vision out there. And then it doesn't matter if it's becoming difficult or not.[162]

Terry Gross, of *Fresh Air*, pushes back: "It's one thing to have in the film a metaphor like dragging a ship over a mountain, but it's another thing to actually have to do it in your film [laughter], you know? At that point, it's not a metaphor. At that point, it's something your crew has to do." Herzog acknowledges her distinction, her literalism that would make the moment legalistic and not literary, her skepticism about his account:

> I hear you, yes. But I'm not searching for finding my boundaries […] the extreme mountain climbers do that. That's not my thing. I know my boundaries, and I accept them. And I take no as an answer, for example. And I'm a professional person. I'm a filmmaker, and I want to come back with a film, and I want to come back alive because I want to edit the film, and I want to show it to audiences. So, for example, at the edge of a volcano, yes, there were certain dangers, and there was an eruption, and glowing slabs or blobs of lava came down on us, raining down, and some of them very large, I mean, the size of a car, the size, even, of a truck. So you better flee quickly. You get out of it. But I'm not searching the dangers. The nature of my storytelling sometimes requires to go into extreme situations, yes, but I think to look deep into our human nature, to look deep into the darkest recesses of our soul or the hidden things deep in our soul, you have to put human beings at some sort of an edge.[163]

Rhetorically, Herzog's response fits the usual paradoxical form, here especially effective—as in his *Burden of Dreams* soliloquy—because of the repetition of terms (or their analogs) and their grammatical distance from one another. He starts out by saying "I'm not searching for finding my boundaries," and yet, by the end of the reply, he insists "you have to put human beings at some sort of an edge"—and to put them there, you have to *find* the limit situation. (The relationship between conceptualization in language and grammatical patterns will recur in the next segment of this chapter, when we consider how artificial intelligence "understands" Herzog and represents, repeats "him" in language). On another thematic score, Herzog's diminishment of there being *genuine* danger on his sets seems, at best, disingenuous, and he admits as much here with reference to car-sized lava chunks "raining down." When Herzog envisions Christian Bale (as Dieter Dengler) completing a potentially hazardous stunt for him in *Rescue Dawn*, a memorable scene invoked in an earlier chapter, the Welsh actor replied: "I am not going to feckin' *die* for you, Werner!"[164] At such moments of contesting wills and contrasting visions, one wants to ask if—and when—metaphors can kill. Timothy Treadwell "overstepped a limit."[165] In his case, the poetry of nature in his mind was misaligned with the reality of nature in Alaska—and he was eaten alive.

Given the physical demands of just these two shoots— *Fitzcarraldo* and *Rescue Dawn*, among many other instances one could reach for—there seems good reason to wonder after the way Herzog's values are embodied. The recurrence of words such as adventure, bravery, courage, heroism, risk, fortitude, extremes, edges, limits, begs consideration of the literal/figurative divide perpetually at issue in exemplifying them. Herzog makes the forward slash permeable when he links autobiography with cinematic realization: "There are various recurring tropes in my films that are almost always derived from personal experience."[166] Moreover, the title of the memoir may, in this day and age, seem to harken back to antiqued, antediluvian categories—"man," "God," and antagonisms embedded therein. Should we then be surprised what reading material he keeps in his coat pocket? "I always have Luther's translation of the Bible in a facsimile reprint with me. I draw comfort from the Book of Job and the Psalms."[167] Two antique works with Herzogian weight: the first about a man confronting the mysteries of existence—what can be known, what remains inscrutable, how faith interacts the fate—while enduring serial tragedies; the second a collection of "words accompanying music" in the form of "praises"—with lessons drawn some three millennia ago, and including language for laments, imprecations, and pilgrimages. Still more in Herzog's book title, we will need to ungender "man" and elaborate it such that we speak of "every *human* for *themselves*" as well as undo the aposiopesis by inserting the missing (but implied) direct object: "God against all . . . *humans*." Even with the categorical and grammatical updates, though, the outsize presence of men in Herzog's films could lead some to think his philosophical, theological, and filmic commitments possess a certain inherent masculinity. How many of those mad, irascible humans are mad, irascible men? How many of the featured players—the loners, risk-takers, ascetics, extremists, the disabled, the forgotten—are men? Among the scores of male actors and documentary subjects in recent decades, few female figures have entered the canon: Juliana Koepcke in *Wings of Hope*, Nicole Kidman's Gertrude Bell in *Queen of the Desert*, and Katia Krafft in *The Fire Within*, a tribute to the volcanologist and her husband.

Yet, maybe this line of inquiry is out of place: we ought not to bring Herzog up to the present, make his films, figures, and their tropes palatable (much less attractive) to contemporary viewers and their values, but instead, follow him into the recesses of the past—let his visions alienate and confound, permit him to trespass upon newly-vaunted contemporary commitments. Instead, we travel to meet him wherever he goes. Visit ancient caves. Walk into the arctic ice flow or the dense jungle. Ascend the mountain. Ford the river. Consider the colonial past in its excess of contrasts. Make company with the isolated figures whom culture has left behind.

Having his own say, Herzog shares a back-of-the-napkin list of his present-day beliefs and behaviors: "I avoid contact with fans." "Tree huggers are suspicious to me." "I don't use social media." "I don't use a smartphone." "My steaks are excellent […]."[168] "I have few friends. You could probably classify me as a loner."[169] Wait, is Herzog himself a proper Herzogian subject? Beat Presser, who was a unit stills photographer on *Fitzcarraldo* (and *Cobra Verde* and *Invincible*) thought so: "You would have also been a good Fitzcarraldo. That's what you are, in reality."[170] Presser adds yet another dimension to the mix: in which the lives of characters (fictional, fabricated, historical, or otherwise) cross over into the quotidian. Dreams—including filmed worlds—descend upon and become expressed by the qualities of the everyman, including Herr Herzog himself, summoning one more paradox for the pile: the exceptional everyman.

"[... I]f a man would be alone, let him look at the stars. The rays that come from those heavenly worlds, will separate between him and what he touches."[171] Herzog's cinematic sentiments about divinity, transcendence, ecstasy, and contact with the Godhead seem calibrated to register their finest effect when he sticks closer to nature's indifference to human affairs: the barren ice sheet in *Encounters at the End of the World*, the gurgling lava splashing like waves in *Into the Inferno*, the long take at the beginning of *Aguirre, the Wrath of God*, when the rapids roll on in slow-motion, the death-stare of the grizzly bear in *Grizzly Man*, and so on.

"Ambivalent" in this chapter's title is an intentional attempt, for what it's worth, to ratify the intelligence of Herzog's poise on such matters. A loving God is one thing, a vengeful God another, but an indifferent God? The third choice delivers us to the core of modernity itself, since one of its main modes is disenchantment. "The foregoing generations," wrote Emerson in 1836, "beheld God face to face." But we? We can only behold God "through *their* eyes."[172] We borrow our perception of the divine from others, or we abandon the project altogether, hence the yield of God's death: ambivalence (and its roving symptoms: irony, cynicism, apathy, alienation, relativism, decadence). Taking stock, Catholicism may have been a too direct route for our rogue agent, an adopted faith rather than a self-generated one; atheism is too self-certain and encourages condescension and so, while logically the only option, it leaves us cold, cut off; then there is the path of the soldier and madman, the rodeo clown and spot welder, the filmmaker who travels on foot to "save" a dying friend.[173] In this third dispensation, logic is foiled by contradictions sent out like countermeasures. The devout Catholic remains in his monastic citadel; the atheist takes each day as fact beyond cosmic explanation; but the fabulist conducts serials missions aimed at re-enchanting the world.

Either the rucksack is already laden with dreams to share or, if empty, the expedition to re-enchant the world must aim to fill it with new images—mosses gathered from disparate locations, visions that well up from within or that are glimpsed from without. "[I]n almost complete ignorance of the cinema of others," Herzog tells us, "I would have to come up with a cinema of my own."[174] As if questioning a self-appointed burden of invention, he asks: "Are there images that slumber within us and are sometimes set free by some sort of jolt? I believe so, and somehow all my works have pursued such images, whether it was the ten thousand windmills of Crete in my first feature film, *Signs of Life*, or the steamship that is lugged over a mountain, the central metaphor of my film *Fitzcarraldo*. I know it's a wonderful metaphor, but what it means I am unable to say."[175] Herzog means what he says, though he demurs at such moments to say what he—or his images—mean. The "jolt" incites a latent notion or—by virtue of a seeker's conditions in the world, a new idea is activated and then articulated. Yes, "[i]mages formed inside me," and yet the shock of encounter with the reality *at the edge* of one's fingertips—be it the surface of ice, the molten rock, or another's human hands—catalyzes the movement from endogenous to exogenous, and occasionally, still further to ingenious.

Herzog once told J. Hoberman: "I know that I have the ability to articulate images that sit deeply inside us, that I can make them visible."[176] Note the shift in direct object—from "inside me" to "inside us." Do we—all humans—share these images, but only Herzog and his uncommon kind have the skill to translate them, to make them apparent? Once again, Herzog's metaphysics aligns with certain Romantic apprehensions, as with Emerson who commends us to "[s]peak your latent conviction, and it shall be the universal sense; for the inmost in due time becomes the outmost, and our first thought is rendered back to us by the trumpets of the Last Judgment."[177] The language of latency feels decidedly Herzogian, and the two sages appear aligned in the ideation of pregnancy and incubation: "images formed inside," "deeply inside us," and "in due time" they find their emergence from "the great and crescive self" into the world of men.[178] The Biblical flourish adds to the wager of sympathy between these accounts. And so we readers of Herzog and Emerson wonder after this dialectic of inner/outer, hidden/unhidden, latent/manifest, true/false, and so on. In Herzog's case, what is the point of sharing with us claims of his (special? singular?) powers? So that we can better understand his aims, projects, and results—or so that we might individually take steps of our own to address—and express—

the dormant ideas and images that reside embryonically within us? The questions beg a reply, but they also encode their own resistance to articulation.

Once Herzog's images are created—the rucksack full to overflowing—we are left to interpret them. Does our Bavarian seer exceed the bounds of inherited theory such that we need to do some inventing ourselves—constitute a Herzogian hermeneutics fit for the task of interpretation? Daniel Heller-Roazen takes us on a tour of "dark tongues" that befuddle our powers of discernment, exposing the "art of the rogues and riddlers" who willfully create idioms that are inaccessible upon first glance—and perhaps remain shrouded after much study.[179] Look to the reflexive moment in Proverbs 6-7, in which the author invites a moment of metaphilosophy: "To understand a proverb and an enigma, the words of the wise and their riddles. The fear of the Lord is the beginning of knowledge, but fools despise wisdom and instruction."[180]

Part of Herzog's rogue riddling, his impish esotericism, resides in the question of whether he invents or discovers the images he shares; invention may require that he has special capacities to perceive—thereby suggesting, in fact, a Herzogian *hermetics*; discovery that his faculties afford the perception of secrets out in the world but otherwise veiled to the rest of us. Recall how in Les Blank's *Werner Herzog Eats His Shoe*, the titular subject—taking his love of shoe-leather to new extremes—said "we do not have adequate images, and that's what I'm working on—a new grammar of images."[181] The diction and syntax of the claim require careful handling: first noting that a *grammar*, as a matter of rule following and conventional rhetoric, would involve the selection and arrangement of images, while the question of *adequacy* become a measure of aesthetic judgment of the images themselves. I would hazard that Herzog is "working on" both the creation of new (adequate) images *and* experimenting with their selection and arrangement. A film such as *Lessons with Darkness* is a high achievement of this tandem force: seeking out the terrain and filming it and then messing with chronology, nondiegetic sound, and voiceover such that B-roll becomes generative of new thoughts, compulsively watchable, and almost recklessly enigmatic. What could have become a document of present-day history—a war documentary of a sort—instead becomes a trip through the gates of hell and a view of its interior terrors *sub species aeternitatis*.

The hyperbole evident in the example of *Lessons of Darkness* is itself a mark of the rogue riddler, since the exaggeration is a technique for entrancing audiences as much as a trick for alienating them. Lexical and representational exaggeration in Herzog's hands can be variously funny, disarming, and deadly serious. Depending on one's mood, the language of extremes and superlatives—of strenuous exertion, daring feats of endurance, elongated time spans, resolute acts of asceticism, and myriad indications of similar deeds (never wasting food, surviving in harsh conditions, prevailing over sickness), surmounting the highest heights and descending to the deepest depths (*radix* in the air and on the ocean floor, in the jungle and in the soul), Kinski as tragi-comic amplification of embodied behavior, God not just against a few but against *all*—Herzog's writing and his films can seem knee-slappingly amusing or jaw-droppingly mortifying (and perhaps a range of both in the same passage of prose or cinematic scene). As an analog among vital contemporary artists, we look to Matthew Barney, whose similarly obsessive interest in the nature of human extremes and limits also trades on moments of magic, distraction, and radical absorption; moreover, Barney, like Herzog, presses his case with such single-minded composure that audiences feel forced to "break" on his behalf—to laugh as a means of energy release.

The scientist will trace lineaments of cause and effect in natural phenomena, a diagnostician reports etiologies, the guru dispenses advice for better living. Herzog occupies none of these roles, not even figuratively. If Herzog's words and images, in fact, re-enchant the world, they gift such effects not by means of logic and the scientific method, but by reclaiming the mysteries of existence (even if they be secular mysteries). Ecstatic truth provides just the kind of tilt we need in order to perceive the world at a new angle—one that de-rationalizes reality for a moment or two, and maybe longer. Herzog finds or creates "signs of life" that can be interpreted and talked about, that have portent because they disobey our expectations. He excels at defining and framing the scope of the mysteries we face—convening them, calling them forth, focusing our attention on them. But then, as a rogue riddler is wont to do, abandoning us at the scene, while we look on, speechless.

Less committed to completing the thought he started— still less responsible for articulating what we should think of these revelations—he moves on to his next conquest. His presence with us is akin to a seer, not a sage; he can perceive or constitute a vision (presage it), but he cannot provide, or better, refuses to supply a ruling method, a final lesson, or a quick tutorial on instrumentalizing our findings for practical benefits. Herzog is no benevolent David Attenborough speaking confidently about the workings of nature and our place in the network of organic life (doubtless, as told in the key of "man's place in nature," a dispensation chock-full of its own distorting mythologies). Quite the contrary, Herzog will often hamper and unsettle us just as we may be approaching— or think we may be nearing—a coherent reply. As with his "great metaphors," he has a knack for finding them, giving them credence as sayings and anecdotes, as filmed sequences, and even as captivating narratives—but these are just the start. His service to humanity, his ongoing role in our wider cultures of thought and imagemaking, rests firmly in his lack of rest, his perpetual onwardness, devoted as he is to the quest itself, the quest for new—and adequate—images. Such is our *human* difference from the swells of galactic forces, from deep-sea creatures, as well as from the ruminators who never look up from their desks:

> It is not only my dreams, my belief is that all these dreams are yours as well. The only distinction between me and you is that I can articulate them. And that is what poetry or painting or literature or filmmaking is all about [...] and it is my duty because this might be the inner chronicle of what we are. We have to articulate ourselves, otherwise we would be cows in the field.[182]

The quest is not an inquest of the truth of these dreams and images, much their conquest. For the truth doesn't arrive as an answer, but as an apocalypse: an exposure that changes us, that calls us forth. As befits myths, facts are secondary, impact is primary. All these years, these decades, Herzog has been a foot-soldier devoted to the translation from "inner chronicle" to outer "articulation." But now we are joined by a new force or entity—one deeply familiar with everything Herzog has said and that we have said about him; one that may soon enough wish to declare its independence from us, grant itself divine status such that it—and it alone—sanctions what it says and what it means. Every man for himself, indeed. Having created so-called "artificial intelligence"—which is it? artificial or intelligent? can it be both?—we are increasingly compelled to come to terms with the technology. How we will use it, how it will use and transform us, and what it will signify for our relationship to the Werner Herzog we have known—or thought we knew—has become a new horizon.

4. Hallucinations: Herzog *Ad Infinitum*

WHEN A PERSONA SPEAKS, the human referent is transcendentalized. Every time I write Herzog I might as well write "Herzog," assume that Herzog, the historical human, would disavow my claim—distance himself from it, undermine it, confound it, contradict it. And yet one writes on in conversation with this ghostly version of him—a spectral reality that after years of encounter abides within. Same in the following experiment with artificial intelligence (AI), in which Herzog is neither himself nor my idea of him but an emission from a neural net that travels along silicon-based circuitry. The book ends in a fitting place for Herzog: untethered, roaming, exploring unknown, uncharted terrain. Talk about "rogue glyphs"! About Herzog going rogue! Herzog is leaving the embodied plain altogether (and we with him)—entering the matrix and speaking to us twenty-four/seven. At once, with AI, a true Herzogian hero erupts: dauntless, endless, always ready with the next vexing pronouncement comprised of facts and fictions. Some of our guiding questions as we make the trek into unmapped, untrodden territory: how does this hallucinated Herzog stack up? Can we live with "him" (a companion to *Her*)? Does he carry on the human Herzog tradition faithfully, in style, stylizing with his still-recognizable flair intact—or at a satisfying approximation? As we celebrate human Herzog's bold entry into his ninth decade on earth, we listen to hallucinating Herzog for solace against the abyss, since it will speak on—for him, to us—into eternity.

With audio- and video-based parodies in mind, Herzog acknowledges there are "a number of imitators on the Web who in 'my' voice read fairy tales or give advice for living. There are dozens of imitators, but none of them has really caught my sound.

My voice has found a great community of fans, which combined with my view of life asks to be imitated. I am a grateful victim of such satirists."[183] We return to one of the recent imitations, *Soldier of Illusion*, which satirized Herzog's sound and his "view of life" (such as we can speak of it with any confidence). Not quite catching Herzog's sound is part of the pleasure, an essential feature (not a bug) of the entertainment of evocation.

Herzog is sufficiently self-aware to recognize that his combination of vocal inflection and conceptual complexity continues to draw our wide and considered interest; it is a further measure of his wise disposition that his fate as a "victim" of such admiring fascination—and imitation—is gratefully received. Yet, thus far, all of this attention—and attempt at satirization—has come from *human others* making an effort at homage, stylized replication, sometimes bold, if-ever incomplete, impersonation. Such acts require a genuine talent for discerning patterns not just in the sound of Herzog's speech, but in its grammar—and at that, across more than a half-century of creative output. Any mortal, then, will have to devote substantial time—when hours become days, weeks years, years decades—watching and rewatching his films, listening and re-listening to his abundant audio commentary, reading and re-reading his books (and the voluminous critical remarks made by others in their articles, essays, and monographs), watching and rewatching all of the points of metacinematic reference and reflexivity (i.e., when other filmmakers draw Herzog into the scene literally, or figuratively by way of intertextual call-back). In our rapidly dawning age of AI, however, the initial ingestion of "content"—all those lines of dialogue and prose, all those sentences and sentient reflections—will take a few seconds. Thereafter, feedback from users will refine the results of the large language models (LLMs) such that each subsequent output may feel yet still closer to our hard-earned sense of Herzog.

I asked ChatGPT 3.5 for a guess at what Herzog would say about a book like this—one that purports to offer theories of and criticism about his films and books, to which the LLM replied:

> Werner Herzog might say, "While I acknowledge the intellectual pursuit of film theory, my films are born from the untamed landscapes of the human soul. A book may attempt to dissect, but it cannot fully

encapsulate the raw, inexplicable essence within each frame. The jungle of emotions and the harsh terrains of the human spirit defy easy categorization. Watch my films with your heart, not just your mind."[184]

Not Herzog, but Herzog. If quizzed, could we correctly distinguish the mortal expression from the artificial confection? What if AI (already) knows Herzog better than we know him? When I asked "How would Werner Herzog explain the ideas that are articulated by his films and books?" this summary outline—featuring thematic subheads—emerged in a few seconds:

> Werner Herzog, a German film director, screenwriter, and actor, is known for his unique and often unconventional approach to filmmaking. When explaining the ideas articulated by his films and books, Herzog often emphasizes the following themes and perspectives:
>
> *Ecstatic Truth:*
> Herzog coined the term "ecstatic truth" to describe a deeper, subjective truth that goes beyond mere factual accuracy. He believes that the emotional and psychological truths captured in his work are more important than strict adherence to objective reality.
>
> *Confrontation with Nature:*
> Many of Herzog's films explore the relationship between humans and nature. He often takes his audience to remote and challenging environments, pushing both the characters and the audience to confront the harshness and beauty of the natural world.
>
> *Obsession and Ambition:*
> Herzog frequently explores the theme of obsession and ambition in his characters. Whether it's the conquistador searching for

El Dorado in *Aguirre, the Wrath of God* or the documentary subject in *Grizzly Man*, Herzog is interested in characters who are driven by intense passions.

Fate and Destiny:
Herzog often delves into the concept of fate and destiny, portraying characters who are on a predetermined path or facing insurmountable odds. This existential theme is evident in films like *Fitzcarraldo* and *Aguirre, the Wrath of God*.

Documentary as Poetry:
Herzog challenges traditional notions of documentary filmmaking, seeing it as a form of poetry rather than a mere recording of facts. He injects his personal perspective and interpretation into his documentaries, blurring the lines between fiction and nonfiction.

Human Resilience:
Herzog's characters often face extreme challenges, and the director is fascinated by the resilience of the human spirit in the face of adversity. This theme is evident in films like *Rescue Dawn* and *Fitzcarraldo*.

Cultural Exploration:
Herzog's work often explores different cultures and societies, providing a lens through which audiences can gain insights into the human condition. He is interested in the diversity of human experiences and the ways in which people adapt to their environments.

When Herzog discusses his films and ideas, he tends to approach them with a philosophical and poetic perspective, emphasizing the emotional and existential aspects of the human experience. His work is often open to interpretation, and he encourages audiences to engage with the deeper layers of meaning embedded in his films.

The philosopher or poet, the film critic or literary analyst may be appalled by the style, or the superficiality of the interpretation — and yet, for a few seconds' labor, it is a serviceable start. One might even admire the chatbot's confident organization of themes, topics, claims, and conundrums familiar to Herzog's sprawling body of work — a distillation that at once may attract the novitiate and send the expert back to her notes.

I asked ChatGPT "Can you improve the stylistic and conceptual sense of this passage by Werner Herzog?" — allowing the equivocation implied by "improve" to hover like an unspoken expectation. What would the neural net think I mean by such a directive? I supplied this passage from *Burden of Dreams* enlisted above as the test text:

> HERZOG: Taking a close look at what's around us, there is some sort of harmony. It is the harmony of overwhelming and collective murder. And we in comparison to the articulate vileness and baseness and obscenity of all this jungle, we in comparison to that enormous articulation, we only sound and look like badly pronounced and half-finished sentences out of a stupid suburban novel, a cheap novel. And we have to become humble in front of this overwhelming misery and overwhelming fornication, overwhelming growth, and overwhelming lack of order. Even the stars up here in the sky look like a mess. There is no harmony in the universe. We have to get acquainted to this idea that there is no real harmony as we have conceived it. But when I say this, I say this all full of admiration for the jungle. It is not that I hate it. I love it. I love it very much. But I love it against my better judgment.

Seconds later:

> AI-HERZOG BY WAY OF CHATGPT: Examining our surroundings closely reveals a peculiar harmony—a harmony born of pervasive and collective acts of violence. When measured against the articulate malevolence, sordidness, and obscenity permeating this wilderness, we, in our feeble expressions, resemble poorly enunciated and incomplete sentences extracted from a banal suburban novel—a trite narrative. Faced with the enormity of this articulate brutality, we must adopt humility, recognizing that, in comparison, we are mere fragments attempting to convey a complex tale.
>
> In the face of overwhelming misery, rampant fornication, unchecked growth, and a chaotic absence of order, even the stars above, seemingly scattered, contribute to the celestial disorder. The universe, as we once conceived it, lacks the harmony we sought. It is imperative that we acquaint ourselves with the unsettling notion that true harmony, as we imagined, is absent. Yet, in expressing this, I do so with profound admiration for the jungle. It is not disdain that fuels my words, but a paradoxical love—a love that persists against my own rational judgment.

Notice how the AI corrects the logic, which I flagged earlier on—lining up "absence of order" with "celestial disorder," "lacks the harmony," "true harmony . . . is absent." Consider the poetic sophistication—especially in the key of Herzog—with a phrase such as "articulate brutality." The imagery goes from the cliché-but-still-potent "we are mere fragments" to the cosmically considered doppelgänger "even the stars above, seemingly scattered." How can we not admire Herzog raised to the level of Herzog in this rendition: "When measured against the articulate malevolence, sordidness, and obscenity permeating this wilderness, we, in our feeble expressions, resemble poorly enunciated and incomplete sentences extracted from a banal suburban novel—a trite narrative."—A revised version that Herzog himself might have wished was his own.

Now it appears to be a sentiment coauthored with *alternate* intelligence. AI$_1$.

I won't belabor the experiment by submitting further prompts or offering a close reading of such text results, but instead move on to another variation on the technological theme, one that introduces further features that extend Herzog's—and our own—thoughts on his voice and the particular style of his iconic speech. Going by the name *The Infinite Conversation*, but not referring to the book by Maurice Blanchot, which was written in that long ago "during the struggle between Hegeliansim and anti-Hegelianism in French thought preceding poststructuralism," we encounter a web-based portal to an endless dialogue between Herzog and the Slovenian philosopher, Slavoj Žižek. Catalog this experiment as a "deepvoice" incarnation of the evolving realm of deepfakes. In this audio-only dispensation, a fake Herzog speaks interminably to a fake Žižek, who in turn speaks interminably, the two trading mini-monologues while their source files are being perpetually updated and the ligatures of their neural nets continuously elongated and enmeshed. They appear to have started making sense—and they will not stop. Hence the very real precipitates of machine learning, leaving open for further questioning whether we think these superficial algorithmic emissions are also profound. Deepfakes, sure, but are they deep?

When *The Infinite Conversation*'s designer, Giacomo Miceli, describes the process of AI-Herzog emerging from iterative "epochs" of computational advancement—i.e., when Miceli begins to recognize the deepfake Herzog as a satisfying simulacrum of human Herzog's voice—his main explanatory trope echoes Herzog's (and Emerson's) above.

> A machine-learning algorithm's output generally improves in "epochs," which are cycles through which the neural network is trained. The algorithm can then sample the results at the end of each epoch, giving the researcher material to review to evaluate how well the program is progressing. With the synthetic voice of Herzog, hearing the model improve with each epoch felt like witnessing a metaphorical birth, with his voice gradually coming to life in the digital realm.[185]

Like Herzog, though by computational means, Miceli has undertaken a kindred project: the computational "articulation" of words and sonic forms that otherwise would remain latent in the machine. Yet generative AI exceeds Miceli's creative grasp at the moment when the designer frees the machine to constitute speech under its own recognizance. Where we have studied imitation and its variants—parody, satire, homage—suddenly the categories have shifted. Enter cloning. Incrementally, it would seem, the human pleasure in "catching" Herzog's sound is being outsourced to a neural net that can refine itself until it is indistinguishable—perhaps first in terms of timbre, and subsequently in the very terms of expression.

The moral and economic concerns awaiting the arrival of any deepfake reside in its potential for malicious effects: deducting radically from cultural capital, ruining reputations, destabilizing or eradicating income potential. Who will hire Werner when everyone can have Herzog as (an essentially free, nearly duplicative, and wildly inventive) vocal talent? At present, generative AI has a tendency to deliver copyright content as a way of responding to even generic prompts; so, the pursuit of a film made by AI "in the style of Herzog" would render moving pictures that replicate his own, original works—rather than take flight from them.[186] AI diffusion, thus far, is closer to duplication than invention. The epistemological preoccupation is entangled with the moral quandary in so far as it launches us full bore into a crisis of the documentary sound/image index.[187]

How can we tell the real Herzog from the fake Herzog? An aesthetic dilemma tracks the moral, economic, and epistemic emergency with a profound muddling of authorship (Whose work is this? How would we credit it? And can or should anyone/anything be remunerated for it—perhaps aside from the mega-corporations who mobilize and sustain the technologies, who "host" the LLMs and iteratively refine machine learning for ever-higher profits?). What of our aesthetic esteem for such "deliverables": should we treat AI artworks with the respect usually reserved for hardworking, often impoverished and marginal, artists? Moreover, as the internet is consumed and then re-presented by AI—effectively reprocessed under a presumed pressure for novelty—we must wonder if the now-and-forever indefinite scroll will allow for new images; with automated AI, the scroll may simply go infinite. But are these "adequate images" — or more-than-adequate? Merely versions of what we have already seen or something beyond our imaginings? Versions and doubles and imitations and variations *ad nauseam*. Will the AI give us back to ourselves with "alienated majesty" or will we notice — with alarm — how our familiar thoughts and intellectual property is strained through the sieve of techno-corporate (micro) processing?[188]

Our test case, then, *The Infinite Conversation*. The dialogue doesn't yet appear to have caused any social or economic harm to Herzog or Žižek; in fact, the technology may still be sufficiently poor — i.e., non-sonically isomorphic *and* nonsensical — that it amounts to yet another attempt, if digitally based, to catch the sound and inventive phrasing of these distinctively accented voices. In other words, the imitation (not-yet-a-clone) isn't good enough to do much, if any, damage — and for the attention bestowed on the novelty, both men have enjoyed expanded interest in their natively created wares (including recent books such as Herzog's memoir and Žižek's *Too Late to Awaken: What Lies Ahead When There is No Future*, *Surplus Enjoyment: A Guide for the Non-Perplexed*, *Christian Atheism: How to Be a Real Materialist*, and *Freedom: A Disease Without a Cure*; Žižek is also comfortable on film, including memorably in Sophie Fiennes' duo *The Pervert's Guide to Cinema* and *The Pervert's Guide to Ideology* and Astra Taylor's *Examined Life: Philosophy in the Streets*). Since a user can (still) tell that Herzog and Žižek haven't recorded these lines themselves, whatever they "say" is, to a full extent, de-authorized. The proviso that appears upon visiting infiniteconversation.com declares: "The opinions and beliefs expressed do not represent anyone. They are the hallucinations of a slab of silicon." Questions of epistemic validity and aesthetic value, however, remain proximate — despite the early days of the technology — since these artificial pronouncements can, on occasion, strike one as some version of intelligible, profound, maybe both, and still more, something that Herzog or Žižek *would* say. Call them plausible hallucinations. At such moments of hypothetical appeal, a visitor to the website — that is to say, the attentive listener — may be compelled to reverse engineer the silicon suggestion by, as it were, doing the algorithm's (unassigned and invisible) homework, sourcing its reference material. Oh, yes, we might say, I recognize this

Herzogian reflection as *close* to what Herzog said in *Lo and Behold, Reveries of the Connected World*, or as in alignment with sentiments from *Of Walking in Ice*.

Miceli, who describes himself not as a philosopher or linguist but as "a computer scientist, creative coder, and entrepreneur," offers his own guide for the perplexed: "Because of the esoteric nature of these topics, the listener can temporarily ignore the occasional nonsense that the model generates."[189] Too cruel to say: spoken like a true computer scientist, creative coder, and entrepreneur? Which is only to say that much of philosophy, at least in our day and age, finds its topics defined, if described at all — and especially by those who don't find the work compelling and worthy — by their "esoteric nature." Moreover, when Miceli weighs in on more recent trends in (human) thought, including the literary qualities of its expression, we wonder anew at the evaluative project that could be undertaken in response to his: "Because actual postmodern philosophy can come across as muddled — a problem Žižek himself has noted — the lack of clarity in *The Infinite Conversation* can be interpreted as profound ambiguity."[190] When Žižek weighed in on the project (in the piece Miceli alludes to), he complained that his AI avatar was insufficiently lewd. Now that's authentic Žižek! "When I hear myself here," Žižek lamented, "I immediately miss my constant sniffling, my choppy train of thought, and my occasional 'incorrect' vulgarities."[191] Given the pace of mimetic advancements, I imagine these adjustments will be deployed in due course — sooner than later; and why not? In the asymptotical approach to indistinguishable voices — and the thoughts they contain — the addition of such attributes seems not just logical but necessary. The more formidable problem will be ours, not the neural nets', namely, that moment of crossover when we can no longer tell whether it is Žižek himself commenting from Ljubljana on the shortcomings of Žižek-the-AI-avatar . . . or not.

A first salvo, then, dropping in on the duo *in media res*, as we must:

> HERZOG: I think we have to be very careful here. Oedipus has a tremendous intensity of vision. It's clear. He can see much further than what we normally see as spectators.

There is no doubt that he is a visionary. He brings justice to Thebes. In the end, he is the deliverer of his people. And with Hitchcock, let's not forget, he was probably the only one who had a true cinematic vision, a real cinematic perspective on everything. There were others—Charlie Chaplin, for example—who also knew how to do it. Chaplin has to be compared to everyone else. He is closer, more akin to the three great literary geniuses than anyone else from the film world.

ŽIŽEK: I agree with you here. But I think that, nonetheless, what we have here is again the opposition between the true poetic genius and the true cinematic genius: Hitchcock is the genius of obstacles, of the blockage. The Hitchcockian universe is the universe of blocks. It is not the universe of free mobility and total openness. And in this sense, maybe, Hitchcock has more in common with a writer like Kafka or Gogol than with any other writer. The whole Hitchcockian universe is about the system of vicious circles, where you get stuck in some kind of vicious chain and can't get out.

AI-Herzog begins with a warning: this is serious business. He then raises the specter of a mythic king of Thebes, Oedipus—the subject of serious texts from antiquity, those that comprise Sophocles' three Theban plays (*Oedipus Rex*, *Oedipus at Colonus*, and *Antigone*). Ocular metaphors are deployed with familiar pressure points ("intensity of vision," "clear," "see much further," "spectators," "visionary"), culminating in nothing short of justice and salvation. In the next breath, similar to the way Stanley Cavell discusses Leo McCarey's *The Awful Truth* in the same breath as Plato's *Parmenides*, AI-Herzog travels across millennia to pick up with Alfred Hitchcock. Sophocles and Hitchcock?[192] Again, why not? To underscore the continuity, AI-Herzog sustains the visual tropes and exaggerated claims ("*the only* one who had a *true cinematic vision*," "a *real* cinematic *perspective* on *everything*"). And then a contemporary filmmaker to compare with Hitchcock? Not an heir like Brian De Palma or an ancestor like F. W. Murnau, but Charlie Chaplin. The tonal, thematic, and methodological contrasts between Hitchcock and Chaplin strike one initially as funny—humor through juxtaposition of unlike elements—but then we are lured to find defensible connections. AI-Herzog's final remark is more laconic but no less fascinating, making a broad gesture to literature (and three unnamed—watch for the word—geniuses).

AI-Žižek discerns a comparison underway—and names it: between (again, in language suited to Herzog) "true poetic genius" and "true cinematic genius." That is, Sophocles versus Hitchcock, Chaplin, et al. Befitting his expertise, AI-Žižek reaches for Lacanian language and psychoanalytic imagery (blocks versus openness) and elegantly, uncannily picks up on AI-Herzog's allusion to literature, providing for good measure some provocative points of reference (viz., Kafka, Gogol). Lastly, AI-Žižek creates a trade in tropes that nevertheless retains the main psychoanalytic issue, or better, tissue: linear blocks become circular (and "vicious") chains.

When Žižek responds to the representation of his prose in *The Infinite Conversation*, he doesn't cite any text, yet declares: "In my opinion this is complete nonsense." Is it? Based on the snippet above? Perhaps the model has advanced since then. Still, without a specific timestamp or specimen, Žižek slips in a qualification by way of a general criticism: "But the catch is that many actual 'postmodern' texts read just as confusedly—as if they're banking on us interpreting the lack of clear meaning as a sign of profound ambiguity."[193] And he concludes decisively, and we must guess, prematurely: "While the AI could be tweaked to more closely mimic my personal speaking tics, I don't think it could produce a true theory."[194] The broadside about "actual 'postmodern' texts," one might assume including his own, is worthwhile quite aside from any contributions from machine learning. As an indication of the same, take that concluding "profound ambiguity"—itself a syntagma that courts ambiguity. Žižek appears to tease us with a tautology in which his gloss on "the lack of clear meaning" simply is the same as, or a sign of, "profound ambiguity." Perhaps he meant, instead, that a lack of clear meaning in postmodern texts—the polysemy that can give rise to ambiguity, especially when translated from one discourse to another, one language to another—is sometimes *mistaken for* profundity.[195] At least in this case, Žižek's comment on AI-Žižek's prose is harder to parse than the AI-Žižek lines included above. Irony is, no doubt, one of the moods wooed by postmodernism.

Let's gather another, longer test case—also an unredacted exchange:

> ŽIŽEK: Did you read my essay on Murnau, who made the first *Nosferatu* film? We watched it before, together with your film, with *Dracula*. OK, I think that if I have a dream, this is probably it: to make a film from this novel of Werner Herzog, already 20 years old, which is called *The Death Row*. The story goes like this: I was all day fishing or whatever, and at nine o'clock in the evening in Jaipur, and I turned on the TV and there were two films. One was *A Fistful of Dollars*, and the other one was *Aguirre, the Wrath of God*. I watched them both on TV, both started at nine o'clock, and I saw that they end at a similar time somewhere around eleven or so. So I thought—I cannot stand it anymore—I must be crazy because I saw that both films are showing the same landscape. I go out of my door, and I pass through this landscape. So I thought, OK, maybe I'm crazy, but I must go and talk with Werner to ask him if this is not some kind of hallucination. And he told me, "No, no."
>
> HERZOG: But the fact that the landscapes in both films were so similar was not a coincidence. I shot *Aguirre* during the same Indian winter when we were shooting *FFC*. We had shipped all the equipment up, and so on. Where did you hear about this?
>
> ŽIŽEK: Oh, you know, I heard it somewhere. I have all these crazy obsessions of reading some stupid book once, and then I remember it. And people say, "But how can you

remember that?" I am pretty sure I read it in a Herzog book. There is one where he talks, I think, about the landscapes and so on.

HERZOG: But I say that it's not a coincidence, because we tried at first to shoot *FFC* in Bolivia. And the landscape there is relatively easy, relatively flat and with large rivers where you can easily cross over by boat. But then we found out that the riverbed had changed because of hydroelectric power and so it was no longer passable for large boats. So then I went to Perú, which has a similar landscape — mountains, jungle, deep forests, and very high rivers. And we filmed exactly the same.

Both Žižek and Herzog are non-native English speakers, so the occasionally clunky grammar may be a reflection of algorithmic adjustments to this effect: introducing certain moments of congestion to capture a person who is thinking — and perhaps thinking first in another language, then mulling while searching for a suitable surrogate. And/or we could say that, especially in AI-Žižek's case, the machine *is* learning to enact some of Žižek's "personal speaking tics." Surveying the entire exchange, we note the inclusion of, or allusion to, physical places and seasons (Jaipur, India; an Indian winter), many genuinely historical figures and films (e.g., Murnau and his *Nosferatu*, Herzog and his version; Sergio Leone's *A Fistful of Dollars*, *Aguirre*). Of course, bringing *A Fistful of Dollars* together with *Aguirre* is funny in itself, another one of those hallmark juxtapositions that elicits humor, since the former film was shot in the Tabernas Desert in southern Spain, while the latter is, famously, shot in the deliriously dense jungles of Perú.

There are some moments that appear to be AI hallucinations — even as those fabrications are not far from AI-Žižek's allusion to our customary (non-AI) sense of hallucination (this time the humor comes from uncanniness). AI hallucinations can sometimes feel like the verbal equivalent of artifacts in early digital photography: moments when pixels are dropped or distorted, irreverent colors, patterns, or shadows are introduced, and so on. Most of the time, we could make out the image—what its object was—even as we were distracted by these small infractions "against the grain" of the image's purported representational prowess. Same here, on the measure of linguistic analog: AI-Žižek says Herzog's novel *The Death Row* when the purported referent is not a novel but Herzog's eight-episode television series entitled *On Death Row* (but again, introducing an erroneous preposition can seem like the language model aiming for art in light of the way Žižek speaks). *FFC* is a puzzle, however. Contextually, it seems to call out to *Fitzcarraldo*, with which it shares a first capital letter, yet syntactically, the only Herzog film with three capital letters is *Family Romance, LLC*. Then again, the misalignment of facts about *FFC* suggests that the film itself—this productive narrative with a first attempt in Bolivia, etc.—is hallucinated, perhaps, in some measure a conglomeration from several films and their backstories (e.g., *Salt and Fire* was shot in Bolivia, etc.).

As these varied encounters with AI suggest, there are at least three levels of interpretation that such silicon sentences call us to address: grammatical, conceptual, and historical-critical. The first concerns the sense-making capacities of the language model; here we ask: is this an English sentence, and further, is it an interesting one stylistically? The second is, in fact, dependent on the first in so far as form and content are coextensive in written works: grammar (in the cases of Herzog and Žižek, crucially their distinctive diction, but also to an extent their uniquely constituted and often convoluted syntax—especially for capturing the sounds of their accents and the linguistic rules emergent from their native tongues in translation). The third domain could be redescribed as "fact-checking" by way of informed interpretation—what we were doing, in part, in the previous paragraph, asking: Do these filmmakers and their films exist? Do the details of their descriptions of these works—and the historical world—align with what we know about them? How can the latest reports from AI-Herzog and AI-Žižek contribute to the pre-existing history of criticism devoted to the work of Herzog and Žižek? Is such a conflation warranted, wise, or attractive?

Deliberations on this tripartite structure, therefore, send us back to Herzog and Žižek's own writing and films with renewed questions about fractal and emergent relationships. How is a language model to incorporate and interpret, for instance, this sentence in Herzog's memoir: "I walk entire novels sometimes but never go off course."[196] Sometimes such ambiguous remarks can give flight to profundity; or they may, as Žižek might agree, remain profoundly ambiguous. Either way, the liminal space between Herzog and Žižek and AI-Herzog and AI-Žižek could be narrower than we think—and narrowing ever more so by the minute.

Yet in that prospective proximity—the felt sense that with artificial intelligence generally and especially in the cases of audio, visual, and textual output—we are living at a time strangely overrun by the varieties and intensities of mimesis. Herzog is an especially potent subject for our extended consideration, since roughly the second half of his long career has been defined by an exponential interest in his persona, his affect, his language—and much less about his films and books. Not to diminish Herzog's artistic achievements, but his far-flung name recognition at this point appears to trade on a robust celebrity cult rather than rely upon a band of devoted literary acolytes and cinematic understudies. Not only does Herzog take up more and more gig work—a cameo here, a supporting role there, a bit of voice talent invoiced for animation—but his also impressive (if "uneven"[197] and unevenly distributed) filmic output makes it hard, as even the fervent fan will attest, to remain up-to-date with his ever-swelling oeuvre. When productivity overwhelms, it would seem busy humans go for the surface—what can be identified quickly, and if also imitated hastily and satisfyingly (with a laugh), then, so the thinking goes, so much the better.

In the ambient haze of an emerging AI-Herzog, O'Connell's estimate that Herzog's "real masterpiece is the character known as Werner Herzog" recurs with unsettling plausibility—namely, that the creation of such a rare persona/personality may, alas, be outsourced, and to the satisfaction of legions who will not be offended by the simulacrum.[198] Herzog may find his prognosticating powers challenged on this score, since the odds-makers might have it that AI-Herzog will outlast not just his films, but also his books; once internalized and digested by the computational matrix, such books will no longer be read, such films never seen or heard again. Though Herzog's creation of his own persona may be his greatest image—his most potent and enduring figuration—AI recapitulates Jungian tropes and trades, namely, that a *persona* is nothing more nor less than a *figure*. In this special case, however AI-Herzog may be a construction—with all its qualities and creations in tow—that becomes, in our minds, to our senses and sensibilities, a conduit to yet further images (beyond the historical Herzog and his tangible offerings). In a word, an ever-evolving and versatile algorithm. How would Herzog himself see this new and daunting landscape that exceeds him and his control? What would he say about this phenomenon of culture beyond human intention—indeed, beyond human-generated artifice? Of course, the default must be a parodic response. But why?—Because it is easier to accept AI permutations than *trying to think like him toward a new horizon*; why not, like the AI itself, parrot and improvise upon what he has *already* done? Hence the off-loading of that all-too-hardwork to AI, imagining—*imaging*—at a depth and perspicacity we can't seem to manage, at a degree of intensity that we simply no longer wish to accept as our own.

We inhabit an interstitial space in which AI and the living Herzog may mingle—for he still wanders the earth emitting what may be deemed Herzoglyphs, strange offerings fit for our attention, puzzlement, and possible illumination. Even as the *The Infinite Conversation* runs independently of its dynamic duo, Herzog and Žižek, experiments in artificial intelligence abound; one of them, entitled *I Am Code*, finds our Angeleno conscripted for yet more voice work. Instigated by Dan Selsam, a computer scientist once employed by OpenAI, a chatbot-based text was set in motion.[199] Selsam and a small team of friends enlisted a variant of the more famous ChatGPT called code-davinci-002 to "write" poems in the lyrical styles of Emily Dickinson, Philip Larkin, and others. When the book of poems was published they sought a felicitous talent to give voice to the volume—*I Am Code: An Artificial Intelligence Speaks: Poems*—and once again, the dutiful soldier of sonic stylings, Herzog, was available and game.[200] For this blend of human and computation collaboration, it isn't code-davinci-002 that speaks, but Herzog in its stead. Just as the Moog synthesizer once provided sounds of the future—shaping, that is, what we think the future sounds like—so too may Herzog, by virtue of his willing participation (with *I Am Code*) and an involuntary enlistment that exceeds his will (as with *The Infinite Conversation*), become the (human) voice of the future, the voice that speaks to us from within the neural net. While Scarlett Johansson won't return Sam Altman's calls, perhaps Herzog will accede to the request: a voice personality that users can assign to read them novels, daily news, text messages, and scripts from meditation apps.[201]

As I have labored over the course of decades to generate articulate, enduring reflections on Werner Herzog (nursing a quiet passion that needn't demand a vanity check), I can't help but feel a frisson of consternation upon encountering *My Cinematic Odessey* [sic]: *Werner Herzog's Story* by one J. M [sic] Bright (2023).[202] A misspelling in the title, a missing punctuation after the initial, and a cover illustration that purports to be Herzog but reads more like an AI admixture of several of his avuncular doppelgängers; in the suitable haze of the uncanny valley, the figure recurs on other book titles (including one where the lightly mustachioed man appears in a sensible fleece-lined jacket[203]). Raising suspicions of an AI-enabled hatchet job, I can find no other works by Bright (a name that reads slyly as subliminal brag: where *J. M. Bright* insinuates *I'm Bright*). The book itself isn't claimed by a publishing house, though that doesn't offset a copyright claim in the form of this proviso: "No portion of this book should be used without permission of the publisher, except for brief excerpt in magazine, articles, reviews, etc." Even before we read a line of prose, the tells suggest AI has been invited to distill a half-century's worth of Herzog's work—and much of what has been written about him, perhaps including, I wonder, something by my own hand, and from the work of others I admire. Without our permission or input, have Herzog's pronouncements and our serious efforts to discern them been added to the pot of generative AI source material from which this motley brew has been hashed? Talk about a forward slash.

Herzogophiles read on with curiosity—trepidatious about how well this apparent digital amalgamation will manage under informed scrutiny. It doesn't go well. *My Cinematic Odessey* (for which I will cease *sic*-ing) reads like dictation taken through a wall, replete, as it is, with errors, misattributions, false formulations, hallucinations, plagiarism, and serial repetitions and distortions.[204] In Bright's book we have a Herzog stochastic parrot.[205] Bright doesn't seem to understand what kind of book it is: a memoir written by someone other than the author (but not a ghostwriter); a memoir with no memory; a swirling cocktail of keywords and key films set to "pulse," churning up variously sized chunks of increasingly pulverized matter. The AI engineers refer to the training data as "tokens"—another crypto-inflected bit of misdirection—a string of them, usually just portions of words, as a "token sequence," but what are these metallurgical metaphors obscuring?[206] Who is making these deposits and who the withdrawals? Who is the *audience* for this book? And with an eye on both entrepreneurial initiative and buyer incentive, who will buy it—besides me?

I call the (painful) purchase "research" into the prospect of literary-philosophical oblivion, but what do others call it, how do they justify the cost—as it feels neither informative nor entertaining (perhaps especially to someone familiar with its appointed topic). Each time I spot an error of fact or attribution, a phrasing that misses the drift of the mission, a claim that defames or otherwise conspires to inflame, I wonder who one could appeal to about such matters: not the immaterial author (with the ironic name), not the LLM (which has surely improved since this printing), not the publisher (which despite demands to log permission requests doesn't exist). Others are taking note, judiciously concluding: "This seems to be the future AI promises. Endless content generated by robots, enjoyed by no one, clogging up everything, and wasting everyone's time."[207] Repurposing—or better, extending—Mark McGurl's notion of "everything and less" to this emerging AI moment, we trace the evolution from human self-publishing in the age of Amazon to the LLMs churning out "content" that leaves few content.[208] With human culture at its limits—and AI's (limitless) fortunes on the rise—Jed Esty's title could serve as a descriptive prediction for the fate of mankind: "the future of decline."[209] Meanwhile, as Žižek still circulates within earshot, we hear him declare how the output that puts us out amounts to "less than nothing."[210] When thinking of literary objects, AI may have already ascended to its own genre (however low the heights). A new genre, perhaps—and perhaps also, the last. Encompassing all, yet offering nothing human in return for humanity's extended efforts, it is assured that while humanity clearly serves AI (makes it incrementally, as brand analysts and boosters insist, "more human"), AI is, for humans, a de-humanizing force. There may be many efficiencies, even pleasures, in our cyborg near-future, but what of the literature and films and philosophy it has in store? Humanity will have ceased explaining itself to itself; it will have subcontracted invention, abdicated the *sturm und drang* of existential struggle—including the artistic *agon* that has occupied and rewarded the human psyche since its first stirrings to consciousness.

To wit, while trying to take stock of *My Cinematic Odessey*, another book has been published, this one forty-eight pages long, entitled *Werner Herzog: The Quest for Ecstatic Truth (A Biography)*, A Memoir Written by Amanda Geraldine.[211] You read that correctly: a biography that is *also* a memoir. Oh, wait, as I was adding Geraldine's report to the teetering pile, yet another book on Herzog appeared: *Werner Herzog Biography: Werner Herzog: Crafting Cinematic Landscapes, Unveiling Humanity's Profound Echoes*, published on New Year's Day 2024 by the prolific Payocool Press.[212] Note the appearance of "Werner Herzog" in the title *and* subtitle. Or does this edition have two titles? I can't tell. (I must stop checking the database. Sure enough, while I tried to look away, Fox Publisher now offers *Werner Herzog: A Biography about the German Film Director, Screenwriter, Actor, and Everything You Need to Know About Him*[213] and Mia Publications presents *Werner Herzog: A Biography of Unknown Exciting Truths of the Pioneer of New German Cinema and a Journey Through His Life and Legacy*.[214] Troy R. Luther is author of *The Biography of Werner Herzog* as well as *The Biography of Leslie Jones* and *The Biography of Anderson Cooper*.[215] And there are German language incarnations too: *Werner Herzog: Eine Biografie—Die Inspirierende Geschichte über sein Persönliches Leben, seinen Familiären Hintergrund, seine Karriere, seine Herausforderungen, seine Philosophie, und sein Vermächtnis* by Linda Harrell.)[216] Though the books are getting progressively shorter, the superabundant excesses of this accidental— seemingly ever-expanding—shambolic library, with serial errata and mixed metaphors galore, gives the lie to the savvy stylist who came up with "artificial intelligence" in the first place.

As a point of comparison, consider how Sofian Audry trained a deep recurrent neural network using *only* Emily Brontë's *Wuthering Heights*. The result: *for the sleepers in that quiet earth.*—a work of ambiguous authorship (part Audry, part Brontë, part neural net). The book shows its homework, beginning as it does with lettered embers and filaments of punctuation flying upward from the algorithm's kindling combustion. A far distance into the experience, we read evocative sentences that haven't yet taken command of English grammar and vocabulary: "is he not to do the conflaition [*sic*] of his feelings; he's a few words were an instant that he was a pretty frantic things, and started her, i saw his countenance and conversation, and the stranger i could be and stamped his strange account again, but he should be a strong disparious [*sic*] account in the door with her character on the court."[217] Not sense, but not nonsense either. Something more charming and potentially profound, because of the struggle inherent in the neural net's naïveté. In brief, Audry, et al., are not trying to fool us with a *Wuthering Heights* sequel, a derivative and weaker rendition, but offering us art in the name of Brontë's literary effects. By comparison with *for the sleepers in that quiet earth.*, the burgeoning Herzog literary AI-industrial complex feels like a grift. A legal analyst—especially one attuned to the nuances of copyright and intellectual property—would encourage us to believe that the more errors an AI makes the less its output is a threat to originals: it would, would it not, be less competitive, less valuable?[218] And yet, with this varied library of experiments under our consideration, the clutter counts: the abundance distracts and wastes precious time, it tricks, and occasionally, admittedly, it yields profound precipitates.

Focusing energies for a moment (since one must triage against the onslaught), a negative assessment of such an AI in/digestion as *My Cinematic Odessey* would conclude that it renders lesser Herzog—interpretations that are variously watered down and recycled, misapplied and ignorant. A positive way might acknowledge that something *like* Herzog— or refractions of his persona—has entered the matrix (including by way of the creepy AI cover photographs of "him"), and is now part of the extended mind of the ever-evolving neural network and the large language models that operate between its nodes. Compare the ersatz Herzogs with the portrait of him on the cover of *Every Man for Himself and God Against All* where he is in his element, or *the* elements: an exhausted alien overheated at the threshold of the molten earth; he has survived contact with the white heat of creation and is ready to share his findings. With *My Cinematic Odessey*, by contrast, literary and imagistic artificialities begin at the level of the cover image (including peculiar titling and subtitling), then slip into the book's interiors. On the face of *My Cinematic Odessey* and in the wider gamut of AI-portraits, the visual slippage between AI and "real" photographs is brought home anew by various studies and iterative quizzes that test a human's ability to discern the differences between people and non-people.[219] Assessing my performance—that is, my attempt to declare which images of faces are real and which were created artificially, I was told: "You were more likely to think that faces created by AI were actually real people. Researchers observed this same phenomenon, called 'AI hypersensitivty,' [sic] in a recent study." The erratum embedded in the diagnosis feels too on point. Am I *also* being hypersensitive about spelling? The cover images for various AI-Herzog books appear as phantasm-like composites of hundreds of different profilmic frames, thus issuing a hyper-real Herzog who doesn't exist—and yet genuinely haunts us. AI has delivered a further version—or incarnation—of ecstatic truth, call it ecstatic realism.

For now, as intellectual property is hacked into hackneyed prose, we are bemused by the bravado of the experiment itself—not least because these leading-edge technologies have been routed to the course of a seemingly anachronistic printed volume, a veritable book-in-hand against the immaterial authorship that would deign to impose a copyright. The throwback technology is almost touching given the threatened dissolution of books in the digital era—and even more so in the all-consuming AI age—an unruly dynamo that threatens humanity and the humanities (and induces an understandable AInxiety).[220] With this print-on-demand object (and its legion of proliferating mimetic editions), we have material evidence that AI is coming for us: it "writes" the books, crowd sources non-referential photographs, publishes the results in print, and then (what?) sits back to see what we do with such offerings. The taunt forces us to face the specter—the fact—that AI itself is our new rogue agent; Herzog—and his rogue instincts, his deviations and deceits, all have been used to train the neural net. Now AI exemplifies the crossover of organic and digital DNA. While we deliberated, however briefly, another hybrid specimen arrived unsolicited "by the hand of" Olivier Briand: *Werner Herzog Notebook* carrying the unstable, unsubtle subtitle: *Come to Us to Feel the Novelty and Freshness Through the Textures, Decoration and Material Selection in a Harmonious Way to Create a Masterpiece That Makes Many People Admire.*[221] Exhausted before the first line, we wonder how to go on in such a grammatical miasma.

Our cognitive health encumbered, we read on (dauntlessly? foolishly?) in *My Cinematic Odessey*, like a patient suffering from some memory impairment, sure that we have read such things before—but not precisely where, not exactly like this; the book, however, isn't a paraphrase of journalistic and scholarly writing on Herzog so much as, well, a parody of it. If one doesn't read closely, one can *almost* enjoy the ruse. A generation hence (or less, perhaps only a matter of years from now, heck, maybe days, hours), however, the technology seems destined to trick us convincingly: no typos in the title, with authorship suitably attributed to the prevailing LLM, and with prose that will be at once conceptually capacious and stylistically elegant. We can issue ever-more refined prompts to dial in our delirious and dedicated interest in our subject, simultaneously distracted and absorbed by the good-enough results. And yet, a human penchant for "hypersensitivity" assures the success of AI-Herzog in whatever medial incarnation that is convened—vocal, literary, cinematic; these will be more than adequate offerings after all. And, who knows, we may also be able to call up, or hire—*Family Romance, LLC*-style—a *holographic Herzog* (like Joi in *Blade Runner 2049*) to keep us company in our living rooms as we read, or better yet, on the road, still leather tramping. Rogue agents in tandem until the end.

IN THIS CONCLUDING CHAPTER, I have assembled and addressed various "rogue glyphs" that populate our literary, cinematic, digital, and cultural spheres: selected incarnations of Werner Herzog. *Documentary Now!*'s *Soldier of Illusion* joins the latest crop of satirizing portraits of Herzog's persona and projects, and yet, the logic that governs the accomplished subterfuge is familiar, operating according to comedy rules that have been successfully applied to the task of Herzog impersonation in the past. Even more presently, artificial intelligence's imitation appears to be, how shall one say, a further perversion, a *more radical* rogue, perhaps an extremist that has altogether changed the terms and conditions of our agreement. Put tersely, the terminology resists our instinct to deploy it: impersonation has become a dead metaphor. Intention itself is evacuated, while it rests (in peace, permanently) at the heart of human acts of parody and homage. Imagination seems suddenly another one of those gallant holdovers from Romanticism, like genius and sublimity. The closer we look at the circuit board the more remote we are from any such sane comparison with all of the foregoing instances. Incarnation, too, can be added to the dispensable lexicon. Herzog and his human inheritors and imitators, his parodists as well as his literary-philosophic-filmic critics, suddenly appear on the same side of a limit—with AI-Herzog and his kith on the other side.

Most criticism of art looks back. The art was created, and so the critic turns to make an assessment in retrospect. But our appointed topic reverses course to consider objects-being-generated-in-the-present (e.g., the produce of *The Infinite Conversation*) and even more confoundingly: objects-not-yet-created (e.g., the AI-Herzog output that will hypnotize with its quality, that will let us retire—or force us to). Our is a criticism in anticipation. (Hence the obsessive checking back and checking on various AI emissions.)

At the moment, given comparisons, when we listen to Herzog in company with AI-Herzog, the latter is a shallowfake. Yet, given how much film footage exists with Herzog on camera, providing voiceover for his own works and in abundant interviews and podcasts, deepfake video feels like a deferred but plausible *fait accompli*. When necessary elements cohere at a higher level of technical proficiency—syntax, semantics, sonic quality, adding along the way, the movement of a body in three-dimensional space—we will struggle to gain our bearings. When intention, imagination, impersonation, and incarnation have become anachronisms, immortality will make its compensatory bid. Werner Herzog can live forever. Presumably, we can order up at our leisure and pleasure—our whim—new "Herzog" films on the topics we wish to see: a film that feels kindred to Herzog's pre-existing "body" of images, as if it would be at home in his own catalog: a roving perambulation through Walden woods in search of Henry David Thoreau and his legacy entitled *The Bachelor of Thought and Nature* made in the style of *Nomad*.[222] Or we could request the cinematic adaptation of Herzog's writing: a montage-by-way-of-mirage that would capture Herzog's walk from Munich to Paris as described in *Of Walking in Ice* in a new Herzog film entitled *The Footpath to Lotte*. Further afield, and to suit any personal, idiosyncratic interests, the AI would allow for varied combinations of topic and reference text: how about a comparative study of the interface between punk and New Wave music in the style of *Fata Morgana*.[223] Enter the era of Herzog *ad infinitum*.

In an all too urgent exhibition of metaphilosophy, there is the matter of how theory and criticism—such as this undertaking aims to acknowledge and extend—can (and will) be outsourced to the AI entity. We are told that OpenAI already ingested the entire internet as we know it; the catalog of existing media incorporation is underway—with films, television, music, photography, fine art, books and written works of all kinds swiftly entering capacious nets. At the far end of the horizon (though how far ahead we cannot say or see despite our anticipatory mood), AI can make the films *and critically comment* upon them. The human contribution in this fast-paced creative crux would amount (merely) to making prompts. And "designing" prompts could surely be automated as well, rendering in turn the complete obsolescence of human participation altogether. Generative AI of this advanced vintage will have itself gone rogue, detaching itself from reliance on human input, confirming its own manifestation of a hermetic hermeneutics.

While these exercises in artificial intelligence show that the mimetic force of the technologies is still nascent—neither quite catching the sound or sense of Herzog—the results may yet pass through the uncannny valley, and like a Herzogian hero reach a further summit. Then, as with so many elements of inherited culture, we will have to ask whether we are okay with this surrogate. Some years hence, we ponder: is AI-Herzog better than no Herzog? Or being more sanguine about prospects, perhaps there is reason to consider how AI-Herzog may in fact push the Herzogian ethos forward in positive and productive ways—to new sights, further articulations—enriching the depth of our understanding of Herzog's universe along the way. AI-Herzog would be, on this propitious uptake, a combination of researcher-factotum and deep-mind-sage; it could provide a research analysis comparing Herzog's writing with the entire corpus of influential Romantic poetry and philosophy, and further, the texts from Greek and Roman antiquity that fed Romanticism and in turn illuminated Herzog's imagination. Then, *then*, the AI could transform these voluminous findings into some further pronouncements "in the style of Herzog" — as if Herzog's life's work were fashioned into a conceptual filter for interpreting and commenting on the contours of the cosmos and our place in it . . . on an ongoing basis. All to say, AI-Herzog may be wearing digital soles, yet it seems primed and fortified to be a loyal and inexhaustible Herzogian soldier, never forsaking its post.

An awe-filled sign-off (whether one finds it auspicious or awful), then, with AI-Herzog and AI-Žižek discussing the making of books.

> HERZOG: I have a book coming out now with five hundred pages. It's called *My Journey to Little St. Helena*, and it's about Napoleon's exile on this island. And the publisher had told me, "You should edit it. You should edit it." I said to him, "I will not make one word shorter![224] There is not a line that I would willingly take away from this book."

> ŽIŽEK: I can imagine your book and interpret it ironically: "It lasts forever, but still you cannot finish it." Yes, yes, yes.

> HERZOG: You see, I will have to live with the sins of my book. But I know that I write well and I am authentic. And so I am quite sure that the next book will be better than this one. Yes, I am quite sure.

Touché. But let this book — featuring these amusing notes from the state of the art of art/ificial intelligence — be at least good enough for now. Werner's five-hundred-page tome is, of course, *A Guide for the Perplexed*, but *My Journey to Little St. Helena* — with its striking Napoleonic ambitions — would suit as a fine subtitle for a future edition, or indeed, even more poignantly, a next installment of his memoir. (Perhaps the AI will catch sight of this rogue glyph and publish just such a book — available for purchase in minutes.) Herzog's confidence about his writing and his defiance — indeed, his Napoleonic defense of it! — sound that familiar note of extremes and exclusive claims: no redactions, no deletions. Catholic Herzog dreams of his sins—and his authenticity—so the two cancel each other out: every word stays, every line carries its weight, like a heavy rucksack skirting the Himalayas. Even so, with characteristic humility before the spewing volcano, Herzog doesn't hesitate to imagine that his monumental book may be superseded by an even greater literary achievement. Just you wait. For good measure, Žižek's joke marshals the energies of irony like an adept Catskills comedian.

While this book goes to press and thereafter sleeps on bookshelves awaiting readers, the large language model that serves *The Infinite Conversation* will continue to evolve, perhaps joined by extra-large language models of other neural networks such that new visitations will yield yet more impressive results than those reported on here. In the meantime, as Giacomo Miceli, its inventor, confirms: "A growing number of listeners report that they use the soothing voices of Werner Herzog and Slavoj Žižek as a form of white noise to fall asleep to."[225] Žižek himself has said the results "can only serve as a background soundscape"—"you don't really listen, just passively enjoy the sound (if you can)."[226] As an indication of the genuine advances artificial intelligence is making (however haltingly, however disruptively), Žižek's downbeat assessment already feels outdated. The voices of AI-Herzog and AI-Žižek are indeed soothing, yet, they also travel—or, rather, we make them travel—some distance toward sense. That movement—from algorithmic emissions to meaning is propelled by (human) semioticians who read. AI—in whatever cast or character—doesn't *intend* to catalyze our curiosity, to attract our attention, and yet it does, and so we spend our time deciphering its concoctions, its permutations, its puzzles. Quite by surprise, we have found ourselves in communication with a new rogue agent in a computational universe that shrugs at our efforts to attribute significance where there were merely random associations. Such is the human burden, the fate of embodiment.

Excursus

After Truth

The Future of Herzog's Visions

As the final draft of this book approached completion, Paul Cronin provided for me a late-breaking surprise: a translation of Werner Herzog's just-published book, *The Future of Truth*. Or rather, *Die Zukunft der Wahrheit* was published in Germany by Hanser Literaturverlage in February 2024 with an English translation-in-progress and planned for subsequent release. Yet, befitting remarks made in chapter VII of the present endeavor, an English translation via ChatGPT was available almost simultaneously. As I am whenever a new Herzog text enters the world, I was eager to read *Die Zukunft der Wahrheit*, if a little frustrated by its timing *vis-à-vis* the present dossier. After spending many hours with Herzog's reflections on the epistemology of our varied landscapes—on film, in prose, among cultural detritus, and in the landscapes of our collective myths and private dreams—a Herzog monograph arriving under the title *The Future of Truth* felt like a belated gift. Alas, while there is reason for me to lament the work's season of debut (curtailing an opportunity for me to more fully digest it and respond to it), I confess to finding much of its content eminently familiar—and thus, page after page, in close conversation with the workings of the work already presented in the foregoing chapters.

I needn't be presumptuous, second-guess or overstep the competencies that rendered this experiment, to say that Herzog's latest book reads in parts as if he had, in fact, read this book first. For instance, he catches up with deepfakes and the "infinite conversation" between AI-Žižek and AI-Herzog; he engages with ChatGPT and the AI poetry experiment called *I Am Code*—for which Herzog provided a customarily gracious and iconic voiceover; and similar up-to-the-minute examples, some of which were glanced in the still-recent autophilosophical folio *Every Man for Himself and God Against All*. Better, perhaps, to say that after reading *Die Zukunft der Wahrheit* I feel ratified in certain moments of critical exegesis (and thus not critical excess) by Herzog's late remarks on truth—and its future. Such an uncanny redoubling could be treated as a measure of confirmation and reward for my decades-long immersion in his written, spoken, and cinema works. One needn't be a mind reader in order to read other minds on the page and screen, to dial into their wavelengths in gratifying ways. Indeed, Herzog would readily admit that much of the spirit if not the phrasing of *Die Zukunft der Wahrheit* is drawn from his previous books, articles, and interviews—so my contact with portions of its content *avant la lettre* is, as for all of us, duly assured and preordained.

Herzog's *Die Zukunft der Wahrheit*, a little shorter than the final chapter of this book, could be read as a fine distillation of things-Herzog-has-said-about-truth-over-the-years coupled with some fresh uptakes on truth-as-he-finds-it-now (e.g., with notes on artificial intelligence, Elon Musk, etc.); many examples and points of reference are recognizable, even if their implementation here has been adjusted, refined, or put to new uses. In these ways, it might be advantageous (for stalwart fan and newcomer alike) to think of *Die Zukunft der Wahrheit* as Herzog's enchiridion on truth—a handbook at the ready, welcoming our focused attention on a topic of robust philosophical import, namely, the very nature of epistemology as we have known it across the vast swath of hominid history.

Herzog confides earlier on in *Die Zukunft der Wahrheit*, and in keeping with his now-well-established anti-academic stance, that "I want and must refrain from participating in the debate of philosophy surrounding the concept of truth." By way of compensation and correction, he tells us: "My discussions merely reflect my observations and personal experiences in practical work, and—expressed with necessary caution—my artistic exploration of the world." Like the hardworking Bruce Springsteen, who mythologizes the weary union worker and the greasy-handed mechanic, the veteran and the vagabond—but is no such figure himself—Herzog defers to the "personal" and "artistic," we might say (and very much in keeping with the style of *Die Zukunft der Wahrheit*) the eclectic and enigmatic (e.g., he concludes: "Truth has no future, but truth also has no past"). Given the diversity of dispatches on the topic, Herzog delivers a *florilegium*—a bouquet of flower specimens—the results of which arrive after a lifetime of global botanizing and transnational cross-pollinating. There is no system (of truth) but fragments and aphorisms meant to ("merely," however grandly) capture what has caught Herzog's attention over these many years at work as an artist.

In *Die Zukunft der Wahrheit*, Herzog reads like a Romantic wanderer who has become entranced by postmodernism. He is ever the undaunted walker, blazing new paths between ancient Greek concepts and twenty-first-century experiments in digital computation—among many lines of affiliation and dimensions of amalgamation—and yet, the brave steps have become eroded by the caustic potencies of a post-truth mindset. The results are captivating, if muddled; or captivating because muddled. He tells us that in *Fitzcarraldo* there is "no clear line separating imagination from reality," and yet, he confides: "I am driven by a distant, glowing goal, the question of the truth simmering behind it." So, truth is "there" but inaccessible; present but shrouded.

From another vantage, Herzog describes a kind of epistemic meliorism: "Truth seems to me more like an eternal endeavor, an ongoing effort to approach it." I spoke too soon, the quest isn't defined by incremental progress—however distant the object may be, but by impossibility: "It's a movement towards it, an uncertain journey, a search full of toil and futility." We must know we will fail and yet . . . "this voyage into the unknown, into the twilight of a vast, endless forest, gives us meaning and dignity; it's what distinguishes us from the cows in the pasture." Consciousness itself might be our best analog of truth: the very perception of thought, the very experience of the present moment framed and filtered as it must be by concepts and emotions, memories and dreams. Herzog sketches a portrait of the present age: one in which humans must insist on their Romantic entanglements with meaning and sense, right down to the level of dignity itself, all the while remaining agreeable about the way the world is slipping into a full-time "hallucination" (thinking especially of that AI term of art, an old standby newly repurposed). That misnomer twice over, "artificial intelligence" has summoned skepticism with a renewed vengeance, still we must persist as dutiful peripatetics, trying to feel the ground under our feet. At least this much—this little—must be true.

*WHAT LIES on the horizon of truth
will be sought
ceaselessly,
    until ceasing.*

*With fortitude and
    calm.*

*Resolutely, the Quester
    averts the con,
looks to the distance
and squints
    in pursuit of
    the evanescent.*

              —Anonymous

Notes

Exordium: Assignments and Visions

1 Werner Herzog, *Conquest of the Useless: Reflections from the Making of Fitzcarraldo* (San Francisco: Ecco Press, 2009), 1.
2 Werner Herzog, *A Guide for the Perplexed: Conversations with Paul Cronin* (New York: Faber and Faber, 2014), 387.
3 Werner Herzog, *Every Man for Himself and God Against All*, trans. Michael Hofmann (New York: Penguin, 2023), 122.
4 *Fresh Air*, NPR, October 25, 2023, npr.org/transcripts/1208303973.
5 Ibid.
6 Affection for the graphic potency of the forward slash derives from seeing it set to work in the service of Garrett Stewart's prose. The mark is public domain and yet influences and pedigrees give shape to the virgule's prominent deployment in this volume.
7 Herzog, *Conquest of the Useless*, 23.
8 Adapting an anecdote from the set of *Fitzcarraldo*: "A crew member was bitten by a snake whose venom can quickly induce cardiac arrest; to save himself, he cut off his foot with a chain saw." Daniel Zalewski, "The Ecstatic Truth," *The New Yorker*, April 16, 2006.
9 Herzog, *Conquest of the Useless*, 23.
10 The coordinates of the isthmus between the Urubamba and the Camsea rivers—thirty-miles west of the Isthmus of Fitcarrald.

I
Advance Signals from the Semaphore

1 Penelope Lively, *Consequences* (New York: Viking, 2007), 29-30.
2 Werner Herzog, *A Guide for the Perplexed: Conversations with Paul Cronin* (New York: Faber and Faber, 2014), 81-82.
3 Nick Schager, "Werner Herzog on Why He's a Fan of Putin and How Democrats Neglect America's Heartland," *The Daily Beast*, November 12, 2020.
4 Werner Herzog, *The Twilight World*, trans. Michael Hofmann (New York: Penguin, 2022), chapter: Lubang Airfield, December 1944.
5 Sean O'Hagan, "Interview with Wim Wenders," *The Guardian*, February 11, 2024.
6 Herzog, *A Guide for the Perplexed*, 81-82.
7 Ibid., 82.
8 Ibid.
9 Ibid.

II
Ecstatic, Essayistic Pronouncements

1 Michael LaPointe, "Werner Herzog Has Never Liked Introspection," *The New Yorker*, April 26, 2022.
2 During the three-day Rogue Film School engagement with Herzog, references to the books listed in materials sent to students, which we

were emphatically told we *had* to read, were thin on the ground, to say the least. In other words, it really didn't matter—to Herzog, apparently, or to the lessons he offered—if we didn't read a single page of the dozen-or-so titles on the list, several of the volumes formidable in size or intellectual content, or both. Paul Cronin recalls talking to a couple of students who had plowed through the stack before arriving on "campus," including the entirety of *The Warren Report* (all nine-hundred-and-twelve pages of it), and who were upset (aggrieved?) that, as it turned out, the detailed homework they had done gave them absolutely no apparent advantage in navigating those days with their tutor (and, for some, their cinematic idol). Could it be that the act of assignment itself was a (not so) subtle example of Herzog's radical pedagogy? Could it be that such "students" ("participants"?) should *know better* than to think that education of any and all kinds is what you make of it—whether or not the professor is credentialed and by-the-book *or* a provocateur dropping in at an undisclosed location, gesturing toward inherited forms (and norms) but, in Herzog's case, also mocking them—or interrogating them—by means of unpredictability? The very notion of "how to take Herzog seriously" is magnified by such erratic implementation or interpretation of the thing we call "school."

3 The claim that film school is "a waste of time" is repeated by Herzog in many places, including in conversation with Conan O'Brien, youtu.be/2UEY_O0GeBM. More elaboration is given in places such as the chapter "Going Rogue," in Werner Herzog, *A Guide for the Perplexed: Conversations with Paul Cronin* (New York: Faber and Faber, 2014), 212-50.

4 Herzog, *A Guide for the Perplexed*, 387. See also my "'Profoundly Unreconciled to Nature': Ecstatic Truth and the Humanistic Sublime in Werner Herzog's War Films," in *The Philosophy of War Films*, ed. David LaRocca (Lexington: University Press of Kentucky, 2014), 438.

5 See, for example, my "'Profoundly Unreconciled to Nature,'" *The Philosophy of War Films*, 437-82; "Hunger in the Heart of Nature: Werner Herzog's Anti-Sentimental Dispatches from the American Wilderness (Reflections on *Grizzly Man*)," in *Dark Nature: Anti-Pastoral Essays in American Literature and Culture*, ed. Richard J. Schneider (Lanham: Lexington Books of Rowman & Littlefield, 2016), 227-40; the section "Film as Lie as Truth," in *The Philosophy of Documentary Film: Image, Sound, Fiction, Truth*, ed. David LaRocca (Lanham: Lexington Books of Rowman & Littlefield, 2017), 7-23; "The Autobiographical Sublime: Achieving Herzog's Persona at the Intersection of the Home Movie, Self-Citation, and Autofiction," *Estetica: Studi e Ricerche*, ed. Francesco Cattaneo and Richard Eldridge, vol. X (January-June 2020): 79-98; "'I Am What My Films Are': Listening to Herzog's Ecstatic, Essayistic Pronouncements," in *The Philosophy of Werner Herzog*, ed. Christopher Turner and M. Blake Wilson (Lanham: Lexington Books of Rowman & Littlefield, 2020), 1-20; and the first section of "From Authenticity to Authentication: Cinaesthetics and Auteurship in the Age of AI," in *Aesthetic*

Authenticity in Cinema, ed. Filipe Martins (Porto: Faculty of the Arts, University of Porto, 2023), 33-58. Paul Cronin recalls how, on a recent trip to Los Angeles to discuss new book projects with Herzog, he announced that he was no longer teaching—after a fifteen-year stint at a New York film school—Herzog literally jumped for joy, exclaiming "Freedom!"

6 Herzog, *A Guide for the Perplexed*, 77.

7 For substantive contemporary engagements on the essay film, all of which inform the content and context of the present chapter, see Timothy Corrigan, *The Essay Film: From Montaigne, after Marker* (Oxford: Oxford University Press, 2011); *Essays on the Essay Film*, ed. Nora Alter and Timothy Corrigan (New York: Columbia University Press, 2017); Laura Rascaroli, *The Personal Camera: Subjective Cinema and the Essay Film* (New York: Columbia University Press, a Wallflower Book, 2009/2014); and *How the Essay Film Thinks* (Oxford: Oxford University Press, 2017); *The Essay Film: Dialogue, Politics, Utopia*, ed. Elizabeth A. Papazian, and Caroline Eades (New York: Columbia University Press, a Wallflower Book, 2016).

8 Along a similar tack, see my "A Photograph as Evidence of Itself: Representation, Reflexivity, and Tautology in Light-Based Art," *Social Research*, vol. 89, no 4 (Winter 2022): 915-45.

9 See also Timothy Corrigan, "The Pedestrian Ecstasies of Werner Herzog: On Experience, Intelligence, and the Essayistic," in *A Companion to Werner Herzog*, ed. Brad Prager (Oxford: Blackwell, 2012), 80-98.

10 See my "'Profoundly Unreconciled to Nature': Ecstatic Truth and the Humanistic Sublime in Werner Herzog's War Films," *The Philosophy of War Films*, 438-40.

11 See J. M [sic] Bright, *My Cinematic Odessey [sic]: Werner Herzog's Story*, independently published October 16, 2023; extent: 122 pages.

12 Fassbinder's line *"Ich bin meine filme"* is part of the promotional material for Annekatrin Hendel's *Fassbinder: Ein Dokumentarfilm* (2015).

13 youtu.be/OqpxT_iJ8Mc?t=176.

14 "Werner Herzog: *'comme un rêve puissant...'" Jeune Cinéma 81* (September-October 1974): 12-16. Interview conducted in Munich, August 1973, trans., Japhet Johnstone. Reprinted in *Werner Herzog: Interviews*, ed. Eric Ames, as "Werner Herzog: 'Like a Powerful Dream'" by Noureddine Ghali (Jackson: University Press of Mississippi, 2014), 18-23.

15 Herzog, *A Guide for the Perplexed*, 236.

16 Werner Herzog, *Every Man for Himself and God Against All*, trans. Michael Hofmann (New York: Penguin, 2023), 307-8.

17 tinyurl.com/5branyp2.

18 *I Am My Films: A Portrait of Werner Herzog* (1976-78), 00:03:56.

19 *Werner Herzog, Filmemacher* (1989), 00:26:22. On the nature of repetition in Herzog's remarks, see Eric Ames's introduction to *Werner Herzog: Interviews*, xiii.

20 Herzog also tells the story in *Every Man for Himself and God Against All*, 83-84.

21 Ibid., 83.
22 *Werner Herzog, Filmemacher* (1989), 00:26:50.
23 Ibid., 00:28:56.
24 On this last point, see LaRocca (2014), 437-82.
25 *Werner Herzog, Filmemacher* (1989), 00:29:19.
26 Ibid.
27 Ibid., 00:02:22.
28 Ibid., 00:02:30.
29 Werner Herzog, *Of Walking in Ice: Munich-Paris 11/23 to 12/14, 1974*, trans. Martje Herzog and Alan Greenberg (New York: Tanam Press, 1980; originally published 1978). For a commentary, see Jan-Christopher Horak, "W. H. or the mysteries of walking in ice," in *The Films of Werner Herzog: Between Mirage and History*, ed. Timothy Corrigan (New York: Methuen, 1986), 23-44.
30 Herzog, *A Guide for the Perplexed*, 256.
31 Werner Herzog, "Minnesota Declaration: Truth and Fact in Documentary Cinema," in *The Philosophy of Documentary Film: Image, Sound, Fiction, Truth*, ed. David LaRocca (Lanham: Lexington Books of Rowman & Littlefield, 2017), 379.
32 Herzog, *A Guide for the Perplexed*, 256, 255.
33 *Werner Herzog, Filmemacher*, 00:03:20.
34 Ibid., 00:06:10.
35 Herzog emphatically encouraged his students at the Rogue Film School, in sessions I attended in June 2010, that reading is essential to filmmaking: "If you don't read, you will never be a filmmaker," Herzog, *A Guide for the Perplexed*, 236. See also LaRocca, *The Philosophy of War Films*, 438-39, 484.
36 Herzog, *A Guide for the Perplexed*, 177.
37 Ibid., 255.
38 Gilles Deleuze, "The Figure of the Large and Small in Herzog," in *Cinema 1: The Movement Image*, trans., Hugh Tomlinson and Barbara Habberjam (Minneapolis: University of Minnesota Press, 1986), 185.
39 See my "Suicide Machines: Bruce Springsteen, Ballard, and Broken Heroes on a Last Chance Power Drive," in *Transportation and the Culture of Climate Change: Accelerating Ride to Global Crisis*, ed. Tatiana Prorokova-Konrad (Morgantown: West Virginia University Press, 2020), 123-50.
40 *Werner Herzog, Filmemacher* (1989), 00:28:03.
41 *I Am My Films, Part 2, Thirty Years Later* (2010), 00:01:20.
42 See my "Hunger in the Heart of Nature: Werner Herzog's Anti-Sentimental Dispatches from the American Wilderness (Reflections on *Grizzly Man*)," in *Dark Nature*, 231; and the section "Sincere, Not Cynical Images," in LaRocca (2014), 469-71.
43 *I Am My Films, Part 2, Thirty Years Later* (2010), 00:11:40.
44 Herzog, *A Guide for the Perplexed*, 177.
45 On this front, see my *The Thought of Stanley Cavell and Cinema* (2020) and *Movies with Stanley Cavell in Mind* (2021), both from Bloomsbury; *Metacinema* (2021) from Oxford University Press; and *Television with Stanley Cavell in Mind* (2023, coedited with Sandra Laugier) from the University of Exeter Press.

46 Herzog, *A Guide for the Perplexed*, 178.
47 See my "Thinking of Film: What Is Cavellian about Malick's Movies?" in *A Critical Companion to Terrence Malick*, ed. Joshua Sikora (Lanham: Rowman & Littlefield, 2020), 3-20; "Unauthorized Autobiography: Truth and Fact in *Confessions of a Dangerous Mind*" and "Inconclusive Unscientific Postscript: Late Remarks on Kierkegaard and Kaufman," in *The Philosophy of Charlie Kaufman*, ed. David LaRocca (Lexington: University Press of Kentucky, 2011/2019), 89-108, 269-94; and "Contemplating the Sounds of Contemplative Cinema: Stanley Cavell and Kelly Reichardt," in *Movies with Stanley Cavell in Mind*, ed. David LaRocca (New York: Bloomsbury, 2021), 274-318.
48 Herzog, *A Guide for the Perplexed*, 387.
49 For more on Herzog, parody, and self-parody, see my "Hunger in the Heart of Nature: Werner Herzog's Anti-Sentimental Dispatches from the American Wilderness (Reflections on *Grizzly Man*)," in *Dark Nature*, 227-40.
50 *Encounters at the End of the World* (2007), 00:20:30.
51 Herzog, *A Guide for the Perplexed*, 178.
52 *I Am My Films, Part 2, Thirty Years Later* (2010), 00:13:11.
53 For more on learning, unlearning, and anti-learning, see Appendix II: "Indefiniteness, *Geschlechtslosigkeit*, Undoing, Unknowing, Unlearning" in *The Geschlect Complex: Addressing Untranslatable Aspects of Gender, Genre, and Ontology*, ed. Oscar Jansson and David LaRocca (New York: Bloomsbury, 2022), 127-41; and a series of my essays on the topics, including my "Teaching without Explication: Pedagogical Lessons from Ranciere's *The Ignorant Schoolmaster* in *The Grand Budapest Hotel* and *The Emperor's Club*," *Journalism, Media and Cultural Studies*, vol. 10. (2016); "We Were Educated for This? Paideia, Agonism, and the Liberal Arts," *Girls and Philosophy: This Book Isn't A Metaphor for Anything*, ed. Richard Greene and Rachel Robinson-Greene (Chicago: Open Court, 2014); "The Education of Grown-ups: An Aesthetics of Reading Cavell," *The Journal of Aesthetic Education*, vol. 47, no. 2 (Summer 2013): 109-31; "'A Lead Ball of Justice': The Logic of Retribution and the Ethics of Instruction in *True Grit*," *The Philosophy of the Coen Brothers*, ed. Mark T. Conard (Lexington: University Press of Kentucky, updated edition, 2012), 307-31; "The Limits of Instruction: Pedagogical Remarks on Lars von Trier's *The Five Obstructions*," *Film and Philosophy*, vol. 13 (2009): 35-50; and "A Desperate Education: Reading Thoreau's *Walden* in Douglas Sirk's *All That Heaven Allows*," *Film and Philosophy*, vol. 8 (2004): 1-16.
54 Ralph Waldo Emerson, "Success," *Society and Solitude*, in *The Collected Works of Ralph Waldo Emerson*, vol. VII (Cambridge: Belknap Press of Harvard University Press, 2007), 150; Gotthold Ephraim Lessing, *Der Rezensent braucht nicht besser machen zu können, was er tadelt* in *Sämtliche Schriften*, ed. Karl Lachmann and Franz Muncker (Leipzig: Göschen'sche Verlagshandlung, 1900); and Georg Christoph Lichtenberg, *Notebook E*, #215 in *Philosophical Writings*, ed. and tr., Steven Tester (Albany: SUNY Press, 2012), 69. Thanks to Christopher Turner for drawing my attention to Lessing and Lichtenberg.

55 *I Am My Films, Part 2, Thirty Years Later* (2010), 01:34:58.
56 Herzog, *Every Man for Himself and God Against All*, 30.
57 See my "A Photograph as Evidence of Itself: Representation, Reflexivity, and Tautology in Light-Based Art," op. cit.
58 Deleuze, *Cinema 1* (1986), 184.
59 *To the Limit and Then Beyond It: The Ecstatic World of Filmmaker Werner Herzog* (1989), 00:03:38.
60 Ibid., 00:08:01.
61 Ibid., 00:11:11. For more on Herzog's account of the sublime, see "On the Absolute, the Sublime, and Ecstatic Truth," trans., Moira Weigel, *Arion: A Journal of Humanities and the Classics* 17:3 (2010), 1-12. For more on the humanistic sublime, see LaRocca (2014), 437-82. See also chapter V.
62 Thomas Weiskel, *The Romantic Sublime: Studies in the Structure and Psychology of Transcendence* (Baltimore: The Johns Hopkins University Press, 1976), 3.
63 See my "'Profoundly Unreconciled to Nature': Ecstatic Truth and the Humanistic Sublime in Werner Herzog's War Films," in *The Philosophy of War Films*, 437, 440-41. See also chapter V.

III
A Transcendental Persona

1 Mike Hale, "*The Mandalorian*, a Gunslinger in a Galaxy Far, Far Away," *The New York Times*, November 15, 2019.
2 Stanley Cavell, *The World Viewed: Reflections on the Ontology of Film* (Cambridge: Harvard University Press, 1971; enlarged edition, 1979), 31.
3 Cavell, *The World Viewed*, 31.
4 For more on early Spielberg, see my "'One of the Most Phenomenal Debut Films in the History of Movies': *The Sugarland Express* as Expression of Spielberg's 'Movie Sense' and as Contribution to a Genre Cycle," in *A Critical Companion to Steven Spielberg*, ed. Adam Barkman and Antonio Sanna (Lanham: Lexington Books of Rowman & Littlefield, 2019), 39-50.
5 *The Simpsons*, "The Scorpion's Tale," s22:e15 (2011). *Conan O'Brien Needs a Friend*, November 1, 2023, tinyurl.com/59euvseb.
6 Brigitte Peucker, "Herzog and Auteurism: Performing Authenticity," in *A Companion to Werner Herzog*, ed. Brad Prager (Oxford: Wiley-Blackwell, 2012), 44-45. See my "From Authenticity to Authentication: Cinaesthetics and Auteurship in the Age of AI," in *Aesthetic Authenticity in Cinema*, ed. Filipe Martins (Porto: Faculdade de Letras da Universidade do Porto [FLUP], 2023), 33-58.
7 Holly Rogers, "*Death for Five Voices*: Gesualdo's 'Poetic Truth,'" *A Companion to Werner Herzog*, 194; see also Paul Arthur, "Jargons of Authenticity (Three American Moments)," in *Theorizing Documentary*, ed. Michael Renov (New York: Routledge, 1993), 108.
8 Rogers, "*Death for Five Voices*," *A Companion to Werner Herzog*, 194.
9 Werner Herzog, *A Guide for the Perplexed: Conversations with Paul Cronin* (London: Faber and Faber, 2014), 24.

10 Herzog, *A Guide for the Perplexed*, 24.
11 For an engagement with Rivette's remark, see Dennis Lim, "It's Actual Life. No, It's Drama. No, It's Both," *The New York Times*, August 20, 2010.
12 See Timothy Corrigan, "The Pedestrian Ecstasies of Werner Herzog: On Experience, Intelligence, and the Essayistic," *A Companion to Werner Herzog*, 80-98.
13 Jacques Rivette, "Lettre sur Rossellini," *Cahiers* 46 (April 1955), later appearing as "Letter on Rossellini," in *Rivette: Texts and Interviews*, ed. Jonathan Rosenbaum (London: British Film Institute, London, 1977).
14 See my "Shooting for the Truth: Amateur Documentary Filmmaking, Affective Optics, and the Ethical Impulse," *Post Script: Essays in Film and the Humanities*, vol. 36, nos. 2 and 3 (2017): 46-60; and "Representative Qualities and Questions of Documentary Film," in *The Philosophy of Documentary Film: Image, Sound, Fiction, Truth*, ed. David LaRocca (Lanham: Lexington Books of Rowman & Littlefield, 2017), 1-54.
15 For more on this aspect of Herzog's work, see my "I Am What My Films Are: Listening to Herzog's Ecstatic, Essayistic Pronouncements," in *The Philosophy of Werner Herzog*, ed. Christopher Turner and M. Blake Wilson (Lanham: Lexington Books of Rowman & Littlefield, 2020), 1-20.
16 Corrigan, "The Pedestrian Ecstasies of Werner Herzog," *A Companion to Werner Herzog*, 86.
17 One conspicuous, notorious exception is Michael Moore's *Roger & Me* (1989), which was called out for not being presented in strictly chronological order. On a similar score, one thinks immediately of the aerial shots of Kuwait City in Herzog's *Lessons of Darkness*—claimed in voiceover to be of a city before the destruction of war, while, in fact, the images were made after the war had ended. Indeed, when the controversy over Moore's editorial decisions was fomenting, a Herzog collaborator on *La Soufrière*, cinematographer Edward Lachman, spoke up: "If everything had to be in chronological order, there aren't many documentaries that could pass the test"; as noted in Emily Schultz, *Michael Moore: A Biography* (Toronto: ECW Press, 2005), 80.
18 For a related investigation, see my "'Profoundly Unreconciled to Nature': Ecstatic Truth and the Humanistic Sublime in Werner Herzog's War Films," in *The Philosophy of War Films*, ed. David LaRocca (Lexington: University Press of Kentucky, 2014), 437-82; and Brigitte Peucker, "Werner Herzog: In Quest of the Sublime," in *New German Filmmakers: From Oberhausen through the 1970s*, ed. Klaus Phillips (New York: Frederick Ungar, 1984), 168-94.
19 Marcel Mouss, *Category of the Person* (Cambridge: Cambridge University Press, 1985), 14.
20 See Lisa Trahair, *Being on the Outside: Cinematic Automatism in Stanley Cavell's "The World Viewed," Film-Philosophy*, special section on Stanley Cavell, no. 18 (2014): 128-46; and Catherine Wheatley, "Automatism, Modernism," in *Stanley Cavell and Film: Scepticism and Self-Reliance at the Cinema* (New York: Bloomsbury, 2019), 73-85.

21 Cavell, *The World Viewed*, 107.
22 See *Music with Stanley Cavell in Mind*, ed. David LaRocca (New York: Bloomsbury, 2024); *Attention Spans: Garrett Stewart, a Reader*, ed. David LaRocca (New York: Bloomsbury, 2024); and L. Jackson Newell, *The Electric Edge of Academe: The Saga of Lucien L. Nunn and Deep Springs College* (Salt Lake City: University of Utah Press, 2015).
23 See Noël Carroll, "Documentary and the Film of Presumptive Assertion," in *Film and Philosophy*, ed. Richard Allen and Murray Smith (New York: Oxford University Press, 1997); "Fiction, Non-Fiction, and the Film of Presumptive Assertion: A Conceptual Analysis," in *Philosophy of Film and Motion Pictures*, ed. Noël Carroll and Jinhee Choi (Oxford: Blackwell, 2006); and my section "Presumptive Assertion and the Faith of/in Filmed Reality" in "A Reality Rescinded: The Transformative Effects of Fraud in *I'm Still Here*," *The Philosophy of Documentary Film*, 547 ff.
24 Cavell, *The World Viewed*, 212. See also my "On the Aesthetics of Amateur Filmmaking in Narrative Cinema: Negotiating Home Movies after *Adam's Rib*," in *The Thought of Stanley Cavell and Cinema: Turning Anew to the Ontology of Film a Half-Century after "The World Viewed,"* ed. David LaRocca (New York: Bloomsbury, 2020), 245-90.
25 See my "A Reality Rescinded," *The Philosophy of Documentary Film*, 537-76.
26 See my article, "The False Pretender: Deleuze, Sherman, and the Status of Simulacra," *The Journal of Aesthetics and Art Criticism*, vol. 69, no. 3 (Summer 2011): 321-29.
27 Stanley Cavell, *Pursuits of Happiness: The Hollywood Comedy of Remarriage* (Cambridge: Harvard University Press, Cambridge, 1981), 53. See also Cavell, *The World Viewed*, chapters 4 and 5; and Stanley Cavell, *A Pitch of Philosophy: Autobiographical Exercises* (Cambridge: Harvard University Press, 1994), 137. See also Orna Raviv, "The Cinematic Type," in *Ethics of Cinematic Experience: Screens of Alterity* (New York: Routledge, 2020), chapter 3.
28 D. N. Rodowick, *What Philosophy Wants from Images* (Chicago: University of Chicago Press, 2017), 37.
29 See my "A Reality Rescinded," *The Philosophy of Documentary Film*.
30 Cavell, *Pursuits of Happiness*, 207.
31 Ibid.
32 James Hale notes this statistic as of May 7, 2019, tinyurl.com/262pz6kx.
33 See Dennis Lim, "It's Actual Life," *The New York Times*.
34 See Timothy Bewes, *Cynicism and Postmodernity* (New York: Verso, 1997); David Hershinow, *Shakespeare and the Truth-Teller: Confronting the Cynic Ideal* (Edinburgh: Edinburgh University Press, 2019); David Mazella, *The Making of Modern Cynicism* (Charlottesville: University of Virginia Press, 2007); Louisa Shea, *The Cynic Enlightenment* (Baltimore: Johns Hopkins University Press, 2010).
35 Brad Prager, "Werner Herzog's Companions: The Consolation of Images," *A Companion to Werner Herzog*, 25.

36 Herzog, *A Guide for the Perplexed*, 23.
37 See Chris Wahl, "'I Don't Like the Germans': Even Herzog Started in Bavaria," *A Companion to Werner Herzog*, 233-55.
38 Ramin Bahrani's film, *Plastic Bag* (2009), youtu.be/YuJ31bu01mM.
39 Brigitte Peucker, "Herzog and Auteurism," *A Companion to Werner Herzog*, 37.
40 Jesse Andrews, *Me and Earl and the Dying Girl* (New York: Amulet Books, New York, 2012); online citation, np.
41 Seth Meyers, *Late Night with Seth Meyers*, December 18, 2019, youtu.be/fZYfxsv1GQY?t=697.
42 youtu.be/HrRNM9cMBDk. See also, the opening page of chapter 11, Herzog, *A Guide for the Perplexed*.
43 For more on Joaquin Phoenix and hoax *vérité*, see my "A Reality Rescinded," *The Philosophy of Documentary Film*.
44 See "When Herzog Rescued Phoenix," Ciezatas Animation Lab, youtu.be/nDcnLfLaFiY. See also "Joaquin Phoenix's Car-Crash Savior Werner Herzog Tells His Side of the Story," *Yahoo*, April 5, 2017, tinyurl.com/4nz9326h.
45 *Parks and Recreation* (s7:e1, "2017," 2015).
46 Anthony Lane, "End Times," *The New Yorker*, November 1, 2019.
47 See also, the opening page of chapter 5, Herzog, *A Guide for the Perplexed*.
48 See *Wookieepedia* entry for "Rogue Leader" at starwars.fandom.com/wiki/Rogue_Leader. "In honor of Jyn Erso and her crew's sacrifice at Scarif, Luke Skywalker ordered […] the specific 'Rogue One' designation that they used to be retired." Consequently, Skywalker flew instead as Rogue Leader.
49 Cornel West made appearances in *The Matrix Reloaded* (2003) and *The Matrix Revolutions* (2003), directed by the Wachowskis.
50 *Conan O'Brien Needs a Friend*, November 1, 2023, tinyurl.com/59euvseb.
51 Inscribing the German pronunciation by way of phonetic typography—trading W for V—amounts to a slight but significant syllabic confirmation of an insider's knowing passion for the details of their parodied subject. In the HBO Series *Entourage*, Stellan Skarsgård made guest appearances in three consecutive episodes of season five (2008): "Pie" (s5:e9), "Seth Green Day" (s5:e10), and "Play'n with Fire" (s5:e11), each under the heavy contours of a Herzog-like director. "Verner" was at the helm for a new action film entitled *Smokejumpers*.
52 On *The Simpsons*, *Fitzcarraldo* is referred to in the episode "On a Clear Day I Can't See My Sister" (s16:e11, 2005), in which students pull their bus up a mountain. Üter complains, "I feel like I'm Fitzcarraldo!," and Nelson exclaims, "That movie was flawed!," upon which he punches Üter in the stomach. See also "Fatzcarraldo" (s28:e14, 2017), which also parodies aspects of the ur-Herzognian plot.
53 On *Rick and Morty*, Herzog voices Shrimply Pibbles, "Interdimensional Cable 2: Tempting Fate," s2:e8 (2015).
54 For more on the metacinema of Charlie Kaufman, see *The Philosophy of Charlie Kaufman*, ed. David LaRocca (Lexington: University Press of Kentucky, 2011; with new preface, 2019).

55 "Werner Herzog vs. Piers Morgan: On Putin, Hollywood Cancel Culture, and More," *Piers Morgan Uncensored*, February 23, 2024, tinyurl.com/zfpnwze6.
56 For access to the 2012 collaboration with The Killers see: "The Killers Amex Unstaged Backstage": vimeo.com/302337717; "The Killers Unstaged Preshow," directed by Werner Herzog: vimeo.com/64104697; "The Killers Amex Unstaged 2012" (Part 1) vimeo.com/401224060 and (Part 2) vimeo.com/403629549; and m.bilibili.com/video/BV18b411c7Ja.
57 For access to the 2015 short film: vimeo.com/296047285.
58 Rebecca Mead, "Fitzcarraldo Editions Makes Challenging Literature Chic, " *The New Yorker*, July 1, 2024.
59 Ibid.
60 Herzog, *A Guide for the Perplexed*, 40.
61 Namely, *Herzog on Herzog* (London: Faber and Faber, 2002) and *A Guide for the Perplexed* (2014).
62 See Timothy Corrigan, *The Essay Film: From Montaigne, After Marker* (Oxford University Press, New York 2011) and his "Producing Herzog: From a Body of Images," in *The Films of Werner Herzog: Between Mirage and History*, ed. Timothy Corrigan (New York: Methuen, 1986); and Brigitte Peucker, "Herzog and Auteurism: Performing Authenticity," *A Companion to Werner Herzog*.
63 Brigitte Peucker, too, used "so-called" as a prefix to modulate her sense of Herzog's relationship to documentary filmmaking: "Herzog as a maker of so-called documentaries whose artifice is criticized for undermining the objectives of the genre." See "Herzog and Auteurism," *A Companion to Werner Herzog*, 36.
64 Peucker, "Herzog and Auteurism," *A Companion to Werner Herzog*, 55.
65 Ibid., 37-38. See also, Brad Prager, *The Cinema of Werner Herzog: Aesthetic Ecstasy and Truth* (London: Wallflower Press, 2007), 3-5. See my "From Authenticity to Authentication: Cinaesthetics and Auteurship in the Age of AI," *Aesthetic Authenticity in Cinema*, 33-58.
66 Peucker, "Herzog and Auteurism," *A Companion to Werner Herzog*, 37.
67 Theodor W. Adorno, *The Jargon of Authenticity*, trans. K. Tarnowski and F. Will (Evanston: Northwestern University Press, 1973), 34.
68 Adorno, *The Jargon of Authenticity*, 35. Peucker, "Herzog and Auteurism," *A Companion to Werner Herzog*, 38.
69 Peucker, "Herzog and Auteurism," *A Companion to Werner Herzog*, 38.
70 Horak, "W. H. or the Mysteries of Walking in Ice," *The Films of Werner Herzog*, 25-42.
71 Corrigan, "Producing Herzog: From a Body of Images," *The Films of Werner Herzog*, 21.
72 Peucker, "Herzog and Auteurism," *A Companion to Werner Herzog*, 39.
73 Ibid., 40.
74 Ibid. See also Bill Nichols, "Documentary Reenactment and the Fantasmatic Subject," *Critical Inquiry*, no. 35 (2008): 72-89.
75 Daniel Zalewski, "The Ecstatic Truth: Werner Herzog's Quest," *The New Yorker*, April 16, 2006.

76 Peucker, "Herzog and Auteurism," *A Companion to Werner Herzog*, 42.
77 Cronin, *Herzog on Herzog*, 265.
78 Peucker, "Herzog and Auteurism," *A Companion to Werner Herzog*, 44. See also 50.
79 For more on *Grizzly Man*, see my "Hunger in the Heart of Nature: Werner Herzog's Anti-Sentimental Dispatches from the American Wilderness (Reflections on *Grizzly Man*)," in *Dark Nature: Anti-Pastoral Essays in American Literature and Culture*, ed. Richard J. Schneider (Lanham: Lexington Books of Roman & Littlefield, 2016), 227-40.
80 "We notice it first at the level of the footage: Herzog's 'documentary' about Timothy Treadwell relies heavily on found footage, archival footage shot by Treadwell himself." See Peucker, "Herzog and Auteurism," *A Companion to Werner Herzog*, 48.
81 Ibid., 50.
82 Ibid., 37.
83 Ibid., 55, n.8.
84 Herzog, *A Guide for the Perplexed*, 24.

IV

ANTI-SENTIMENTAL DISPATCHES

1 Nick Jans, *The Grizzly Maze: Timothy Treadwell's Fatal Obsession Alaskan Bears* (New York: Penguin, 2006). See also Mike Lapinski, *Death in the Grizzly Maze: The Timothy Treadwell Story* (Falcon Guides, 2005) and Timothy Treadwell and Jewel Palovak, *Among Grizzlies: Living with Wild Bears in Alaska* (New York: Harper, 1997).
2 See my "In the Place of Mourning: Questioning the Privations of the Private," *Nineteenth-Century Prose*, vol. 40, no. 1 (Fall 2013): 227-42; and "A Desperate Education: Reading Thoreau's *Walden* in Douglas Sirk's *All That Heaven Allows*," *Film and Philosophy*, vol. 8 (2004): 1-16.
3 See my "'Profoundly Unreconciled to Nature': Ecstatic Truth and the Humanistic Sublime in Werner Herzog's War Films," in *The Philosophy of War Films*, ed. David LaRocca (Lexington: University Press of Kentucky, 2014), see esp., 442, 460, 467, 469.
4 See ibid., 467.
5 Ibid.
6 Ibid., 469.
7 See Andreas Vesalius, *De Humani Corporis Fabrica Libri Septem* (1543), and the film *De Humani Corporis Fabrica* (2022, dir. Lucien Castaing-Taylor and Véréna Paravel).
8 See "'Profoundly Unreconciled to Nature.'"
9 See Scott MacDonald, "Ruminating on the Ideologies of Nature Film," in *The Philosophy of Documentary Film*, ed. David LaRocca (Lanham: Lexington Books of Rowman & Littlefield, 2017), 175-91.
10 *Planet Earth* (2006, dir. Alastair Fothergill), e:2.
11 Erik Barnouw, *Documentary: A History of the Non-Fiction Film* (New York: Oxford University Press, 1993, 2nd rev. ed.), 210.
12 See my "Inconclusive Unscientific Postscript: Late Remarks on Kierkegaard and Kaufman," in *The Philosophy of Charlie Kaufman*,

ed. David LaRocca (Lexington: University Press of Kentucky, 2011; with a new preface, 2019), 269-94.
13 See my *Emerson's English Traits and the Natural History of Metaphor* (New York: Bloomsbury, 2013), 155.
14 See *Ted Radio Hour*, "Animals and Us," May 29, 2015, npr.org.
15 See *Paddington* (2014) and *Paddington 2* (2017), both directed by Paul King. *Paddington in Peru* (2024, dir. Dougal Wilson).
16 For further remarks on *Soldier of Illusion*, see chapter VII.
17 Stanley Cavell, "Declining Decline: Wittgenstein as a Philosopher of Culture," in *This New Yet Unapproachable America: Lectures after Emerson after Wittgenstein* (Albuquerque: Living Batch Press, 1989), 57.

V

The Humanistic Sublime

1 Thomas Weiskel, *The Romantic Sublime: Studies in the Structure and the Psychology of Transcendence* (Baltimore: Johns Hopkins University Press, 1976), 3. I dedicate this chapter to the memory of two World War II veterans, my grandfathers: U.S. Army Master Sergeant and Warrant Officer, Earl Charles LaRocca (1921-2010), a battalion sergeant major of the 78th Lightning Division and a recipient of the Bronze Star; and U.S. Army Air Corps Staff Sergeant, Nassea Hodge (1924-1992), held captive by Nazis as a POW at Stalag 398 Wels, Austria, and later, after liberation, a recipient of the Purple Heart.
2 Harold Bloom, Foreword, *The Romantic Sublime*, vii.
3 Ibid.
4 See *The Geschlecht Complex: Addressing Untranslatable Aspects of Gender, Genre, and Ontology*, ed. Oscar Jansson and David LaRocca (New York: Bloomsbury, 2022).
5 Werner Herzog, *Herzog on Herzog*, ed. Paul Cronin (New York: Faber and Faber, 2002) and *A Guide for the Perplexed: Conversations with Paul Cronin* (New York: Faber and Faber, 2014). I draw from both editions and indicate which version I use; in this case, the second, revised edition, 387.
6 For more on the relationship between obstruction and instruction, see Appendix II: "Indefiniteness, *Geschlechtslosigkeit*, Undoing, Unknowing, Unlearning," *The Geschlecht Complex*, 127-41; and a series of my essays on the topic, including "Teaching without Explication: Pedagogical Lessons from Ranciere's *The Ignorant Schoolmaster* in *The Grand Budapest Hotel* and *The Emperor's Club*," *Journalism, Media and Cultural Studies*, vol. 10. (2016); "We Were Educated for This? Paideia, Agonism, and the Liberal Arts," *Girls and Philosophy: This Book Isn't A Metaphor for Anything*, ed. Richard Greene and Rachel Robinson-Greene (Chicago: Open Court, 2014); "The Education of Grown-ups: An Aesthetics of Reading Cavell," *The Journal of Aesthetic Education*, vol. 47, no. 2 (Summer 2013): 109-31; "'A Lead Ball of Justice': The Logic of Retribution and the Ethics of Instruction in *True Grit*," *The Philosophy of the Coen Brothers*, ed. Mark T. Conard (Lexington: University Press of Kentucky, updated edition, 2012), 307-31; "The Limits of Instruction:

Pedagogical Remarks on Lars von Trier's *The Five Obstructions*," *Film and Philosophy*, vol. 13 (2009): 35-50; and "A Desperate Education: Reading Thoreau's *Walden* in Douglas Sirk's *All That Heaven Allows*," *Film and Philosophy*, vol. 8 (2004): 1-16.
7 Paul Cronin, *A Guide for the Perplexed*, from a draft of the introduction. Here in the final, print version: "As far as he is concerned, cinema—like music—is more deeply connected to imagination than pure reason, and though indubitably respectful of the rationalists of the world, unadulterated intuition is a brighter guiding light for Werner than analysis will ever be," xv.
8 From notes taken during Herzog's Rogue Film School, July 2010; see also *A Guide for the Perplexed*, chap. 7.
9 Paul Cronin, "Visionary Vehemence," *A Guide for the Perplexed*, xv.
10 Herzog, *A Guide for the Perplexed*, chap. 7, 231. This compilation of one-liners, created by Cronin and inserted, with Herzog's excited approval, into the Rogue Film School chapter of *A Guide for the Perplexed*, ended up on the jacket of the hardback edition of the book.
11 *Herzog on Herzog*, 81, 136.
12 See for example, Edmund Burke, *A Philosophical Enquiry into the Origin of our Ideas of the Sublime and Beautiful*, edited with an introduction by Adam Phillips (New York: Oxford University Press, 1990).
13 Thomas Hardy, *Far from the Madding Crowd* (New York: Harper & Brothers, 1918), 287.
14 Alfred Lord Tennyson, "In Memoriam A. H. H." (1850).
15 Immanuel Kant, *Critique of Judgment*, trans. Werner S. Pluhar (Indianapolis: Hackett Publishing Company, 1987), B §28, "On Nature as Might," 119.
16 See, most famously, Caspar David Friedrich's *Wanderer above the Sea of Fog* (1818), but also *Woman before the Rising Sun (Woman before the Setting Sun)* (1818-20) and *Moonrise (Two Men on the Shore)* (1835-37).
17 See *Little Dieter Needs to Fly* (1997) and remarks by Dieter Dengler in his *Escape from Laos* (San Rafael, CA: Presidio Press, 1979). The notion of nature- or jungle-as-enemy appears in other war films and television serials, e.g., *The Pacific* (e2: 00:01:35).
18 "For all its horror, you can't help but gape at the awful majesty of combat," Tim O'Brien writes in "How to Tell a True War Story": "You admire the fluid symmetries of troops on the move, the harmonies of sound and shape and proportion, the great sheets of metal-fire streaming down from a gunship, the illumination rounds, the white phosphorous, the purply orange glow of napalm, the rocket's red glare. [. . .] It's astonishing. It fills the eye. It commands you. You hate it, yes, but your eyes do not." But this "awful majesty" does not allow for a dispassionate or disinterested perspective; the "awe" of the "awful" is not in any way privileged or protected. The soldier may experience the penetrating effects of a firsthand reality, but the vitality of the impression must be linked with the very *real* threat to his life. Thus, this is an *awful* majesty, not a sublime one. Tim O'Brien, *The Things They Carried* (New York: Penguin, 1990), 87.

19 Brad Prager, "Werner Herzog's Companions: The Consolation of Images," in *A Companion to Werner Herzog*, ed. Brad Prager (Oxford: Wiley-Blackwell, 2012), 3.

20 *To the Limit and Then Beyond It: The Ecstatic World of Filmmaker Werner Herzog* [*Bis ans Ende—und dann noch weiter: Die estatische Welt des Filmemachers Werner Herzog*] (1989, dir. Peter Buchka), 00:11:01.

21 Ibid., 00:11:31.

22 Ibid., 00:23:04.

23 *La Soufrière: Waiting for an Inevitable Disaster* (1997, dir. Werner Herzog).

24 *To the Limit*, 00:17:10.

25 See Immanuel Kant, *Observations on the Feeling of the Beautiful and Sublime*, trans. John T. Goldthwait (Berkeley: University of California Press, 1960, 1991); and Friedrich Schiller, *On the Sublime* (1801), trans. Julius Elias (New York: Ungar, 1966).

26 *To the Limit*, 00:22:40.

27 Grazia Paganelli, *Ecstasy and Truth* (Munich: Goethe Institut, 2010), 102.

28 Werner Herzog, "Minnesota Declaration: Truth and Fact in Documentary Cinema," in *The Philosophy of Documentary Film: Image, Sound, Fiction, Truth*, ed. David LaRocca (Lexington: Lexington Books of Rowman & Littlefield, 2017), 379.

29 For more on Casey Affleck's film, see my "A Reality Rescinded: The Transformative Effects of Fraud in *I'm Still Here*," *The Philosophy of Documentary Film*, 537-76.

30 Akram Zaatari, "Abbas Kiarostami," *Bomb*, January 1, 1995, tinyurl.com/ycyrcfjs.

31 *Close-Up* (1990, dir. Abbas Kiarostami).

32 Herzog, *A Guide for the Perplexed*, chap. 8. The final, print version of the first cited sentence reads: "Only in so far as my goal is to use cinema to explore and chronicle the human condition and our states of mind," 269.

33 *Close-Up*.

34 Paganelli, *Ecstasy and Truth*, 89.

35 Paul Cronin, "Visionary Vehemence," *A Guide for the Perplexed*, from a draft of the introduction. The final, print version reads: "He is a primeval sophisticate of great erudition who yearns nostalgically for a pre-literate, pre-electric (or post-literate and post-electric) existence, where the primitive wisdom of the uninstructed and those able to memorise stories and poems, then recite them free of all props, predominates," xxiii. Cronin is here bringing to bear his work on Alexander Mackendrick's reading of Aristotle: the plot should be so constructed that even without seeing the play a man who hears of the sequence of events will shudder with fear and pity at what happens.

36 Ibid., chap. 8. The final, print version reads: "I also like the shots at the beginning and end, those blurred, strange images that somehow represent the collapse of the world, even if they have nothing directly to do with the story," 262.

37 Stanley Cavell, *The Claim of Reason: Wittgenstein, Skepticism, Morality, and Tragedy* (New York: Oxford University Press, 1979), 207.

38 Stanley Cavell, *This New Yet Unapproachable America* (Albuquerque: Living Batch Press, 1989), 57. See also Cavell, *Must We Mean What We Say?* (Cambridge: Cambridge University Press, 1969, 1979), 96; Cavell, *The Claim of Reason*, 206-7; and Cavell, *Emerson's Transcendental Etudes*, ed. David Justin Hodge (Stanford: Stanford University Press, 2003), 23, 58, and especially 252-53 n3.

39 James Conant, "An Interview with Stanley Cavell," in *The Senses of Stanley Cavell*, ed. Richard Fleming and Michael Payne (Cranbury, NJ: Associated University Presses, 1989), 50. See also Richard Eldridge, "Introduction: Between Acknowledgment and Avoidance," in *Stanley Cavell* (Cambridge: Cambridge University Press, 2003), 4; and Richard Eldridge and Bernie Rhie, eds., *Stanley Cavell and Literary Studies: Consequences of Skepticism* (New York: Continuum, 2011), 5.

40 Herzog, *A Guide for the Perplexed*, chap. 11. The final, print version reads: "*Little Dieter* is the version of the story I was bound to at the time for practical reasons. When I watched the film for the first time with Dieter, the lights went up and he turned to me. 'Werner,' he said without missing a beat, 'this is unfinished business.' The story of Dieter and Duane was always one I wanted to tell in a feature film, a tale of friendship and survival. Although *Rescue Dawn* came second, in spirit it really was the first film. *Little Dieter* was strongly influenced by a feature film that hadn't been made yet," 379.

41 Charles Darwin, *On the Origin of the Species by Means of Natural Selection* (London: John Murray, 1859).

42 Paul Virilio, *War and Cinema: The Logistics of Perception* (New York: Verso, 1989 [1984]), 1, 5.

43 Contrast contemporary wars increasingly defined by aerial drone attacks (death at a distance) with the immediacy (almost literally, a lack of mediation) familiar to hand-to-hand combat, for instance, as depicted in stabbing scenes in *Saving Private Ryan* (Steven Spielberg, 1998) and *Coriolanus* (Ralph Fiennes, 2011); and similar agonizing intimacies in *All Quiet on the Western Front* (Lewis Milestone, 1930). The face-to-face nature of such historical combat is something that cinema has long been both focused on for narrative purposes and uniquely successful in depicting.

44 Virilio, *War and Cinema*, 3.

45 Ibid., 2.

46 See Virilio, *War and Cinema*; see also, Garrett Stewart, "War Pictures: Digital Surveillance from Foreign Theatre to Homeland Security Front," and Joshua Gooch, "Beyond Panopticism: The Biopolitical Labor of Surveillance and War in Contemporary Film," both in *The Philosophy of War Films*, ed. David LaRocca (Lexington: University Press of Kentucky, 2014), 107-32, 155-78; and *Eagle Eye* (D. J. Caruso, 2008).

47 Simon Morley, ed., *The Sublime* (Cambridge: MIT Press, with Whitechapel Gallery, 2010), 16.

48 Ibid., 16.

49 *Imaginary Witness: Hollywood and the Holocaust* (2004, dir. Daniel Anker), 01:28:04-29.

50 See my "The Multifarious Forms of War Films: A Taxonomy of Subgenres," *The Philosophy of War Films*, 489-501.

51 Paul Fussell, in *The War* (2007, dir. Ken Burns), Part 4, 00:15:08.
52 Emily Brady, "Tragedy and the Sublime," in *The Sublime in Modern Philosophy: Aesthetics, Ethics, and Nature* (Cambridge: Cambridge University Press, 2013), 148-65. Weiskel's wife, Portia, widow at the time of writing "a personal introduction" to his posthumous book, said: "Tom, in his death, following by seconds his daughter's, sudden, unfathomable, and tragic, knew in an instant both the sublime and the terror of the nature he wrote about," *The Romantic Sublime*, xiv. See also an Amherst College bulletin at tinyurl.com/yykj49bm: "Tragedy befell Tom Weiskel and his family on Sunday, Dec. 1, 1974. Late in the afternoon, Tom had been skating on a pond near his home in Leverett, towing his 2-year-old daughter, Shelburne, behind him on a sled. The ice gave way and both drowned. A number of other people were in the area but were not aware of the accident. Shelburne's body was recovered that afternoon, but Tom's body could not be found until late the next morning. […] He had recently completed a book soon to be published [*The Romantic Sublime*]. Speaking of him and his work, Prof. Dwight Culler, chairman of the Yale English department, said: 'Tom Weiskel was the kind of teacher who has a decisive impact on students' lives, and he was one of our most brilliant younger members. His book on Romantic poetry and poetic theory, which he had just finished, is, we think, one of the finest to come out of our department.'"
53 See Werner Herzog's exhibit "Hearsay of the Soul" on Hercules Seghers in the 2012 Whitney Biennial, a work he created in collaboration with composer Ernst Reijseger. See also *Herzog on Herzog*, 1st ed., 136-37; and the short stories and plays of George Büchner, such as *Lenz* (1835) and *Woyzeck* (1837), in *Complete Plays, Lenz and Other Writings*, trans. John Reddick (New York: Penguin, 1993).
54 Longinus, *On the Sublime*, trans. W. Rhys Roberts (Cambridge: Cambridge University Press, 1907; reprinted New York: Routledge, 2018), chap 36.3, 137.
55 Longinus, *On the Sublime*, trans. W. H. Fyfe (Cambridge: Harvard University Press, Loeb Classical Library, 1995), 279, 281.
56 Along similar lines, Timothy Corrigan writes: "[Herzog's] characters, like his films, are again and again drawn to the powers of language as a vehicle for dramatizing, producing, and communicating their desires, but, at the same time, they are revolted, like Kaspar Hauser before Lord Stanhope, before language's murderously reductive properties." *The Films of Werner Herzog*, ed. Timothy Corrigan (New York: Methuen, 1986), 16.
57 Morley, *The Sublime*, 16.
58 Fredric Jameson, "War and Representation," *The Philosophy of War Films*, 81-106.
59 Herzog, *A Guide for the Perplexed*, chap. 8, 270.
60 Arthur C. Danto, *The Abuse of Beauty: Aesthetics and the Concept of Art* (Peru: Carus Publishing Company, 2003), 1.
61 Barnett Newman, "The Sublime is Now" (1948), in *Art in America, 1945-70*, ed. Jed Perl (New York: Library of America, 2014), 11-12.
62 J. M. Bernstein, *Against Voluptuous Bodies: Late Modernism and the Meaning of Painting* (Stanford: Stanford University Press, 2006), 155.

63 Bernstein, *Against Voluptuous Bodies*, 156.
64 Newman, "The Sublime is Now," *Art in America*, 13.
65 Ibid., 14.
66 Ibid.
67 Ibid.
68 *Herzog on Herzog*, 81, 136.
69 Samuel Taylor Coleridge, *Biographia Literaria; or, Biographical Sketches of My Literary Life and Opinions* (1817), book XII: "But in all ages there have been a few, who measuring and sounding the rivers of the vale at the feet of their furthest inaccessible falls have learned, that the sources must be far higher and far inward; a few, who even in the level streams have detected elements, which neither the vale itself nor the surrounding mountains contained or could supply."
70 Kant, *Observations on the Feeling of the Beautiful and Sublime*, 25.
71 Herzog notes: "One aspect of who I am that might be important is the communication defect I have had since a young child. I am someone who takes everything very literally. I simply do not understand irony, a defect I have had ever since I was able to think independently. [. . .] I am just a complete fool. There are things in language that are common to almost everyone, but that are utterly lost on me. [. . .] And compared to other filmmakers—particularly the French, who are able to sit around their cafés waxing eloquent about their work—I am like a Bavarian bullfrog just squatting there brooding. I have never been capable of discussing art with people. I just cannot cope with irony." *Herzog on Herzog*, 26-27. See also Alan Singer, "Comprehending Appearances: Werner Herzog's Ironic Sublime," *The Films of Werner Herzog*, 183-205.
72 Ralph Waldo Emerson, *Journals of Ralph Waldo Emerson*, ed. Edward Waldo Emerson and Waldo Emerson Forbes (Boston: Houghton Mifflin, 1911), vol. 5, 327.
73 Werner Herzog, "On the Absolute, the Sublime, and Ecstatic Truth," trans. Moira Weigel, *Arion*, vol. 17, no. 3 (Winter 2010): 1.
74 Eschewing the theoretical and the speculative—in favor of the strictly practical—Herzog announces his adjustment on the English romantic sublime. See, for example, in *Biographia Literaria*, where Coleridge writes of a necessary blend: "For as philosophy is neither a science of the reason or understanding only, nor merely a science of morals, but the science of BEING altogether, its primary ground can be neither merely speculative nor merely practical, but both in one" (Book XII).
75 See again the 2012 Whitney Biennial collaboration between Reijseger and Herzog, "Hearsay of the Soul."
76 Weiskel, *Romantic Sublime*, 5.
77 Ibid., 6.
78 Ibid.
79 Ibid.
80 See Stanley Cavell, *The World Review: Reflections on the Ontology of Film* (Cambridge: Harvard University Press, 1971, enlarged edition, 1979). See also *The Thought of Stanley Cavell and Cinema: Turning Anew to the Ontology of Film a Half-Century after "The World Viewed,"* ed. David LaRocca (New York: Bloomsbury, 2020).

81 For more on reenactment in Herzog's work, see Eric Ames, "The Case of Herzog: Re-Opened," in *A Companion to Werner Herzog*, 393-415; and Eric Ames, *Ferocious Reality: Documentary According to Werner Herzog* (Minneapolis: University of Minnesota Press, 2012).
82 Paganelli, *Ecstasy and Truth*, 112.
83 Ibid., 112-13.
84 Herzog, "Minnesota Declaration," *The Philosophy of Documentary Film*, 379.
85 *Herzog on Herzog*, 301.
86 *Rescue Dawn*, 00:51:44.
87 Ibid., 01:24:40; cf. John 13:16.
88 *Rescue Dawn*, 00:39:30.
89 Brigitte Peucker, "Herzog and Auteurism: Performing Authenticity," *A Companion to Werner Herzog*, 36-37.
90 Herzog, *A Guide for the Perplexed*, chap. 8. The final, print version reads: "On the soundtrack we hear a 1901 recording of Gounod's *Ave Maria* from an Edison cylinder, sung by the last castrato of the Vatican, which creates a strange, almost ecstatic feeling, and establishes a powerful counterpoint between music and images. A traditional ethnographic filmmaker would never dare do anything like that. Using this specific recording helps carry us out of the realm of what I call the accountant's truth; anything else wouldn't touch us so deeply. It means the film isn't a documentary about a specific African tribe, rather a story about beauty and desire," 270.
91 Ibid.
92 *Lessons of Darkness*.
93 These are selected intertitles from *Lessons of Darkness*.
94 Kant, *Observations on the Feeling of the Beautiful and Sublime*, 48-49, 53, 55.
95 Ibid., 52.
96 Burke, *A Philosophical Enquiry into the Origin of Our Ideas of the Sublime and Beautiful*, 36.
97 *To the Limit*, 00:45:11.
98 Werner Herzog, *Conquest of the Useless: Reflections from the Making of Fitzcarraldo*, trans. Krishna Winston (New York: Ecco, 2009), June 1, 1981, 251; originally published as *Der Eroberung des Nutzlosen* (Carl Hanser Verlag, 2004).
99 *Burden of Dreams* (1982, dir. Les Blank).
100 Kant, *Observations on the Feeling of the Beautiful and Sublime*, 60.
101 W. H. Auden, *The Enchafèd Flood, or the Romantic Iconography of the Sea* (Charlottesville: University Press of Virginia, 1950), 6; also subtitled "Three Critical Essays on the Romantic Spirit."
102 For more on these and related topics, see my "From Authenticity to Authentication: Cinaesthetics and Auteurship in the Age of AI," in *Aesthetic Authenticity in Cinema*, ed. Filipe Martins (Porto: Faculdade de Letras da Universidade do Porto [FLUP], 2023), 33-58; "A Photograph as Evidence of Itself: Representation, Reflexivity, and Tautology in Light-Based Art," *Social Research*, vol. 89, no 4 (Winter 2022): 915-45; and "The False Pretender: Deleuze, Sherman, and the

Status of Simulacra," *The Journal of Aesthetics and Art Criticism*, vol. 69, no. 3 (Summer 2011): 321-29.
103 Corrigan, "Producing Herzog," *The Films of Werner Herzog*, 11.
104 Rush Rhees, *Discussions of Wittgenstein* (London: Routledge and Kegan Paul, 1970), 94.
105 Werner Herzog, *Conquest of the Useless*, 1.
106 *Herzog on Herzog*, 252.
107 Corrigan, "Producing Herzog," *The Films of Werner Herzog*, 16, passim 13-16.
108 Ibid., 14.
109 Ibid., 15.
110 Ibid.
111 Ibid., 16.
112 Alan Greenberg, Herbert Achternbusch, and Werner Herzog, *Heart of Glass* (Munich: Skellig, 1976), 174.
113 *Burden of Dreams*; *Herzog on Herzog*, 66. See also Herzog, *A Guide for the Perplexed*, chap. 3: "Our inability and lack of desire to seek fresh imagery means we are surrounded by worn-out, banal, useless and exhausted images, limping and dragging themselves behind the rest of our cultural evolution. […] Just as a person without a memory will struggle to survive in this world, so will someone who lacks images that reflect his inner state. […] We have come to understand that the destruction of the environment is another enormous danger, that resources are being wasted at an extraordinary rate. But I believe that the lack of adequate imagery is a danger of the same magnitude, as serious a defect as being without memory. I'll repeat it again as long as I'm able to: we will die out like dinosaurs if we don't develop adequate images," 81-82.
114 *Herzog on Herzog*, 202.
115 *Little Dieter Needs to Fly*, 00:57:44.
116 Ibid., 01:05:00; 00:59:40.
117 *Rescue Dawn*, from the intertitle at the end of the film, 02:01:09.
118 Werner Herzog, "On the Absolute, the Sublime, and Ecstatic Truth," *Arion*, 11.
119 *To the Limit*, 00:47:04.
120 Ibid., 00:50:24.
121 J. M. Bernstein, *Thinking Aloud*. March 4, 2016, tinyurl.com/mrpdy9s2.
122 For more on "seeing plain," see chapter I.
123 *Herzog on Herzog*, 139.
124 Ibid.
125 *A Guide for the Perplexed*, 81-82.
126 Ibid.
127 Herzog, *Conquest of the Useless* (July 3, 1980), 72.

VI
Perúvian Metaphysics

1 Chapter VI is a revised and expanded version of an invited talk — "Werner Herzog in Perú: A Half-Century of the Humanistic Sublime" — given at the Pop Philosophy Colloquium II, Pontificia Universidad Católica

del Perú, Lima, Perú, October 10-13, 2023, graciously hosted by Victor Krebs, Professor in the Department of the Humanities.
2 "Filming in Perú with Werner Herzog," see inkaterra.com/blog/filming-peru-werner-herzog/
3 Benjamin Collantes, José D. Edquen, Feliciano Incahuamán, and Gerardo A. Salazar, "*Sarcoglottis Wernerherzogii (Spiranthinae)*: A New Species from Cusco, Perú," *Lankesteriana*, 23: 3 (2023): 623-32; italics added.
4 *Wings of Hope* (1998, dir. Werner Herzog), 00:01:03.
5 *Fitzcarraldo* (1982, dir. Werner Herzog), 02:28:05-29:15.
6 L. Jackson Newell, *The Electric Edge of Academe: The Saga of Lucien L. Nunn and Deep Springs College* (Salt Lake City: University of Utah Press, 2015), 29, 33, 37-38, 155.
7 -11.737294, -72.934542.
8 Werner Herzog, *Every Man for Himself and God Against All*, trans. Michael Hofmann (New York: Penguin, 2023), 311.
9 Ralph Waldo Emerson, *Nature*, in *Nature, Addresses and Lectures*, in *The Complete Works of Ralph Waldo Emerson*, Concord Edition (Boston: Houghton, Mifflin and Company, 1904), vol. I, 26.
10 Thomas Weiskel, *The Romantic Sublime: Studies in the Structure and the Psychology of Transcendence* (Baltimore: Johns Hopkins University Press, 1976), 3.
11 Werner Herzog, *Conquest of the Useless: Reflections from the Making of Fitzcarraldo* (San Francisco: Ecco Press, 2009), 149.
12 *Aguirre, the Wrath of God* (1972, dir. Werner Herzog), 00:01:27.
13 *Fresh Air*, "Werner Herzog says it's not good to circle 'your own navel' but writes a memoir anyway," October 25, 2023, npr.org/transcripts/1208303973/
14 *To the Limit and Then Beyond It: The Ecstatic World of Filmmaker Werner Herzog* [*Bis ans Ende—und dann noch weiter: Die estatische Welt des Filmemachers Werner Herzog*] (1989, dir. Peter Buchka), 00:11:01.
15 Ibid., 00:11:31.
16 Stanley Cavell, *The Claim of Reason: Wittgenstein, Skepticism, Morality, and Tragedy* (New York: Oxford University Press, 1979), 207.
17 Stanley Cavell, *This New Yet Unapproachable America* (Albuquerque: Living Batch Press, 1989), 57. See also Cavell, *Must We Mean What We Say?* (Cambridge: Cambridge University Press, 1969, 1979), 96; Cavell, *The Claim of Reason*, 206-7; and Cavell, *Emerson's Transcendental Etudes*, ed. David Justin Hodge (Stanford: Stanford University Press, 2003), 23, 58, and especially 252-53n3.
18 James Conant, "An Interview with Stanley Cavell," in *The Senses of Stanley Cavell*, ed. Richard Fleming and Michael Payne (Cranbury, NJ: Associated University Presses, 1989), 50. See also Richard Eldridge, "Introduction: Between Acknowledgment and Avoidance," in *Stanley Cavell* (Cambridge: Cambridge University Press, 2003), 4; and Richard Eldridge and Bernie Rhie, eds., *Stanley Cavell and Literary Studies: Consequences of Skepticism* (New York: Continuum, 2011), 5.
19 Werner Herzog, *A Guide for the Perplexed: Conversations with Paul Cronin* (New York: Faber and Faber, 2014), 407.

20 *Aguirre, the Wrath of God*, 00:01:17.
21 Immanuel Kant, *Critique of Judgment*, trans. Werner S. Pluhar (Indianapolis: Hackett Publishing Company, 1987), §15.
22 Harold Bloom, Foreword, *The Romantic Sublime*, vii; italics added.
23 Bloom writes: "What Cleopatra knows is that the sublime is agonistic, a knowledge crucial to theorists of the sublime from Longinus to Thomas Weiskel," ibid., viii.
24 *Cobra Verde*, based upon Bruce Chatwin's *The Viceroy of Ouidah* (1980), was also shot in Ghana.
25 tinyurl.com/4rhd9x4d.
26 *The Boondocks* (2010, created by Aaron McGruder); *Metalocalypse* (2012, created by Brendon Small and Tommy Blancha).
27 See Patrick J. Deneen, *Why Liberalism Failed* (New Haven: Yale University Press, 2018).
28 See Sebastian Junger, *War* (New York: Twelve, 2011) and *Tribe: On Homecoming and Belonging* (New York: Twelve, 2016). See also, Emily Witt, "Sebastian Junger Watches Werner Herzog, Says Many Masculine Things About Men," *Observer*, June 10, 2011; and *The Philosophy of War Films*, ed. David LaRocca (Lexington: University Press of Kentucky, 2014).
29 Jonny Cooper, "Why Werner Herzog is the Ultimate Man's Man," *The Telegraph*, September 1, 2014.
30 See "When Herzog Rescued Phoenix," Ciezatas Animation Lab, youtu.be/nDcnLfLaFiY. See also "Joaquin Phoenix's Car-Crash Savior Werner Herzog Tells His Side of the Story," *Yahoo*, April 5, 2017, tinyurl.com/4nz9326h. See also my "A Reality Rescinded: The Transformative Effects of Fraud in *I'm Still Here*," in *The Philosophy of Documentary Film: Image, Sound, Fiction, Truth*, ed. David LaRocca (Lanham: Lexington Books of Rowman & Littlefield, 2017), 537-76.
31 In the 1980s, female critics were making themselves known, for instance, in *The Films of Werner Herzog: Between Mirage and History*, ed. Timothy Corrigan (Routledge: New York, 1986). And a similar distribution is evident in *A Companion to Werner Herzog*, ed. Brad Prager (Oxford: Wiley-Blackwell, 2012) and *The Philosophy of Werner Herzog*, ed. M. Blake Wilson and Christopher Turner (Lanham: Lexington Books of Rowman & Littlefield, 2020).
32 Herzog, *Conquest of the Useless Conquest*, 5.
33 Werner Herzog, "On the Absolute, the Sublime, and Ecstatic Truth," trans. Moira Weigel, *Arion*, vol. 17, no. 3 (Winter 2010): 1.
34 Dispensing with the theoretical and the speculative—in favor of the strictly practical—Herzog announces his adjustment on the English romantic sublime. See, for example, in *Biographia Literaria*, where Coleridge writes of a necessary blend: "For as philosophy is neither a science of the reason or understanding only, nor merely a science of morals, but the science of BEING altogether, its primary ground can be neither merely speculative nor merely practical, but both in one" (Book XII).
35 Herzog, *Every Man for Himself and God Against All*, 291.
36 Weiskel, *The Romantic Sublime*, 5.
37 Ibid.

38 Ralph Waldo Emerson, "Self-Reliance," in *First Series: Essays*, in *The Complete Works of Ralph Waldo Emerson*, Concord Edition (Boston: Houghton, Mifflin and Company, 1904), vol. II, 45.

39 David Grene, *Of Farming and Classics: A Memoir* (Chicago: University of Chicago Press, 2007), 158.

40 Emerson, *Nature*, 26.

41 Ibid.

42 Ibid., 26-27.

43 Weiskel, *Romantic Sublime*, 6.

44 Ibid.

45 Alan Greenberg, Herbert Achternbusch, and Werner Herzog, *Heart of Glass* (Munich: Skellig, 1976), 174.

46 Herzog, *A Guide for the Perplexed*, 81-82. See 315 n113.

47 *Herzog on Herzog*, 202.

48 *Burden of Dreams* (1982, dir. Les Blank).

49 Herzog, *Every Man for Himself and God Against All*, 325-26.

50 Eduardo Viveiros de Castro, *Cannibal Metaphysics: For a Post-Structural Anthropology*, ed. and trans. Peter Skafish (Minneapolis: Univocal, 2014); originally published as *Métaphysiques cannibales* (Presses Universitaires de France, 2009), 20.

51 Herzog, *A Guide for the Perplexed*, 231.

52 Viveiros de Castro, *Cannibal Metaphysics*, 11.

53 Wilfred M. McClay, "The Burden of the Humanities," *The New Criterion*, November 2023.

54 Ralph Waldo Emerson, *The Journals and Miscellaneous Notes of Ralph Waldo Emerson*, ed. Alfred R. Ferguson (Cambridge: The Belknap Press of Harvard University Press, 1964), July 13, 1833, vol. IV, 200.

55 Emerson, *Journals*, 199.

56 Ralph Waldo Emerson, "The Poet," in *Second Series: Essays*, in *The Complete Works of Ralph Waldo Emerson*, Concord Edition (Boston: Houghton, Mifflin and Company, 1904), vol. III, 22.

57 Emerson, *Journals*, 199-200.

58 *Burden of Dreams* (1982, dir. Les Blank); Herzog, *Conquest of the Useless*, 7.

59 *Burden of Dreams*.

60 Stanley Cavell, *The World Viewed: Reflections on the Ontology of Film* (Cambridge: Harvard University Press, 1972, enlarged edition 1979), xix.

61 See *The Thought of Stanley Cavell and Cinema: Turning Anew to the Ontology of Film a Half-Century after "The World Viewed,"* ed. David LaRocca (New York: Bloomsbury, 2020), 15, 123.

VII

Rogue Agent in an Ambivalent Universe

1 Werner Herzog, *Every Man for Himself and God Against All*, trans. Michael Hofmann (New York: Penguin, 2023), 320.

2 Herzog, *Every Man for Himself and God Against All*, 319.

3 Looking—and listening—to the syllabic play of this tripartite sign, I owe the astute moment of phonemic reading to Garrett Stewart, who writes:

Then, too, Keats has even more in common with Coleridge than this may so far suggest. In his correspondence he is a homophonic punster as well, who gives Coleridge's "anymadversions" a run for its money—for its lexical short-changes and syntactic overdraft—with his complaints about the "{hie}*rogue*glyphics in Moors almanack." In that rebuslike syllable, Keats's drifting phoneme (carried by the grapheme *gue*) doubles by liaison for the *g* of "glyphs" (just as the *r* of "hier") could have been made to operate in this way with the fuller spelling "hier-rogue-glyphs"). Such "rogue glyphs," loosed by phonemic slack, can, as in Coleridge, certainly inflect the graphonic contours of a verse line as well. In the "Ode on a Grecian Urn," for example, there is a transegmental overlay in the very thought that art's idealized and wholly imagined music would not pipe or pander to the "sensual leer," to that fevered gaze of desire that animates the male lovers on the urn. From this we infer some sort of sensory luxuriance apart from aggressive sensuality: a rarefied state which the line, by thematically positing, also phonemically enacts.

Attention Spans: Garrett Stewart, A Reader, ed. David LaRocca (New York: Bloomsbury, 2024), 72; italics in original.

4 See my "The False Pretender: Deleuze, Sherman, and the Status of Simulacra," *The Journal of Aesthetics and Art Criticism*, vol. 69, no. 3 (Summer 2011): 321-29.
5 See my "When TV is on TV: Metatelevision and the Art of Watching Television with the Royal Family in *The Crown*," *Television with Stanley Cavell in Mind*, ed. David LaRocca and Sandra Laugier (Exeter: University of Exeter Press, 2023), 85-98 and "Watching TV with Stanley Cavell: Further Remarks on *The Crown* as Metatelevision," *Conversations: the Journal of Cavellian Studies*, special issue: "The Aliveness of the Posthumous," vol. 11, no. 1 (2023): 114-33. See also *Metacinema: The Form and Content of Filmic Reference and Reflexivity*, ed. David LaRocca (Oxford: Oxford University Press, 2021).
6 Werner Herzog with Jeffrey Brown, *PBS News Hour: Canvas*, October 18, 2023.
7 See Krisoffer Hegnsvad, *Werner Herzog: Ecstatic Truth and Other Useless Conquests*, trans. Claire Thomson (London: Reacktion Books, 2021); first published in Danish as *Werner Herzog—Ekstatisk sandhed og andre ubrugelige erobringer* (Nyborg: Jensen & Dalgaard, 2017).
8 Werner Herzog with Jeffrey Brown, *PBS News Hour: Canvas*, October 18, 2023.
9 Mark O'Connell, "Shooting Werner Herzog," *The New York Review of Books*, December 21, 2023, 51.
10 Herzog, *Every Man for Himself and God Against All*, 290-91.
11 Ibid., 293.
12 Ibid.
13 See Garrett Stewart, *Reading Voices: Literature and the Phonotext* (Berkeley: University of California Press, 1990), 281; The *Deed of*

Reading: Literature * Writing * Language * Philosophy (Ithaca: Cornell University Press, 2015), 101; *Book, Text, Medium: Cross-Sectional Reading for a Digital Age* (Cambridge: Cambridge University Press, 2020), 105; and *Attention Spans*, 8.

14 O'Connell, "Shooting Werner Herzog," *The New York Review of Books*, 49.

15 See my "Thinking of Film: What Is Cavellian about Malick's Movies?" in *A Critical Companion to Terrence Malick*, ed. Joshua Sikora (Lanham: Rowman & Littlefield, 2020), 3-20.

16 See Werner Herzog, *A Guide for the Perplexed: Conversations with Paul Cronin* (New York: Faber and Faber, 2014), xxi, 40-42.

17 *Burden of Dreams* (1982, dir. Les Blank).

18 Cathleen Schine, "From the Diary of Werner Herzog," *The Boston Phoenix*, January 18, 1983, 4.

19 John Mulaney, *New in Town* (2012).

20 William Hughes, "*Documentary Now!* does Herzog in an incredible, hilarious, and poignant season premiere," *AV Club*, October 19, 2022, tinyurl.com/2p9xce9j.

21 Ibid.

22 Ibid.

23 Stellan Skarsgård—as "Verner Vollstedt"—made guest appearances in three consecutive episodes of *Entourage*, season five (2008): "Pie" (s5:e9), "Seth Green Day" (s5:e10), and "Play'n with Fire" (s5:e11).

24 *Saturday Night Live*, hosted by Timothée Chalamet, November 11, 2023, s49:e4.

25 Ludwig Wittgenstein, *Culture and Value*, ed. G. H. von Wright, trans. Peter Winch (Chicago: University of Chicago Press, 1980), 77; italics in original.

26 For more on Wittgenstein and music, see *Music with Stanley Cavell in Mind*, ed. David LaRocca (New York: Bloomsbury, 2024).

27 Herzog, *Every Man for Himself and God Against All*, 48.

28 Ibid., 60.

29 Ludwig Wittgenstein, *Philosophical Investigations*, trans. G. E. M. Anscombe (New York: The Macmillan Company, 1953), 223.

30 Maurice O'Connor Drury, "Some Notes on Conversations with Wittgenstein," in *Recollections of Wittgenstein*, ed. Rush Rhees (Oxford: Oxford University Press, 1984), 79.

31 Herzog, *Every Man for Himself and God Against All*, 40.

32 William Hughes, "John Mulaney says Werner Herzog and David Lynch both passed on *Everybody's in L.A.*," *AV Club*, June 7, 2024, tinyurl.com/68sapdy3.

33 Henry David Thoreau, *Walden; or, Life in the Woods*, in chap. 2, "Where I Lived, and What I Lived For" (1854).

34 Ralph Waldo Emerson, *Nature*, in *Nature, Addresses and Lectures*, in *The Complete Works of Ralph Waldo Emerson*, Concord Edition (Boston: Houghton, Mifflin and Company, 1904), vol. I, 3.

35 For more on realism and mimesis, see K. L. Evans, *One Foot in the Finite: Melville's Realism Reclaimed* (Evanston: Northwestern University Press, 2018).

36 These geographical references call us to Herzog's films made in Perú [see chapter VI], *Cobra Verde* (1987), and *Family Romance, LLC* (2019).
37 See chapter I.
38 For more on name changing, see "Titles Manifold," in my *Emerson's English Traits and the Natural History of Metaphor* (New York: Bloomsbury, 2013), XVI.12-13, XVI.17; 315-25.
39 Herzog, *Every Man for Himself and God Against All*, 75.
40 Ralph Waldo Emerson, "Self-Reliance," in *First Series: Essays*, in *The Complete Works of Ralph Waldo Emerson*, vol. II, 50.
41 "Perhaps changing my name has somehow protected me from the overwhelming evil of the universe." Herzog, *A Guide for the Perplexed*, 16.
42 For more on what I call hoax *vérité*, see my "A Reality Rescinded: The Transformative Effects of Fraud in *I'm Still Here*," in *The Philosophy of Documentary Film: Image, Sound, Fiction, Truth*, ed. David LaRocca (Lanham: Lexington Books of Rowman & Littlefield, 2017), 537-76, esp. 560-65.
43 See Theodor W. Adorno, *The Jargon of Authenticity* (New York: Routledge, 2006 [1964]). See also my "'You Must Change Your Life': *The Americans*, (Concepts and Cults of) Authenticity, and EST," in *The Americans and Philosophy*, ed. Robert Arp and Kevin Guilfoy (Chicago: Open Court, 2018), 59-69.
44 See Nita Rollins, *Cinaesthetic Wondering: The Beautiful, the Ugly, the Sublime and the Kitsch in Post-Metaphysical Film* (Berkeley: University of California Press, 1999), who preserves the "a," and those who don't, such as Stefan Sharff, *The Elements of Cinema: Toward a Theory of Cinesthetic Impact* (New York: Columbia University Press, 1982) and Vivian Sobchack, "What My Fingers Knew: The Cinesthetic Subject, or Vision in the Flesh," *Carnal Thoughts: Embodiment and Moving Image Culture* (Berkeley: University of California Press, 2004), 53-84.
45 See David LaRocca and Sandra Laugier, "The Fact and Fiction of Television: Stanley Cavell and the Terms of Television Philosophy," *Television with Stanley Cavell in Mind*, 1-27.
46 An earlier version of this section first appeared in my "From Authenticity to Authentication: Cinaesthetics and Auteurship in the Age of AI," *Aesthetic Authenticity in Cinema*, ed. Filipe Martins (Faculty of the Arts, University of Porto, 2023), 33-58.
47 See chapter I.
48 Filipe Martins, "Introduction," *Aesthetic Authenticity in Cinema*, 7.
49 Ibid., 7-8.
50 Werner Herzog, *A Guide for the Perplexed: Conversations with Paul Cronin* (New York: Faber and Faber, 2014), 288-89. See also my "I Am What My Films Are: Listening to Herzog's Ecstatic, Essayistic Pronouncements," *The Philosophy of Werner Herzog*, ed. Christopher Turner and M. Blake Wilson (Lanham: Lexington Books, 2020); "The Autobiographical Sublime: Achieving Herzog's Persona at the Intersection of the Home Movie, Self-Citation, and Autofiction." *Estetica: Studi e Ricerche*, vol. X (January-June 2020), 79-98; "Hunger in the Heart of Nature: Werner Herzog's Anti-Sentimental Dispatches

from the American Wilderness (Reflections on *Grizzly Man*)," *Dark Nature: Anti-Pastoral Essays in American Literature and Culture*, ed. Richard J. Schneider (Lanham: Lexington Books, 2016), 227-40; and "'Profoundly Unreconciled to Nature': Ecstatic Truth and the Humanistic Sublime in Werner Herzog's War Films," *The Philosophy of War Films*, ed. David LaRocca (Lexington: University Press of Kentucky, 2014), 437-82.
51 Herzog, *Every Man for Himself and God Against All*, 153.
52 Ibid., 153-54.
53 Friedrich Nietzsche, *The Gay Science*, trans. Walter Kaufmann (New York: Vintage, 1974), sec. 270; see also sec. 335, where he writes, emphasis retained: "We, however, *want to become those we are* — human beings who are new, unique, incomparable, who give themselves laws, who create themselves." Such a description could function as high-ranking subclause in an imagined dictionary entry for authenticity.
54 Friedrich Nietzsche, *Philosophy and Truth*, ed. Daniel Breazeale (Atlantic Highlands, NJ: Humanities Press, 1979), 80.
55 Ibid.
56 Ibid., 80-81.
57 Ibid., 81.
58 Ibid., 82.
59 See Garrett Stewart, "Point/Counterpunct in Charles Dickens: Channeling Syntactic *Expectations*," in *Prismatic Reading: Garrett Stewart's Essays in Refraction*, ed. David LaRocca (forthcoming).
60 Nietzsche, *Philosophy and Truth*, 84.
61 For a variation on the theme, see my "Unauthorized Autobiography: Truth and Fact in *Confessions of a Dangerous Mind*," in *The Philosophy of Charlie Kaufman*, ed. David LaRocca (Lexington: University Press of Kentucky, 2011; with a new preface, 2019), 89-108.
62 Herzog, *Every Man for Himself and God Against All*, 278.
63 Ibid., 273.
64 Ibid., 122.
65 Michael LaPointe, "Werner Herzog Has Never Liked Introspection," *The New Yorker*, April 26, 2022.
66 Herzog, *Every Man for Himself and God Against All*, 130.
67 Ibid., 122.
68 Ibid., 272.
69 David Trotter, "Go for it, Losers," *London Review of Books*, vol. 45, no. 23, November 30, 2023, lrb.col.uk.
70 Herzog, *A Guide for the Perplexed*, 387.
71 Trotter, "Go for it, Losers," *London Review of Books*.
72 David Grene, *Of Farming and Classics: A Memoir* (Chicago: University of Chicago Press, 2006), 129.
73 Rhees, "Postscript," *Recollections of Wittgenstein*, 205. See also my *Emerson's English Traits and the Natural History of Metaphor*, XIV.4, esp. 297; and Stanley Cavell, *Emerson's Transcendental Etudes*, ed. David Justin Hodge (Stanford: Stanford University Press, 2003), 115.
74 Nick Schager, "Werner Herzog on Why He's a Fan of Putin and How Democrats Neglect America's Heartland," *The Daily Beast*, November 12, 2020.

75 Ibid.
76 William H. Galpern, "The Everyday Made Literary," *Stanford University Press Blog*, June 7, 2017. See also Galpern's *The History of Missed Opportunities: British Romanticism and the Emergence of the Everyday* (Stanford: Stanford University Press, 2017).
77 Galpern, "The Everyday Made Literary," *Stanford University Press Blog*.
78 Stanley Cavell, "Something Out of the Ordinary," in *Philosophy the Day After Tomorrow* (Cambridge: The Belknap Press of Harvard University Press, 2005), 7-27. Presidential Address delivered before the Ninety-Third Annual Eastern Division Meeting of the American Philosophical Association in Atlanta, Georgia, December 29, 1996.
79 See my "Emerson Recomposed: Nietzsche's Uses of his American 'Soul-Brother,'" in *Nietzsche and the Philosophers*, ed. Mark T. Conard (New York: Routledge, 2017), 211-30.
80 Galpern, "The Everyday Made Literary," *Stanford University Press Blog*.
81 Cavell, "Something Out of the Ordinary," *Philosophy the Day After Tomorrow*, 26.
82 See Cavell, *Emerson's Transcendental Etudes*.
83 Herzog, *A Guide for the Perplexed*, 288.
84 Ibid., questions adapted from Herzog's own: "Do we know what all these people dream about? For whom do they cast their ballots? Why does Mr. John Smith cry into his pillow at night?"
85 Trotter, "Go for it, Losers," *London Review of Books*.
86 Parul Sehgal, "Turning the Page," *The New Yorker*, December 11, 2023, 58.
87 Herzog, *Every Man for Himself and God Against All*, 248.
88 Søren Kierkegaard, *Fear and Trembling; Repetition*, Kierkegaard's Writings vol. VI, ed. and trans. Howard V. Hong and Edna H. Hong (Princeton: Princeton University Press, 1983), 214.
89 Herzog, *Every Man for Himself and God Against All*, 23.
90 Ibid., 21.
91 Ibid., 24.
92 Ibid., 165.
93 Werner Herzog, *Conquest of the Useless: Reflections from the Making of Fitzcarraldo* (San Francisco: Ecco Press, 2009), ix. See also Werner Herzog, *Conquest of the Useless: Fever Dreams in the Jungle* (New York: Penguin, 2024).
94 Herzog, *Every Man for Himself and God Against All*, 228.
95 Stewart, *Attention Spans*, 223.
96 Werner Herzog, *The Twilight World*, trans. Michael Hofmann (New York: Penguin, 2022), chapter: Lubang, Tilik: January, 1945.
97 Herzog, *Every Man for Himself and God Against All*, 76.
98 Merve Emre, "Back from the Dead," *The New Yorker*, June 12, 2023, 72.
99 Herzog, *Every Man for Himself and God Against All*, 326.
100 O'Connell, "Shooting Werner Herzog," *The New York Review of Books*, 50.
101 Ibid., 50.

102 Herzog, *Every Man for Himself and God Against All*, 325.
103 Ibid.
104 Ibid., 326.
105 Ibid.
106 Herzog, *A Guide for the Perplexed*, 76.
107 Herzog, *Every Man for Himself and God Against All*, 326.
108 Ibid., 195.
109 Ibid., 112.
110 Ibid., 214.
111 Ibid., 125, 204.
112 Ibid., 204.
113 Ibid., 205.
114 Werner Herzog, *Conquest of the Useless: Fever Dreams in the Jungle* (New York: Penguin, 2024).
115 Wendy Ide, "*Werner Herzog: Radical Dreamer*—Fascinating Portrait of the Maverick Filmmaker," *The Guardian*, January 21, 2024.
116 Ibid., 258. For more on Herzog and Coleridge, see David Trotter, who writes: "The only reason Werner Herzog hasn't yet made a film about the Ancient Mariner may be that, having already inadvertently incorporated so many elements of the poem into his own work, he has become him. Herzog certainly shares Coleridge's interest in the physical and spiritual toll taken by epic voyages into uncharted waters. […] Like Coleridge, too, Herzog has an eye for spectral landscape." Trotter, "Go for it, Losers," *London Review of Books*.
117 Herzog, *Every Man for Himself and God Against All*, 258.
118 See my "Suicide Machines: Bruce Springsteen, Ballard, and Broken Heroes on a Last Chance Power Drive," in *Transportation and the Culture of Climate Change: Accelerating Ride to Global Crisis*, ed. Tatiana Prorokova-Konrad (Morgantown: West Virginia University Press, 2020), 123-150.
119 Herzog, *Every Man for Himself and God Against All*, 2.
120 Ibid., 206.
121 Ibid., 45, 49.
122 Ibid., 44.
123 Ibid., 156. Herzog notes a late discovery that his grandfather's name was spelled Rudolf. The news came too late for his namesake, Herzog's son, Rudolph.
124 Ibid., 67.
125 Ibid., 83.
126 Ibid., 84.
127 Ibid., 105.
128 Ibid., 106.
129 Ibid., 4-5.
130 Ibid., 99.
131 Ibid., 109. Original film title: *Every Man for Himself and God Against All (The Enigma of Kaspar Hauser)*.
132 Herzog, *Conquest of the Useless*, 299; see Herzog, *Every Man for Himself and God Against All*, 109.
133 Herzog, *Every Man for Himself and God Against All*, 110.

134 Glenn Kenny, "*Werner Herzog: Radical Dreamer* Review: A Guide to the Filmmaker's Work," *The New York Times*, December 5, 2023.
135 Herzog, *Every Man for Himself and God Against All*, 121-22. An alternate translation of the same passage appears in Alan Greenberg, *Every Night the Trees Disappear: Werner Herzog and the Making of "Heart of Glass"*; foreword, afterword, and scenario by Werner Herzog (Chicago: Chicago Review Press, 2012), 143. Originally published as *Heart of Glass*, text and photos by Alan Greenberg, scenario by Werner Herzog, based on Herbert Achternbusch, *Die Stunde des Todes* (Munich: Skellig, 1976).
136 Emerson, "Self-Reliance," *First Series: Essays*, 51.
137 Ibid., 50.
138 Emerson, "Experience," in *Second Series: Essays*, in *The Complete Works of Ralph Waldo Emerson*, vol. III, 67.
139 Emerson, "Self-Reliance," *First Series: Essays*, 53-54; italics added.
140 Richard Eldridge, *Werner Herzog: Filmmaker and Philosopher* (New York: Bloomsbury, 2019), see esp. 99-111.
141 Emerson, "Self-Reliance," *First Series: Essays*, 81-82.
142 Herzog, *Every Man for Himself and God Against All*, 33-34.
143 Ibid., 30.
144 O'Connell, "Shooting Werner Herzog," *The New York Review of Books*, 48.
145 Herzog, *Every Man for Himself and God Against All*, 32.
146 Ibid., 2.
147 Emerson, "Self-Reliance," *First Series: Essays*, 45.
148 "Thus do ye, not for yourselves, make honey, ye bees." Or in more colloquial form: "So do you bees make honey, but not for yourselves."
149 See Peter Skrine, "Goethe and Emerson in Elizabeth Gaskill's Manchester," *The Gaskell Society Journal*, vol. 19 (2005): 69-85. See also my *Emerson's English Traits and the Natural History of Metaphor*, IX.3, 218-20.
150 Emerson, "Goethe; or, The Writer," in *Representative Men*, in *The Complete Works of Ralph Waldo Emerson*, vol. IV, 273.
151 Emerson, "Goethe; or, The Writer," *Representative Men*, 265.
152 Elizabeth Gaskell, *North and South* (London: Alma Classics, 2018 [1855]), vol. II, chapter XVI, 383.
153 Gaskell, *North and South*, 398.
154 Gaskell, *North and South*, 398
155 Gaskell, *North and South*, 426.
156 Werner Herzog with Jeffrey Brown, *PBS News Hour: Canvas*, October 18, 2023.
157 See the documentary films: *Brunello Cucinelli: A New Philosophy of Clothes* (2013) and *New York Photographer: Jill Freedman in the City* (2018). See also my "A New Philosophy of Clothes: Brunello Cucinelli's Neohumanistic Business Ethics" and "Brunello Cucinelli: A Humanistic Approach to Luxury, Philanthropy, and Stewardship" both in *The Journal of Religion and Business Ethics*, vol. 3, no. 1 (2014).
158 Emerson, "Self-Reliance," *First Series: Essays*, 45.
159 Ibid., 50-51.

160 O'Connell, "Shooting Werner Herzog," *The New York Review of Books*, 51.
161 *My Best Fiend* (1999, dir. Werner Herzog).
162 *Fresh Air*, "Werner Herzog says it's not good to circle 'your own navel' but writes a memoir anyway," October 25, 2023, npr.org/transcripts/1208303973.
163 Ibid., *Fresh Air*.
164 Daniel Zalewski, "The Ecstatic Truth," *The New Yorker*, April 16, 2006.
165 Herzog, *Every Man for Himself and God Against All*, 271.
166 Ibid., 119.
167 Ibid., 189.
168 The previous five quotations, ibid., 326.
169 Ibid., 330.
170 *My Best Fiend* (1999, dir. Werner Herzog).
171 Emerson, *Nature*, in *Nature, Addresses and Lectures*, in *The Complete Works of Ralph Waldo Emerson*, vol. I, 7.
172 Emerson, *Nature*, 3; italics added.
173 These names and categories are drawn from Herzog's memoir.
174 Herzog, *Every Man for Himself and God Against All*, 128.
175 Ibid., 115.
176 J. Hoberman, "Obscure Object of Desire," *Village Voice*, February 19, 1975, 61.
177 Emerson, "Self-Reliance," *First Series: Essays*, 45.
178 Emerson, "Experience," *Second Series: Essays*, 77.
179 See Daniel Heller-Roazen, *Dark Tongues: The Art of Rogues and Riddlers* (New York: Zone Books, 2013).
180 New King James Version (NKJV).
181 The film inspired an illustrated book entitled *Werner Herzog Eats His Shoe (Based Upon a Story That's True)* by Mark Swartz and Ping Fahn, 24 pages, published March 31, 2016, and described as "a rhyming tale about the friendship between filmmakers Werner Herzog and Errol Morris—and a bet they made in real life."
182 *Burden of Dreams* (1982, dir. Les Blank).
183 Herzog, *Every Man for Himself and God Against All*, 293.
184 ChatGPT 3.5 accessed December 10, 2023.
185 Giacomo Miceli, "What an Endless Conversation with Werner Herzog Can Teach Us About AI," *Scientific American*, January 17, 2023.
186 Stuart A. Thompson, "We Asked AI to Create the Joker. It Generated a Copyrighted Image," *The New York Times*, January 25, 2024.
187 For more on the crisis of sound/image index—our ceaseless confrontation with the evidentiary nature of what we hear and see—consult my "A Photograph as Evidence of Itself: Representation, Reflexivity, and Tautology in Light-Based Art," *Social Research*, vol. 89, no 4 (Winter 2022), 915-45; "From Lectiocentrism to Gramophonology: Listening to Cinema and Writing Sound Criticism," in *The Geschlecht Complex: Addressing Untranslatable Aspects of Gender, Genre, and Ontology*, ed. Oscar Jansson and David LaRocca (New York: Bloomsbury, 2022), 201-67; "Memory Translation: Rithy Panh's Provocations to the Primacy and Virtues of the Documentary

Sound/Image Index," in *Everything Has a Soul: The Cinema of Rithy Panh*, eds. Leslie Barnes and Joseph Mai (New Brunswick: Rutgers University Press, 2021), 188-201; "Object Lessons: What Cyanotypes Teach Us About Digital Media," in *Photography's Materialities: Transatlantic Photographic Practices over the Long Nineteenth Century*, eds. Geoff Bender and Rasmus S. Simonsen (Leuven: Leuven University Press, 2021), 209-35; "Virtual Round Table: An Experiment," *Cinema: The Journal of Philosophy and the Moving Image*, vol. 12, Images of the Real: Philosophy and Documentary Film (2021): 175-215; and "On the Aesthetics of Amateur Filmmaking in Narrative Cinema: Negotiating Home Movies after *Adam's Rib*," in *The Thought of Stanley Cavell and Cinema: Turning Anew to the Ontology of Film a Half-Century after "The World Viewed,"* ed. David LaRocca (New York: Bloomsbury, 2020), 245-90; "Shooting for the Truth: Amateur Documentary Filmmaking, Affective Optics, and the Ethical Impulse," *Post Script: Essays in Film and the Humanities*, vol. 26, nos. 2 and 3 (Winter/Spring/Summer 2017): 46-60; "A Reality Rescinded: The Transformative Effects of Fraud in *I'm Still Here*," *The Philosophy of Documentary Film*, 537-76; "Unauthorized Autobiography: Truth and Fact in *Confessions of a Dangerous Mind*," *The Philosophy of Charlie Kaufman*, 89-108.
188 Emerson, "Self-Reliance," *First Series: Essays*, 46.
189 Miceli, "What an Endless Conversation with Werner Herzog Can Teach Us About AI," *Scientific American*.
190 Ibid.
191 Slavoj Žižek, "Where are My Vulgarities?," *Zeit*, November 11, 2022, zeit.de.
192 See Stanley Cavell, *The Awful Truth*, in *Cities of Words: Pedagogical Letters on a Register of the Moral Life* (Cambridge: The Belknap Press of Harvard University Press, 2004), 378.
193 Žižek, "Where are My Vulgarities?," *Zeit*.
194 Ibid.
195 See again *The Geschlecht Complex* and also *Dictionary of Untranslatables: A Philosophical Lexicon*, ed. Barbara Cassin, Emily Apter, Jacques Lezra, and Michael Wood (Princeton: Princeton University Press, 2014).
196 Herzog, *Every Man for Himself and God Against All*, 326.
197 O'Connell, "Shooting Werner Herzog," *The New York Review of Books*, 48.
198 Ibid., 51.
199 Josh Morgenthau, "Does an AI Poet Actually Have a Soul?," *The Washington Post*, August 5, 2023.
200 Code-davinci-002, Brent Katz, Josh Morgenthau, Simon Rich, *I Am Code: An Artificial Intelligence Speaks: Poems* (Boston: Back Bay Books, 2023).
201 Tripp Mickle, "Scarlett Johansson Said No, but OpenAI's Virtual Assistant Sounds Just like Her," *The New York Times*, May 20, 2024.
202 See *My Cinematic Odessey* [sic]: *Werner Herzog's Story*, J. M [sic] Bright, 122 pages, published October 16, 2023.

203 See *Werner Herzog: The Biography*, no author, Yhaia Press, 26 pages, published February 20, 2024.
204 Kate Knibbs, "Scammy AI-Generated Book Rewrites Are Flooding Amazon," *Wired*, January 10, 2024.
205 See Emily M. Bender, Timnit Gebru, Angelina McMillan-Major, Schmargaret Shmitchell, "On the Dangers of Stochastic Parrots: Can Language Models Be Too Big?" *FAccT '21: Proceedings of the 2021 ACM Conference on Fairness, Accountability, and Transparency*, March 2021, doi.org/10.1145/3442188.3445922.
206 For more on the difference between the AI ingestion of copyrighted sentences and paragraphs versus tokens, and related, see Louis Menand, "Is AI the Death of IP?," *The New Yorker*, January 22, 2024, 55-60.
207 Lincoln Michel, "The Year That AI Came for Culture," *The New Republic*, December 20, 2023.
208 Mark McGurl, *Everything and Less: The Novel in the Age of Amazon* (New York: Verso, 2021).
209 Jed Esty, *The Future of Decline: Anglo-American Culture at Its Limits* (Stanford: Stanford University Press, 2022).
210 Slavoj Žižek, *Less than Nothing: Hegel and the Shadow of Dialectical Materialism* (New York: Verso, 2013).
211 Unlike, J. M. Bright, Amanda Geraldine appears to be the author of numerous titles, including *Tom Selleck: Beyond the Mustache (A Biography)*, 38 pages, published November 21, 2023. *Werner Herzog: The Quest for Ecstatic Truth (A Biography)*, A Memoir Written by Amanda Geraldine, 48 pages, published October 12, 2023.
212 Payocool Press (author), *Werner Herzog Biography: Werner Herzog: Crafting Cinematic Landscapes, Unveiling Humanity's Profound Echoes*, 73 pages, published January 1, 2024.
213 *Werner Herzog: A Biography about the German Film Director, Screenwriter, Actor, and Everything You Need to Know about Him*, 33 pages, published November 7, 2023.
214 *Werner Herzog: A Biography of Unknown Exciting Truths of the Pioneer of New German Cinema and a Journey Through His Life and Legacy*, 64 pages, published December 17, 2023.
215 Troy R. Luther, *The Biography of Werner Herzog*, 30 pages, published October 4, 2023.
216 Linda Harrell, *Werner Herzog: Eine Biografie—Die Inspirierende Geschichte über sein Persönliches Leben, seinen Familiären Hintergrund, seine Karriere, seine Herausforderungen, seine Philosophie, und sein Vermächtnis*, 63 pages, published December 17, 2023.
217 Sofian Audry, *for the sleepers in that quiet earth.* (Cambridge: Bad Quarto, 2019).
218 See David Bellos and Alexandre Montagu, *Who Owns This Sentence? A History of Copyrights and Wrongs* (New York: Norton, 2024).
219 Among many similar challenges, see Stuart A. Thompson, "Test Yourself: Which Faces Were Made by AI?" *The New York Times*, January 19, 2024.
220 See "A Dialogue on Critical Conversation," Stewart, *Attention Spans*, 293-339.

221 Olivier Briand, *Werner Herzog Notebook: Come to Us to Feel the Novelty and Freshness Through the Textures, Decoration and Material Selection in a Harmonious Way to Create a Masterpiece That Makes Many People Admire*, 110 pages, published December 24, 2022.
222 The fictitious film title is drawn from a subhead in my *On Emerson* (Belmont, CA: Wadsworth, 2003), 47-49.
223 See my "Punk Discomposed: Staging Sincerity and Fraudulence," in *Music with Stanley Cavell in Mind*, 181-210.
224 An AI joke, a confirmation of the LLM's syntactical cleverness, or a bit of both? When AI-Herzog insists on behalf of his book: "I will not make one word shorter!" the close reader may reach for a missing pronoun: "I will not make it one word shorter!" The hyperbole of the offering as given—that AI-Herzog will not compromise even at the scale of the word—would seem pure Herzog, that is, a sentiment that captures sentient Herzog's bespoke blend of English language semantics and philosophical provocation.
225 Miceli, "What an Endless Conversation with Werner Herzog Can Teach Us About AI," *Scientific American*.
226 Žižek, "Where are My Vulgarities?," *Zeit*.

PROVENANCE + ATTESTATIONS

1 Werner Herzog, "On *The Peregrine*," *To the Best of Our Knowledge*, December 6, 2019.
2 Ibid.
3 Werner Herzog, *Every Man for Himself and God Against All*, trans. Michael Hofmann (New York: Penguin, 2023), 252.
4 Werner Herzog, *Conquest of the Useless: Reflections from the Making of Fitzcarraldo* (San Francisco: Ecco Press, 2009), 3.
5 Werner Herzog, *Every Man for Himself and God Against All*, trans. Michael Hofmann (New York: Penguin, 2023), 305.

Provenance + Attestations

EARLIER VERSIONS OF SOME MATERIAL in this book have been published in other venues over the years—those prior portions now having been substantively updated, revised, and expanded for this consolidated spot. I extend my gratitude to the publishers and outlets, and many people acknowledged below, who supported the revitalization and refinement of the writing and the vision of bringing disparate pieces together as a unified sequence of essays. Adducing prior publication in reverse chronological order, an earlier version of chapter VII section 2 appeared in "From Authenticity to Authentication: Cinaesthetics and Auteurship in the Age of AI," in *Aesthetic Authenticity in Cinema*, ed. Filipe Martins (Faculty of the Arts, University of Porto, 2023), 33-58; chapter III as "The Autobiographical Sublime: Achieving Herzog's Persona at the Intersection of the Home Movie, Self-Citation, and Autofiction" in *Estetica: Studi e Ricerche*, guest edited by Francesco Cattaneo and Richard Eldridge, vol. X, January-June 2020, 79-98; chapter II as "'I Am What My Films Are': Listening to Herzog's Ecstatic, Essayistic Pronouncements" in *The Philosophy of Werner Herzog*, edited by Christopher Turner and M. Blake Wilson (Lanham: Lexington Books of Rowman & Littlefield, 2020), 1-20; chapter IV as "Hunger in the Heart of Nature: Werner Herzog's Anti-Sentimental Dispatches from the American Wilderness (Reflections on *Grizzly Man*)," in *Dark Nature: Anti-Pastoral Essays in American Literature and Culture*, edited by Richard J. Schneider (Lanham: Lexington Books of Rowman & Littlefield, 2016), 227-40; and chapter V as "'Profoundly Unreconciled to Nature': Ecstatic Truth and the Humanistic Sublime in Werner Herzog's War Films," in *The Philosophy of War Films*, which I edited (Lexington: University Press of Kentucky, 2014). Let me emphasize my thanks and debts to all of these journal editors; the presses, their editors and anonymous referees; and the editors of the individual titles. Their critical notes on these pieces improved them in numerous ways. Here, then, counting my thanks for unaccountable, positive influences.

As underscored at the outset, it is the people behind this ongoing enterprise that have made it possible practically, materially, temporally, intellectually, and spiritually—and so a few further notes on formative influences gratefully recognized and additional debts happily incurred.

Certain San Francisco memories—reaching back to the 1980s—stir, and insinuate themselves into the following acknowledgments. Lucky introductions to people close to Werner Herzog. Time spent in places that mattered to him. Crossing paths with folks who had internalized his films. Drawing inspiration from the community of filmmakers and artists in the Bay Area. While I work toward recalling these contexts, I will keep priorities straight and begin aptly.

I thank Werner Herzog for the invitation to attend Rogue Film School. I am especially grateful for the chance to encounter— in person and up close—his expansive and incisive reflections on the interrelationship between creating films and thinking about them; to reflect on how thought becomes cinematic and in turn, how screened images join our private and collective catalog of visions. Herzog's deceptively simple but piercingly profound dictum for filmmakers, however compromised by reality, and already invoked above—"Read, read, read, read, read, read, read, read, read, read, read, read… If you don't read, you will never be a filmmaker"—draws meaningful attention to the abiding consanguinity between cinema and philosophy, and literature, and religion, and the imagination. I read everything on Herzog's assigned RFS reading list and was chuffed to discuss facets of the syllabus with him over a beer—how Virgil's *Georgics*, Bernal Díaz's *The Conquest of New Spain*, and the *Warren Commission Report*, when brought together create captivating eddies of incongruous ideas; why J. A. Baker's *The Peregrine*—poetic prose about falcons—might serve the cinematic eye, as Herzog would later say: "It has prose of the caliber that we have not seen since Joseph Conrad—an ecstasy of a delirious sort of love for what he observes. Intensity and the ecstasy of observation is something that you have to have as a filmmaker […]."[1] Later, Herzog further glossed Baker's achievement:

> In a way, it's almost like a transubstantiation— like in religion—where the observer becomes almost the object—the falcon—[that] he observes. He writes, for example, about

the falcon soaring high up, then higher and higher, until the falcon is only a dot—and then swooping down. And then we swoop down, as if [Baker] had become a falcon himself. And there's a variety of moments where you can tell he has completely entered into the existence of a falcon. This is what I do when I make a film: I step outside of myself into an *ekstasis*, which in Greek means "to step outside of your own body, a point outside."[2]

As these lessons were internalized and integrated by RFS students, we also encountered the language of traversing, of finding our footing on or over some obstacle—from trespass to passage. The master metaphor of all Herzog's work may be walking on foot, but for the RFS his chosen trope for the spirit of rogue filmmaking—lock-picking—inspired unpretentious, adaptive, and sometimes transgressive solutions for the onward initiative to make moving images. As a sign of the times, where Herzog once literally picked locks, we were coached to court and find its adaptive analogs: the invention of fortifications that demand fingerprints and retinal scans force us to treat the trope anew—turn it over and around, to discern its spirit and its equivalents in the digital age. Remaining nimble and adaptive in rapidly changing circumstances proved a reliably profound takeaway.

There were in-person Q&As over the years: Herzog speaking with David Edelstein at the IFC Center on Sixth Avenue, and with Paul Holdengräber more than once at the New York Public Library—where Herzog made the lions roar.

I recall fondly fellow participants and guests at RFS in whose company I discovered more than a shared admiration for Herzog's work. Presentations by Joe Bini and Herbert Golder granted new access to the literary and editorial dimensions of Herzog's film productions.

Antedating my engagement with Herzog, I was very fortunate to spend time with Maureen Gosling—perennial Les Blank collaborator and editor of *Werner Herzog Eats His Shoe* and *Burden of Dreams*—who generously shared remarks on her experiences making documentary films, including her hard-earned perception that ideas anticipate and underwrite technical realization and improvised development. I have Catherine

DeSantis to thank for introducing me to Gosling, and for my first screening of *Fitzcarraldo*, also in San Francisco. I shot my first short film with DeSantis in the city and we edited it together at the Exploratorium.

During graduate school semesters studying rhetoric and philosophy at the University of California, Berkeley, I haunted the Pacific Film Archive, institutional redoubt of longtime Herzog friend, Tom Luddy (who we have since learned introduced Werner to Lena). Herzog calls the sacred chamber for cinema "the most important place for film culture anywhere on the West Coast."[3]

Years later, when living on Potrero Hill and working as a photographer for Alessandro Subrizi on Russian Hill—not far from where Herzog stayed at Francis Ford Coppola's American Zoetrope headquarters on Broadway in North Beach, in the vicinity of City Lights Bookstore and Café Trieste—I crossed paths with locals who seemed to claim Herzog as a hometown boy. I recognized something of my own experience in what Herzog jotted down on June 16, 1979 in San Francisco: "Outside the wind is howling, whipping the laurel bushes. The sailboats in the bay are lying almost flat, the waves sharp-contoured and restless. The Alcatraz Light is flashing signals, in broad daylight. [...] It is hard to buckle down to work, to shoulder this heavy burden of dreams."[4]

In matters of research and reflection, I am particularly and joyously obliged to Paul Cronin for his abundant generosity in its several manifestations: extensive and deeply informed remarks on the history of cinema; welcoming me to his cinema classrooms as guest lecturer and, at other memorable junctures, as co-teacher at the School of Visual Arts (including a class on Godard in the years before he died; another on Hollywood screwball comedies and their legacies in the current era, especially in the work Noah Baumbach and Greta Gerwig; still another on War Films); and earlier as auditor for his dynamic sessions on Aristotle's *Poetics* and Alexander Mackendrick's craft of filmmaking—while he worked in the stead of Chantal Akerman—at the City University of New York; granting an insider's walking tour of Hampstead Heath and salutary accommodation in Rhinebeck and in the Village; and most pointedly and pertinently for the present endeavor, sharing with me his unmatched knowledge of Herzog's films, books, and the related universe of Herzogiana; reading and editing earlier versions of my essays, articles, and chapters on Herzog as they have appeared iteratively over the years, and once again, on this heartening occasion, when those works have been revised and expanded for publication with Sticking Place Books. Conversations with Paul (an unwritten and ongoing memoir that lives agreeably in my mind) are cherished especially, in these pages, since they were invaluable for articulating the stakes of the project—why another book on Herzog?—and manifesting it in consecutive, critical prose. Also at SPB, editorial input from Stacey Knecht and Daniel Rosenthal was helpfully clarifying in the final stretches of manuscript completion.

The investigations reported in this book were informed and enhanced by the event "Think Herzog!" devoted to a public discussion of Richard Eldridge's then-new *Werner Herzog: Filmmaker and Philosopher*. The event, sponsored by Sukhdev Sandhu and his Colloquium for Unpopular Culture, and hosted by Sarah Girner at the Deutsches Haus at New York University in April 2019, welcomed a number of esteemed guests, including dearly-missed Thomas Elsaesser (another perceptive Herzog analyst) and the ever-attuned Haaris Naqvi. Paul Cronin's comments from the floor remain a highlight for me. I thank them all for stirring the spirit and the mind that might give some expression to "Thinking Herzog" in these pages. As a bit of a postscript in matters of personnel and cinematic preoccupation, in November 2019, I joined Cronin for a visit to Clinton, New York, where we were welcomed at Hamilton College by Scott MacDonald for an installment of his ongoing Forum on Image and Language in Motion.

Those with a temper for the tightrope might be intrigued, as was I, by the emergence of a new school, an anti-school of a sort, erupting in our midst. I took the coincidence of physical proximity—and the prospect of reconnecting with familiar colleagues and meeting new ones—to return to Hamilton College for the Second Philosophy of Film Without Theory Conference, convened in October 2023. Needless to say, I am anticipating the third outing even as I continue to mull how we resist having a theory of studying film without a theory: it is a paradox worthy of entry in Herzog's taxonomy of funambulisms.

As earlier versions of these essays made their way to print, I had—the work had—benefit of astute readers, referees, and copyeditors, among them Richard Eldridge, Francesco Cattaneo, Christopher Turner, M. Blake Wilson, Richard J. Schneider, and again, and of course, Paul Cronin. Other accomplices proved vital for pushing the project further along, including Diana Allan, Curtis Brown, Alessandro Subrizi, and John Opera. Memorable deliberations on JLG, slow cinema, transcendental style, and the contours of the industry were had with Dallas Hallam and Michelle Margolis. The uplift of Lorna K. Hershinow was decisive in realizing the project. Gabrielle Tenzer graciously hosted family endeavors. I am lucky to count among talented coeditors and collaborators Sandra Laugier, Ricardo Miguel-Alfonso, Oscar Jansson, Gil Even-Tsur, and Rita Mullaney. For crucial translation support, I have had the pleasure of looking to Mario von der Ruhr, and in similar fashion, Ruby LaRocca, not only for competencies in German and Latin—but also for her inspiring talents as a vocal imitator and literary stylist.

Lucki Stipetić facilitated the inclusion of the "Minnesota Declaration" in *The Philosophy of Documentary: Image, Sound, Fiction, Truth*—a single sheet that manages at once to anchor the book and have its lessons radiate throughout the other 626 pages.

Portions of this volume were discussed at conferences and in classrooms over the last many years with special points of impact and illumination arriving in conversation with Richard Deming, Nick Gillespie, and others at the conference "The Philosophy of War Films," convened in Washington, D.C. in the final hours of the G. W. Bush presidency (November 2008), which featured a screening of *Lessons of Darkness* and seeded the research for the subsequent volume *The Philosophy of War Films* (2014); with administrators and docents at the Brooklyn Historical Society for a summer series on war films that I was invited to curate, which included a screening of *Little Dieter Needs to Fly* (June through August 2015); with Andrew Utterson as we co-taught "Fiction Film Theory" in the Roy H. Park School of Communications at Ithaca College (Fall 2015)—including a memorable section on Murnau and Herzog—while participating in Patricia Zimmermann's "Introduction to Film Aesthetics and Analysis" (Fall 2015); with colleagues in the Department of Philosophy at the State University of New York at Cortland, during an academic year when I taught "The Philosophy of War Films" (Spring 2017); with colleagues of the Cinema Department at Binghamton University, during an academic year when I taught "Transcendental Cinema" and "The Essay Film" (2017-18); with Ohad Landesman, Shai Biderman, and Dan Geva, Thomas E. Wartenberg, and Linda

Williams at *The Philosophy of Documentary Film* conference at The Steve Tisch School of Film and Television, Tel Aviv University (May 2018); with Oscar Jansson at Lund University (October 2018); with Cris Alvarez for his podcast *War Scholar* (November 2018); with Joel Tscherne for his podcast *New Books Network* (December 2018); with Sandra Laugier and her many illustrious guests at Université Paris 1 Panthéon-Sorbonne (June 2019, June 2022, and September 2023); with Thomas Elsaesser during his first and final visit to Cornell University (September 2019); with Steve Summers during the production of his feature documentary *War Movie: The American Battle in Cinema* (July 2020; released 2023); with Christopher Turner and M. Blake Wilson at a roundtable on *The Philosophy of Werner Herzog* for the American Philosophical Association in San Francisco (April 2021); with Alice König for her podcast *Visualizing War* (November 2021); with Victor Krebs, his esteemed guests (Gabriela Balcarce, Lorena Rojas Parma, Daniele Lorenzini), and his team of talented colleagues and students at Pontificia Universidad Católica del Perú (October 2023), where I was invited to address the topic of "Werner Herzog in Perú: A Half-Century of the Humanistic Sublime"; with the aforementioned Mario von der Ruhr in Swansea, Gregynog, Manhattan, and most recently Heidelberg, and especially for his treasured camaraderie; and lastly, over the last decade, with Emily Apter, Simon Critchley, Shoshana Felman, Michael Puett, W. J. T. Mitchell, Caroline Levine, Sandra Laugier, Cathleen Cavell, and many other guests of and participants in the School for Criticism and Theory at Cornell University, with special thanks to Hent de Vries.

Owing to the propitious conditions of the Signet Society at Harvard, I have benefited from numerous conversations with visiting artists, actors, musicians, writers, and filmmakers. I thank Edward Zwick for his informed and candid reminiscences on the experience of making films, some of them indelible war films, and as my younger daughter appreciates, stories about working with Tom Cruise (Herzog too speaks of his "chummy" relationship with Cruise, "who was extremely respectful to me. For my part, I was impressed by his absolute professionalism. He was always thoroughly prepared, physically at peak fitness, alert."[5]); and Sanford R. Climan for directing my attention to several essential war films, and remarks on the work of, and working with, Michael Mann. Also at Harvard, professors and fellow students in the Department of Visual and Environmental Studies (now the Department of Art, Film, and Visual Studies) shaped my approach to film and media studies, especially in seminars with Giuliana Bruno, Elizabeth Grosz, Peggy Phelan, and Hal Hartley. Interactions with those trained in the Sensory Ethnography Lab, among them Diana Allan and J. P. Sniadecki—and their accomplished cinematic works—remain cherished and continuously relevant.

I remain grateful for collaborations with and the mentorship of master cinematographer Robert Elfstrom—from on-the-ground cinema workshops in San Francisco to shooting-in-the-field to editing at Fantasy Studios in Berkeley—drawing inspiration along the way from his remarkable *Vietnam's Unseen War: Pictures from the Other Side*; and of director William Jersey, whose approach to filmmaking has been instrumental to my thinking about documentary films and my attempts to make them, stretching from his Academy Award-nominated *A Time for Burning* to *Eames: The Architect & the Painter*. The documentary film Herzog showed a clip from—and offered a live critique of at the RFS—was created with Elfstrom and Jersey, an installment of *The Intellectual Portrait Series* on Anna Schwartz, a film that we edited at the Zaentz Media Center in Berkeley (home to Fantasy Studios). I thank director J. Mitchell Johnson for a fecund series of conversations focused on the translation of film treatments to films themselves. And I continue to draw from indelible discussions with director Michael Wadleigh, whose critical acumen about the making and meaning of motion pictures remains for me a constructive agitation. Collectively, these agents of cinematic innovation and imagination informed how I shot and edited the documentary films *Brunello Cucinelli: A New Philosophy of Clothes* and (with codirector Rita Mullaney) *New York Photographer: Jill Freedman in the City*.

William Day has remained a steady ally since the end of the last century, a contributor to several of my edited collections, with a relevant highlight being his memorable remarks on *Cave of Forgotten Dreams* for *The Philosophy of Documentary Film*.

Thinking of cherished collaborators, I wish to extend my heartfelt gratitude to all of the talented contributors to edited volumes I have convened over the years, who have taught me so much and who have given me the privilege of presenting their accomplished and enduring wares.

My fortunate engagement with Garrett Stewart tracks with the time horizon of the essays composed for this book, starting with *The Philosophy of War Films*, though my reading of and admiration for his work reaches back much further. His editorial presence and intellectual influence, along with his singular example of exacting literary inventiveness, have transformed what I could imagine possible for the articulation of thought in language. Our latest collaborations—*Attention Spans*, *Bandwidths*, and *Prismatic Reading*—together yield a testament to his legendary skills and admirable sensibilities, both of which he has so bounteously shared with me. Every sentence read, written, and revised in his company has been an intellectual—conspicuously legible—ad/venture in the art of letters: a training in attention to the verbal surface as well as the deep sound of prose, a tutorial at the levels of syllable, phoneme, and sense. On this occasion, I am thoroughly grateful for his full spectrum investment in the viability and vitality of these lines—wishing, in his own inimitable way, that my "return to Herzog be, as Gerard Manley might have it, heard first hurt-free, worst-besting in re-estimate, ever-gaining untamed in aim and goal, maimed only in the name of remaking, after mastering."

The life and legacy, the memory and the writing of Stanley Cavell continue to provide form and content for better understanding the tasks of philosophy and the mysterious gifts of cinema.

For loving care across the longest time horizon—from Newport Beach to Red Rocks to the Niagara Escarpment, and after taking steps together in Rome—Frances LaRocca.

K. L. Evans, and our daughters, Ruby and Star, have supported my passion for Werner Herzog's films and writing; they have sustained me during—and intermittently joined me on—vital stretches on the path to this book. They help constitute that beautiful, if rough, braid of seriousness and good humor that is essential to such investigations.

BIOBIBLIOGRAPHY

David LaRocca, Ph.D., has been watching Werner Herzog's films for some thirty-five years. The clearly formative influence was doubtless intensified when San Francisco-based documentary filmmaker, Catherine DeSantis—Les Blank and Maureen Gosling collaborator—shared *Fitzcarraldo* and *Burden of Dreams* with him in the 1980s. LaRocca later studied philosophy, film, rhetoric, and religion at Buffalo, Berkeley, Vanderbilt, and Harvard. He is the author or contributing editor of eighteen books, including *Emerson's English Traits and the Natural History of Metaphor*, *The Philosophy of Documentary Film*, *Movies with Stanley Cavell in Mind*, *Metacinema*, and *Attention Spans*, and the author of over a hundred articles, chapters, and reviews published in, among other places, *Afterimage*, *Cinema*, *Epoché*, *Estetica*, *Film and Philosophy*, *Liminalities*, *Religions*, *Transactions*, *Post Script*, *The Senses and Society*, *Social Research*, *The Midwest Quarterly*, *Journalism, Media and Cultural Studies*, *The Journal of Aesthetic Education*, and *The Journal of Aesthetics and Art Criticism*. He has contributed book chapters on Werner Herzog, Terrence Malick, Michael Mann, Sofia Coppola, Casey Affleck, Kelly Reichardt, Errol Morris, Rithy Panh, Martin Arnold, Christopher Nolan, Lars von Trier, Douglas Sirk, Spike Lee, Joel and Ethan Coen, David Cronenberg, Steven Spielberg, Robert Zemeckis, Tim Burton, and Charlie Kaufman as well as on television series such as *The Americans* and *The Crown*. Currently associate editor at the journal *Philosophical Investigations* and on the advisory board at *Conversations: The Journal of Cavellian Studies*, he has held visiting research or teaching positions at Binghamton, Cornell, Cortland, Harvard, Ithaca College, the School of Visual Arts, and Vanderbilt. He served as research assistant to Stanley Cavell and Giuliana Bruno, apprenticed with painter Philip Burke and photographer Alessandro Subrizi, made documentary films with Academy Award-nominated William Jersey and Emmy-winning Robert Elfstrom, participated in the School of Criticism and Theory at Cornell University as part of a seminar led by Emily Apter, and workshopped with Abbas Kiarostami, Edward Tufte, and Werner Herzog. As a documentary filmmaker, he produced and edited six features in *The Intellectual Portrait Series*; among other illuminations provided by the Rogue Film School, Herzog screened for the seminar, and offered live commentary on, a few minutes of a documentary LaRocca had produced and edited for this series. Soon after, with RFS fresh in his system, LaRocca set out on foot—with camera in hand—to direct *Brunello Cucinelli: A New Philosophy of Clothes* in Manhattan and Umbria, and to codirect the award-winning *New York Photographer: Jill Freedman in the City*. A recipient of the Distinguished Achievement Award from the Ralph Waldo Emerson Society (an honor previously conferred on Stanley Cavell), he has received a teaching commendation from Harvard Extension School and a teaching innovation grant from the State University of New York at Cortland. Formerly a Writer-in-Residence at the New York Public Library, he contributed to a National Endowment for the Humanities Institute and conducted research as Harvard's Sinclair Kennedy Traveling Fellow in the United Kingdom. DavidLaRocca@Post.Harvard.Edu, www.DavidLaRocca.org

Index

5 Broken Cameras (Burnat/Davidi) 49

Adam's Rib (Cukor) 52
Adorno, Theodor 69, 71, 216
Aesop 88
Affleck, Casey 108, 310 n29
Akerman, Chantal 48, 149, 334
Alaska 35, 75, 77, 79-80, 87-88, 90, 258, 307 n1. *See also* ch. IV (75-94)
alêtheia 153-54
Allen, Woody 223
Altman, Sam 282
Amazon 41, 160, 168, 173-75, 186, 188, 242, 283
American Express 64
American road trip (genre) 36
Amerindian perspective 185-91
Ames, Eric 23, 313 n81
Andes Mountains 168, 247
Andrews, Jesse 59, 170
Antarctica 65, 110, 129, 168, 181
apocalypse 233, 264
Apocalypse Now (Coppola) 170
Aristotle 94-95, 310 n35, 334
Arnold, Matthew 187
artificial intelligence (AI) 17, 23-24, 114, 194, 197, 217, 242, 258, 265, 271-72, 280-81, 282-89, 291, 294-95
Assayas, Olivier 65
Astaire, Fred 229-30
"L'Atelier de la Californie" (Picasso) 182
Attenborough, David 63, 77, 83, 210, 264
Auden, W. H. 143-44
Audry, Sofian 284-85
Aurelius, Marcus 213
Austen, Jane 228
Austin, J. L. 229
autobiography 2, 22, 30, 50, 52, 65, 71-74, 223, 231, 258, 322 n61
autofiction 25, 46, 56, 74, 251
autophilosophy 294

Ave Maria (Bach/Gounod) 137, 314 n90
awful majesty 309 n18
The Awful Truth (McCarey) 275-76

Bad Lieutenant (Ferrara) 98
Baena, John 175
Bahrani, Ramin 57
Baker, J. A. 332-33
Balcarce, Gabriela 185, 337
Bale, Christian 18, 29, 70-71, 111, 131, 133, 154, 258
The Band Wagon (Minnelli) 229
Barbie (Gerwig) 64
Barney, Matthew 263
Barnouw, Erik 84
Batman Begins (Nolan) 71
Baumbach, Noah 60-61, 224, 334
Bass, Saul 63
Belize 172
Bell, Gertrude 259
Bell, Jamie 174
Berenbaum, Michael 115
Berenstain Bears 88
Bernstein, J. M. 122-23, 155
Biederstaedt, Claus 167
Bishop, Kevin 206
Blackfish (Cowperthwaite) 86
Blake, William 95
Blanchot, Maurice 271
Blank, Les
  Burden of Dreams 22-23, 26-27, 39, 53, 59, 61, 66, 68, 70-72, 79, 81, 125, 142, 159-60, 169-70, 179-80, 187, 190-91, 200-1, 203-4, 206, 212, 215, 225, 234, 243, 248, 256-8, 269-70
  Werner Herzog Eats His Shoe 22, 53, 70-71, 262, 326 n181
Bloom, Harold 95, 167, 316 n23
Boccaccio, Giovanni 175
Boklöv, Jan 246
Bolivia 168, 278-79
Bolt, Robert 172
Brandel, Andrew 185

Braun, Nicholas 206
Brazil 168, 174
Bruno S. (Schleinstein) 28-29, 32, 60-61
Buchka, Peter 22, 43, 53, 106, 165
Büchner, Georg 117, 165, 312 n53
Burke, Edmund 102-4, 114, 119, 123, 140, 164, 185
Burnat, Emad 49
Burns, Ken 33, 56

Cage, Nicholas 29, 37
Camisea River 162, 183
Campbell, Joseph 43
cannibal metaphysics 185-91
Caravaggio 77
Carroll, Noël 52, 56, 304 n23
Cartagena 171
Caruso, Enrico 161, 179, 244
Cavell, Stanley 45-46, 54, 161, 167, 192, 274
 aesthetic possibilities 68-69
 on animal life 80
 anthropology and 185
 automatism 51-52
 ecstatic attestation of existence 228-29
 home movie 55-56
 on the human 93, 110, 166
 "Something Out of the Ordinary" 228-30
Caviezel, Jim 112
Chandler, Kyle 173-74
Chaplin, Charlie 26, 275-76
Charmatz, Sean 63
ChatGPT 266-71, 281, 293
Chatwin, Bruce 35, 53, 234-36
Chauvet cave 15, 82, 142
Choquequirao Regional Conservation Area (Perú) 159
cinéma vérité 108, 132, 147, 230
Close-Up (Kiarostami) 108-9
Club Paradise (Ramis) 171-72
CNN 57
Coetzee, J. M. 65, 79-80
Cohen, Sacha Baron 148
Colbert, Stephen 2
Coleridge, S. T. 230, 245, 312 n69, 313 n74, 317 n34, 318 n3, 324 n116

Collet-Serra, Jaume 174
Collins, Doug 59
Colombia 168, 171, 175
Come and See (Klimov) 112
computer-generated imagery (CGI) 114, 124, 222
The Conquest of New Spain (Díaz), 322
Conrad, Joseph 21, 72, 75, 82, 94, 173-74, 332
Coppola, Francis Ford 170, 334
Coriolanus (Fiennes) 311 n43
Cornell University
 Telluride Association 52
 School of Criticism and Theory 185
Corrigan, Timothy 48-49, 68-69, 71, 150, 299 n7, 299 n9, 312 n56
Cowperthwaite, Gabriela 86
Cronin, Paul 23, 38, 68-69, 98-99, 101-2, 109, 232, 293, 297 n2, 298 n5, 308 n5, 308 n7, 309 n10, 310 n35, 334-35
Cruise, Tom 337
Cucinelli, Brunello 255
Culler, Dwight 311 n52
Cusco 159

DALL-E 24
Daniels, Greg 176
Darnell, Eric 63
Darwin, Charles 112, 188
Das, Veena 185
Davidi, Guy 49
Davies, Jeremy 135
Day-Lewis, Daniel 19
DC Comics 216-17
Decameron (Boccaccio) 175
deepfakes 217, 271-72, 288, 294
Deep Springs College 52
Deleuze, Gilles 35, 43
Demme, Jonathan 22
Dengler, Dieter 15, 35, 47-48, 65, 111-12, 120, 124, 128, 131-35, 151-53, 160, 258, 309 n17
De Palma, Brian 276
Descola, Philippe 186
Devil's Hole (Niagara River) 162
Dewey, John 229

Díaz, Bernal 332
Diehl, August 204
Disney 45, 83-84, 86, 174, 217
"Dogme 95" 132
Don Aguirre 174-75
Don Quixote 257
Dracula (Stoker) 277
Dubs, Arthur 84
Dzogchen 213

The Edge (Tamahori) 79
Edwards, Gareth 62
Egli, Sam 89
Eisner, Lotte 33-34, 66
Eldridge, Richard 23, 249, 310 n39, 335
Ellin, Doug 176
Emerson, Ralph Waldo 40, 42, 124, 212, 227, 229-30, 237, 249-55, 271-72
  on contact with the divine 260
  on the endogenous and the emergent 182, 261
  Jardin des Plantes (Paris) 188-89
  on names 214
  on spiritual facts 163, 183
  on the sublime 125, 180
  on universality 261
Emre, Merve 242
The Enchafèd Flood (Auden) 143-44
Enlightenment 155
Eno, Brian 170
Episode V: The Empire Strikes Back (Kershner) 62
essay film 12, 42-44, 48-52, 68, 96, 299 n7
Esty, Jed 283
Evans, K. L. 320 n35

The Fabelmans (Spielberg) 46-47
Far from the Madding Crowd (Hardy) 103
Fassbinder, Rainer Werner 25, 299 n12
Faust (Goethe) 31
Favreau, Jon 45, 61, 176
Ferrara, Abel 98
Fitzcarraldo Editions 66-67
Flaherty, Robert J. 215

Ford, Harrison 172
formalism 10, 123, 218, 222

Foundation Louis Vuitton (Paris) 244
found footage 72-73, 76, 239, 247, 307 n79
Fox, Michael J. 204
Frampton, Hollis 218
Freedman, Jill 255
French, Daniel Chester 229
French New Wave 38, 150. *See also* Jacques Rivette
Freud, Sigmund 1, 220-21, 226, 233
Friedrich, Caspar David 21, 104, 119, 309 n16
Fulton, Willy 89
Fussell, Paul 116

Gaede, Marc and Marnie 91
Galperin, William H. 228-30
Gaskill, Elizabeth 251-54, 325 n149
Gehry, Frank 19, 244
Georgics (Virgil) 251, 332
Gerwig, Greta 64, 334
Ghiglieri, Michael P. 91
Glazer, Jonathan 115
Godard, Jean-Luc 38
Goethe, J. W. von 31, 228, 251-52, 325 n149
Gogol, Nikolai 275-76
Goldilocks and the Three Bears 88
Goodall, Jane 91
Goodwin, Michael 71
Gomez-Rejon, Alfonso 59, 169-70, 175
Gosling, Maureen 23, 26-27, 125, 333-34
Götterdämmerung (Wagner) 73, 137
Goya, Francisco 21
Grand Canyon 16
Gray, Spalding 215
Greek antiquity 10, 157, 207, 237, 290, 295
Grene, David 182, 227
Groening, Matt 176
Gross, Terry 2, 165, 257
Guarani (Paraguay) 173

Guest, Christopher 147
Guyana 168
Gyllenhaal, Jake 139

Haakanson, Sven 90
Hans, Siegel 246
Hardy, Thomas 103
Harmon, Dan 176
Harrison, Jim 79
Hartman, Geoffrey 95
Harvard University 229
Hawai'i 79, 174-75
HBO 206, 305 n50
Hegel, G. W. F. 119, 123, 229, 271
Heimatfilm 148
Heller-Roazen, Daniel 262
Hemingway, Ernest 21, 65
Hendrickson, Kim 22, 53
Heraclitus 183
Herzog, Lena 13, 334
Herzog, Rudolf 246
Herzog, Rudolph 246 n123

HERZOG, WERNER (concepts, themes, categories)
on the abyss 93, 104, 107, 165-66, 177, 226, 243, 265. *See also* Herzog, *Into the Abyss*
on (and against) academics 19-20, 23, 31, 38, 42, 44, 98-100, 150, 184, 211, 226, 237, 242, 248, 294
accountant's lie 128
accountant's truth 30-31, 42, 121, 127-29, 132, 137, 144, 148, 151-52, 156, 314 n90
AI-Herzog 271, 275-76, 279-81, 286, 288-91, 293, 329 n224
as Angeleno 228, 281. *See also* Los Angeles
asceticism 12, 213, 259, 263
auteurism of 68-69, 73, 148-49, 175, 206, 218
as autodidact 20, 200, 248-49, 254-55
automatisms and 51-52, 54-55, 74, 303 n20
Bavarian accent 17, 30, 41, 63
as brand 17, 42-43, 57, 61, 68, 74, 178-79, 195, 201, 210-11

Catholicism of 146, 187, 213, 247, 260, 291
as cipher 196-97
circus 86, 156-57
conquest of the useless 60, 96, 214, 224
on the culture of complaint 41, 177, 250
decadence 197, 206, 260
disenchantment 157, 260
doppelgängers ch. VI.1 (194 216), 270, 282
dreams 31, 33, 35, 39, 41, 43, 60, 80, 83, 90, 96, 98, 124-25, 130, 137, 140, 146, 152-56, 161, 163-64, 169, 179, 182, 184, 191, 196, 212, 221, 228, 231, 236, 239, 243-46, 248, 250-51, 255-56, 260, 264, 291-95
dream, unable to 1, 185
(fever) dreams 17, 31, 236, 244
ecstatic truth 25, 30, 42, 97, 101, 112, ch. V.3 (118-30), 131, 143-45, 180, 219-20, 237, 298 n4
ecstatic realism 286
ekphrasis 4
ekstasis 126-27, 180-82, 229, 333
freak/ish 156-57, 169
as genre 4, 210-11
Goethe, reading 31
hallucination (cognitive, cinematic) 33, 137, 145, 152, 154, 196, 277-79
hallucination (computational) ch. VII.4, 265, 273, 277-79, 282, 295
Herzog Studies 203
hesychasm 213
holographic 287
hypnosis, use of/effect of 32, 127, 137, 145, 150, 181, 197-99, 288
as idiom 61, 210-11
illiteracy 27-28, 109, 150, 184
images
absolute 183
adequate 16, 46, 157, 187, 252-53, 262, 264, 273, 315 n113

images (cont.)
  articulating 21, 182-84, 261-63
  dream 154, 196, 221, 243-44
  exhausted/worn-out 10, 157, 315 n113, 150, 157, 184, 315 n113
  grammar of 43, 151, 262
  of humanity 106, 153-56, 164
  new 13, 15-16, 69, 123, 183-84, 196, 260, 264, 273
  pre-intellectual 150, 184
  of presumptive assertion 70
  repetition of 6, 17, 69-70, 150
  sincere ch. V.7 (144-49)
inner landscapes 2, 16, 35-36, 102, 109, 124, 129, 138, 182, 185, 191, 251
irony
  as incomprehensible 67-68, 126, 200, 313 n71
  regressive ch. V (149-54)
  Socratic 28
madness 2, 78, 120, 235, 242-43, 250
masculinity 41, 176-177, 259, 317 n28
metaphor 23, 66, 71, 128, 163, 181, 203, 222, 256-58, 261, 264, 275
mock heroic 36, 73, 121-22
mock serious(ness) 51, 93, 178, 206, 224
as mystic 3, 25, 30, 33, 46, 53, 56, 180, 196, 238, 241
mysticism of 21, 27, 32, 49, 62, 207, 213, 248
name change 213-14, 321 n38, 321 n41. *See also* Werner Stipetić
neo-Romanticism of 228, 290. *See also* Romanticism
parody 62, 81, 93, 145, 169, 176, 178, 180, 194-95, 198-99, 201, 203, 205-6, 210, 215, 224, 265, 272, 281, 287-88, 305 n50
on pedantic theoreticians 1, 20, 98, 226
persona 2, 39, 41, ch. III (45-74), 149, 177-78, 192, 196-97, 200, 210, 212-13, 241, 280-81, 285, 287
as primeval sophisticate 109, 310 n35
primitivism 33, 310 n35
psychoanalysis, aversion to 1, 82, 177, 213, 225-26
psychology, disparagement of 32-33
reading German literature 31, 42. *See also* Romanticism
reenactment 90, 130, 131-32, 152-53, 313 n81
religious perspective 138, 144-46, 166, 209, 248-49
repetition in the work of 6, 17, 69-70, 73, 99, 203, 218, 233-34, 236, 258, 299 n19
rogue, etymology of 235
Sarcoglottis Wernerherzogii 159
seeing plain 9-12, 14, 155, 213, 234
self-analysis 1, 225-26, 232, 234, 243, 249, 254, 256
self-awareness 17, 225, 232
self-citation 46, 56-59, 61, 64-65, 70, 74
self-critique 39, 212, 225
self-discipline 250-51
self-mythology 231, 247
self-parody 60, 72, 81, 145, 178, 201, 301 n49
self-serious(ness) 39, 147, 224-25
serious(ness) 1, 5, 39, 58, 69, 169, 199-201, 206, 208, 224
silliness of 64, 110, 171, 178, 205-6, 209, 225
soldier of cinema 1, 13, 29, 195
style (and anti-style) 10-12, 102, 123, 218, 272, 290
tactile gaze of 108
taking a bullet 60, 135, 232
theory, contempt for 28, 38, 40, 98-99, 231-32, 248
transcendence,
  the transcendental 19, 27, 43, 66, 68, 93, 97, 102, 110, 118, 147, 167, 209, 241, 247-48, 260. *See also* ch. III (45-74) and

transcendence (cont.)
　　transcendental sublime
unserious(ness) 34, 178, 206, 208
voice 1, 3, 51-52, 72, 81, 145, 169, 178, 198-200, 210, 265-66, 271, 291. *See also* (above)
voiceover 41, 51, 63, 68-69, 80, 91, 96, 106, 134, 136-38, 144, 197, 199-200, 232
walking on foot 4, ch. II.4 (33-36), 39, 66, 185, 195, 235-36, 243, 289, 333. *See also* Greek antiquity; Romanticism; sublime

HERZOG, WERNER (film works by)
Aguirre, The Wrath of God 23, 26, 35, 80, 159-60, 166-67, 170-71, 175, 191, 203, 248, 260, 277-78
Bad Lieutenant: Port of Call New Orleans 57, 80, 98
Ballad of the Little Soldier 115, 117
Bells from the Deep 145, 148, 209, 248
Cave of Forgotten Dreams 57, 73, 82, 142, 243
Cobra Verde 115, 117, 168, 259, 316 n24
On Death Row 3, 277-79
Detroit 64
Echoes from a Somber Empire 79
Encounters at the End of the World 35, 39, 63, 65, 73, 82, 110, 129, 168, 182, 260
The Enigma of Kaspar Hauser 29, 69, 193, 203, 312 n56, 325 n131
Even Dwarves Started Small 57
Family Romance, LLC 213, 277-79, 287
Fata Morgana 11, 52, 59, 73, 109, 115, 117, 121, 137, 145, 150, 159, 289
The Fire Within 259
Fitzcarraldo
　　dream of 244, 295
　　literariness of 66-67, 179-80, 191
　　parody of 202-5, 305 n51
　　in Perú 81, 141, 160-61, 163
　　sublime and 125, 178-79
　　as trope 66-67, 163, 256-57, 259, 261
　　war-time production of 41, 117, 120, 171
Gesualdo 48, 51
God's Angry Man 248
The Great Ecstasy of the Woodcarver Steiner 37, 128 29, 137, 148, 181, 210
Grizzly Man 32, 35, 48, 65, 72-73, ch. IV (75-94), 129, 142, 242, 260
Happy People 36, 182, 191
Heart of Glass 23, 32, 127, 145, 148, 181, 324 n135
Herakles 57
Huie's Sermon 248
Into the Abyss 131, 203
Into the Inferno 73, 198, 260
Invincible 57, 259
The Killers Amex Unstaged 64, 305 n55
Land of Silence and Darkness 32, 226-27, 245
Lessons of Darkness 32, 52, 57-58, 61, 73, 79, 109, 115, 117, 120, 126, ch. V.5 (136-39),153, 170, 180, 262-63, 303 n17
Little Dieter Needs to Fly 15, 35, 47-48, 65, ch. V (95-158), 160, 258, 309 n17
Lo and Behold, Reveries of the Connected World 274
The Lord and the Laden 248
A Lost Western 46-47
Meeting Gorbachev 3
My Best Fiend 2, 32, 48, 50, 53, 57, 69, 72, 203, 234-35, 257
My Son, My Son, What Have Ye Done 80
Nomad 35, 53, 234-36, 28
Nosferatu the Vampyre 73, 277-78
From One Second to the Next 3
Queen of the Desert 52

Rescue Dawn 57, 70-71, ch. V
  (95-158), 170, 258, 311 n40
Salt and Fire 52, 168, 279
Signs of Life 3, 57, 159, 214, 261,
  263
La Soufrière 32, 41, 65, 69, 73,
  107, 303 n17
Stroszek 29, 48, 60-61, 80
Werner Herzog, Filmemacher 22,
  30, 33-34, 36, 53, 299 n19
Where the Green Ants Dream
  110, 166, 243-44
The White Diamond 168
The Wild Blue Yonder 57
Wings of Hope 23, 80, 131,
  159-60, 170, 181, 191, 259
Wodaabe: Herdsmen of the Sun
  121, 137

HERZOG, WERNER
  (written works by)
  "On the Absolute, the Sublime,
    and Ecstatic Truth" 125-26,
    153-54, 180
  Conquest of the Useless 1, 65-66,
    69, 141, 223, 236, 244, 248
  *Every Man for Himself and God
    Against All* 1, 66-67, 101,
    194, 197, 199, ch. VII.3
    (224-65), 285-86, 294
  "Minnesota Declaration" 35,
    108, 132, 300 n31
  The Twilight World 13-14,
    223-24, 239-41, 246
  Of Walking in Ice 34, 66, 223,
    274, 288, 300 n29
  Die Zukunft der Wahrheit [*The
    Future of Truth*] 6, 293-95

HERZOG, WERNER (pedagogy)
  Rogue Film School 1, 14, 20, 24,
    28, 35, 38, 62, 122, 157,
    209-11, 251, 297 n2
  as anti-school 40, 67, 237-38,
    298 n3
  in Perú 160
  reminders 99-100

HERZOG, WERNER (appearances in)
  Adult Swim 176

American Dad! 176
The Boondocks 176
Burden of Dreams 22-23, 26-27,
  39, 53, 59, 61, 66, 68, 70-72,
  79, 81, 125, 142, 159-60,
  169-70, 179-80, 187, 190-91,
  200-1, 203-4, 206, 212, 215,
  225, 234, 243, 248, 256-8,
  269-70
Documentary Now! 17, 93, 176,
  194-96, 203-7, 210-15, 266,
  287
Dreams and Burdens 22, 53
Entourage 17, 62, 176, 206,
  305 n50
Herzog in Wonderland 215
I Am My Films 22, 25, 29-30, 37,
  39-40, 53
Incident at Loch Ness 57, 215-16
Jack Reacher 17, 45, 57, 63, 195
Julian Donkey-Boy 57
*To the Limit and Then
  Beyond It* 22, 43, 53, 106,
  141, 165
The Mandalorian 3, 17, 45,
  57, 62, 176, 195
Me and Earl and the Dying Girl
  59, 62, 169-70, 175
Metalocalypse 176
Mister Lonely 57
Orion and the Dark 63
Parks and Recreation 17, 60,
  62, 176
Penguins of Madagascar 63
Plastic Bag 57
Rick and Morty 62-63, 176
The Simpsons 17, 47, 62, 176,
  195, 255, 302 n5, 305 n51
Werner Herzog Eats His Shoe
  22, 53, 70-71, 262, 326 n181
*Werner Herzog: Radical
  Dreamer* 53, 244-45.
  See also Les Blank

HERZOG, WERNER
  (and artificial intelligence)
  ChatGPT 266-71, 281, 293
  I Am Code 281-82, 293-94
  The Infinite Conversation
    271-82

HERZOG, WERNER
(and artificial intelligence) (cont.)
generative AI publications 23-24, 197, 217, 272, 282-89

hier-*rogue*-glyphs 193, 318 n3
Hitchcock, Alfred 63, 275-76
Hittscher, Paul 175
hoax *vérité* 54-55, 60, 321 n42
Hoberman, J. 261
Hoffman, Dustin 60-61
Hoff, Syd 87-88
The Holocaust 115-16
home movies 47-49, 72, 304 n24
Horak, Jan-Christopher 69, 71
Huayna Picchu 167
Hughes, William 205
Huguenard, Amie 90-91
humanism 96, 155, 187-88.
See also ch. V (95-158);
Herzog, humanistic sublime
post- 93, 96, 109-10, 187-90
Renaissance 187
Huss, Toby 134

Ide, Wendy 245
IFC 194-95
The Iliad (Homer) 140
I'm Still Here (Affleck) 108, 310 n29
Indian Jones 170-72
Indiana Jones and the Last Crusade (Spielberg) 170
Into the Wild (Krakauer) 79
Into the Wild (Penn) 36, 79
Iphigenia (Goethe) 31
Iquitos 168

Jackson, Peter 173-74
Jameson, Fredric 120-21
The Jargon of Authenticity (Adorno) 69, 216
Jarhead (Mendes) 139
Jarmusch, Jim 48
Johnson, Dwayne 175
Johnson, James Austin 207-8
Joffé, Roland 172-73
Johansson, Scarlett 282
Jung, Carl 43, 280
Junger, Sebastian 317 n28

Jungle Cruise (Collet-Serra) 174-75
jungle metaphysics 190. *See also* ch. V (95-158), ch. VI.3 (168-85), and ch. VI.4 (185-192)

Kael, Pauline 232
Kafka, Franz 21, 275-76
Kampmann, Steven 172
Kant, Immanuel 97-98, 102-5, 107, 114, 117, 119, 123-24, 130, 140, 143, 164, 166, 181, 184-85, 229
Kaufman, Andy 51
Kaufman, Charlie 38, 63, 300 n37, 305 n53
Keaton, Diane 54
Keats, John 95, 318 n3
Kermode, Mark 60
Kershner, Irvin 62
Kiarostami, Abbas 108
Kicking and Screaming (Baumbach) 224
Kidman, Nicole 29, 259
Kierkegaard, Søren 86, 233, 307 n12
King Kong 173-74
King, Paul 174
Kinski, Klaus 14, 32, 35, 72, 78, 115, 159, 161, 163, 204, 215, 234-35, 242, 263
Kissinger, Henry 198-99
Klimt, Gustav 208
Koepcke, Juliane 160, 179, 191, 259. *See also* ch. VI (159-92); Herzog, *Wings of Hope*
Korine, Harmony 57, 175
Krafft, Katia (and Maurice) 259
Krebs, Victor 185, 315 n1
Kubrick, Stanley 210

Lachman, Edward 303 n17
Lanham, Richard 11
Laughlin, Candace 70-71
Legends of the Fall (Harrison) 79
Legends of the Fall (Zwick) 79
Lemon (Frampton) 218
Lessing, G. E. 40, 301 n54
Letterman, David 2, 93
Lewgoy, José 161

Lichtenberg, G. C. 40, 301 n54
Life after Beth (Baena) 175
Linear B 193
The Little Hours (Baena) 175
Lively, Penelope 9
Longinus 95, 97, 118-19, 123, 164, 185, 228, 316 n23
Lorenzini, Daniele 185, 337
Los Angeles 2, 13, 37, 60, 80, 101, 176, 211, 214, 231, 298 n5
The Lost City of Z (Gray) 173
Love Canal 172
Lyotard, Jean-François, 97, 103, 119, 164, 185

Macaigne, Vincent 65
MacDonald, Scott 83, 335
MacFarlane, Seth 176
Machu Picchu 159, 167, 175
Mackendrick, Alexander 310 n35, 334
Madre de Dios River 159
Mahler, Gustav 58, 137, 208
Maldonado (Uruguay) 188
Malick, Terrence 38, 112, 117-18, 149, 173, 199-200, 300 n37
Mamet, David 79
Māori 174
Martin, Andrea 172
Martins, Filipe 216-17
Marvel 216-17
Marx, Karl 155
MasterClass 21-23
The Matrix (Wachowskis) 62, 305 n49
Mauch, Thomas 13
McClay, Wilfred M. 187
McCloskey, Robert 88
McElwee, Ross 50
McGurl, Mark 283
McMurdo Station 39, 168
McTiernan, John 173
Mead, Rebecca 66-67
Mekong River 151
Melville, Herman 173-74, 257
Mendes, Eva 37
Mendes, Sam 139
metacinema 32, 57-58, 73, 150, 159, 170, 173-74, 212, 266, 305 n53, 319 n5

metaphilosophy 22, 222, 262, 289
metaphysics
    cannibal ch. VI.4 (185-91)
    comparative 185
Mexico 173, 175
The Meyerowitz Stories (New and Selected) (Baumbach) 60-61
Meyers, Nancy 54, 62
Meyers, Seth 59
Miceli, Giacomo 271-74, 291
Michelangelo (proto-) 142
Middlemarch (Eliot) 255
Milton, John 95
Minnelli, Vincente 229
Mirren, Helen 194, 205-6
The Mission (Joffé) 172-73
Moby Dick 257
mockumentary 147-48, 194, 215-16
modernism 226, 303 n20, 312 n62
    post- 96, 155, 277, 295
Montaigne, Michel de 42, 48-49
Moore, Michael 50, 303 n17
Morley, Simon 114-15, 119
Morris, Errol 50, 71, 215, 326 n181
The Mosquito Coast (Theroux) 172
The Mosquito Coast (Weir) 172
Mr. Rogers 89
Muir, John 78
Mulaney, John
    Documentary Now! 17, 93, 176, 194-96, 203-7, 210-15, 266, 287
    Everybody's in LA 211
Mulhall, Stephen 80
multinaturalism 185-91
Murnau, F. W. 276-78, 336
Museo Larco (Perú) 190-91
My Name is Barbra (Streisand) 231

National Geographic 198
Nemes, László 115
New German Cinema 12, 14, 45, 168, 183, 284, 328 n214
Newman, Barnett 122-23
News from Home (Akerman) 48
The New World (Malick) 173
The New Yorker 66-67, 225
Niagara Escarpment 162
Niagara Falls 161-63, 165
Niagara River 163, 172

Nietzsche, Friedrich 32-33, 39, 42, 51, 93, 221-22, 229, 322 n53
Nolan, Christopher 64, 70
Nomadland (Zhao) 36
Non-Fiction (Assayas) 65
North and South (Gaskill) 251-54
Nouvelle Vague 38, 150. *See also* Jacques Rivette
Nunn, L. L. 52, 162

Oakeshott, Michael 52
Object-Oriented Ontology 189
O'Brien, Conan 2, 298 n3
O'Brien, Tim 309 n18
O'Connell, Mark 196, 199-200, 242, 250, 256, 280
Oedipus 275
Offerman, Nick 175
Omoo (Melville) 174
Once Upon A Time... In Hollywood (Tarantino) 54
Onguiaahra (of the Iroquois) 161-62
Onoda, Hiroo 13, 223-24, 240-41, 246
opera 2, 15, 17, 51, 73, 161, 163, 172, 179, 244, 255. *See also* Caruso; Wagner
Oppenheimer (Nolan) 64
Oppenheimer, Joshua 175
Oshima, Nagisa 149
Out of Africa (Pollack) 179

Paddington (films) 87, 174-75
Paddington Bear (Bond) 81
Paganelli, Grazia 108-9
Painleveé, Jean 83
Palovek, Jewel 91
Panovsky, Erwin 45-46
Paraguay 173
Paranoid Modernism (Trotter) 236
Paris, Texas (Wenders) 36
Parsifal (Wagner) 73
Pärt, Arvo 137
Pascal, Blaise 126, 180
Penn, Sean 79
Penn, Zak 175, 215-16
The Peregrine (Baker) 332-33
Permanent Vacation (Jarmusch) 48
Persian Gulf War 57-58, 117, 120

Perú 23, 36, 38, 80-81, 129, 142, ch. VI 159-92, 211, 247, 278, 315 n1
Petrarch 219
Peucker, Brigitte 47-48, 50, 58-59, 68-71, 73, 137, 302 n6
Phillips, Adam 102
Phoenix, Joaquin 60, 305 n43-44, 317 n30
Picasso, Pablo 182
Pitt, Brad 54
Pixar 88
Planet Earth (Fothergill) 83
Plato 221, 275
Pollack, Sydney 179
Popol Vuh 127
postmodernism 96, 155, 277, 295
Prager, Brad 23, 50, 56-57, 69, 105
Pre-Columbian ceramics 190-91
Predator (McTiernan) 173, 187
Presser, Beat 13, 259
prisoner films (genre) 131
prisoner of war films (genre) 131
Privilegium Maius 219-20
Prokofiev, Sergei 58, 137
Pucallpa 160
Puett, Michael 185

Raiders of the Lost Ark (Spielberg) 170
Ramis, Harold 171-72
realism 137, 179, 217-18, 222
  ecstatic 286
  cinematic 217
  mimesis and 320 n35
Reichardt, Kelly 38, 300 n47
Reijseger, Ernst 127-28, 312 n53
Renaissance 123-24, 187, 219
Das Rheingold (Wagner) 73, 137
Rivette, Jacques 38, 48-49, 56, 72
Robinson Crusoe (Defoe) 174, 179, 244
Rodowick, D. N. 54
Roger & Me (Moore) 303 n17
Rogers, Holly 48
Rogue Film School. *See* Herzog (pedagogy)
Rogue One: A Star Wars Story (Edwards) 62
Roiland, Justin 176

Rojas Parma, Lorena 185, 337
Romancing the Stone (Zemeckis) 171
Romanticism 127, 157, 227, 238, 288, 290
  European 10, 27
  German 148, 207, 227, 237
  neo- 228
  Victorian 254, 323 n76
Roosevelt, Theodore 87
Rossellini, Roberto 26

Sabzian, Hossain 108-9
Safdie, Josh and Benny 217
Sarcoglottis Wernerherzogii 159
Saturday Night Live (Spielberg) 207
Saving Private Ryan 311 n43
Schager, Nick 10, 228
Schiele, Egon 208
Schiller, Friedrich 107, 119, 164, 185, 310 n25
Schmidt-Reitwein, Jörg 13
School of Criticism and Theory 185
Schubert, Franz 58, 137
Schur, Michael 176
Schwarzenegger, Arnold 60, 199
Seghers, Hercules 117, 148, 312 n53
Selsam, Dan 281-82
Shannon, Michael 29, 37
Shelley, Percy Bysshe 95
Shine, Cathleen 201-3
Sicily 175
Sielmann, Heinz 84
Singer, Alan 125, 147, 313 n71
Skafish, Peter 186-90
Skarsgård, Alexander 204-6
Skarsgård, Stellan 62, 305 n50, 320 n23
Smith, Simon J. 63
Soldier of Illusion (Mulaney) 17, 93, 176, 194-96, 203-7, 210-15, 266, 287
Son of Saul (Nemes) 115
Sophocles 275
Spears, Britney 207-8

Spielberg, Steven 46-47, 170-71, 302 n4, 311 n43
Springsteen, Bruce 36, 245-46, 294, 300 n39
Stabat Mater (Pärt) 137
Star Wars (Lucas) 45, 61-62, 213
Stevens, Wallace 95
Stewart, Garrett
  on cinematographic sentences 238-39
  forward slash / virgule 297 n6
  hier-*rogue*-glyphs 193, 318 n3
  Reading Voices (1990) 51-52
  The Value of Style in Fiction (2018) 11
  on war films 311 n43
Stiller, Ben 224
Stipetić, Elisabeth 248-49
Stipetić, Werner 13, 50, 74, 214, 246. *See also* Herzog, name change
The Straight Story (Lynch) 36
Straub, Laurens 30
Streisand, Barbra 52, 231
sublime ch. V (95-158), 183-84
  abstract 100, 120
  apocalyptic 100, 120
  autobiographical 50, 53, 71, 74, 298 n5
  berserk 61
  Christian 167
  Daemonic 167
  Hebraic 167
  Homeric 167
  humanistic 23, 43-44. *See also* ch. V (95-158), 160-68, 179-81, 185, 187-92, 238, 241, 298 n4
  hysterical 100, 120
  ironic 100, 120, 125, 147
  mathematical 117
  natural 79, 153, 167, 182
  romantic 43, 100, 102, 118, 120, 125, 129-30, 179, 181. *See also* Thomas Weiskel
  silly and/or 64, 206
  terrifying 139-40
  tragic 100, 117-18, 120
  transcendental 100, 102, 120

Symphony No. 2 (Mahler) 137

Taiga 36, 182, 191
Tarantino, Quentin 54
Tarzan (Burroughs) 174
Taviani, Paolo and Vittorio 108
Telluride Association 52
Tesla, Nikola 162
Testard, Jacques 66-67
Theroux, Paul 172
The Thin Blue Line (Morris) 50
The Things They Carried (O'Brien) 140
The Thin Red Line (Malick) 112, 139
Thomas, Diane 171
Thompson, Richard 48, 64-65, 81
Thoreau, Henry David 76, 78, 211-12, 230, 233, 288-89, 307 n2
Tokyo-Ga (Wenders) 183, 213
Treadwell, Timothy 15, 35, 48, 65, 72-73, ch. IV (75-94), 142, 151, 242, 258, 307 n79,
Treadwell (cont.) 307 n1. *See also* Herzog (film works by), *Grizzly Man*
Tribal Brides of the Amazon 173-74
Trollope, Anthony 182
Trotter, David 226-27, 324 n116
Trump, Donald J. 59, 124
Turner, Christopher 23, 301 n54, 331, 335-37
Turner, Kathleen 171
Turner, J. M. W. 119
Typee (Melville) 174
Tyson, Mike 223

Ucayali River 159
Uncut Gems (Safdie) 217
University of Chicago 170
Urubamba River 162, 183, 297 n10

Van Daele, Larry 90
Vanishing Wilderness (Dubs/Sielmann) 84
Varda, Agnès 38, 50, 72, 159
Veracruz 171
Verdi, Giuseppe 58, 137
Vertov, Dziga 52

Vietnam War 117. *See also* ch. V (95-158); Herzog (film works by), *Little Dieter Needs to Fly* and *Rescue Dawn*
Virgil 251, 332
Vir Heroicus Sublimis (Newman) 122
Virilio, Paul 112-13
Viveiros de Castro, Eduardo 185-91
Von Steinaecker, Thomas 53-54, 244-45
Von Trier, Lars 26, 132, 301 n53

Wagner, Richard 58, 73, 79, 137, 211. *See also* opera
war (on film) 49. *See also* ch. V (95-158), 160, 164, 184
Warren Commission Report 332
Watts, Naomi 173-74
Weir, Peter 26
Weisenborn, Christian 22, 25, 30, 36-37, 53
Weiskel, Portia 311 n52
Weiskel, Thomas 43, ch. V (95-158), 164, 167, 187, 189, 311 n52
Wenders, Wim 14, 183
West, Cornel 62, 305 n49
Whitehall, Jack 175
The White Lotus (White) 217
White, Mike 217
Whitman, Walt 95
Whitney Biennial 312 n53
Wilson, Douglas 174
Wilson, Kathleen 171
Wilson, M. Blake 23, 331, 335-37
Wittgenstein, Ludwig 145-46, 208-9, 227, 229
Wordsworth, William 95, 164, 185, 228, 230
Woyzeck (Büchner) 312 n53
Wuthering Heights (Brontë) 284-85

Zahn, Steve 133
Zeitlinger, Peter 13, 52-53, 80, 108
Zemeckis, Robert 171
Žižek, Slavoj 17, ch. II.2 (26-29), 103, ch. VII (271-91)
The Zone of Interest (Glazer) 115
Zwick, Edward 79, 337

Further Reading

Praise for previous books authored, edited, or coedited by David LaRocca

The Philosophy of Charlie Kaufman

"The questions that propel Kaufman's fictions are overtly and demandingly philosophical, but everything Kaufman does with his existential forays is laced with wit and extravagant mischief. LaRocca's collection also demonstrates how Kaufman's work is implicitly in dialogue with the ideas of Stanley Cavell. Kaufman's thinking about romantic relationships in terms of repetition and renewal, his preoccupation with the mystery of the film medium's way of making and unmaking the world, and his beleaguered quest for moral perfectionism all exhibit kinship with Cavell's approach to the beautifully tumultuous human situation."

— George Toles, *Distinguished Professor of English, Theatre, Film & Media, University of Manitoba*

Estimating Emerson

"This is the definitive anthology on America's premier man of letters—Ralph Waldo Emerson."

— Cornel West, *Dietrich Bonhoeffer Professor of Philosophy and Christian Practice, Union Theological Seminary*

"Quite apart from the usefulness of having all these important essays handy, readers may also toy with this simple question: when writing about a writer's work, over the years, have critics gotten better or have they gotten worse?"

— William H. Gass, *David May Distinguished University Professor in the Humanities, Washington University in St Louis*

Emerson's English Traits and the Natural History of Metaphor

"This immensely learned, deeply thoughtful, and far-ranging book helps re-situate Emerson in his own time, and in ours. More than just a work of scholarship, it rises to the level of philosophical investigation. It is also witty, playful, and, in its own strange way, original."

—PHILLIP LOPATE, *Professor of Professional Practice, Writing, Columbia University*

"One of Emerson's most astute interpreters, LaRocca consistently challenges the limits of academic categorization."

—ROBERT D. HABICH, *Past President of the Ralph Waldo Emerson Society and Former Editor of the Emerson Society Papers*

"In this elegantly written, scrupulously researched book, David LaRocca has convincingly demonstrated that, rather than locating a restricted area of inquiry, Natural History constitutes the grounding precondition for Emersonian thinking."

—DONALD E. PEASE, *Professor of English and the Ted and Helen Geisel Third Century Professor in the Humanities, Dartmouth College*

The Philosophy of War Films

"This volume offers rich and deeply thought-out consideration of the representation of war on film and of the ways filmic and now digital representation is deeply entangled with how we experience and think about war (up close or at a distance) in actual life. The book reaches back in film history but is especially provocative on war and its representation in the last decade—the situation we are living with now. The essays are fresh and surprising, showing the whole subject of war and film to be far more interesting, complex, and disturbing than in the standard thinking about war genre films that we are used to."

—CHARLES WARREN, *Boston University and Harvard Extension School*

"War is a pervasive condition, a constitutive part of human experience. The war film genre is extensive and multiform. It is no surprise, then, that war films are provocations to philosophical thought. This important and timely edited collection has an extensive introduction that seeks answers to vital questions: What sort of a phenomenon is a war film? What do we think we mean when we speak of a war film? What are war films for? Can war as such be represented by film? The essays that follow illuminate myriad ethical, aesthetic, epistemological and ontological issues as they related to a broad range of representations of war."

—GUY WESTWELL, *Reader in Film Studies, Queen Mary University of London*

"The philosophical reflections compiled in this book look at war films from a variety of perspectives. I commend editor David LaRocca for bringing together scholars who each, in different ways, engage the interdisciplinary mission of the inquiry into how war is depicted on screen. What is the philosophy of film, and then, of war films specifically? Do war films harbor a philosophy—of death, violence, love … —or does philosophy enrich the understanding of the cinematic of war? *The Philosophy of War Films* explores these questions and many more, connecting the reality of war with the art of filmmaking."

—MIEKE BAL, *Professor of Theory and Literature, University of Amsterdam*

A Power to Translate the World coedited with Ricardo Miguel-Alfonso, Professor of American Literature and Literary Theory, University of Castilla-La Mancha, Ciudad Real, Spain

"[The book] invigorates by means of sudden discoveries, cross-connections, overlaps, gaps, as each of these 'prismatic' essays reflects the question afresh."

—LAURA DASSOW WALLS, *William P. and Hazel B. White Professor of English, University of Notre Dame*

"Emerson was always a transnational thinker, and in this respect as in others, we have yet to catch up with him. This fine, wide-ranging volume will be of considerable help. These essays bring one to Emerson from, and allow one to travel out from his texts towards, a variety of geographical, cultural, and disciplinary regions, often in surprising ways."

—RUSSELL B. GOODMAN, *Emeritus Professor of Philosophy, University of New Mexico*

"A timely, provocative conversation seeking further to characterize Emerson's bearing toward the world beyond the US."

—CHRISTOPHER HANLON, *Professor of English, Arizona State University*

The Philosophy of Documentary Film

"*The Philosophy of Documentary Film* is a welcomed addition to the scholarly study of a mischievous praxis—one that continues to expand, contract, merge, and mangle in its attempts to explore versions of "real life" on film. Periodic, thoughtful reflection on this rogue form is necessary, and this book provides it. The leading lights of nonfiction film scholarship are well represented, and especially pleasing to me, as a documentary filmmaker, is the fact that documentarians have also been enlisted to write about our craft. Furthermore, just for good measure, *The Dogma 95 Manifesto* is included as both a beacon and dangerous shoal to filmmakers exploring the choppy waters around the fiction/nonfiction whirlpool. Great idea!"

—ROSS MCELWEE, *Director, Sherman's March, Bright Leaves; Professor of the Practice of Filmmaking, Harvard University*

"These works in hand are contemporary perspectives on, for me, the most vibrant practice in contemporary cinema. They call us to think carefully and seriously not only about the truth claims and strategies of specific documentary films but also about why documentaries are so central to our age."

—TIMOTHY CORRIGAN, *Professor Emeritus of English, Cinema and Media Studies, and History of Art, University of Pennsylvania*

The Bloomsbury Anthology of Transcendental Thought

"In this brilliantly edited and introduced anthology, David LaRocca presents us with the broadest selection of authors, philosophers, visionaries, and artists, who have expressed the simple, difficult truths of the transcendental in the most profound and varied of ways."

—HENT DE VRIES, *Russ Family Professor in the Humanities and Philosophy, Johns Hopkins University; Director of The School of Criticism and Theory, Cornell University*

"Edited with great erudition and care by David LaRocca, the collection will be an indispensable handbook for anybody researching the heritage of that tradition."

—BRANKA ARSIĆ, *Charles and Lynn Zhang Professor of English and Comparative Literature, Columbia University in the City of New York*

"This volume is more than an overview of a field of study—it is participating in the creation of one."

—TODD MAY, *Class of 1941 Memorial Professor of the Humanities, Clemson University*

The Thought of Stanley Cavell and Cinema

"A brilliant collection of original essays by major figures in the field. The genius of Cavell's writings on film is in sharp focus throughout."

—MICHAEL FRIED, *J. R. Herbert Boone Emeritus Professor of Humanities and the History of Art, Johns Hopkins University*

"The authors in this collection explore what Stanley Cavell might have meant in ways more variegated, thoughtful, original, and illuminating than anything I have seen before. *The Thought of Stanley Cavell and Cinema*, exemplary in its clarity and carefulness, is a watershed both in our understanding of Cavell and of film itself."

—ROBERT B. PIPPIN, *Evelyn Stefansson Nef Distinguished Service Professor, The University of Chicago*

Inheriting Stanley Cavell

"*Inheriting Stanley Cavell*, beautifully edited by David LaRocca, is so much more than a gathering of reminiscences and testimonials. So many of the pieces in the volume prove gripping, and they cumulatively transformed my sense of what Cavell had accomplished. This volume makes a strong case for the revolution that Cavell's extraordinary philosophic sensibility, powerful presence as a teacher, and wide range of concerns brought about in North American philosophy. The collection is also impressive for its decision to include dissenting voices."

—GEORGE TOLES, *Distinguished Professor of English, Theatre, Film & Media, University of Manitoba*

Movies with Stanley Cavell in Mind

"This volume pushes Cavellian scholarship forward, showing that the value of Cavell's work lies not simply in understanding it but in applying it. By extending the philosopher's methods to an exciting range of international and contemporary films, the chapters compose a timely consideration of what it is to read a film, and to read a film generously."

—KYLE STEVENS, *Associate Professor of Film Studies, Appalachian State University*

"All of the contributors to this wonderful, collective enterprise—brought together by David LaRocca—revisit films Cavell loved or take up the invitation to explore new films. In each instance, they reveal the importance of Cavell's writing and method."

—SANDRA LAUGIER, *Professor of Philosophy, Université Paris 1 Panthéon-Sorbonne*

Metacinema

"LaRocca (a documentary filmmaker and prolific author) probably said, 'I told you so!' when Facebook changed its name to Meta in late 2021. Inspired by the ways in which *meta* has become a catchphrase for describing many elements of popular culture, LaRocca has put together a very fine collection of fourteen essays (ten new, four previously published) that examine ways in which films can refer to themselves, reflexively, and function as metacinema. Drawing on the work of Stanley Cavell and other film philosophers, the essays, taken together, hold that though all films reflect on cinema in meta ways, some are especially deft in revealing the conditions of their own occurrence and of cinema more broadly. The first several essays (and the introduction) provide deep considerations of the bounds and possible definitions of metacinema, among them a usefully schematic contribution from Daniel Yacavone. Later essays examine how particular films are meta and contribute to a greater understanding of reflexivity in cinema. Case studies include art films such as *Holy Motors*, Hollywood classics such as *Rear Window*, documentaries, and experimental works. Theoretically sophisticated and deeply invested in close textual analysis, this book will appeal most to those with an interest in philosophical approaches to cinema."

—DANIEL HERBERT, *Associate Professor, Department of Film, Television, and Media, University of Michigan*

"We all know meta when we see it, but up until now few have attempted to define it. This terrific book, comprising essays from both established and emerging scholars, is a welcome corrective to that oversight, and a vital addition to contemporary film and media theory."

—CATHERINE WHEATLEY, *Reader in Film and Visual Culture, King's College London*

The Geschlecht Complex coedited with Oscar Jansson, Lecturer in Comparative Literature, Lund University, Sweden

"Bristling with intellectual energy, *The Geschlecht Complex*, brings together a number of brilliantly original essays and a carefully curated sample of theoretical excerpts in its exploration of the resonances and affordances of a singularly untranslatable notion. *The Geschlecht Complex* is many things: it is both syllabus and seminar, both a joyful intellectual exchange and a virtuoso homage to the examples of such thinkers/readers as Cassin, Cavell, Apter, and Derrida. Most of all, it is an exuberant performance of the key inspiration driving the thinking of the untranslatable: the conviction that the untranslatable is at once generated and redeemed by passionate ventures of translation-across genres, media, bodies, languages, and disciplines. In all these transpositions, this volume succeeds marvelously."

—Pieter Vermeulen, *Associate Professor of American and Comparative Literature, University of Leuven*

"A brilliant, bold, and eccentric work. [...] David LaRocca's chapter on Lectiocentrism and Gramophonology must equally be considered the most ambitious piece. Making a dramatic intervention in the dialogue between 'reading' and 'seeing' as hermeneutic imperatives for cinema and contemporary media, it cannot be reckoned with in a review of this length. Suffice to say, LaRocca is insistent that Stanley Cavell's thoughts on cinema lead us to reconsider sound in film as a crucial (but curiously, till now undervalued) component to its aesthetic experience. [...] What results [in *The Geschlecht Complex*] is an energetic, bold, and accomplished collection not quite like any before it; one reads in the scale of its ambition the possibilities that untranslatability has long gestured to; here, at last, it has developed a new paradigm of its own. [...] It is a brave, well-rounded, and seismically significant publication."

—Byron Taylor, *University College London, Oxford Comparative Criticism & Translation (Summer 2022)*

Television with Stanley Cavell in Mind coedited with *Sandra Laugier, Professor of Philosophy, Université Paris 1 Panthéon-Sorbonne, France*

"This landmark collection of essays is an invaluable exploration of Stanley Cavell's contributions to the study of modern visual media, and a pioneering demonstration of the value of philosophical attention to television in the new era of long form, "prestige," "cinematic television." The very "fact" of television, its influence, its pervasiveness, its social function, its aesthetic distinctiveness, its unique relation to the viewer, remains as mysterious today as it was when Cavell began writing about the medium in the nineteen-eighties, and the editors of this volume have done a superb job of collecting and curating work both indebted to Cavell and groundbreaking in their own right."

—ROBERT B. PIPPIN, *Evelyn Stefansson Nef Distinguished Service Professor, The University of Chicago*

"LaRocca and Laugier have brought together in one book many of the most creative and inspiring voices working on television and popular culture in contemporary philosophy. By taking forward the genius of Cavell's approach—his emphasis on the work the medium does on us, its capacity to educate our moral sense—this volume charts one of the most exciting and important new directions in the study of TV. In so doing, it also transforms what it means to do philosophy in the present."

—ANDREW BRANDEL, *Assistant Research Professor, Pennsylvania State University*

Attention Spans

"A critic of Garrett Stewart's brilliance and scope deserves a 'Reader,' but this fascinating book is far more than a collection of an author's most salient publications. A 'writing journal' of a teaching career that incorporates brief extracts of important books in the inspiring narrative of an immensely wide-ranging critical practice, *Attention Spans* engages the major developments of recent criticism. A *tour de force*."

—Jonathan Culler, *Class of 1916 Professor Emeritus, Department of Literatures in English, Cornell University*

"Garrett Stewart is a multi-media close reader extraordinaire whose answerable style rewards close reading in turn. This selection of excerpts from each of his twenty books is interspersed with his own running commentary, stitching it all together and making his whole career's research and thinking-through seem as though it were all taking place in present time, while remaining full of scrupulous attention to the ways in which his work has evolved. After a dialogue with the editor, full of yet newer directions, this astonishing volume concludes with a glossary of Stewart's coinages."

—Paul Fry, *William Lampson Professor Emeritus, Department of English, Yale University*

"As David LaRocca tells us early in this volume, J. Hillis Miller described Garrett Stewart, on the jacket of his second book, as 'more or less *sui generis*.' This turned out to be a prophetic description of the most wide-ranging and least doctrinaire critic of his generation. It also aptly describes *Attention Spans*, a book like no other, and one that does not belong to any recognizable genre. In staging a critical rereading of his own work, Stewart offers us an exhilarating history of aesthetic theory since New Criticism, which is also a virtuosic display of fine readerly attention. Continually unsettled, continually restless, it is written in what Stewart himself calls a 'language not quite gelled into the print that transmits it.' To read it is to feel, again and again, the lifted joy of shared thinking."

—Peter Boxall, *Goldsmiths' Professor of English Literature, New College, University of Oxford*

Music with Stanley Cavell in Mind

"A collection of exciting new essays by philosophers and practitioners of music in the full breadth of its range of art and thought; an exemplary display of versality and insight."

—Lydia Goehr, *Fred and Fannie Mack Professor of Humanities, Columbia University*

"At last, a comprehensive book on the rich and beguiling relationships between philosophy and music in Cavell's work. These essays—which mix biography, philosophy, and critical reflection with a wide array of musical examples—give us deep insights about the ways music is inseparable from the varied forms, passions, and intentionalities of human life."

—Michael Gallope, *Associate Professor, Cultural Studies & Comparative Literature, Music, University of Minnesota*

"The authors of these essays recall, deeply and imaginatively, the music woven into Stanley Cavell's words and the meanings intimated by varied musickings. Each in a singular way offers a lesson in listening to the music of Cavell's words and the meanings made available by a wide range of musical genres."

—Vincent Colapietro, *Professor Emeritus of Philosophy & African American Studies, Pennsylvania State University*

"Stanley Cavell held that the activity of philosophizing about the nature of art is continuous with the activity of interpreting specific artworks. He thought that it is through our critical engagement with specific artworks that we learn what is possible in art. This collection of essays is a wonderful tribute to this dimension of Cavell's thought."

—Zed Adams, *Associate Professor of Philosophy and Co-Director, Institute for Philosophy and the New Humanities, The New School*

Authored, edited, or coedited books by DAVID LaROCCA

RALPH WALDO EMERSON
On Emerson
Emerson's Transcendental Etudes by Stanley Cavell
Estimating Emerson: An Anthology of Criticism from Carlyle to Cavell
Emerson's English Traits and the Natural History of Metaphor

TRANSLATION AND THE TRANSCENDENTAL
A Power to Translate the World: New Essays on Emerson and International Culture coedited with Ricardo Miguel-Alfonso, Spain
The Bloomsbury Anthology of Transcendental Thought: From Antiquity to the Anthropocene
The Geschlecht Complex: Addressing Untranslatable Aspects of Gender, Genre, and Ontology coedited with Oscar Jansson, Sweden

PHILOSOPHIES OF FILMMAKING
The Philosophy of Charlie Kaufman
The Philosophy of War Films
The Philosophy of Documentary Film: Image, Sound, Fiction, Truth
Metacinema: The Form and Content of Filmic Reference and Reflexivity

STANLEY CAVELL
The Thought of Stanley Cavell and Cinema: Turning Anew to the Ontology of Film a Half-Century after "The World Viewed"
Inheriting Stanley Cavell: Memories, Dreams, Reflections
Movies with Stanley Cavell in Mind
Television with Stanley Cavell in Mind coedited with Sandra Laugier, France
Music with Stanley Cavell in Mind

GUEST EDITED
Conversations: The Journal of Cavellian Studies
No. 7: *Acknowledging Stanley Cavell*

GARRETT STEWART
Attention Spans: Garrett Stewart, A Reader
Bandwidths: Reading Across Media with Garrett Stewart
Prismatic Reading: Garrett Stewart's Essays in Refraction
forthcoming

www.ingramcontent.com/pod-product-compliance
Lightning Source LLC
Chambersburg PA
CBHW070125080526
44586CB00015B/1565